THE ADVENTURES OF AMOS WRIGHT
MORMON FRONTIERSMAN

THE ADVENTURES OF AMOS WRIGHT
MORMON FRONTIERSMAN

GENEVA ENSIGN WRIGHT

Council Press
Provo, Utah

Dedication

To my husband, Charles Coulsen Rich Wright

Contents

Chapter		*Page*

Acknowledgments

I am indebted to my husband who left a wealth of written commentary about his father Amos R. Wright whom he knew imtimately. Warren Wright generously made available extensive information gathered by his brother David L. Wright in 1956 when first-generation sources were still available. David had begun to write his grandfather's story when the work was interrupted by his untimely death. Conover Wright wrote the first story. Gwen Anderson's followed.

My three sons: Amos, Earle and Thomas provided inspiration and encouragement and Amos' wife Gloria, is my indispensable advisor, reader and critic.

Many family members and friends contributed vital information, among them Loella Jacobson, Nettie Humphery's, Faun Weaver King, Mark and Mary Weaver, Kathryn Stephens Jensen, Nona Green Brown, Virginia Mitchell, Martie McLean and Patricia Burdick.

Gratitude is also expressed to librarians and assistants at the L.D.S. Church Historical Archives for their expert and kindly assistance.

Lee Nelson merits special mention for his friendship and faith in me and the biography. Without him the book would probably not have been published.

Geneva Ensign Wright

Prologue

This story is true. The time is a century and a half ago. The place is the Great American West and the man is Amos Russell Wright. So much of what happened to him came about because of the kind of parents he had, that the tale must begin with them.

At twenty-three Jonathan Wright quit his job as a bartender on a Mississippi riverboat, determined to become a minister like his father before him.

But one night Jonathan had an unusual dream that was to shape his destiny more than any noontime daydream ever could. When he awakened, the picture was indelibly imprinted on his mind and heart as clearly as a photograph. He recorded the details, being careful to include the date, March 23, 1831.

I dreamed I went to a large splendid building, but the door was locked and the key was lost. The door flew open at my command and as I went in, it closed behind me. But the strangest thing was that I saw a woman named Rebecca who was supposedly my wife. She was a beauty with dark hair and flashing eyes. I'd never even thought of getting married, but there she was, dressed all in white, and looking like an angel. I never felt so happy in all my life.

As he pondered it over and over in his mind, the dream remained a mystery to him until finally he gave it up, tossed his notes into an old footlocker and forgot all about it. It didn't cross his mind again until seven years later and then he knew there *was* something to it.

No one remembers what business took Jonathan to Waynesville, Illinois that spring day in March, 1838, other than that he knocked at the door of Dr. David Wheeler, a widower. He was greeted by a pretty blonde named Charlotte, one of the four

Wheeler daughters, the two eldest of whom were married.

After their business was concluded, Dr. Wheeler invited Jonathan to stay for dinner and spend the night.

Jonathan was ushered into the dining room, and after introductions to the youngest daughter, lovely dark-eyed Rebecca, the host noticed that his guest was suddenly silent, preoccupied, and showed little interest in the delicious food before him. Efforts to draw him out in conversation were unsuccessful and the meal ended on an uncomfortable note. Jonathan excused himself as soon as possible and went to his room.

Next morning, however, the dark-eyed brunette was surprised when the handsome guest asked if he could see her alone for a moment or two. She was all the more surprised when he announced, "You don't know me. I am a complete stranger to you. But I would like to marry you. I will be back this way a week from today and you may give me your answer then."

He just as abruptly walked out of the room, mounted his waiting horse, and galloped off down the road.

As his horse trotted along the muddy trail, Jonathan pondered the happenings of the previous evening. It was all so fantastic he shook himself to see if it were a dream from which he would suddenly awaken. No. *This* was real enough. It was the dream of seven years before which gripped his emotions, tied his tongue and stole his appetite the night before. He must have made a miserable impression upon Rebecca, to say nothing of her father. He hadn't slept all night trying, unsuccessfully, to put the puzzle together. Nothing made sense, any more than it had seven years before, but there was no mistaking that he had just seen the girl who had been his wife in the dream.

He was four months past twenty-nine. Perhaps it *was* time he got married. Besides, if the Lord wanted him to marry Rebecca, why should he object? She was lovelier than any girl he had ever seen. After the rashness of what had happened, she may have thought him insane, but somehow, even then, he knew what her answer would be.

Seven days later, Rebecca met Jonathan at the door of her father's home with a smile and shyly admitted her answer was, "Yes!"

Dr. Wheeler, however, wasn't so easily convinced. He insisted his daughter take time to reconsider this proposal. But twenty-five-year-old Rebecca had a mind of her own. When her father remained adamant, she packed her belongings and left with her husband-to-be without her father's consent or his blessing.

The young couple went to live at Exeter, kept in touch with Dr. Wheeler, and eventually made their peace with him.

Those first days and nights together as husband and wife were sweet beyond expression. Jonathan explained his irrational behavior that first evening they had met. Rebecca listened quietly and said at last, "After you left, it was as if someone were at my elbow whispering ... 'go ahead, say yes ... it's all right ... he's Mr. Wright!' I didn't dare tell Charlotte or Father, but I could think of nothing else."

Together they read, talked about Jonathan's dream, and were delighted to discover that the cogs of their deep-seated desires, likes and dislikes, meshed perfectly. It wouldn't be true to say they lived happily ever after, because they didn't. But the groundwork of love was solid and it molded the life of their beloved first son, Amos Russell Wright.

Chapter One

Beginnings

Jonathan and Rebecca welcomed their firstborn into the world of "battle and blood" eleven days late to be a New Year's baby in that New Era of 1840, and like the clamorous times he was born into, he would grow to participate in clamorous times as long as he lived.

Right from the first he tried to push aside the time curtain. He needed to see what was ahead and to understand the whys and wherefores. As a ten-year-old boy he walked from Nauvoo to Great Salt Lake, a distance of fifteen hundred miles, often driving a yoke of oxen. He recalled in later years wondering if he would have to go entirely naked when the clothes he was wearing were gone. The pants that were too long when he got them, came to his knees and were raveling off the ends when he reached the end of the trail. The comfort of socks and underwear was unknown to him.

As he watched the stars on a clear night, looking up from his bed on the hard ground, he asked them to tell him about the future and what it held for him. If they had told him he probably wouldn't have believed! He would have seen himself riding with the restless urge of a pony express rider, driving a ten-mule team freighting outfit, being chased by officers of the law; learning to speak the language of three different Indian tribes and a universal sign language; fighting them, hating them, loving them and teaching them, often coming within an inch of losing his life at their hands. The full moon might have whispered about his becoming a Mormon bishop, having two wives and two dozen children of his own, but if it did he probably didn't hear.

Amos could hardly have been aware of the stupendous events going on around him. The early nineteenth century was in Carl Sandburg's words, a time when "windy and clamorous forces blew across America. The future held unknown cross-paths."

It was a new era for the infant Mormon Church, newly
organized in 1830. The powers of darkness hovered over its cradle,
hoping to snuff out the life which would eventually transform the
world. By 1840 the young Prophet Joseph Smith was in chains in
Liberty Jail, the Saints driven out of Missouri, threatened with
extermination. Appealing for redress the leaders were told "your
cause is just but we can do nothing for you."

Jonathan Wright was an apprentice to his father, a Methodist
minister, with a flock of believers seemingly content with their
brand of religion. He heard of the young prophet Joseph Smith
and of the strange and powerful doctrines he taught.

"Rebecca," he said, looking earnestly at her, "I must see this
man Joseph Smith!"

"I wish you would," she replied. "If you don't, you will go
crazy."

Thus it was that thirty-five-year-old Jonathan C. Wright faced
the decision whether "to be or not to be" one of those damned
Mormons. He must have been well aware of the hatred and
disgust in which that peculiar sect was held. He had probably
shared the popular feeling himself for a decade or more as Joe
Smith and his followers had been front-page news during their
unhappy attempts at settlement in Ohio, Missouri, and now
Illinois.

Brought up from childhood in the Methodist faith, his father
an exhorter, Jonathan very naturally adopted the same religion
and himself prepared to become a minister. Here was a mature
man following in the footsteps of a respected father, making his
living honestly as he believed, serving as the mentor of his small
flock. By 1843 he had a wife and family to support. His life pattern
was firmly set. His religious philosophy, adopted in childhood,
had never been seriously questioned. Then suddenly this utterly
despised Mormon cult said in effect, "You have no business
accepting pay for what you are doing. Much of what you are
preaching is false. You have no authority for what you do. There
is only one true Church on the earth. God the Eternal Father and
his Son Jesus Christ have appeared to this 'prophet' Joseph
Smith. He receives revelations and has written a book which
purports to be as sacred as the Bible," and a dozen other
seemingly outrageous dogmatic assertions.

Such a situation might not have precipitated mental turmoil
in some men's minds, but Jonathan, naturally of a religious
nature, felt the challenge too keenly to shrug it off. Failing to find

the truth about such fundamental concepts was to him, unthinkable. If Mormons were right, he would in honesty have to give up his means of livelihood. The settled pattern of his life would be turned topsy-turvy. He would incur the ridicule of family, friends, and parishioners. His own small world would tumble about his ears. Such ideas simply couldn't be true. He set out for Nauvoo to find a way to prove them false.

Tradition has it that his first direct exposure to Mormonism occurred when Jonathan was traveling on a stagecoach. A man about his own age got on and found a place beside him. Soon they were engaged in a religious discussion. The man said his name was Brigham Young and that he was a Mormon. He thereupon launched into an explanation of some of the peculiar beliefs they held.

Shortly thereafter, Lyman L. Corey, a Mormon who had married Jonathan's sister Elizabeth, asked for the privilege of preaching in the little church over which Jonathan was presiding. Corey was uneducated and unqualified in the language of the ministry, but he had been sent out as a Mormon missionary. A little disconcerted at having a brother-in-law pop up posing as a preacher, Jonathan was nevertheless broad-minded enough to say to Corey, "All right, you can come." Corey said, "I want you to come and listen to me." Jonathan agreed to do that and took his seat right by the door. Lyman got up and gave out a hymn. Jonathan wasn't interested. But when Lyman commenced to pray, he began to listen. After the prayer Corey began to preach. He hadn't spoken more than fifteen minutes when his listener began to feel as if all his sturdy objections to Mormonism were being knocked down one by one. Of course he didn't tell Lyman that, but as soon as Lyman left he began reading the Book of Mormon. Bedtime came and he *still* read. It was at this point that he made his decision to go see Joseph Smith, and told his wife about it.

Shortly thereafter Jonathan got on his horse and started for Nauvoo some eighty miles away. He rode early and late to make the trip and it was necessary to bate the horse frequently. Each time he stopped he would take the saddle off, let him graze and then get his Book of Mormon and read as he waited. Then he came across something that didn't suit him. He shut the book and said to himself, "I will not go another step! I'm going back home. I don't believe the story!" He put the book away and went for his horse. As he approached, the animal started with his mouth wide open in a most vicious manner, determined to fight. He whirled and kicked at Jonathan, then broke loose and galloped away. Jonathan knew in a minute the devil had taken possession of his horse. He started after him, making slow progress on foot. Finally, he met some men who stopped and asked if it were his horse they had just seen. "He is sure full of the devil," they said. "We caught him and tied him in a corner of the fence in the lane, but he is in an awful condition."

Jonathan thanked the men for their assistance and hurried on. As he neared, the horse came toward him again, mouth stretched wide and eyes bulging. Ordinarily he was as gentle a horse as anyone would wish to own. Jonathan promised the Lord regardless of what happened, he would go and see Joseph Smith, if he would take the devil out of his horse. When he made that promise, the horse dropped his head and opened his mouth to receive the bit and bridle just as quiet and docile as could be. Jonathan mounted him and rode away without further difficulty until he reached Nauvoo.

Nauvoo was the largest settlement in Illinois in 1843. As Jonathan topped the final rise, he pulled his horse to a stop and gazed on the scene before him. The Mississippi River, about a mile wide at that point, swept around the City of the Saints in a curve which emphasized the beauty of the river and the city itself. It seemed to nestle there as if the Father of Waters were encircling it with his mighty arm.

The traveler inquired as to the whereabouts of Joseph Smith and was told Joseph would be gone for a few days. He was taken, however, to the office of the "Nauvoo Neighbor" where he was introduced to Elders John Taylor, Wilford Woodruff, Elias Smith and others. A tall blondish gentleman who introduced himself as Joseph's brother Hyrum, invited him to supper and they made their way along the tree-shaded street talking animatedly as they went.

After a refreshing bowl of bread and milk served by Hyrum's wife, the two men settled themselves in earnest conversation, Jonathan plying Hyrum with questions and Hyrum answering them simply and thoroughly. The evening hours melted into midnight and the two men were unaware of the passage of time until dawn approached and they heard the crowing of a neighborhood rooster. This was indeed the most far-reaching experience in the life of this thirty-five-year-old apprentice preacher.

While he felt it was his duty to embrace the Gospel, he started again for home but was struck down with a severe sickness as if death were upon him, and he soon found himself back in the home of Hyrum Smith. Being fully convinced that in the "waters of Jordan" there was healing to be found for body and soul, Jonathan proceeded to the banks of the Mississippi where he was baptized by Hyrum Smith and ordained an elder on May 29, 1843, after which he returned to his home in Exeter a happy man, but a man who faced a completely new world. Anxious to share this new-found truth with Rebecca, knowing she would support him in his action, he was not so sure of his religious flock, but he determined to go and try. He had a wife to support and two small children, with Rebecca expecting in another four months. Now he feared he would be out of a job for joining the Mormons.

It was soon noised about that he had really done so. He asked for the privilege of holding a meeting and invited the former members of his Methodist flock to come and hear him preach. Some of his faithful followers said they would if he would let their old Methodist minister reply to his remarks. This man had a life's experience of preaching behind him and Jonathan was worried.

The day of the meeting came. Jonathan stopped on the way behind a shed and poured out his soul in thanks to the Lord for the testimony he had gained of the truthfulness of the Gospel. He begged the Lord in case the minister started to argue after he finished speaking, to close his mouth. "Don't let him speak," Jonathan prayed. "If you will do this, I will accept it as additional proof of its truth and will be willing to give my time, money, talents, and all that I have, to build up thy kingdom."

When he finished his prayer, he went into the church and the meeting started. Jonathan got up and talked an hour and a half and felt good about what he said. When he finished, the minister arose to his feet. He stepped to the pulpit, looked around the congregation, turned and looked at Jonathan and sat down. He never uttered a word.

The urge to gather with the Saints in Nauvoo came strongly upon Jonathan and Rebecca, but one more test of faith remained to be met. When Rebecca's father, Dr. David Wheeler, heard of Jonathan's conversion to Mormonism he was deeply troubled about the future of his daughter. At length he determined to make a personal visit to Exeter hoping to persuade her and Jonathan to abandon their foolish notions.

The young couple greeted him warmly on his arrival, though they were surprised to see him. Rebecca hurriedly prepared supper

as her father and Jonathan chatted. Dr. Wheeler waited till after
the meal was over to broach the subject which so troubled him.
Rebecca tucked baby Virginia Ann Charlotte in bed. Three-year-
old Amos begged to stay up and sit on Grandpa David's lap.
Gathering the little fellow into his arms, he began guardedly by
questioning Rebecca about their plans for the future. Jonathan
didn't wait for his wife to reply. Uncrossing his legs and leaning
toward his father-in-law he replied, "We're going to Nauvoo just
as soon as possible. I'll go on ahead and find a place for us to live
and Rebecca will stay here till after her confinement in September, and then I'll come back to get her and the children."

Realizing it was now or never, David cleared his throat and
began. "I'm an old man. My four daughters are all married now.
I've had to be both father and mother to all of them for many
years. As you know their mother died soon after Rebecca was
born and since then she has always been first in my heart,
perhaps because she was the baby. I cannot bear to see her move
even farther away and especially to join the Mormons."

Amos looked up quickly and said, "Don't feel bad, Grand-
fadder," and putting his arms around the old man's neck, he gave
him a wet kiss. David hugged the child closer and a tear slid down
his cheek. It took a few minutes for him to find his voice again.

"I've worked hard since I moved to Waynesville and bargained
for my farm. I've finally paid off the mortgage, and I'm out of
debt. It's a good piece of land and will make a living for anybody
who works it carefully. Now this is my proposition." His voice
was husky as he continued. "I can't hope to live much longer, but
I will make out a deed in Rebecca's name if you two will move to
Waynesville and take over the place and let me live with you the
rest of my life. There's just one string attached.... Let those
Mormons alone ... don't have anything more to do with them!"

An uneasy silence settled over the little room. Amos squirmed
out of David's arms and climbed into his mother's lap. As Rebecca
ran her fingers through the little boy's hair she prayed silently for
wisdom.

Maybe it would be best to accept Father's generous offer, she
thought to herself. It would provide security for Jonathan and our
children and make a home for Father at the same time. But how
could I ask Jonathan to give up Mormonism when it means so
much to him? How could *I* give it up when I know it is true? But
Jonathan waited, feeling this had to be Rebecca's decision.

At last she broke the heavy sound barrier which hung over

them. "Can we wait until morning to decide this important question, Father?" Her father quickly agreed and with a few words they bade one another good night.

It was anything but a good night for Rebecca and Jonathan and David Wheeler. Jonathan told Rebecca this decision had to be hers since it was her father who made the offer. He said he would abide by her answer.

Conversation during breakfast next morning was in monosyllables. Dark circles under Rebecca's eyes told of sleepless hours. David said he had to get back to Waynesville and must be going. Jonathan shook hands with his father-in-law and Rebecca helped him into his greatcoat. Tearfully, she hugged and kissed him as Amos and Charlotte clung to her skirts.

"Father, you know how much I love you, but I must go with my husband. I want these children to grow up with the teachings of Joseph Smith in their hearts. I know he is a prophet. The Mormons will be my people and their God, my God." Jonathan whispered thankfully, "Amen ... so be it!"

David Wheeler went wordlessly and alone back to Waynesville.

Chapter Two
Nauvoo

Little Amos' first memories of Nauvoo were of being shushed in meeting as he and Charlotte squirmed during a long-winded sermon, for the many and varied routines and concepts of the restored Gospel were inbibed along with his mush and milk.

He was early aware of tension in the neighborhood, hearing words like "mobbing", "tar-and-feathers", "burnings," in his parents' guarded conversation. His father had been appointed marshal of Nauvoo and a member of the city council shortly after their arrival.

Imprinted in his four-year-old memory was the fearful summer day when Edwin Markham rode through the streets shouting, "Brother Joseph and Hyrum have been killed by a mob at

Carthage!" Women screamed, children cried, even the dogs barked and howled, while cows bawled mournfully. Through her tears Rebecca tried to explain. Most clearly, Amos remembered attending a viewing of the martyrs next morning in the Mansion House. Jonathan was gone all night helping to arrange for the burial, but in the early hours of daylight, little Amos rode behind his father on a big white horse to see Brother Joseph and Hyrum. There were long lines of people ahead of them and everybody was crying. When they got near enough, Jonathan lifted the boy in his arms so he could look into the familiar faces lying in their black velvet-covered caskets. His child-mind etched a lasting picture of the pale, still forms in white robes.

Tiny brother David was often put in Amos' charge, as Rebecca hurried about her household tasks or helped with the needs of her neighbors. Charlotte, too, had to be kept from running away, so Amos early learned to take responsibility and to sense the needs of others.

These were the days when Rebecca's influence made its greatest imprint on the soft wax of Amos' young spirit. Her dependence on him because of her ill health developed his manly qualities and his desire to protect her. By a tender word or glance she expressed her love for him, making him even more anxious to care for her.

Their new home in Nauvoo had a fireplace in it. Rebecca and the children loved to feel its warmth and watch the dancing firelight as she read to them. Each evening after baby David was tucked away to sleep, Amos and Charlotte brought the Book of Mormon or the Bible to her, saying, "It's reading time, Mother!" Charlotte climbed into her mother's lap and Amos pulled a chair close to her rocker.

Nephi and Laman and Lemuel came alive as they went back to Jerusalem to get the brass plates from mean old King Laban. Amos shivered when Rebecca read how the Lord told Nephi to kill Laban when he was lying drunk on the street, so Nephi could take the brass plates back to his father Lehi. The story of Joseph Smith's vision was another favorite. If God answered Joseph's prayers, he reasoned, he can answer mine as well. When Father Jonathan was at home they always knelt together for evening prayer. But the times when he, his mother and Charlotte knelt together seemed more intimate. Rebecca let him take his turn, prompting him when he hesitated, but he early learned to talk to the Lord by himself, expecting to have his prayers answered.

It was about this time that he became acquainted with death. His tiny brother Hyrum, named after the man who had baptized his father, lived only a few hours. He touched the wee little hands before the lid of the coffin was closed. They were stiff and cold. Through her tears, his mother explained that the real baby Hyrum had been called back to heaven and wouldn't need his body until he was resurrected. These were big thoughts for a small boy, but he was comforted to know the baby wouldn't feel when the dirt was shoveled over his little grave on the hillside.

Rebecca was weak and tired after that. Many days when she stayed in bed Amos brought her cool drinking water, and listened for her voice when she called.

"They said they'd let us stay in Nauvoo until next spring, but it looks like we'll have to leave sooner than that," explained Jonathan to Rebecca, sadly. Amos was nearly six years old by then and although he didn't understand the increasing persecutions, he felt his parents' sorrow and worry with all the tender vulnerability of childhood. He remembered clinging to his father's big hand and trying to keep up with his long steps as they walked past the big white building made of stone called *The Temple*. It was still not finished and he knew his parents went without so they could donate money to help pay for it. His father told him it was The House of the Lord and when he grew up he could go there if he was a good boy. He said Brother Brigham wanted to finish it before the Saints had to leave, and Amos wondered why, if they were going to go anyway.

On the very last day of 1846, Rebecca left Amos to take care of Charlotte and David while she and Jonathan went to the temple to be sealed as husband and wife for eternity in the "large splendid building" that Father Jonathan had dreamed about fifteen years before.

Amos loved to go over to the blacksmith shop and watch the men building wagons for the journey West. It was warm inside even in the winter time. There was a big bright fire and something they called a bellows which made fire burn hot enough to melt iron to put around the outside of a wagon wheel. There was lots of sawing and hammering as the men assembled the different parts of a wagon. His father said it cost about two-hundred-and-fifty dollars to buy one of the wagons and a pair of oxen and enough food and clothing to start on the journey with the other Saints. That sounded like more money than Amos could imagine, but they sold their house and lot and most of their possessions at far less than they were worth, so they could go.

One winter morning in 1847, Amos remembered particularly how cold it was when they said goodbye to their beautiful home in Nauvoo. He was bundled up in two coats, with a cap to cover his head and ears, and mittens for his hands. All three children were packed in the wagon box with sacks of wheat and flour around them. Jonathan had the oxen hitched to the wagon and their breath looked like fog. Rebecca was crying steadily but Amos couldn't help feeling excited even as he tried to comfort her.

When they got to the steep bank that went down to the Mississippi River, however, he shut his eyes tight and put his head under a quilt so he wouldn't have to look. He thought sure they would all be drowned. After awhile when nothing happened, he peeked out between the canvas cover and the wagon box. It wasn't water at all . . . just white ice as far as he could see, with the sun shining on it till it hurt his eyes. He looked ahead and behind and saw a long line of wagons and oxen just like their own and they got across safely.

After that, his memory got all mixed up and he couldn't remember what happened then. He could remember a terrible storm with thunder and lightening and wind and rain. A woman was sitting on the ground holding her baby. She was shivering and crying. A boy bigger than Amos asked her where her husband was and she said, "He's gone off to Mexico to fight for Uncle Sam who drove us out here in the wilderness to die." Amos asked Rebecca who that mean old Uncle Sam was, but it wasn't until years later that he could understand what the woman meant.

When the weather got a little warmer, the snow and ice melted and everything turned to mud. The ground was still partly frozen so the heavy wagons would bog down if the oxen didn't keep moving; but even so, the wheels made such deep ruts that each wagon had to make a separate track, or it would sink in clear to the hubs. Jonathan said he was going to see how deep the mud really was. He took a long pole and started pushing it down into one of the ruts. He pushed and pushed till it went out of sight.

It took so long to get across Iowa, the Saints stopped after they crossed the Missouri and started to build a mud and log town called Winter Quarters. Jonathan took a shovel and started digging a hole in the bank of the river. A lot of men were doing the same thing. Amos helped to carry the dirt out until there was a place as big as a room and that was their house. They called it a dugout. Some of the families had houses made of logs and it made quite a big town. His father said there were about three thousand people there, and three hundred of them were sick.

As soon as Jonathan got the dugout finished, he built two bunk beds inside with ropes stretched across to put the straw tick on. Then he made a door out of slabs, and left Rebecca and Amos to unload the wagon and start keeping house. Brother Brigham had asked him and Newel K. Whitney to go back and buy supplies for the Saints with money from Uncle Sam because five hundred of the Brethren had joined the Mormon Battalion. It was hard to understand all the big new words he heard and he wondered why Uncle Sam suddenly turned out to be a good fellow.

Amos was proud when his father got back from buying goods for the Saints, because he helped him distribute flour and sugar and beans and bacon to each family, so they all felt rich for awhile. While the Wrights were at Winter Quarters they occasionally heard reports from the Valley of the Great Salt Lake where the Saints were going to settle and be free from persecution. Amos thought they might go there right away, but Brother Brigham called Jonathan on a mission back to Illinois where Amos was born, and he didn't know how long his father would be gone. It seemed to Amos he was always left to look after his mother and Charlotte and Dave and do all the chores. Another baby was born while Jonathan was gone and he was named Enoch, but like Hyrum, he only lived a few days. Some kind neighbors made a coffin and dug a grave in the cemetery alongside a lot of others. Amos didn't feel as bad this time as he did when Hyrum died. Rebecca spent a lot of time lying on the bunk bed in the dugout after that.

Whenever he could leave her, Amos went to school in one of the log houses. That was fun and the teacher praised him because he learned quickly. He loved to get home after school to tell his mother all the new ideas he was learning about in school.

On January 11, 1848, Amos turned eight. He wanted to be baptized but his father was gone and so he waited. January, February, and March crept slowly and the very last day of that month his father surprised everybody by walking in unannounced from his ninety-day mission. Almost before Jonathan got his overcoat off, Amos left off hugging his father's legs and pulled at his trousers. "Father, will you baptize me tomorrow?"

"Baptize you! ... tommorow? Why, it's cold enough out there to freeze the horns off a goat." And that settled it for the time being. But Amos never forgot that expression and often used it to clinch a point for his own children.

Jonathan found things in a mess on his return. Debts had accumulated. Rebecca was as bad or worse than when he left. April slid by and so did May before a time came to even think about baptism. But the first of June was clear and warm and so was Amos' heart because his father said this was *THE DAY* at last.

The Johnny-jump-ups were thick on the prairie as the two walked hand in hand toward the big river and picked their way down the steep bluff. The bottoms were lined with brush, cattails and marsh grass. Amos excitedly stripped off his shirt and pantaloons ... he never wore shoes ... and waded out into the water until it came up to his armpits, making him catch his breath. Even in June the water was cold. His father followed him and as they stood facing each other, he showed Amos how to hold on to his big left hand. Jonathan's right one was raised to the square. Then he began solemnly:

"Amos Russell Wright, having been commissioned of Jesus Christ, I baptize you in the name of the Father, and of the Son, and of the Holy Ghost, Amen." Then he quickly laid his son under the water, making sure he was completely immersed, and set him back on his feet. The boy sputtered and wiped the water out of his hair and eyes with a swift motion, as he climbed the steep bank. Both were out of breath as they reached the top. Still under his father's direction, he knelt on a grassy spot and felt Jonathan's hands on his head to confirm him a member of the Church of Jesus Christ of Latter-day Saints, saying, "receive the Holy Ghost." Then followed a few words of blessing and promise which would ring in his ears many times in the future when he was being tempted, or felt discouraged. At length, they turned toward the village again.

Chapter Three
Life and Death

A strange thing happened as Rebecca and her family were huddled in their sod house or dugout at Winter Quarters. Rebecca's health continued to deteriorate until it was unthinkable for them to go with the next company of Saints. Besides, they had scarcely enough food to last a week, let alone make a trek into the wilderness. Jonathan was moody, sometimes cross with the children and short-tempered even with Rebecca.

Rumors reached Jonathan's ears almost immediately after he came to live at Nauvoo about a wierd new doctrine called polygamy, but he brushed it off as gossip and the usual lies about Mormonism. He had left Rebecca at Exeter awaiting the birth of David Darwin, while he went on ahead to arrange a place for the family to live.

However, when he was invited shortly afterward to a meeting with some of the leading brethren, he heard for the first time the official doctrine of plurality of wives. The revelation, they were told, had been dictated by Joseph Smith to his scribe William Clayton, July 12, 1843, a year before the Prophet became a martyr. It had actually been received twelve years earlier in 1831.

At the mention of that date Jonathan's mind flashed back to his dream, recalling words which had been without meaning all that time. "One of the elders in authority said to each of the brethren, go ... make haste, get your wives." ... and on about the new basket and the lost key and the door which flew open at his command. His mind reeled as he tried to comprehend all the implications. In memory he saw at the top of the page he had written all those years ago, the date, 'Mar. 23, 1831.' He forced himself to think back step by step. God had graciously chosen Rebecca for him. He had no doubts the moment he saw her that she was the woman in his dream. Time had proved his action right. Now this thing seemed to be something else pointing directly at him. The thought of it made his scalp prickle. He sat there stunned, weak and trembling.

Should he tell Rebecca? She had read the copy of his dream when they were first married, but like him, she failed to understand it. It was out of the question to tell her. Such a repugnant doctrine might turn her against the Church altogether. She was only recently baptized. At least he'd wait until she heard it herself and broached the subject. Now that it was official, she was bound to know about it sooner or later.

Rebecca broke the ice early one morning after they had both spent a sleepless night. "Is something bothering you dear?" She waited a full minute for his reply. Then the dam broke and he poured it all out without stopping. He explained about the dream. That the lost key was the authority of the priesthood now restored to the earth. Doors long locked can be opened by a word. He told her he had known about this a long time but dared not talk about it ... about what the dream said, "go, make haste, get your wives." I don't want to do it. How can I do this to you?"

Her reply amazed him. "I've been wondering when you would talk to me about it," she said simply. "It might make things easier for both of us. I get so tired now and the children need a mother more than ever. Maybe another woman in the house would help. Do you have anyone in mind?"

So together they agreed on a Sister Sarah Boyce, if she was willing. Jonathan felt surprisingly relieved in spite of himself. At least the uncertainty was over, and he could talk freely with Rebecca. Things were arranged, Sarah said yes, and a simple ceremony was performed in the presence of "Elders in authority." "Aunt Sarah" came to live with the family in the tiny mud house.

It was an impossible situation from the first, though the children accepted their new "Aunt Sarah" without questions, as children do. But tensions began to build. At least the babies could be shooed outside during the summer, but when snow began to pile up around the dugout and they all crowded around the little stove in one tiny room, the bomb exploded.

"Whose slave do you think I am?!!" said Sarah. "I'm sick and tired of being ordered around all the time. You can't put on your airs around me any more. I won't take it. You lie there all day and I do all the work. I'm just as good as you are. I'm through and neither you nor your Jonathan can make me change my mind!" And with that she picked up her few belongings and left. There were undoubtedly other reasons than jealousy and frustration,

but they would have been enough. So that was that. Jonathan
arranged a divorce a few months later to make it legal and the
family settled back into the old, more comfortable pattern. All
that remained to be remembered was the entry in Jonathan's
Bible in faded ink on a yellowed page: "Jonathan C. Wright and
Sarah Conklin Boyce married May 1847; divorced 1848."

Winter Quarters had been built on land belonging to the
Omaha Indians and the federal Indian agent began to fear the
possibility of an Indian war if the Saints were allowed to stay
much longer. The "Authorities," therefore, agreed to vacate
Winter Quarters in the spring. Those who had enough supplies to
start for Salt Lake Valley would do so then. The "poor" as they
were called, would have to recross the Missouri and start another
temporary mud town along the East bank in Pottawottamie
County. And so it was, that spring found them making fresh
dugouts in a settlement named Kanesville in honor of the Saints'
friend, Col. Thomas L. Kane. The town was later re-named
Council Bluffs. "The poor," including Jonathan and family,
hoped soon to scrounge enough supplies to follow the lucky ones
to the valley. Jonathan wrote to his friend Brigham Young:

"My wife has been sick ever since we left Winter Quarters and
it will be twenty-three months tomorrow since she has been
constantly confined to her bed. She now lies before me in the same
afflicted condition.

"Last spring I made every effort in my power to go to the
valley, but failed for the want of one yoke of oxen. After I had
loaded up my things and drove out as far as the ferry, the
examining committee decided that I must have one more yoke of
oxen and being entirely unable to procure them, after having
made every exertion in my power to do so, I returned to this land
with a heavy heart to await the troubling of the waters the next
time—which time is again near at hand, and I hope through the
blessing of Brother Hunter et al I shall be enabled to step in this
time, and to this end I am now daily laboring.

"In relation to Kanesville, I will say that it is at this time a
stage, whereon is acted a great amount of various vices and
virtues, and a more checquered scenery I have never beheld in my
life. About 2000 gold diggers alias mobocrats, are now tarrying in
Pottawattamie waiting for the grass to permit them to go on to the
mines, via Salt Lake. Their conduct to me in the main appears
hateful, deceitful and beastly, and are not unlike Alexander,
almost ready to tear their hair in rage that there is no more to

conquer. They have committed a number of depredations here and the general breathing of their sentiments is 'Damn the Mormons'.... I frequently ask myself, who can help sickening at the sight; yet, still it is true that there are those who appear more happy in this kind of society and under this state of affairs than under any others." (Original letter on file, Journal History, LDS Church Historical Archives.)

Kanesville was a lonely and miserable waiting place. The Saints made the best of it most of the time. They prayed and danced and sang and suffered, whether they were there or anywhere, but their hearts were already in the valley ... in Zion. The days and weeks and months wore on and winter turned to spring, with its mud and misery. Jonathan's vigil over Rebecca's fight for life took most of his attention and all his courage. He found himself almost hoping she would die for her own relief. Meanwhile, Rebecca gave birth to son Jonathan, May 24, 1848, at Harris Grove, Pottawattamie County, Iowa and two years later to the month at Kanesville, Lyman Van arrived.

On a cold day in December, 1849, Jonathan took a breather away from the noise. and confusion of the children, and the distressing sight of his wife Rebecca lying pale and weak on the bunk bed in their little dugout in Kanesville. His breath was visible in the zero air as he made his way down the narrow snow-lined path. This waiting was the most frustrating of all. If he could just get going! But with Rebecca getting weaker every day there was little chance for that. He noticed a group of people down the road talking excitedly. He crowded closer to hear what was going on. Then he recognized Bishop Edward Hunter, who was doing the talking.

"President Young has sent me from the valley to help bring families to Salt Lake next spring. Ed Wolley and I have orders to go to Philadelphia and exchange gold for currency there and come back here in the spring. We'll buy some cattle to take along, make up a company and head for the West. Brother Brigham has worked out a plan called The Perpetual Emigration Fund to help those who need it. The Saints in the Valley and in the East have chipped in so there is a sizable amount already collected. Those who receive help will be expected to pay it back as soon as possible when they get to Salt Lake."

Jonathan's heart did a double somersault as he listened. Could it be that his family's turn had come at last? He turned to retrace his steps, deep in thought.

"Brother Wright ... wait a minute, I want to talk to you." He turned to see Brother Hunter following him.

"You and your family are on my list to go to Salt Lake next spring. You'll have time to get some supplies before then, provided by the Emigration Fund."

Jonathan couldn't bring himself to voice his gratitude nor his doubts about his wife, and simply nodded a proper thank you. But he'd have to keep the news to himself. It wouldn't do to raise the family's hopes at this point. And this he did, hugging the thought and bringing it out a dozen times a day to examine and wonder about, and then burying it again.

Meanwhile Rebecca's condition worsened rapidly. Bearing eight children in twelve years and burying three of them as infants was more than her delicate heart and body could survive. She knew she was dying. Jonathan knelt by her sagging bed, his hand holding her frail cold one. Her words came, halting and in whispers. He leaned close to hear.

"Find a ... mother ... for the children ... soon. I must ... go ... now. The dream!!!!! Don't let me ... sleep ... too long. It will be like it says ... all together again ... and ... happy." As always she was the wise one, the strong one. His tears fell unashamedly as he gathered her in his arms and the children around them.

As her hands and feet grew colder, her pulse slower, she clasped week-old Lyman Van to her breast and the children leaned over the cobbled-up bunk bed to hear her last whispered words. Her frail hand caressed each one in turn, and lingered lovingly on Amos' sandy hair. The children's tears fell on her cold cheeks as they kissed her crying, "Mother, Mother, don't leave us, don't go, don't go!"

But the woman, Rebecca Wheeler Wright, had to go, a pioneer sacrifice, mother of eight, with memories of monotonous days and nights of pain and suffering, of joy and sorrow, of love for her man and babies and her God.

Rebecca's body was laid lovingly in a simple coffin and lowered into her frozen grave. Amos, now familiar, although not comfortable, with death, carried the image and pain of the 29th of May, 1850 for the rest of his life.

Chapter Four
Exodus

Rebecca's death signaled a series of events which demanded the attention of the widower and his five children, leaving no time for mourning or looking back. Word had been received a few days earlier that Bishop Hunter's company would leave no later than June 1st. Inevitable delays postponed starting until the 25th, giving Jonathan barely enough time to make the deadline. He made sure that before leaving he had the three indispensable items: a rifle, an ax and a plow, together with seeds for planting, and this time he met all the other requirements.

A final census showed 261 souls, 67 wagons, 106 yoke of oxen, 133 cows, 10 horses, 19 sheep, 19 dogs, 6 cats, 6 doves and 40 loose cattle. Of these, 5 wagons, 55 yoke of oxen, 41 cows and 27 loose cattle belonged to the Perpetual Emigration Fund. Brother Hunter was captain of the whole group with sub-captains of 50's and 10's under his command. Jonathan was one of the latter.

Careless teamsters and wild unbroken cattle drove the herders crazy at first. The loose cattle were always getting away during the night, and nearly every morning they had to be rounded up before the company could make a start. The roads, if sloughs and hollows can be given that name, became almost impassable after constant and heavy storms. Animals and people sickened and died from exposure, exhaustion and disease. Bishop Hunter's list of graves left behind mounted into the sixties, mostly cholera victims. At the close of a day's travel, nearly seventy wagons formed a corral to try to keep the cattle inside.

There must have been those in the company whose motherly wings continued to enfold the five little Wright children, but six weeks of daily travel was all the tiniest could endure. He too fell asleep and could not be wakened, joining the mother from whom he had been so recently separated. Jonathan dug another lonely little grave, filled it and left it behind.

Even the shrill notes of a trumpet at 5:30 each morning didn't always pull Amos out of the depths of sound sleep, but when he heard his father's voice he didn't waste time getting up. There were chores assigned to him such as rolling up the bedding, loading the wagon and checking to see that nothing was left behind. David Darwin was his shadow. He idolized his big brother, and imitated everything Mose did, as he fondly called Amos. Virginia Ann Charlotte and little Jonny turned to Amos when they needed help as Father Jonathan was often busy helping one of his ten families and it was up to Mose to be "Captain" of his brothers and sister.

Rounding up the cattle and getting the slow-witted oxen into their yoke took some doing. One of the "Fund" cows was fresh, and it was fun to hear the ping of the milk in the bottom of the bucket as Bossy gave down her milk. The muscles of his arms grew strong as he learned how to make an inch or two of foam by the time he had her stripped.

Warm milk and sourdough biscuits, or "lumpy-dick" left over from the night before, provided his breakfast and stuck to his ribs. By seven o'clock everything was loaded and with a "gee" and a "haw" he guided the wagon into line for the day's march.

Driving a team of oxen demanded some skill in itself and he learned quickly, though not without pain. Weeks of walking in the hot sun and drizzling rain could not have been easy for a boy of ten. He listened avidly to his father's conversation, and watched his every move, gleaning wisdom that might come in handy in the future. He came to understand the desert loneliness through body, ear, eye, and his own beating heart.

He looked ahead with anticipation to the conferences around the campfire before bedtime when plans for the next day unfolded, and when men's minds and hearts turned to things beyond cold, or heat or hunger or weariness. This was food for the next day's thinking, which made the miles shrink as he walked.

There were lean times and fat, all depending on the weather or where they were. They ate fish and buffalo steak whenever they could, but when they had to get along on johnny cake, he hoped the next world would be better than this one. He was always hungry it seemed, and thoughts of food often crowded out the larger questions of philosophy and religion which he preferred to consider. He laughed when his father told about the smart woman cook who was so clever she could toss a pancake off the skillet up through the top of the chimney and run outdoors and catch it coming down.

He drank in what Jonathan told him about his father, Peter Bice Wright, and *his* father before him, Samuel B. and how he married a lady who could hardly speak English. About Daniel Shed, who fought in the Revolution, and how the name of the mother country thus became the United States of America, and that freedom was worth fighting for.

The days, weeks and months crept by. The boy walked. The simple act of placing one foot in front of the other, the feel of the ground beneath his feet, the endless sand and sagebrush stretching out in every direction went dully on. His legs ached from the monotonous motion.

Just before reaching Ft. Laramie they stopped to visit an Indian village. There was a whole string of tepees with children and dogs playing around the campfires. Amos' keen eyes took in everything and he recalled what he saw many times afterward. It seemed he had an unexplainable yen for anything Indian.

The women were drying buffalo meat and tanning the hides. One old squaw was packing away the dried meat in a sack made of buffalo hide. The hair had been scraped off and the skin polished till the sack looked like shiny leather. It was painted with bright colors. This was his first chance to learn a little sign language and he loved it. An Indian boy about the same age as Amos, pointed to an elderly white sister of the company who had no teeth. This was strange to him, because Indians of all ages had handsome large teeth. Amos made signs to his new-found Indian friend expressing his approval of the tantalizing odor of savory campfire stew.

Bishop Hunter and Edwin Wooley drove the provision wagon into Fort Laramie to replenish it. They reported they had to pay seventeen-fifty per hundred pounds of flour when it was only six dollars at Kanesville. But it was rumored to be twenty-five dollars in the valley and sometimes as much as a dollar a pound.

Time wore on into August and September. Monotony, the heat, small and large irritants, brought inevitable clashes and disagreements among the travelers. Being thrown so closely into one another's daily lives was itself an irritant. Bishop Hunter wrote of some of his own frustrations in his journal, or reports to Brigham Young. He complained about some of the Saints who were slow to take responsibility, leaving to others the daily chores which made travel possible.

Ultimately came the day when Amos' yoke of sweating,

grunting oxen topped the last rise and his unbelieving eyes gazed with fascination on the scene before him ... Zion!...Place of Refuge. All the waiting weariness melted away as his eyes dwelt hungrily on the broad sweep of sagebrush and scrub cedar. A cluster of log houses could be made out in the distance, with the great shimmering Salt Lake on the horizon in the glow of the October sun.

Chapter Five
Zion

History records that Jonathan lost no time getting into the thick of life in the valley.

"The Hunter party arrived in Salt Lake City, Oct. 13, 1850, 3 months and 9 days after leaving the Missouri River, and settled somewhere as a unit in South Cottonwood, a small settlement just south of Salt Lake City. In 1848-50 the little colony grew steadily and prospered as well as any neighborhood in Utah at that time. The first meetinghouse built in the Ward was a small adobe building, known as Jonathan C. Wright's schoolhouse. It was built in 1851. Previous to this, all meetings had been held in private houses. In the fall of 1851 the majority of the people went to San Bernardino. Jonathan C. Wright stayed and was appointed bishop. He presided until the fall of 1852. Later in the fall of that year he was made counselor to Abraham O. Smoot. When Bishop Smoot was absent, J.C.W. took charge.

"26 July 1851: A political meeting was held in the Bowery in G.S.L. City. Nominations were made: Jonathan C. Wright for Judge in G.S.L. County." (Vol. I. Jonathan Calkins Wright, *Ancestors and Descendants*, p. 70.)

Newly arrived in Cottonwood, a schoolteacher, judge and bishop, he must have been keenly aware of the need of his children for mothering. That, besides his own hunger for a companion determined him to try again. On December 18, 1850, two months after their arrival in the valley, an item in the Church

Journal History shows: "At 8 p.m. Pres. Young, Heber C. Kimball, Willard Richards, Parley P. Pratt and ladies met at John Van Cott's residence and married Jonathan C. Wright. The Brethren had a good supper and danced till about 10 p.m."

The name of the bride was evidently not important. She was a widow, Cynthia Martin Nichols. How the two met or any of the details of their marriage is not known. That it was sanctioned by the Church leaders is self-evident, but that it was unsuccessful is shown by the entry in the Wright family Bible: Jonathan C. Wright and Cynthia Nichols, Married Salt Lake City, Utah, Dec. 18th, 1850. Divorced May 7, 1851. She bore twins, Henry and Cynthia on 12 August. They took the name of Wright.

After this disappointing episode, Jonathan must have been wary of another marriage, but he remembered Rebecca's last words, and nine months later he brought home another mother to his children.

Amos looked up into the kindly face of nineteen-year-old Mary Jane Neeley. Jonathan was forty-three. As one of her hands held his head against her skirt, Amos felt a sense of homecoming; the maternal warmth he had needed so much had so long been denied.

Jonathan's third try at a new mother for his children and a companion for himself was a winner on both counts. Mary Jane and her parents came to the valley the same year as Jonathan. Their meeting wasn't itemized, but as usual Jonathan didn't mince words or waste time. The wedding was arranged for February 25, 1852 in President Brigham Young's office. Mary Jane explained later, "I didn't marry Mr. Wright for love, but to help him rear four motherless children, Amos, David, Charlotte and little Jonathan, and to get my little sister, Harriet Neeley, away from a cruel stepmother."

Mary Jane had a few pieces of furniture to bring to the house. Amos ran his fingers over the slick wood of the bureau, pushed his fist into the feather pillows, sat in the new chair and wondered to himself, because this was the first time he could remember touching such fine things, such soft slick things. Life felt different from then on. He seemed to have found some shelter from the storms of everyday living. At last he had a chance to think about things like new friends, school, and books. Ah, books! They indeed opened new worlds for this knowledge-hungry boy.

One evening after supper his father pulled a coin out of his pocket. Money of any kind was scarce and Amos examined it carefully. It was about the size of a modern dime of shiny yellow metal. The words "Holiness to the Lord" were stamped on one side, and on the other, two clasped hands with the letters G.S.L. P.G. (Great Salt Lake, Pure Gold) and the date 1840. He later saw but did not own, coins of five, ten and twenty-dollar denomination. They were minted from gold dust brought by Mormon Battalion boys from the gold fields in California. Except for such isolated reminders, Amos would have known little of the mad rush for quick wealth in California.

In contrast, the Mormons pooled their hard-to-come-by money to help bring more exiles from Illinois and foreign shores. Amos remembered making small donations to the Emigration Fund himself. But as new converts flooded into the valley from all parts of the world it was the Indians which fascinated Amos most. In their first home in Cottonwood this counsel from Brigham Young was posted for all to read:

> Stockade your fort and tend to your own affairs and let the Indians take care of theirs. Let your women and children stay in the fort and the Indians stay out. But while you mix with them promiscuously you must continue to receive such treatment from them which they please to give. This is what we have told you continually and you will find it true.

It was probably at this time that Mose began to pick up snatches of their language, which served him so effectively a few years later as a peacemaker and interpreter.

Then one day his father announced that they were going to move. "Where to? When? Why?" The year was 1854 and Amos was fourteen. They were going to one of the new settlements north of Salt Lake. It was called Brigham City.

The insides of Amos' hands took on calluses thick as leather. He learned to swing an ax. He grew hard, tough, wiry, and his nerves and muscles became instruments of his will. He learned to ride a pony, Indian style, laying his body close to the horse, clutching the mane with one hand and only one leg over the horse's back and suddenly switching to the other side, to avoid stray bullets. There was plenty for a strong young fellow to do in this new country. It was back to fort-survival living for awhile.

Each head of family was later apportioned a good-sized lot in town and twenty acres of farmland on the outskirts. Jonathan's twenty was north, about two or three miles. Cow and horse pasture was also available. Each family had a corral on the home lot for a cow or two. A herder was paid a few cents a day to drive them along the street down to the meadow for the day's grazing. At about five in the evening, they were brought back to the homestead in time for milking. This was kid stuff for Amos, so young Jonathan or "Pony" as he was later called, and David, usually got that assignment.

There was plowing, planting, irrigating, and harvesting aplenty for the big boys. Between times Amos could always be found with his nose in a book, or hanging around the Indian tepees on the edge of town, playing mumble-peg, stick game, and learning new words in Shoshone and Bannock. It was fun to try the odd-sounding gutteral syllables, and he worked hard to reproduce the correct intonation. He also enjoyed the graphic sign language used between Western tribes who spoke different vocal languages. Sometimes his brown brothers laughed at him for his mistakes, but they recognized his persistence and came to stand a little in awe of his achievement.

He watched the squaws tan buckskin by rubbing the hide with calf brains for hours at a time until it came out velvet soft and white. If they wanted the skin to be tougher for moccasins, they smoked it over a wood fire, making it a light brown color. It was a great day when one of the Indian women made him his first pair of moccasins, paid for with a quart of berries picked from Mary Jane's patch.

Amos found it difficult to concentrate on school, although Jonathan sometimes taught. The kids learned their lessons by saying them aloud to themselves till it was time to recite. Alphabets, multiplication tables, and letters of spelled words were all in the air at once. Amos said it was a waste of time when he could learn it by himself with a lot less noise. Still, it was about the only time he had a chance to play. Before and after school was work and more work, so he made the most of his time in the classroom. He learned his lessons.

He also learned, though, it wasn't in the curriculum, to jump and click his heels before he hit the floor. He could whistle through his teeth by putting his two fingers in his mouth a certain way and blowing. There were dozens of tricks he learned from both Indians and Whites, and he used them all. But always in the back of his head he knew he'd better walk it pretty straight, because he was the eldest son of Bishop or Judge or Honorable Jonathan Calkins Wright, who might even give him a thrashing if he didn't.

Time came when he looked across the room at a cute little girl sitting by Virginia Ann Charlotte, named Susanna Moran whose long black braids he liked to jerk whenever he got near enough. Lois Susanna—that was the prettiest name he'd ever heard and she was as pretty as her name. And when he talked to her, he thought he was a man for sure.

Chapter Six
The Test

Childhood and early youth had been anything but easy, yet to Amos it tasted sweet. He loved life and craved all it could give. But now he sensed a change. There was a quickening, an urgency in his approaching manhood. The strange dream which had encircled and chiseled the life of his father Jonathan and mother Rebecca, as well as Sarah Boyce, Cynthia Nichols and Mary Jane Neeley, suddenly drew him into its embrace.

It was spring once more, this time 1856. Amos was sixteen-going-on-seventeen. He had finished the fifth reader and anybody who got that far was considered educated. He seemed too young to get a real job but old enough to want one. One day he ran into Lewis Shurtliff. He was twenty-one and had just got the contract to carry mail up through the northern settlements. He and his partner Nate Leavitt were about ready to leave.

"But we need someone who can talk Shoshone and Bannock in case we have any trouble. We'll cut you in on the pay. We have an extra pony you can use and a pack mule for your belongings and grub. Better bring your own bedding," he said, "and be ready to leave day after tomorrow." Amos said he'd talk to his father and let him know for sure.

Down at the courthouse he waited in line. When it was his turn, he walked into Jonathan's office and announced, "Father, I've got a chance for a job," and explained the proposition. "It won't pay much but I think it would be better than just loafing around here all summer." Jonathan looked surprised and pleased.

"When are you leaving?"

"Day after tomorrow," replied Amos.

Jonathan reached in his pocket, pulled out a five-dollar gold piece and handed it to his son. "Take care of yourself, Mosey." The two men embraced, and Amos was gone.

When he told Mary Jane, she began scrounging around among his few possessions, washing his clothes and putting things in order. She sat up all night making him an extra shirt and pair of pants. He traded some odds and ends for a buckskin coat from one of his Indian friends, and got a pair of moccasins thrown in. There was also a good camp quilt which he could take, Mary Jane said.

As time for his departure drew near, she found herself dreading his going. He had become very dear to her in the past three years. He would be in danger and she knew it. "His mind and mine," she thought to herself, "what little I have, seem to run together." She was twenty-three, expecting her third child and he was sixteen. But seven years under those conditions made a world of difference, so her role as mother seemed logical to both of them. He was "her boy" as much or more than any yet born to her. As he said goodbye she hoped he would sometimes get homesick enough to long for a piece of her bread hot out of the oven with butter running down between his fingers.

Mary Jane's baby was a boy and they named him Lehi, after the prophet in the Book of Mormon. Summer chores like gardening, bottling fruit, making butter and taking care of chickens merged yesterday into today, and before she knew it, flakes of snow were falling outside. Jonathan came home one evening looking especially thoughtful and sat through the meal without saying anything. Finally, he blurted it out:

"I guess I'll be taking another wife. The authorities advise it."

Mary Jane was naturally surprised but offered no objection. She understood plural marriage, believed it was right and was willing to obey it. She asked him who he had in mind. He said he didn't know.

Virginia Ann Charlotte, Jonathan's fourteen-year-old daughter and Lois Moran, the little girl whose braids Amos liked to pull, were bosom companions, practically inseparable. They had been born only two days apart. Lois was in and out of Mary Jane's house every day, often staying overnight. Mary Jane would hear the two girls laughing and whispering long after they went to bed. They were at that "romantic age" and often talked about getting married. They heard a lot from the older folks about the honor it was to marry a prominent man who already had another wife or two. He could furnish them a good home and their children would be "born under the covenant," which sounded good. In one of their heart-to-heart talks they promised each other they would do this if they ever had a chance. Lois' chance came sooner than she expected.

When Brother Wright asked her to marry him, she remembered her pledge to Charlotte and said, "Yes, if Mother is willing." Her mother gave her consent. As soon as he left, Lois thought, "Wouldn't it be fun to tell Charlotte and make her guess who I'm going to marry!" She'd say first, "He's a bishop." Charlotte would right away wonder if it was Bishop Nichols, the man she had her eye on already. Next she'd tell her he was a judge. There was one other judge in town. If she couldn't guess by that time, Lois would tell her he was in the stake presidency ... that would be three to wonder about. And finally she would say he was a member of the state legislature, and Brother Wright was the only one it could be. She was really very proud to have a chance to marry such an important man. Charlotte guessed and guessed and finally Lois had to tell her and then she could believe it.

It was a cold mid-January day, 1857, in the little village of Brigham City, Utah, that Mary Jane noticed a horse and buggy stop out front. She saw her husband carrying a suitcase in one hand and holding the arm of a woman as they made their way across the slippery road toward the house. In a moment she heard her husband's booming voice say, "Mary, this is my new wife, Lois Moran!"

Jonathan was forty-nine ... a big, handsome, impressive man, accustomed to the recognition accorded those in authority. The child-bride at his side was fifteen. She stood there looking like a little doll, her dark eyes framed with long lashes, and black glossy hair falling in waves about her shoulders. She was tiny, yet her winter coat could not disguise the soft curves of her body. She was a beauty!

As Mary Jane looked at her, she was suddenly aware of her own appearance. She ran her hand quickly through her hair, realizing she hadn't even combed it, and looked down at her soiled, torn dress. Well, there was no use standing there acting as terrible as she looked and felt.

"Hello, Lois. Have off your coat and sit down. Have you had dinner? If you'll wait a minute I'll scramble some eggs and the bread's just out of the oven." Then turning to her husband she said, "Brother Wright," for she always called him that, "the cow got out this morning and I've been chasing her all over the lot and finally got her back in the corral. Maybe you can fix the fence so she won't get out again." At least he'd know why she looked so awful. It didn't seem quite fair for him to bring this child here without telling her ahead of time.

After they ate, Jonathan told Mary Jane he had to be at the courthouse in fifteen minutes. Could she make a place for Lois for awhile till he could arrange things? She did, and Lois stayed in Mary Jane's home for the rest of her life.

The news set the little town abuzz for a few days, but was soon accepted as just another in a string of events which frequently took place among the Saints those days, who had come to be known as "a peculiar people."

To Mary Jane it was like taking another child to raise. Lois and Charlotte were together all the time, laughing and giggling like the little girls they were, and leaving most of the work to her. There was going to be a ward dance for Valentine's day and that was only two weeks away. The girls talked incessantly about what they would wear. They decided they'd each make a new dress for the occasion. They worked every spare minute and the dresses were finished the day before the dance.

The next day, who should walk in but Amos himself, looking a lot bigger and handsomer than when he left almost a year ago. Everybody said they were anxious to hear about him but nobody had time to listen. Father Jonathan had a call to go to Willard for a day or two and had to leave in a hurry. Lois was upset because Brother Wright wouldn't be there to take her and Charlotte to the dance. Their new dresses were all ready to wear and now they couldn't go. As they sat on the bed crying, Charlotte suddenly stopped and said, "I know what we'll do ... I'll ask Amos to take us!" A sly grin spread over Lois' face. "Let's not tell him I'm married until afterwards, and surprise him."

Amos caught his breath as the girls walked out of the bedroom ready for the dance. His sister looked beautiful in her long blue gown with her hair done up in a blond swirl. He couldn't believe she was so grown up in just a year. But it was Lois Moran who took his breath away, as she stood there smiling up at him. She had on a bright red dress with a tight bodice and full skirt down to the floor, trimmed with black lace around her white neck and shoulders. It was evident she, too, was a woman. And she was *his* girl. Mary Jane said she was too tired to go, so the three young ones said goodbye and were out the door.

The ward hall was decorated in grand style with big red hearts hung from the ceiling. There was a big crowd, too. Ezra Dunn had his accordion and Zeke Nebeker was tuning up his fiddle. There was Moroni Box in the caller's corner, and everything was ready to start.

After the opening prayer by Bishop Nichols, the music started. There were so many, everybody couldn't dance at once so the boys drew numbers and danced when their turn came. Only one waltz was allowed. The rest were quadrilles, French Fours, and Schottisches. Amos danced a square with Charlotte while Lois watched. He looked like a good dancer and she could tell he was having fun by the way he swung Charlotte and put in little extra movements without missing a beat. He reminded her of Brother Wright, only of course he was a lot younger.

Amos had to wait several dances until his number came up again. Charlotte was dancing with Bishop Nichols but nobody asked Lois so she and Amos sat and talked. He said it was wonderful to be back in civilization again after almost a year among the Indians. Lois was fascinated as she listened with both eyes and ears to the strange and exciting stories. Before they knew it, Amos' number was called again. It was a quadrille and he asked Lois to dance. The caller announced this would be a new tune called "Oh, Susanna." It was a good swinging tune and the two were carried away as they fell into perfect rhythm. They were both out of breath as the music stopped.

"They made that one just for me!" laughed Lois. "My name is Susanna you know!" Amos knew. The name just fit her ... Lois Susanna Moran, all run together like a little tune.

They had both gone to the same one-room school. She was the only one who could spell him down. She had to be good to do that. It stung his pride but intrigued him at the same time. He watched her as she walked, swinging her dark braids which hung below her waist. He knew where she lived and wanted to walk home with her, but was afraid of being made fun of by the other boys. He couldn't resist sometimes after dark, walking past her house hoping to catch a glimpse of her. But most often the shades were drawn, and he could only imagine how she looked sitting there at the table, studying her spelling so she could spell him down again. She didn't know it but she was *his* girl, and some day he would tell her. Meanwhile he kept that precious thought buried deep inside, to think about just before going to sleep, or on special quiet occasions when he was all alone. Nobody ... but *nobody* could be trusted with this precious secret of his, and that made it all the sweeter.

There were a couple of dances after that. Charlotte was dancing with Bishop Nichols again, so Amos and Lois sat them out, finding lots to talk about in the meantime. Then "Pop Goes The Weasel" and "I Danced With a Girl With A Hole In Her Stocking," kept them do-si-do-ing and promenading and they were both sorry when it was over. Each time they met and the caller said, "SWING YOUR PARTNERS!" Amos made the most of it and gave her an extra twirl. His arm could have gone all the way around her tiny waist, but even halfway was heavenly.

When the dance was over Charlotte came and whispered something to Lois, and they both giggled. She called over her shoulder to her brother, "I'm going home with somebody else. You can look after Lois. Bring her to my house, she's staying with me. See you later."

It was late when he finally said good night. He wanted to kiss her but didn't quite dare so soon. There would be another time, and another and another, and the anticipation would make it worth the waiting.

As he crawled between the camp quilt and a buffalo robe in the hayloft at the back of the house, he wondered where he had been all his life up to now. Even his secret imaginings about Lois Susanna seemed pale and insignificant now. It wasn't imaginings any more ... it was real and for sure, and a hundred times more wonderful.

He awoke early next morning and lay there without moving, not wanting to break the spell. It was a new world ... a new day! He bounded out of bed and down the ladder from the hayloft. No king could have slept on a finer couch so far as he was concerned.

Father Jonathan was already up. He had got home late after everybody else was in bed. Mary Jane already had the cow milked and was straining the white foamy stuff into the shallow tin milkpans in the pantry.

"I'll have breakfast ready in a jiffy," she called. "We're going to have pancakes."

Amos and his father gave each other a hug and started to talk. They hadn't seen each other for nine months or so. Yes, it had been a pretty good experience. He'd learned a lot. It was hard work and a few narrow escapes, but on the whole he was glad he went. Now he was ready to settle down and get a job if he could find one.

Mary Jane announced breakfast and told Jonathan to call Charlotte and Lois. They came out of the bedroom, their eyes heavy with sleep. Jonathan went over and put his arms around Lois and swung her around before kissing her and letting her down again.

"Well, Honey, did you have a good time last night? Sorry I wasn't here to take you." Then turning to Amos he beamed, "Well son, what do you think of my wife?"

Amos glanced at her. The blood drained out of her face and he would never forget the tragic look she gave him. Without a word, Amos turned and walked out of the house. He had to get away. His brain was paralyzed as he tried to comprehend what it was all about. Was it a trick? He started to run, it didn't matter where. He'd climb the mountain, away from everything and as far as he could get.

There had been a Chinook a few days before and the snow was nearly gone ... just a few patches left here and there in the shady places. His legs were numb and his lungs were bursting but he drove himself mercilessly. On he went, up and up and up, throwing himself at last on the sandy flat half way up the mountain. He lay motionless and gasping. His mind was exhausted along with his body and for a time a blessed unconsciousness settled upon him. Then the blur of questions began again. What had happened? Was it a trick? Who was to blame? How did it happen? Whose fault was it? Was it Charlotte or his father or Lois or all of them? Or was he losing his mind? What right did his father have to marry her? Amos turned over on his back. How could he get even? He'd go and fight him. But he couldn't do that. He loved and trusted his father. It couldn't be *his* fault. Was it Lois? That delicate little girl couldn't hurt anybody or anything. Buy why didn't she tell him herself? But of course ... she didn't know how he felt about her, he had never told *anybody*. How did *she* feel? She was already married ... an impossible thought, but she seemed to like him last night. It must have been all his own imagination. If this is what girls did to you he'd never look at one again. There was nothing to base judgment upon. How could he know? Who could help him? He pushed the palms of his hands against his eyes, rubbing them back and forth as if to clear his vision.... Mary Jane, maybe. She was different... Mother Rebecca ... yes, she *was* different. The warmth and peace she had given him he'd never had enough of. She satisfied a hunger nothing else could ... except God. Yes, that was what she taught him ... he'd ask God! *He'd* know. He'd understand!

Oh, the blessed relief to pour it out in a flood without trying to reason it through. All the hurt and torment, just pour it out ... pour it out, pour it out! "Oh, Heavenly Father help me, help me ... and forgive me!"

The sun was low in the west. He was cold. He shivered. He was hungry. Mary Jane could do something about that. He made his way down the mountain, stumbling, slipping, sliding. The turbulence was gone from inside him now; only numbness remained.

When he walked in, the house was quiet for a change. The children must be in bed. Yes, there was Mary Jane knitting away as usual. She looked up and said simply, "Your supper's waiting for you in the oven." She spread a fresh cloth on the table with deft fingers; set out mashed potatoes and meat and brown gravy and slices of her wholewheat bread. He *was* hungry! Two, three helpings disappeared.

"There's something about food," he grinned as he leaned back in his chair. Then a silence. He had to find out. "Tell me what happened." And Mary Jane in her quiet way tried to explain. They'd been married since the middle of January. She too was surprised, though Brother Wright had told her he was going to get married again. The authorities had urged it. Lois was so young ... still a little girl. Nobody thought to tell you about it when you came so unexpectedly. It all just seemed to happen.

Quietly, Amos thanked Mary Jane for the good supper, said goodnight and went out to his hayloft bed. He'd made his bed; he'd have to lie in it! It was all his own fault anyway. He didn't mean anything to her. It was all his imagination. He'd built up this thing in his own mind and just supposed she felt the same way he did. He got all hot inside at the thought and threw the buffalo robe off to cool himself. At least nobody else knew about his stupid dreams, he was thankful for that much. And nobody ever would!

Jonathan later had a chance to talk to Lois alone. He approached the subject gingerly, but after a few questions she looked at him piteously and burst into tears. He gathered her into his arms and pulled her down on his lap, wiping her eyes with his big handkerchief.

"Now, my dear, don't cry, just tell me what happened." She laid her head on his shoulder and told her story between sobs.

"Oh, Brother Wright, Charlotte and I just thought it would be a good joke to wait till after the dance to tell Amos about you and me, and you weren't here so we got him to take us. We wanted to surprise him. It seemed like things just happened after that. I didn't want to hurt his feelings ... it seemed like he really liked me." She bit her lip and the tears came again. "I guess it was just my imagination. Charlotte and Bishop Nichols got home before we did. He left, and Charlotte went in the house. It seemed like Amos didn't want to say good night ... we didn't do anything, only talk. But the way he looked at me at breakfast time next morning and walked out when he found out, made me think he hated me. I guess you hate me too and I don't blame you!" Then squirming out of his arms she ran out of the room crying hysterically.

Jonathan came home late that evening after Amos had gone to bed. His father asked about him. Mary Jane told him as much as she knew, that he'd asked her what had happened, but didn't say anything afterward and went out to bed. She could tell he was upset though he tried not to show it. She and Jonathan decided to fast, since next day was Sunday. It was conference and Brother Brigham would be there as the visiting authority. Jonathan got to see him a few minutes after meeting. They went over to the courthouse together. Jonathan unlocked the door to his office and they went in and sat down.

"President Young, I think you know I don't go in for tall tales, but I won't blame you if you don't believe what I have to tell you. I need your advice and counsel." Then he related the story.

The president was very solemn as he sat pondering and stroking his chin. It seemed a long time before Brother Young cleared his throat and said, "I ought to have some time to think about this. I won't be leaving till tomorrow. I'll see what I can do in the meantime." And with that he left Jonathan to wrestle by himself.

Brother Lorenzo Snow, president of the Box Elder Stake and one of the Council of the Twelve, who lived in Brigham City, sent word next morning he wanted to see Amos at his office right away. Amos often ran errands for his father or Brother Snow, since Jonathan was Brother Snow's first counselor. As he walked in the office that day he was surprised to see two other gentlemen there also. Then he recognized President Brigham Young who spoke to him kindly and said, "You probably know Elder Thomas Smith already." He came right to the point.

"Amos, Brother Smith is serving a mission to the Indians up at Ft. Lemhi. I understand you have been up there this past year carrying the mail and that you can speak Shoshone like a native. Brother Smith needs a good interpreter. Would you be willing to go back up there again as a missionary this time?"

Amos sucked in a quick breath and his mind went blank—another question to answer. He hesitated and then said, "Could I have time to talk it over with my father first?" "Of course," replied President Young. Then putting his arm around Amos and turning to Elder Smith he continued.

"Now if Amos decides to go, you take care that not a hair of this boy's head is harmed. He is not only a fine young man, coming from a fine father, but he is a very useful lad as well. He will serve you well and faithfully." And then to Amos again, "I'll be leaving for Ft. Lemhi myself the middle of April with a large company. How would you like to go with Captain Jefferson Hunt's Cavalry? You could be mustered in beforehand. They'll be going ahead as an express to carry the mail and notify the settlers we're coming. You can think it over and let me know." The three men shook hands and Amos left.

He'd better see his father right away, Amos thought to himself. So he headed for the courthouse. Jonathan was sitting at his desk reading a letter.

"Close the door and sit down, Son," he said as he handed the letter to Amos. "I found this in the door when I came this morning." Amos took the letter wonderingly, as he read:

Dear Brother Wright:

After careful consideration I suggest we call Amos on a mission if he will consent, and when he comes home, if they haven't gotten over their feelings for each other, you will have to give her up to him.

Yours,

Brigham Young

Jonathan waited awhile after Amos had finished reading. "I talked to Brother Brigham yesterday. Maybe we can take time to think this over and then decide what to do."

"I just saw him over at Brother Snow's office," replied Amos, and walked out.

Everybody seemed to be walking on eggs in those days, talking in monosyllables, moving nervously. Little Lorenzo and Lehi caught the tenseness in the air, too. They even cried quieter. Mary Jane was the go-between. If one had a message for the other, he told *her* to tell *him*. "When Father is ready to talk to me I hope I'll know what to say," muttered Amos. Lois and Charlotte tip-toed in and out and stayed out of sight most of the time.

Amos had crawled up into his hayloft hideaway one late afternoon, when he heard a heavy tread on the ladder. Looking up from under his buffalo robe he saw his father's face peering inquiringly around.

"Oh, there you are, son. I was looking for you." He crawled up and hoisted his heavy body onto the soft hay. He searched for a way to begin. "I got a letter from Brother Brigham today," he began slowly. "There's some probate work needs taking care of in Salt Lake the last of the month and I'll need to go down. He said if you decide to go on that mission, it would be a good time to go for your endowment."

Stalling for time so he wouldn't have to commit himself, Amos asked, "What is this endowment, Father? Why would I have to have it before I go?"

"The endowment is a gift to prepare you for exaltation in the Celestial Kingdom. The Lord gives his sons the authority to act in the name of Jesus Christ in a sacred ceremony held in the Endowment House. If you decide to go on a mission you need authority to act for him and you will be ordained an Elder holding the Melchizedek Priesthood."

Waiting for a little of this to sink in, Jonathan backed toward the ladder on his hands and knees, felt for the top rung and began lowering himself. "If you think you'd like to go, I'll be leaving here the 28th of March. We could have the ordinance performed at the Endowment House on the 31st."

A few days later Amos had a few minutes alone with Jonathan. "I've been thinking about this endowment business. It sounds pretty serious, Father. I don't believe I could go through with it if I was still thinking I might come back and take Lois away from you. I believe it will be easier if I just chop it off now and know I have to forget about her for good and all." The two men clasped hands, and Jonathan's voice was husky. "God bless you, my boy!"

With this turn of events, Jonathan had a brainstorm. If he could get Lois' consent, she could go along and they could be sealed at the same time. He talked to her, explaining that Amos didn't hold any hard feelings against her, and that it had all been a misunderstanding and best forgotten now. And since he and Mary Jane had been married before the completion of the Endowment House, she could come along and be sealed to him as

well. He assured Lois he loved her deeply and hoped she would
consent to be his wife for eternity. She listened, her eyes
swimming in tears.

"Let me talk to Charlotte, Brother Wright, and then I'll
decide."

Charlotte thought it would be a good idea, especially if she
could go along too. Bishop Nichols had asked her to marry him
the night of the dance, and her father had given his consent. She
could get her endowment ahead of time if she went with Lois and
they could have a nice trip together besides. And that's the way it
worked out, the five of them going together, Lois and Virginia
Ann Charlotte and Amos in the back seat of the white-top buggy,
and Mary Jane and Jonathan in front.

It was a subdued, serious group that entered the sacred
building on the day March went out like a lion. The record shows:

Jonathan Calkins Wright, sealed for eternity to Mary Jane
Neeley and Lois Susanna Moran, by Brigham Young, March 31,
1857.

And on May 29, 1857, in Brigham City, Utah, Virginia Ann
Charlotte Wright became the third wife of Alvin Nichols. Thus,
the two fifteen-year-old girls fulfilled their pledge to each other.

Chapter Seven
The Salmon River Mission

Amos was mustered into Capt. Jefferson Wright's
Company A, Utah Cavalry in Brigham City, Utah, April 23, 1857.
He was among a few hand-picked men who left the same day to
notify the settlers and missionaries at Ft. Lemhi, on the Salmon
River that President Brigham Young with a large company was
coming to visit.

The year before, Amos had been carrying mail on the same
route with Lewis Shurtliff and Nate Leavitt and they were often
threatened by Indians. They had a few narrow escapes but
managed to get through unharmed each time. Amos made several

trips back and forth from Utah to Ft. Lemhi, the northern-most settlement, during 1856 and came to know the trail unerringly. The three companions stayed each time at the Fort for a month or so, getting acquainted with both missionaries and Indians and helping out with planting and harvesting, fishing, hunting and practicing Shoshone and sign language. The time went fast. Amos didn't make much money, but he didn't need much, either.

This time things were different. Though still the youngest of the group, only seventeen, he felt ten years older. He was looked to as a knowledgeable leader, especially since he was the only one who spoke Shoshone and Bannock. Besides, now he was a missionary. Camp life had always fascinated him. He loved the smell of sweaty horse flesh, campfire smoke, sourdough biscuits out of a bake-kettle, and the banter of good-natured jesting that took place among the men.

His heart quickened in spite of himself with a mixture of youthful anticipation and anxiety about the unknown. In addition, there was the stabbing ache whenever he thought even fleetingly about Lois Moran. True, he realized it was all over between them, but thoughts have a way of intruding on the screen of memory at the most unexpected moments, to torment and tantalize. He understood, too, that he and the other missionaries had been given a large order, as written instructions verified:

> To settle among the Flathead, Bannock or Shoshone Indians or anywhere that the tribes would receive them, and there teach the Indians the principles of civilization; teach them to cease their savage customs and to live in peace with each other and with the Whites; to cease their roving habits and to settle down; also to teach them how to build houses and homes; in fact to do all they could to better the conditions of those fallen people, and bring them to a better life. (Kate Carter, *The Salmon River Mission*, p. 4.)

The specific methods were left to the ingenuity and skill of the missionaries. They were promised if they would work humbly and faithfully, God would bless them and crown their labors with success. This was indeed a test of faith.

The express was organized somewhat like the pioneer companies, with a captain and various aides during the trip. Amos was assigned to a six-man group called a "mess" with certain chores to be done each day. The men gathered morning and evening for prayer, each member taking his turn according to roll call.

After they crossed the 8,000-foot-high divide near the head-

waters of the east fork of the Salmon River, the beautiful oblong
valley lay before them. It would be home for the indefinite future.
It was three-hundred miles or more to hell-and-gone, but the
country captured his heart and he determined to do his best at the
job he'd agree to try, teaching the Gospel of Jesus Christ to the
Indians, or Lamanites as the Book of Mormon called them.

As the Express Company rode into the camp at Ft. Lemhi,
they were met by excited and curious men, women and children.
When they heard that President Young was making that long
trek to see them, they reacted like the company-starved people
they were. Running from door to door they shouted, "Great day in
the morning! Brother Brigham's coming! He'll be here in a few
days ... can you believe it? He's coming all this way just to see
us!"

President Young's entourage *was* impressive. Altogether
there were one hundred and fifteen men, twenty-two women, five
boys and a hundred and twenty-six horses and mules, twenty-
eight carriages, twenty-six wagons and two light boats for
ferrying across the Snake River. The purpose of the journey,
according to plans, was "to visit the settlement on the Salmon
River, to rest minds, to invigorate bodies, and to examine the
intervening country." Brigham Young told the brethren at the
fort, he thought they had come too far from home to build the fort,
as in case of trouble, immediate help could not be sent. He was of
the opinion that the Snake River Valley would have been better.
(Conover Wright, "History of Amos Wright," ms. p. 19.)

He probably felt, however, that since the mission at Ft. Lemhi
had been set up two years already, it would be discouraging to the
settlers after working so hard, to insist on their abandoning it.
Therefore, he advised them to build a blockhouse on a knoll east
of the fort, with a mud wall around the fort itself. He and the
brethren with him seemed to sense coming trouble with the
natives.

They were counseled also to be patient and kind, to encourage
and teach the Indians, set a good example for them and never
bring reproach on themselves by their actions. The visit proved to
be very encouraging and helpful to the struggling missionaries.
(Carter, *Salmon River Mission*, p. 13.)

One afternoon, Snagg, the head chief of the tribe of Bannocks,
and several other Indians, came into the fort and had a smoke
and a long friendly talk in which Arapeen, head chief of the
Utahs, who accompanied the expedition, took part.

The most surprising and exciting bit of advice during the visit
was given by Heber C. Kimball and Daniel H. Wells when they
urged the young men to marry native women. They said the
marriage tie is the strongest one of friendship that exists.
However, President Young, in his inimitable style, modified this
advice by saying they should not be in a hurry, and should marry
young girls, if any, because said he, "If you brethren were to
marry those old 'vanigadoes' they would be off with the first
mountaineer that came along. (Wright, "History of Amos
Wright," ms p. 20.) A few of the young men did as suggested.
Amos probably listened with interest. Had he followed that
advice, his story would have been a very different one.

After the meeting on Sunday, President Young caught sight of
Amos and came over to speak to him. He shook hands warmly
and asked how he was getting along. He seemed pleased that
Amos had decided to come as a missionary. "Did you get your
endowment before you left?" Amos assured him he did. "Well,
were you set apart?" "No sir, I didn't know I should be." "You
must be. Wait here a few minutes and we'll take care of it right
away." Whereupon he approached some of the other visiting
brethren and shortly President Lorenzo Snow came over and said,
"Please come with me, Brother Wright." He led the way over to a
large tent and lifted the flap. Inside President Snow introduced
Amos to Elders Orson Hyde and J.D. Richards. A camp stool was
provided and he was asked to sit down. The three brethren placed
their hands on his head, with Elder Orson Hyde speaking. When
he finished, Brother Thomas D. Brown said, "If you'll wait just a
few minutes, Brother Wright, I'll have a copy made for you." It
read:

> Apostolic Blessing upon the head of Amos R. Wright, given under
> the hands of Orson Hyde, Lorenzo Snow, and J.D. Richards, Orson
> Hyde being voice:
> Brother Wright, in the name of Jesus Christ, we lay our hands on
> thy head and set thee apart to this mission and calling. Thy name
> shall stand upon the records of the Church and Kingdom of God
> amongst thy brethren. Thou shalt be a comfort to them, being a part
> of this mission and bearing a portion of the labor in strengthening
> this Fort and laboring among the remnants of Israel. Seek for the
> Holy Spirit to lighten thee, and them in darkness. We pray the Lord
> to aid thee in keeping the commandments of God. Gird on the armor
> of truth and righteousness and keep it bright. Thy heart shall yearn
> for the salvation and redemption of the sons of the forest. You pray in
> faith and angels of God shall guard and comfort you, and the

Lamanites that behold in thee truth and light shall apply unto thee for instruction. We dedicate and consecrate thee to this mission that the blessings and all pertaining to this mission shall rest on thee, in the name of Jesus Christ, Amen.

Thomas D. Brown Scribe. May 12, 1857
Salmon   River Mission

These words spoken by an apostle of the Lord, in whom he had implicit trust, became scripture to Amos, especially the part about the Indians. He found himself often repeating the words in his mind: "Thy heart shall yearn for the salvation and redemption of the sons of the forest. And the Lamanites that behold in thee truth and light, shall apply unto thee for instruction." Was this to be a lifetime job, he wondered? If they would come to him for instruction, he'd better be ready to give them what they wanted and needed, and whenever they wanted it.

Before Brother Brigham left, he advised the missionaries to build a stockade on the brow of the hill above the fort, and also to make a wall around it. His suggestion was carried out and a dozen or so men including Amos went to work building what was called a Spanish wall.

Amos had become acquainted with a couple of Indian boys the year before, and now he hunted them up again. They looked to be about the same age as he was. In Shoshone, he explained that the large white man "Peah Tibo" (President Young) had told them to build a wall and asked if they'd like to help. They nodded and followed him. The tall ruddy-skinned boy said he was Anka-Toah, which Amos translated as "Red Boy." The other was small and very shy and said his name was "Tab-Boots" which meant "Rabbit."

The Spanish wall was to be built three feet thick at the bottom and taper to two feet at the top and it would be nine feet high. The forms for the wall were to be planks sawed out of logs, and the logs had to be hauled from the canyon. This would be quite a project and Amos had a plan to get his friends to work while he taught them the gospel. They were very shy at first, and said they didn't know how to do what he was doing. But he was patient and kind and, by and by, Anka-Toah and Tab-Boots became his constant shadows.

They watched in fascination as he cut down a tree, swinging the axe so the chips flew like feathers in a wind, and making the tree fall right where he said it would. They helped him wrap a big chain around the trunk, hitch a mule on and snake it down the mountain. It took days to get logs enough for the forms. There were times in between when Amos said it was time to rest.

As his friends lay on their backs, with the breeze drifting through the quaking aspens, Amos told them about a boy named Joseph Smith, even younger than they were who went into the forest of trees like these quaking aspen. He wanted to know which Church was the right one. "The Great Spirit came and stood in front of him and he had a body like a man, but he was very white and shining. His son, Jesus Christ, came and stood by his Father. Jesus told Joseph Smith the true Church wasn't on the earth yet, but when it was, he must tell the Indians about it. It is on the earth now and that is why I came over three hundred miles to tell you about it. I know it is true. Think about what I have told you today. Now I will pray like Joseph Smith did. We call the Great Spirit, God."

The boys listened very intently seeming to believe all Amos told them. From then on each rest period became a learning time and the Indians began calling Amos "Toop-Shi-*Pó*-Ide," meaning "Young Man From Above."

After many days of working in the canyon they had a big pile of logs lying by the side of the fort. It was time to begin sawing. Everything had to be done the hard way—by muscle and brawn. For two years the missionaries had been going to the canyon to get logs so they could build houses. They dug a hole as deep as a grave and twice as long and called it a saw pit. One man jumped down in one end of the hole. Another man laid a long log lengthwise over the saw pit and straddled across the log. With a two-handled saw they began sawing at one end of the log, each man pushing and pulling on his handle until the log was finally ripped clear to the other end and a slab fell off. They repeated this, making the slabs about two inches thick, until there was no more log. Then they did another one. This was even harder work than cutting and hauling the logs.

The slabs were finally sawed, the forms built part way up and it was time to make the mortar or "stuffing" as they jokingly called it. There was a clay pit near by. Wheelbarrows full of the sticky gray stuff were hauled and dumped in a cleared off space. Then armfuls of grass were cut with a sickle and piled on top of the clay. The next part of the recipe called for bucketfuls of marble-size rocks, and finally a bucket or two of water. That was when the fun began. Red Boy, Rabbit and Amos were the mixers, scrunching over the pile with their bare feet back and forth, round and round getting clay up to the knees and farther.

When it was well mixed, the wheelbarrows were again loaded and the gooey mass dumped into the forms. Then poles were used for tamping, until a solid mass filled the forms nine feet high. That meant a lot of clay and grass and pebbles and water and scrunching and hauling and tamping. As soon as it dried, the forms were taken off and lo and behold, there was a wall that would resist snow and ice and cold and rain and heat and any other kind of weather you could think of. Best of all it would hold any bull or wild pony you could put inside.

About that time it was grasshopper season. The hoppers came in hordes, rolling, hopping, flying, crawling. The tender green wheat stalks were their favorite meal. They advanced like a swather, laying waste the fields of grain. All methods of battling them seemed hopeless and when the men saw it was no use trying any longer, a dozen men and teams started back to the Utah settlements for seed grain and supplies, so they could plant wheat next spring and feed the hoppers again. At least it seemed that way to Amos and his two Indian companions. In the meantime they had milk and choagus roots and salmon if their stomachs could stand it. Most of the men had eaten so much salmon when they first came they couldn't eat a fish to save their lives.

Before President Young's visit, the people had planted and harvested and gardened as a group, but he advised them to try doing it each man for himself. A man could have as much land as he could take care of. This spread them out so they needed a "lower fort" which they proceeded to build. Eighteen men and their families moved down there. Anka-Toah and Tab-Boots stayed in the fort and came to appreciate some of the White men's ways. They learned from the missionaries and the missionaries learned from them.

In June and early July the big salmon came in shoals up the river, gene-urged, swimming from the ocean to deposit their spawn into the Snake and the Salmon Rivers and finally almost to the headwaters of their own little Lemhi River.

This was the time for real Indian fishing. A net of peeled willows, woven together with bark, was stretched across the river on a framework of poles. In this net or dam, an opening of willows was made, large at the down-stream side and narrow where the fish had to pass through into the trap. A second dam was built about fifty feet above without any gate or opening.

Amos was fascinated as he watched the salmon swim into the

trap, through the narrow opening and into the enclosed waters above, nosing frantically for a place to squeeze through on their always up-stream journey. The fish sometimes jumped six or seven feet out of the water, their silver sides flashing in the sun in their attempt to cross the barrier. Those which did get over were caught by a willow basket-like work on the upper side, and soon the water was alive with the threshing dammed-up captives.

This made tedious angle-worm methods look stupid. All that was left to do was jump into the water and begin throwing the twenty to sixty-pound beauties out on the bank. Amos learned, however, there was a trick to grabbing a slippery mass of churning power like that and hanging on long enough to heave it onto shore. He watched the agile Indian, Long Tom, slip his fingers into the fish gills before trying to hoist it out of the water, and found it worked nearly every time. Amos won approval, this time from Long Tom himself who gave him a name in Shoshone meaning "good fisherman."

It didn't take long for a crew of men to throw out two or three hundred silver salmon to be cleaned inside and out, sliced thin and hung up to dry on willow frames with a small fire underneath to smoke the flesh. It was later thoroughly dried and finally stored in the tough skins of the larger salmon, tied up in bales and put away for winter. This method insured a supply of food which could be kept indefinitely. Amos learned to relish it when eaten either raw or cooked. Much of the time it was not what you *liked*, but what you could *get*.

As time went on, the missionaries learned more of the difficult Shoshone words mixed with a little sign language. But even then it was hard to explain such indefinite things as faith and repentance. A mission school for the Indians was started with three sessions a week. Men and squaws, boys and girls from three to thirty-three came and the missionaries learned more than the pupils. Then on Sunday there was singing, preaching and prayer for the benefit of both. There were some dramatic successes. G.W. Hill's journal recorded:

> The following Sunday there was quite a crowd of Indians at our meeting and after we got through, the president called on me to preach to them which I tried to do in my weak way, telling them if they believed, we would baptize them if they wanted it. They all cried out, 'I do! I do! I do!' all over the crowd. So we went to the water and I baptized fifty-six.

By the end of 1857 the missionaries felt some progress had

been made. They were fairly comfortable in their make-shift cabins. There was little or no illness or distress, and they had sufficient clothes and food.

Harvest time began in late August. There was grain to cut, bundle and thresh. A circle about twenty or thirty feet in diameter was leveled and tamped hard. Amos, Red Boy and Rabbit helped haul the bundles of grain from the field to the big threshing circle. They laid them lengthwise around the edge about six sheaves wide. The center of the ring was left bare. Five or six yoke of oxen were then fastened together, two abreast, forming a circle while a driver stood in the center to keep them moving. When the wheat was thoroughly tramped out, the straw was pitched away while the chaff and grain was pushed into the center of the ring. The edge was again filled with fresh sheaves and the process repeated until a large pile of chaff and grain filled the center of the ring. After that, each man took his turn with the fanning mill. This was moved from place to place during the winter until all the grain had been cleaned.

But all was not well despite such pastoral scenes. Pleasant Green Taylor had a premonition of trouble while he was left in charge of the Fort. When President Smith returned he told him about his dream. "It seemed I saw a dark cloud, small but very black, and with lightning rapidity it rose in the north and came directly to the Fort, after which it turned and took off in an easterly direction, settling down on the horizon." Taylor succeeded in persuading all the families at the lower or New Fort to move up to the old one. By nightfall, about thirty people came. President Smith did not object to this change but he thought all would be well.

Amos, too, felt uneasy. He had heard of the mountaineer named Powell and about his goings-on with the unfriendly Indians. Long John told him Powell was a troublemaker, and said he dressed up and painted himself like an Indian and encouraged them in their devilry. He must have found out what they were up to and too late repented of his part in it, because early in February Amos saw him come to the fort and talk to President Smith for half an hour. He seemed excited and waved his hands and made sign language. The president later mentioned him in one of their council meetings, saying Powell had warned him that the Indians were planning some mischief. But Brother Smith being a very kindly and unsuspecting man, passed his warning off as "just one of Powell's ideas."

Activities began at the fort early as usual on the morning of February 25, 1858. Some of the brethren took their ox teams and hayracks down to the new fort to get hay for the cattle. The cattle were kept in the corral at the fort during the night and turned out each morning. It had been an open winter and the stock grazed on the bunch grass during the day and were fed extra hay each night. Amos was taking his turn as a herder so he turned the cattle out as usual. He noticed the men down at the lower fort loading their wagons and it looked as if they were about ready to return.

It was then without warning that "the cloud from the north" which Pleasant Green had dreamed about, became more than a dream. About a hundred painted Indians swooped out of the canyon on their horses, yelling and shooting at the men who were loading hay. The shots ignited the tinder-dry hay, and Amos saw the frantic oxen run wildly through the timber toward the river, trying to get away from their burning loads.

Just as suddenly, another band of warriors rode over the hill and began driving off the stock. Amos was on foot and hurried to try to head the cattle back toward the corral. George McBride was on a horse nearby. Waving his hat around his head a few times with a yell, he spurred his horse over the hill and galloped down among the Indians trying to turn the cattle back. Amos watched in horror as the Indians surrounded him. A bullet struck McBride in the chest and he fell from his horse. Hearing their wild yells, Amos could easily guess what was happening as they stripped George's clothes from his body and scalped him. A few minutes later the Indians mounted their horses and rode away, taking McBride's clothes, revolver and horse with them.

Orson Rose was another herder. He happened to be on the side of the herd nearest the fort, and dropped into a heavy sagebrush when the firing commenced. The Indians riddled the brush with shot but did not hit him. Later he escaped and ran down the creek where he hid until night and then sneaked back to the fort.

Amos and several other men from the fort tried to save the stock but they were pressed back by the fire from the Indians. Colonel Smith and Ezra Barnard were just returning from a canyon timber run. They hurriedly unharnessed their horses, mounted two of them and galloped toward the herd.

As soon as the Indians saw them, six warriors opened fire. One of the bullets passed through Smith's suspenders and lodged in his horse's jaw. The horse lurched and Smith was thrown to the ground. The Indians, supposing he was shot gave an exulting yell. He got back on his horse however, but was shot in the right arm. Smith and Barnard both reached the stockade without further harm. There they found Amos and several other men who had been driven to cover.

Shortly afterward Fountain Welch was brought in severely wounded. He had been shot in the back and stripped of his shirt, ammunition and gun. The savages struck him over the head with a gun and left him for dead. The Indians proceeded to drive off the entire herd, consisting of 235 cattle and 31 ponies.

After President Smith and Barnard reached the fort, the president called for volunteers to go as a search party looking for Quigley who was still missing. Amos, Miller Taylor and two others offered to go. The Indians had disappeared and the men fanned out to look for the missing man. As Amos waded the little creek south of the fort he caught sight of some of the cattle huddled in the willows. Calling to Miller to help, they succeeded in rounding up seventeen head which had been left behind by the Indians, and ran them into the corral. The rest of the search party finally found Quigley about a mile from where McBride was killed. He had been scalped and his naked body riddled with bullets.

That night six men, including Amos, were stationed as guards though it was felt there was little danger of the fort being attacked. Fourteen more head of cows and calves returned during the night. Long John, Amos' friendly fisherman, released them while the rest of the other Indians were excitedly doing a scalp dance. Red Boy and Rabbit hadn't been seen for about a week at the Fort.

The sudden tragic turn of events completely demoralized the remaining brethren. Two of their number were dead, five more wounded, two severely. A large number of the cattle and horses were gone and the beleaguered whites were over three-hundred miles from help. At this point President Smith decided on a strategy which he hoped might work. At that time he had no idea what had prompted the attack. He knew the cattle must be recovered if possible, and the fury of the Indians calmed.

Calling the men together, Smith proposed two actions, asking for volunteers to carry them out. First, at least two men were needed to ride as fast as possible—it was still mid-winter—to Salt Lake and ask for relief from Brigham Young, explaining that their situation was desperate and proposing that the fort be abandoned. Second, a man who could speak and understand the Indian language was to be sent to parley with the natives now camped about five miles across the river. He should remind them of the kind treatment they had received the past three years and appeal to them to stop the present fighting and return the stolen cattle and horses.

B.H. Watts and E.J. Barnard volunteered for the first mission and departed under cover of darkness with a letter to Brigham Young. The remaining men, thirty-two in all, were organized into four equal units under captains to act in defense of the Fort. As Smith looked over the less than three-dozen men, waiting for a volunteer to cross the river and talk to the now savage attackers, a silence settled over all of them and Amos imagined they were all looking at him. All at once his heart felt as big as a circus balloon inside his chest. He remembered the saying which seemed to apply. "It's a good rule never to send a mouse to catch a skunk or a pollywog to tackle a whale." But he knew he could speak and understand Shoshone better than any man among them; he seemed to have a way with Indians; and the words of the Lord to him through an apostle so recently given, told him this was his job. He pulled himself off the ground and heard himself saying, "Brother Smith, if you will promise me I'll come back alive, I will go."

The face of the leader turned pale as sweat broke out on his forehead. After a solemn moment, quietly he spoke the necessary two words: "I promise."

There was only one little two-year-old pony left at the fort which had somehow escaped being run off with the others. Amos untied the bandana handkerchief he was wearing around his neck, slipped it into the pony's mouth for a bridle, threw his leg over the horse's back and started for the river. He disappeared through the brush. Later they made out a dark object moving slowly toward the other side among the chunks of ice and debris. Finally, with a sigh of relief, they saw the pony and rider climb the steep bank on the other side.

The Indians were camped about five miles down river and as Amos approached he could hear their shouts. He dug his heels into the pony's flank and galloped toward the camp. As soon as the Indians saw him they ran toward him shooting arrows. A big Shoshone covered with war paint pulled him off his horse and dragged him into the circle. Amos understood yells of "Kill him, burn him!" Soon a pile of dry sagebrush was collected and he was laid over it, his hands and feet tied to stakes in the ground. He felt strangely calm amid all the hubbub, even when he glimpsed out of the corner of his eye, a man approaching with a lighted torch.

At that moment Anka-Toah and Tab-Boots came running into the circle shouting "Wait Wait," in Shoshone. And then in English as Amos had taught them they bowed their heads and cried, "In the name of Jesus Christ, Amen." Tab-Boots looked around at the fierce fighters and for once he didn't act like a rabbit. A sudden quiet settled on the crowd. Pointing to Amos he said, "This is Toop-Shi-Po-Ide!" Red Boy said, "He is my friend. He speaks straight. Let him talk!" The chief came forward and put his hand on Anka-Toah's shoulder. "You are brave boy. Untie him," said the chief pointing to Amos.

Now all eyes were upon the prisoner as he climbed off the brush pile and turned to Chief Pocatello. Speaking slowly and quietly he said, "I come to talk peace. Missionaries don't want war. Why do you fight us? Why do you drive our cattle away? You have killed our men, others are hurt."

There was talking among the Indians. Then Pocatello replied, "Powell tells us missionaries come to steal our land. He says you lie. Johnson's soldiers tell us to kill you and steal your cattle so you will go away. They give us money for your cattle and horses."

Amos looked around at the men and boys he had taught in Sunday School; the ones he worked with and played games with. On the other side of the circle were squaws and children who knew him well. "Do you say I lie?" The men and boys shook their heads and the squaws yelled, "Papoose, Papoose!" meaning he was a young boy and wouldn't lie.

"Then why did you fight us?" asked Amos quietly. Pocatello shook his head and said, "We get bad spirit. We listen to Powell and soldiers."

"Missionaries always have a good spirit," replied Amos. Peah-Tibo Young sent missionaries to teach you about God."

Pocatello nodded. "Come in my lodge. We will talk." In a moment Red Boy was at Amos' side as they walked toward the tepee, and whispered, "They tied us up so we couldn't warn you. Long John let us loose just in time."

Inside the lodge together, Pocatello said some of the cattle were already butchered and eaten, and a band of Indians had driven most of the others into the mountains. They would try to get them back. He didn't know whether he could stop the fighting but would try. Then he said, "You ride good horse back. Yours no good," and boosting Amos on the back of an Apaloosa mare he said, "Cross river here," pointing directly ahead. "Water not deep like above."

As Amos rode toward the fort, he believed he had quelled their anger for a little while at least and hoped they would keep their promise to return some of the cattle and horses. The fierce warlike habits of generations lay close to the surface, smothering any good influence and teaching they had received.

Meanwhile, Watts and Barnard reached Utah with the plea for help. Brother Brigham responded in his usual prompt way. A couple of weeks later a guard at Ft. Lemhi sighted horsemen approaching and thinking they might be another party of hostile Indians, sounded the alarm. When ten white men rode into camp, they were immediately surrounded by the relieved missionaries, anxious to know who they were and why they came. The captain dismounted and shook hands with President Smith; the rest crowded around to listen. Amos was close enough to hear what was said.

"We are here on orders from President Young. Our express left Salt Lake ten days ago and we have been riding almost night and day. Help is on the way. You are directed to abandon the fort as soon as possible. We will help you get ready to leave by the time the relief expedition arrives."

A spontaneous shout went up from the men and women in the crowd. Amos could hardly believe his ears. Time for going home had seemed so far away until this moment and he was almost ashamed to feel so happy. The happenings of the past few weeks had cast a pall over the little community. This word immediately changed gloom to exuberance. Women hugged each other; men slapped one another on the back and grinned. Amos did a little war dance all by himself and gave the Shoshone war whoop.

March 4th was fast day and the fast meeting was held partly in the house, partly outside, on watch for Indians who might cause trouble. At this time those who had been baptized but who had apostatized or had taken a hand in the robbery and murders were cut off from the Church.

When the relief expedition arrived at the fort they helped gather up a few more head of cattle that had not been with the big herd at the time of the raid. Thomas Smith gave a thousand bushels of mission wheat to Chief Snagg or Shoogan. This old man was a nephew of Sacajawea, the famous Bird Woman who guided Lewis and Clark to the Pacific. He and a few of the faithful

Mormon Shoshones wept before the missionaries left. One young male Indian joined the party returning to Utah and also one Indian woman who had married one of the settlers. The others refused to accompany their missionary husbands.

Amos was pleased to be chosen as one of eleven men to ride ahead as an express headed for Salt Lake. They were to take word to President Young that the fort was being abandoned according to his orders and that the relief expedition had reached Lemhi in good time. He was glad to be one of this select group, and that he would reach Utah sooner than the main body of missionaries. This party set out March 26, 1858, with a wagon and twenty-six horses, planning to travel as fast as possible.

As they rode up Bannock Creek on the last day of March, they saw about a dozen Indians riding in the same direction. Later several of them turned from their course and shortly afterward Amos sighted a smoke signal on the west mountains. A little later six Indians came toward the company. The missionaries signaled to them to find a ford across the river and come over to talk. They acted like they were going to do so. But the next thing Amos heard a bullet zing past his ear and he saw the Indians running for the willows along the creek.

Wm. B. Lake rode up the bank after crossing the creek and was shot in the head and killed instantly. The Indians also shot three horses and a mule. Seventeen other horses got away during the fight. This left only six horses for ten men. They could take only enough food for one meal and head for Utah. They reached Call's Fort on April 1, 1858, exhausted, cold, hungry, and marveling to have come out alive.

Amos got permission from the captain to ride ahead to Brigham City so he could say hello to his father, Jonathan, and then continue on with the express to Salt Lake. He could hardly contain his joy at being only eight miles from home. He had completed a difficult and dangerous assignment under most unusual circumstances.

Thoughts of home and family urged him on and on and soon he left the rest of the party far in the rear, not sparing his sweating horse. As he came in sight of his father's land, he felt an uncomfortable stirring of emotions he had hoped had been buried permanently. Maybe it was a mistake to go back. He could stay with the express even now and go on to Salt Lake with it.

Ahead were the familiar poplars reaching into the blue sky and marking the windbreak near his father's farm north of

Brigham City. Hungrily he took it all in as he approached the gate.

Suddenly, he sensed something wrong, something different. No smoke was curling from the chimney. Old Hank, his dog, was nowhere around. Looking toward the corral he whistled to his favorite pony Buck, but Buck didn't show up either. Then he noticed that the boards were half off the chicken coop; the house looked deserted and lonely.

An all-embracing silence seemed to have settled over everything. He swung down from the saddle and tied his horse to a tree, pushed open the unlocked door and looked around the kitchen. The table stood bare and lonely in the middle of the floor without its usual oilcloth cover. There was a musty smell of rotting apples and cabbage coming up the stair well from the cellar. The stove was stone cold. He walked into the bedroom, scratching his head in wonder. The bedstead had been stripped of springs and bedtick and the chamber pot stood nakedly revealed. Everyone was gone for sure.

Mounting his horse, he proceeded toward town. He glanced toward both sides of the road for somebody to talk to, but saw no one. Then he saw the familiar square-topped roof of the courthouse ahead on Main Street with a lone man leaning against the iron fence out front. Drawing his horse to a stop he called out, "What's happened; where *is* everybody?"

"Didn't you know? Where've you been? They've all gone south! The army is coming and Brother Brigham ordered everybody to desert their farms and homes. Brother Jensen and I were left to guard the town and light a match to it if the soldiers come this far."

Dismay and disappointment flooded over Amos. What should he do now? Maybe he could find his father and Mary Jane "down south" wherever that might be. The two guards shared a loaf of bread and some jerky with him. By this time the other members of the express had caught up to him and together they continued on toward Three Mile Creek and Willard. They said they thought "south" meant somewhere beyond Salt Lake, so his journey wasn't over by a long shot.

Every little town looked the same ... deserted, deadly quiet. Siding and slabs had been torn from barns and houses to make boxes to pack belongings in. "Yes, help yourself," the movers had said, "We'll probably never come back anyway. We'll be going to Jackson County right away so no use worrying about what's left here!" By Jackson County they referred to that part of Missouri which revelation said was "Zion" the place where the Savior would appear at the beginning of the Millenium.

The eleven-man express finally reached Salt Lake, reported to President Young and assured him the main company was on its way from Salmon River with the help of the relief expedition sent from Utah. They told him of their narrow escape in the fight with the Indians on the way, and sorrowfully related how William Lake lost his life. They had packed Lake's body in ice and hauled it in a wagon all the way back to Utah and his family for burial.

Everybody was involved in the move south. The road south of Salt Lake was choked with loaded ox-drawn wagons, bawling cattle and baa-ing sheep in a welter of dust which blinded and covered animals and humans alike. Amos passed a dozen such groups. His own horse was as gray as an elephant with his sweaty dust-caked sides and Amos knew he must look the same way. He longed for a drink of water but there wasn't any so he pushed on. He also met scores of empty wagons with drivers heading back north to help those ready to move but without teams to join the exodus. Were his father and Mary Jane among these hordes?, Amos wondered. It was impossible to see clearly for the dust. He knew they had left Brigham City, so he decided to continue following his nose and hope for the best.

As he approached Provo, the countryside was a mass of tents, brush huts and even tepees thatched with straw, where families were camped to await further directions. Many wagon boxes had been lifted off the running-gears and set on the ground with the canvas wagon cover for a roof to be used as bedroom or makeshift shelter during a storm. Little cook stoves set out in the open were belching smoke as mothers tried to get a fire going to warm up some food for their hungry families. A hum and buzz of voices could be heard, but Amos was surprised that people seemed cheerful, going about their business as if nothing unusual had happened.

A watering trough in Provo gave Amos and his horse a welcome chance to stop and rest. The pony sucked in deep draughts of the cool water and Amos filled up at the spring which trickled into the trough. He inquired about Judge Wright from a man who stopped for a drink, who said he was from Willard, but he shook his head and said he hadn't seen anybody from Brigham. Amos scrounged a loaf of bread from a kind-looking lady in Provo who told him people had been going through town for days. She didn't know how far south they were going, but probably Spanish Fork and further if necessary. The road to Spanish Fork was a strip-tent city on both sides but, inquiry didn't give Amos any clues till he got just outside town. In response to another try, an old man with no teeth grinned and said, "Yeth, thereth quite a bunch of folkth from Brigham Thity here: Packerth, Ensignth, and Dunnths. Mebbe Wrighths, too." The old man was still lisping away when Amos was half a block away. He felt in his bones he was going to find his family soon.

He finally discovered Mary Jane and the children in a cellar just outside of town. They looked as if they were seeing a ghost when he climbed down the ladder into the dark, smelly room. He swung Mary Jane off her feet and the children chattered like magpies. Jonathan would be back pretty soon she said. He was away most of the time helping other folks from Brigham City. She looked thin and worn but didn't complain. Between interruptions by the children, Mary Jane told him about leaving home. Said they'd been in Spanish Fork for about three weeks. The Brigham City folks traveled together to start with and then some couldn't keep up so they got scattered. Lois was still with her. Mary Jane was holding a six-month-old baby belonging to Lois and named after Heber Jedediah Grant. She said Lois had just gone to the neighbors and would be back soon. She said Brother Wright had married his sixth wife last November. She was a Danish girl who had come across the plains with two of her sisters pulling a handcart. Her name was Caroline Olsen.

As Mary Jane chatted on, giving Amos the news, his old nostalgia returned. He thought he had his feelings for Lois Moran buried, but the mere mention of her name revived it all as strong as ever. This was no place for him.

When Mary Jane got around to asking about himself and what he was going to do he said, "I haven't the slightest idea." She realized this time he didn't need her any more as he impatiently kissed her goodbye and not even waiting to see his father, mounted his horse and rode away without a backward glance. Mary Jane followed him out to the road, and watched until horse and rider disappeared over a rise in the distance away to the north, then turned back, wondering when and if she would ever see him again.

Amos rode slowly on, giving the horse his head, as his thoughts reverted to the strange mission he had just completed in Salmon River country, and his return to Utah under such unhappy circumstances.

What was the purpose of it all he wondered? What had been accomplished? It all seemed a total loss and defeat. He spurred his horse impatiently at the thought and then lapsed again into more wondering. Amos asked himself hard questions. He worried about himself and about his family. What would Mary Jane and the children do in the face of this persecution? But for them it was not to be so difficult as it seemed.

The "scorched earth" policy carried out by Brigham Young aroused the sympathy of the American people in favor of the Mormons for the first time in their long history. President Buchanan eased himself out of an embarrassing position by declaring them to be officially pardoned for their "rebellion." The Utah War was over and the Saints packed up their wagons and headed for home.

Chapter Eight
On the Loose

To the lonely traveler, it seemed that each time he tried to fit the pieces of his life into a design which made sense, frustrating events stepped out of the unknown and kicked his plans all to thunder, leaving him worse off than before. In the depths of discouragement and self-pity, he decided he would just run with the tide. No use making plans. His life was rudderless. He took any job that came along, worked for a day or a week or a month while the job lasted and then drifted on to another without purpose or goal, lacking sense of time or place. He turned gypsy once more. But he didn't realize how deeply his early teachings affected him, even when he thought he had forgotten such things.

Once while he was bringing a cargo of gold from the mines in Nevada, the men with him came to a fork in the road and debated which way they should go. Amos was impressed to go one way, but there was a difference of opinion. He said, "Let's stop here and rest a few minutes and give the horses a breather." He hardly dared suggest prayer to this group, but prayed fervently for guidance himself. When they were ready to start again, Amos said, "I'm impressed to go this way," and almost in unison they agreed. At the end of the day they were overtaken by some riders who told of a group of bandits seeking gold. These outlaws had attacked a party on the trail that Amos and his companions had rejected.

He recognized a vast difference between the brethren he'd been around for so long, and the tough soldiers of fortune; mule-skinners and those who plied the freighters trade. At first he felt uncomfortable around them. Their rough language and evil ways shocked and pained his sensibilities. A few times he tried rebuking their uncouth actions, but he met with such ridicule and scorn he gave it up as useless. He discovered that some men lied as easily as licking a dish. Indians called it "speaking with a forked tongue" and came to distrust all whites as a result, and even learned to speak that way themselves. But he discovered there was a certain look in a man's eye—just the way he walked, even, which told he was a liar. Amos wished sometimes he could do it himself, it seemed to work for others, but the teachings at Rebecca's knee were too deeply etched.

Others noticed he was different and were puzzled. They either respected, or hated him for his differences. He had two shifting moods, one the ebullient, waggish storyteller and hilarious companion, and the other a gravity beyond penetration. But despite these unusual characteristics, he was always able to get a job. He wasn't afraid of work. He *wanted* to work and so uncommon a want usually found immediate gratification.

The transition from oxen to mules in the freighting business came gradually, but the slow-moving dumbness of the ox contrasted unfavorably with the quick-witted stubbornness of a tough mule, and the latter eventually won out.

"The driver of a long-line team had to be a skilled teamster, a man whose job it was to control the entire team by means of a jerkline, a quarter or half-inch braided cotton cord running from the hand of the driver more than one hundred feet to the bit of the nigh leader or left wheel animal.

"Aside from his freighting ability, the teamster had to be resourceful enough to take care of himself, his wagons and his team; to be able to treat a sick horse or shoe a kicking mule and even on occasion to repair roads with pick and shovel. He lead a life that would wither the soul of the best of men." ("Men in Death Valley," *Arizona Highways*, October 1978.)

The Deseret News for October 11, 1859, reported: "Yesterday, A.R. Wright with a train of eight wagons arrived from the states, all well and in good condition." Then a year later almost to the day, (Oct. 18, 1860, Thursday) an item in the same paper showed:

"A.R. Wright arrived wtih his train consisting of 11 wagons and 63 head of cattle. He had performed the journey from the States in sixty traveling days." And a few days later in the same paper, (October 31) the story headlined as follows, continued:

> The Last Merchant Train: Mr. A.R. Wright, who went to the States last spring to purchase goods for himself and others, arrived on his return a few days ago, with a train of ten wagons, each drawn by three yoke of oxen, which was the last train of merchandise expected to arrive from the east this season. He had been very fortunate with his cattle, having lost but one or two oxen on the trip, but having purchased them on the Missouri high prices as we understood, the presumption is that a fortune has not been realized by the operation.

So, whether driving oxen or mules, it was all in the day's work. Amos would shrug his shoulders and say, "Just as well try to stop a snowslide with a teaspoon."

Then there were always Indians. They and Mose Wright were drawn together as by a magnet. The "chemistry" was right and they understood each other. He spoke Shoshone perfectly and had a working knowledge of Bannock and Nez Perce. He was able to perfect his knowledge of western sign language and communicate satisfactorily with any that he ran across.

He became a skilled detective and sleuth, being able to track both animals and men when necessary, learning the tricks from his Indian companions. Renegades, thieves, murderers and adventurers were common, both Indian and white, and Amos learned how to take care of himself among them and find out what he needed to know.

When the Pony Express was started, young men dreamed of becoming riders. Along with the rest, Amos' imagination was fired immediately. This was for him if they'd hire him. Maybe he could ride faster than his thoughts and be free of the nagging ache that left him only as he slept, and even then he sometimes dreamed of Lois Moran.

Old men sat around potbellied stoves in stores and saloons telling and re-telling stories of the narrow escapes these invincible young men made, embroidering them generously at each repetition. Mothers prayed their sons would return safely, and young girls prayed they'd be lucky enough to get a letter from a rider to display to their jealous girlfriends. Budding journalists wrote about the Pony Express in prose and verse.

Everybody was caught up with the wonder that news and mail could be carried so swiftly. Newspapers splashed headlines about it all across America.

> On the afternoon of April 3, 1860, at a signal cannon shot, a pony rider left St. Joseph, Missouri; and the same moment another left Sacramento, California, one speeding west, the other east over plains and mountains and deserts. Night and day the race is kept up by the different riders and their swift horses until the mail is carried through. Then they turn and dash back over the same trail again. Not many riders can stand the long, fast riding at first, but after about two weeks they get toughened up. (Wilson-Driggs, *The White Indian Boy*, p. 141.)

Amos learned that Major Howard Egan, one of the early pioneers who knew his father, was in charge of the riders going from Salt Lake to Rush Valley. Egan had a ranch in western Utah and knew more about the country between Salt Lake and Sacramento than any other person. He had made fifty trips to the coast before the Pony Express even started. He had an office in Salt Lake and Amos made a beeline for it.

He recognized some of the men lined up waiting to be interviewed. "So I'm not the only crazy one," he muttered. He was handed a printed form to fill out, giving his age, weight, experience with horses, health etc. It said a man couldn't be over twenty.... well he was just under the wire on that. He couldn't weigh over a hundred and twenty-five. Maybe that would cut him out. He weighed closer to a hundred and thirty-five. That about horses was easy ... no problem there. He'd been on a good many Expresses already. And as for health, he was as tough as the mules he drove.

When his turn came to be interviewed, he felt his knees shaking. Major Egan looked him over carefully. He wondered if Egan could tell he weighed over the limit.

"So you're Judge Wright's son, eh?" said Egan. "See if you want to sign. If so you're hired." The form went like this:

> I do hereby swear before the great and living God that during my engagement, and while I am an employee of Russell, Majors and Waddell, I will under no circumstances use profane language; that I will drink no intoxicating liquors; that I will not quarrel or fight with other employees of the firm and that in every respect I will conduct myself honestly ... be faithful to my duties, and to direct all my acts

as to win the confidence of my employers. So help me God. (1860 version)

Amos signed.

"You men are the pick of the frontier. Your work will be dangerous. This is no job for a tenderfoot, so quit now if you're scared. You'll be fighting Indians as well as carrying mail. You may get killed. You'll be riding about seventy-five to a hundred miles a day. This means six or more changes of mounts. You'll make the round trip twice a week. You will be held responsible for safe delivery of the mail you carry, and it must be on time. You will be given a bed and grub at company expense. Your pay will be forty dollars a month to begin with and up to sixty if you can prove you are worth that much.

"Here's a pair of Colt revolvers, a holster, a dagger and a Spencer rifle. They'll be charged to your account. You'd better know how to use any or all of them. You will be issued a red flannel shirt and blue trousers for special occasions, but you can dress any way you like otherwise. We suggest a buckskin hunting shirt, cloth or buckskin pants, high boots ... tuck your pants inside, and a cap or slouch hat. If you can, get hold of a complete buckskin suit with the hair on the outside; it will come in handy in stormy weather."

Amos learned as he rode. The stations were about twenty-five miles apart, placed as near to a spring or other watering place as possible. There were two kinds of them: the 'home station' and the 'way station.' At the way stations, the riders changed horses. At the home stations, which were about seventy-five miles from each other, the riders were changed; and there they ate their meals and slept.

"Their saddles, which were provided by the company but charged to the rider, had nothing to them but the bare tree, stirrups and cinch. Two large pieces of leather about sixteen inches wide by twenty-four long were laced together with a strong leather string and thrown over the saddle tree. Fastened to these were four pockets, two in front and two behind. The two hind ones were the largest. The one in front on the left side was called the 'way-pocket.' All of these pockets were locked with small padlocks and each home station keeper had a key to the 'way-pocket.' When the express arrived at the home station, the keeper would unlock the 'way-pocket' and if there were any letters for the boys between the home stations, the rider would distribute them as he went along. There was also a card in the 'way-pocket' that the station

keeper would take out and write on it the time the Express arrived
and left his station. If the Express was behind time, he would tell
the rider how much time he had to make up. It cost $5.00 for half
an ounce of mail and twenty pounds was the limit the horse could
carry." (Wilson-Driggs, *The White Indian Boy*, World Book
Company pp. 139-40.)

When Amos dashed into a way station he jumped off the
horse. The attendant pulled the mochilla with the padlocked
pockets off and threw it over the tree of the already saddled fresh
horse and he was off again. Only two minutes was allowed for
changing mounts.

Amos found out about ponies, too. These animals were swift,
fiery and fractious. They had sworn not to abuse them. Ira
Nebeker was a friend of Amos'. He and a couple of other boys had
the contract to break the ponies for riding. They had to ride at
least ten ponies a day, all buckers. But when a horse got through
bucking for these trainers, he didn't buck much again.

Amos learned to give 'em the spurs right from the start and
kept 'em going. If they were buckers, it soon took the meanness
out of 'em. He got to love those little devils though. He knew they
could save his life when he was in a tight spot and they were
speedy enough to beat any the Indians usually had. They seemed
to know they had a big job to do and gave it all they had. Riding
along at night it was hard to see the road. There was often a
strong wind blowing from the north carrying sleet that cut a
man's face while he was trying to look ahead. But as long as he
could hear the pony's feet pounding the road, Amos sent him
ahead full speed.

One night, as he thundered toward Mill Creek, he heard the
pony's feet strike the plank bridge. The next minute horse and
rider both landed in the creek. He was wet all over, but the next
second, with one spring, that faithful little pony was out and
pounding the road again with Amos still on his back.

The hostler's job was to have a fresh mount saddled and ready
half an hour ahead of time, so when a rider came galloping in
with a whoop and a holler to let him know he was coming, he
didn't lose any time. Some of the riders carried a horn to blow, but
Amos had a good built-in one that could raise the dead.

Riders had to be on constant lookout for Indians and thieves.
If they got to a station and the relief man wasn't there, it was
another twenty-five miles to the next one and they had to ride it. If
he wasn't used to the saddle, a man would get so sore he felt like

he was riding a porcupine. Not only was it hard work, but it was the lonesomest kind of a job. Amos got sleepy ... oh so sleepy! He pinched himself, sang old songs, gave the Shoshone war whoop, told whopping lies to keep himself awake. He almost tumbled off a dozen times during the long, long night. But he had to keep going and he knew it.

Major Egan had brought a fine pair of mules from Kentucky and somebody stole them. He offered Amos a big reward if he could find out who did it and bring the mules back to him in Salt Lake. The extra money sounded good, and it was the kind of a job he liked to tackle. He kept riding the express but kept his eyes and ears open for clues about the animals. It took him almost a year to find out they were at a ranch in the Sierra-Nevada Mountains. When he found that out, he asked for a lay-off and proceeded with his plan.

Amos discovered the mules were always turned loose in the evening to drink at a spring about half a mile from the ranch. He hid in a bunch of tules at the edge of the spring and waited. His lariat slid easily over the head of the lead mule without alarming him. In an instant Amos jumped on his back and started off. As he hoped, the other followed. After a couple of miles he stopped to tie the other end of the rope around the mule's neck and kept going. He rode those mules off and on bareback for about two hundred miles without stopping, thinking only of the distance he wanted to put between himself and that ranch.

An oasis in the desert offered respite and he and the mules made the most of it. He slept the clock around and started off again, traveling by night and hiding by day. He delivered the mules safely, though a little bedraggled, to an elated Major Egan.

Then the Indians started giving trouble. They hated the whites for taking over their country. They'd ambush, burn the stations, and kill as many attendants as they could. The riders depended on the swiftness of their ponies more than anything, and didn't fight the Indians if they could get away fast enough. One time, a little mourning dove saved Amos' life.

He was riding through bad Indian country and from the top of a bluff he looked back and caught sight of the dust of some horsemen across the valley. He knew they were chasing him. He had been riding for hours and both horse and rider were plum give out. He spied a grassy meadow about a quarter of a mile away and made for it as fast as his tired horse could. When they got there, he slid off into the cool grass at the edge of a beautiful little creek. He lay there and filled up on that cold water till he thought he'd bust, and so did his horse.

By that time he didn't care about anything but sleep. He heard little Buck grazing away and that's the last thing he remembered. He must have slept about five or ten minutes when he was dragged out of it by the sound of a mourning dove doing his sad little song. He opened his eyes and there perched on his arm was that bird, just like he was saying, "Better get going little brother, or it'll be too late!" Amos raised up and saw the Indians not more than half a mile away. Little Buck was rested and so was he. They took off fast back to safety. And he had that little mourning dove to thank for saving his life.

One day he'd been making good time and his pony was tired. He decided to stop and take a quick dip in a little pool of water along the trail. There weren't many like that and he couldn't resist the temptation. He stripped off and jumped in. He turned over on his back and closed his eyes as he floated in the cool water. It was heavenly after about four hours on a sweaty horse in the hot sun. Then something made him open his eyes. An Indian stood at the edge of the pool, bow drawn tight with the arrow pointing straight at him. He didn't move a muscle and looked the Indian straight in the eye. He thought his time had come for sure. It seemed like an hour the man stood there, but it was probably only a couple of minutes. Then without a word he turned around and disappeared in the brush. Amos made a grab for his pistol, but the red man made a clean get away and Amos wasn't sorry.

It was natural that word of anything unusual got around fast. The riders liked to pass on gossip at the home stations where they spent the night. Rumors reached Ruby Valley Station that a famous English world traveler, linguist and writer named Richard Burton was in Salt Lake on his way to California by stagecoach. The Mormons were always a curiosity because of their strange beliefs and this gentleman was there to see for himself and write about it. The stage followed the same trail as the Pony Express and travelers stopped at Home Stations.

Ruby Valley was a halfway house about three hundred miles from Salt Lake City and the same distance from Carson Valley. Amos had been with the Express about five months and was sometimes delegated as a Station employee between rides. It was October 1860 when Burton got out of the stagecoach at Ruby Valley after a long dust ride across the Nevada desert. Dressed in a black frock coat, white shirt, cravat, and stovepipe hat, he immediately attracted attention.

Amos happened to be on duty at the station that evening. The traveler and his attendants were ushered into the bare waiting room and signed the register with a flourish, "Richard Burton, London, England." So this was the man all had heard about!

After a supper of beef stew and baking powder biscuits, washed down with strong coffee, the Englishman peppered everybody with questions.

"I want to do some shooting. I understand there is a lake somewhere in this vicinity. Can you tell me about it? Is there anybody I could hire as a guide? What is the elevation here? How cold does it get?"

Amos assured him there was such a place about two miles from the station. It was famous for the variety of birds, from the wild swan to the rail. He said he couldn't go with him since he would be on duty the next twenty-four hours, but answered the other questions about weather, etc.

Burton then asked about the Indians, hereabouts. "What tribe do they belong to?" Amos told him they were principally Shoshones, with a few Utes mixed in.

"I've been studying the Shoshone language while I've been in Salt Lake," said Burton, "but I find it very difficult. I wish I had an Indian who could teach me."

Amos rose to the bait. "I speak Shoshone, a little. Maybe I can help you."

"Well, I declare. Why don't you start talking and see if I understand any of it." Whereupon Amos launched into the story about his friend Nick Wilson, the White Indian boy, telling it in Shoshone.

"Hold up, my lad," interrupted Burton, "you go too fast! Now start again slowly and let me try to repeat each sentence after you." He was an eager student and a clever one. His ear caught the slightest change in accent and intonation. He wasn't satisfied until he pronounced each word correctly and understood its meaning. Afer an hour or more of this intensive language lesson, Burton paused and looked wonderingly at his teacher.

"Where did you learn to speak Shoshone? You look like a white man and speak like an Indian."

"I learned it when I was a young boy as I played with Shoshone children," replied Amos.

"Is that the only dialect you speak?"

Amos told his eager pupil that he also spoke Bannock,

understood Arapahoe, Nez Perce and sign language. It was like being given the third degree as Burton probed about his past, present and future. He told Burton his name was Mose Wright, that he was from Illinois, and admitted he was largely self-educated so far. His questioner at length leaned back in his chair and fixing his eye directly on Mose, said, "Mr. Wright, could I hire you to work with me tomorrow, here at the Station, since you have to be on duty, and continue to teach me? I am greatly impressed by your knowledge of languages. I'll gladly pass up the chance for a shooting expedition tomorrow, even if I could get a wild swan, if you'll spend the day making a real Shoshone out of me."

Mose was naturally pleased, and agreed to the proposition. It was a day he would not forget. Burton's thirst for information was unquenchable. Even insignificant items met with interest and approval. Mose told him about the time he beat up a man with a billiard cue who was cheating at the game, and another time how he climbed a telegraph pole to find out what the wire was saying, at which Burton laughed uproariously. The day was spent almost wholly in Shoshone language study, with Burton making copious notes. The traveler didn't seem to be in any hurry to go on, and when he found out that Mose would be working at Sheawit Creek, the next Home Station on the trail, he decided to stop there also, and continue his study of Shoshone.

Such appreciation from this cultured gentleman pleased Mose and prompted him to put on a real show that evening as Burton and a number of other travelers sat before the huge stone fireplace at the uncompleted Sheawit Creek Station, where a roaring fire warmed their bodies and hearts. He dramatized events which had happened at Salmon River so recently in the sudden attack by the Indians. He climaxed it by doing a bear dance for his enthusiastic audience. They bombarded him with questions about Indians in general, and wanted to know about poisoned arrows, and how to survive in the desert.

That Burton was impressed, Mose was sure, but how impressed he would never know. It was many years later that Burton's "City of the Saints" was published, containing an account of the Englishman's visit to Salt Lake, of his visit with Brigham Young and other notables there. Two pages of his journal account told what happened out there in the Nevada desert with Mr. Mose Wright from Illinois as his tutor:

Ruby Valley, 7th Oct. 1860: . . . About two miles from this station there is a lake covered with waterfowl, from the wild swan to the rail.

I preferred, however, to correct my Shoshone vocabulary under the inspection of Mose Wright, an express rider from a neighbouring station. None of your 'one-horse' interpreters, he had learned the difficult dialect in his youth, and he had acquired all the intonation of an Indian. Educated beyond the reach of civilization, he was in these days an oddity.

Sheawit Creek, 10th October. ... Mr. Mose Wright again kindly assisted me with correcting my vocabulary. We spent a cozy pleasant evening round the huge hearth of the half-finished station.

Mose Wright recounted his early adventures in Oregon, (Salmon River) how when he was a greenhorn, the Indians had danced the war dance under his nose, had then set upon his companions, and after slaying them had displayed their scalps. He favored us with a representation of the ceremony, an ursine (bear dance) performance whilst the right hand repeatedly clapped to his lips, quavered the long loud howl into broken sounds:—'Howh! Howh!— howh! ow! ow! Ough! ough! aloo! aloo! loo! loo! oo!'

Mose Wright described the Indian arrow poison. The rattlesnake is caught with a forked stick planted over its neck, and is allowed to fix its fangs in an antelope's liver. The meat, which turns green, is carried upon a skewer when wanted for use: the flint-head of an arrow, made purposely to break in the wound, is thrust into the poison, and when withdrawn is covered with a thin coat of glue. Ammonia is considered a cure for it, and the Indians treat snakebites with the actual cautery. The rattlesnake here attains a length of eight to nine feet and is described as having reached the number of seventy-three rattles, which supposing—as the theory is—that after the third year it puts forth one per annum, would raise its age to that of man. It is much feared in Utah Territory. We were also cautioned against the poison oak, and given detailed information about its painful rash that lasts three weeks. Strong brine was recommended as treatment to us by our "prairie doctor." (Fawn M. Brodie, ed., *City of the Saints*, pp. 527-29.)

The *Deseret News* printed an item about Amos, dated April 17, 1861, "Late Indian Depredations."

Mr. Wright, who came in with the last California mail, reports that the Indians on the route, in some places were becoming quite belligerent, and that they drove off all the animals belonging to the mail company that were at the Cold Spring station about midway between this city Salt Lake and Carson, on or about the 25th of March. At other points they had made threats and there was a fair prospect that the scenes of last season would shortly be renewed all along the road, if no measures be taken to conciliate the disaffected bands that inhabit that desert region.

Mr. Wright was doubtless on his way home from Pony

Express riding for good. It was evident that the day of that glamorous episode in western history was on its last leg. The telegraph was almost completed across the nation and would spell an end to express riding in October of that year.

Mose, or Ame Wright, as he was now sometimes called, was out of a job again. At twenty-one, he had been a missionary, a freighter, Pony Express rider, detective, linguist, Indian lore specialist, and raconteur.

Chapter Nine
Cate

The familiar landmarks along the Wasatch Mountains to his right set his heart to thumping with thoughts of home. Amos whistled the old song, "Then It's Home Again, and Home Again, and Home Again for Me."

There'd be his father's big booming voice and a hearty hug. Mary Jane always melted him to tears in spite of himself. Virginia Ann Charlotte would be all grown up, married, with a baby or two. Hard to realize. David would be glad to see him. Amos was always a hero to his younger brother. And little Jonathan would be, let's see ... twelve by now.

His heart purposely skirted even a thought of Lois Moran. The latest letter from his father told of her sudden death two days before Christmas and a couple of weeks or so after the birth of her third child. What had caused her death? The usual risk of childbirth? Exposure? Want? Or was it, he half hoped, a broken heart? At least her death made it possible to go home again at last. He took a deep breath and shook off his daydream.

Spring in the air. Sego lilies and Indian paint brush peeped out between the gray-green sagebrush which stretched away to the north. Meadowlarks were spilling their lilting song, "Brigham City's a Pretty Little Town," from each scrub cedar and fence post along the way. The juices of manhood were rising within him like sap in a sugar maple.

Two weeks isn't long between meeting a girl and marrying her, but those Wright boys weren't ones to wait around when there was a job to be done. So when Mose saw eighteen-year-old Catherine Roberts at the first dance he went to in Brigham City, he literally swung her off her feet between the do-si-do's and promenade alls. He had rhythm without having to learn it. And 'Cate' fell for it with all her heart!

He said, "Will you?"

She answered, "*Will* I!"

And Father Jonathan tied the knot on April 28, 1861.

The wedding reception was held in the bowery. The long tables were piled high with coconut and chocolate cakes and lots of other good food. And that new couple, they could dance like a dream. They danced, and everybody else danced, and it was a taste of heaven for all of them.

Catherine's mother, Gwen, was a widow emigrant from Wales who buried her first husband on the way to Zion. He died of cholera and took his little three-year-old son with him from the same dread disease. They were buried on the banks of the Mississippi at the lower tip of Kentucky. But the widow and her two daughters, Catherine and Eliza, kept on going till they got to Zion. Gwen later married David R. Evans in Brigham City and had two sons.

Being Welsh and belonging to a family of stepbrothers noted for their thrift and business acumen, Cate developed into a smart and thrifty woman, herself.

Mose, which she called him from the beginning, was delighted to note she could not only cook a good meal, but put it together like a miracle out of practically nothing. It was great, suddenly to find his socks not only washed, but neatly darned and folded. There was a shining warm spot inside him now, which drew him straight to his little gray home in the west, where a sweet woman waited for him at the end of the day.

Home was a little two-room cabin across town from Cate's mother, down on Forrest Street. It was for rent after Sister Jenkins passed away. They were lucky to get it partly furnished, which meant a little cookstove propped up on one side with a stick of wood in place of a leg, a rickety table and two stools, an iron bedstead with a straw tick on it and some faded curtains.

Cate's mother gave her some bedding and a framed motto in cross-stitch saying *God Bless Our Home*. Mary Jane raked up some unsilver silverware and Jonathan told Cate to go down to

Stubb and Twist's and get up to ten dollars worth of whatever she needed most. These things were all received with pure gratitude. Wants were simple and needs few, and love provided the furniture polish which made the place gleam before the eyes of Mose and Cate.

Getting to know each other during honeymoon days followed the magic pattern discovered again and again by each pair of lovers since time began. Sharing ideas they had never before put into words became a precious ritual between them. They marveled that they could have thought such tender thoughts or dreamed such delightful dreams independent of each other. This ritual removed the half-mask both had worn until now. It opened the private side door which each of them carefully guarded, and through which only one completely trusted and loved could enter. The resulting vision became a revelation to both. Such true knowledge of each other manufactured a balm which healed wounds made thoughtlessly or even purposely in the days which followed.

Sometimes when Cate pouted over some trifling offense, Amos kissed her tenderly on top of her head and said, "I didn't know I was marrying a little mourning dove," and Cate would say in her quaint Welsh brogue, "That's what you bargained for, Mose Wright!" To which he replied, "It's a good bargain."

Mose was pleased and gratified to find that he and his father could now talk freely, man-to-man as never before, and they made the most of it.

Mary Jane was happy to have her man-boy back again. But things weren't the same for either of them. She was completely immersed now in her own four children, ranging from seven to two. In addition, there were Heber and Edward Hunter belonging to Lois, now left for Mary Jane to mother. Her own year-old daughter Rachel had to be weaned when Lois died, so nine-day-old Edward Hunter could take her place at the breast. Then there was still twelve-year-old Jonathan, or Pony as they came to call him, which made a family of seven children dependent on her. And when David was around, it meant eight to care for.

With Cate to look after and provide for, Amos knew he'd have to find a job. Summer days slid into autumn and he managed to pick up a few odd jobs and dollars here and there, but Cate was put to it to make ends meet in the middle.

He could always freight, but he hated to be away from home now. A three-week trip from Corinne to Butte sometimes netted as

much as three hundred dollars and that was big money. All
married men vied for the chance to drive teams for some freight
outfit.

The scheduled time between Corinne and Helena, Montana
was twenty days and nights, one thousand miles round trip. Fare
for passengers one-way was seventy-five dollars for a distance of
five hundred miles. The freight rate was seven dollars per
hundred pounds. If the goods were unloaded at any other station
along the route, the charge was the same. There were about four
hundred miles and eighty heavy wagons going and coming from
Corinne. Some horses and oxen were also on the road, but the
most common way of freighting was four mules on one wagon,
although some of them had as many as ten mules to one wagon
with two or three trailer wagons coupled to it.

Father Jonathan was aware of his son's need of a job. One
day he dropped by to tell Amos that President Snow needed a
flock-master to look after some Church cattle out near Portage.
There was plenty of winter feed for them, but the Indians were
likely to make off with some of them unless there was someone
around to keep an eye open.

"But I'd be away all winter, Father ... and Cate's expecting,
you know." "Well, beggers can't be choosers, better talk to Brother
Snow about it." And so he did.

Brother Snow thought Cate would get along all right. She had
her own mother and could always fall back on Jonathan if she
needed help. Maybe she could get coal and wood at the tithing
office.

There were about 1500 head of cattle from Davis, Weber and
Box Elder counties to be looked after. The range was to be to the
west of Bear River and along the Promontory east side. He'd have
to rough it, of course. Better take along some warm clothing and
bedding. He might find a cabin somewhere out there, but if not, a
tent would have to do. The job was to be considered as a mission
although he would be allowed to collect herd bills from the cattle
owners.

It didn't sound too promising to Amos, but it was the only
alternative he had. There were no roads or bridges spanning the
Bear River, but a suitable ford was found which California gold
seekers used in 1849, and swimming the cattle across the river
and following them with a horse was rather an exciting job. There
were no houses anywhere around, but a few Indian tepees
indicated there would be Indians.

Chief John and his Shoshone tribe at Fort Washakie in North Box Elder County were peaceful and soon became friends Amos could depend on. Whenever the quarrelsome Bannocks came roving into the vicinity, Old John came to warn Amos to round up the cattle and take them to safer quarters.

Snow came early and stayed late. There wasn't a cabin anywhere, and a tent didn't keep much cold out or heat in. For the first time Amos knew what bodily pain was. It settled in his joints with stabbing thrusts like a lodged bullet. He made it through January and February and part of March, but the pain got so bad he finally packed up his mule, saddled "Peanuts" and started for home. The cattle would have to get along without him. He had to get home to be with Cate. Her baby was due in April. With what the cattle owners owed him, they'd get by until he could find something else to do.

Things hadn't turned out well for Cate, either. She was proud and didn't want to impose on her mother or Jonathan. She got a little coal and wood from the tithing office, but made out with as little as possible. It had been a long, cold, sometimes hungry, lonesome winter. Finding her in this condition put Mose in a fighting mood at once. Hadn't "they" promised to look after her?

He set about trying to collect herd bills from the cattle owners, but money was scarce and he was put off more often than not. He went to see President Snow, but he was gone and the clerk said he didn't know anything about the agreement. So Amos had to wait. When he finally got to see Brother Snow, he seemed disappointed that Amos had left the cattle unattended. He said he had a dozen things to see to first, and he'd get around to paying him as soon as he could.

Amos left, feeling very low in spirits and a little hot under the collar. He guessed it *was* hard to take care of everybody's needs. He'd try to be patient another few days. He borrowed a team and wagon and got some wood out of the canyon so at least they could keep warm. Cate was miserable in her last month of pregnancy and worried about getting diapers and clothes for the new baby. Each day Amos awoke, thinking, "Today I'll hear from President Snow." But no word came. He tried to formulate what he would say next time he saw him. "Cate will be confined any day now. There will be the midwife to pay, as well as medicine and clothes to buy for her and the baby. The food is mostly gone, too."

When he happened to meet President Snow on the street, he began his prearranged speech. But Brother Snow was in a hurry and said he couldn't stop to talk. Amos grabbed him around the waist, threw him down, took what money he had in his pocket and left without even helping the old man up.

Brother Snow was a small man and no match for Amos. The suddenness of the attack left him breathless. He was not a fighting man, but possessed a certain feisty quality. He was known to have had some encounters with his own grown sons, occasionally, and not just word battles. Ordinarily, he was a mild-mannered gentleman, but now he was anything but that.

Amos didn't tell Cate what had happened. Already ashamed of the whole affair, he just handed her the money.

"Now you can get some things you need for the baby. There should be enough to pay the midwife, too."

Months of exposure at Promontory brought Mose down with a severe case of pneumonia. A mustard plaster on his aching chest didn't help much.

The baby came April 22, a boy they named Silas. Amos was too sick to care, even though he heard Cate's groans and screams. Dear, reliable Mary Jane left her own brood and came to nurse Cate, the new baby and Amos, with Cate's mother taking a turn.

Things couldn't get worse. But they did. A note in the mail announced, "As of April 30, 1862, Amos Russell Wright has been excommunicated from the Church of Jesus Christ of Latter-day Saints." No reason given nor by whom authorized. (L.D.S. Genealogy Film, General Library Member Service, Box Elder Stake, Brigham City microfilm.)

The first Jonathan heard was when it was announced in priesthood meeting on Sunday. He told Mary Jane when he got home. David heard too, and without a word headed straight for his brother's little cabin. Cate answered his knock with the baby in her arms looking pale and worried. Mose had had a bad night.

David pulled a stool close to the bed and took Amos' hand.

"What's this I hear about you being cut off the Church? What happened? What for?"

"I guess I asked for it," admitted the sick man, shamefacedly explaining the situation.

David started to laugh. "Why you old son-of-a-gun! I wish I'd been there to see it. I'd have punched his nose at the same time. He had it coming," and slapping his knee he roared again. He glanced at his brother's drawn face with lines of suffering evident and his heart melted. "You look pretty peaked. Have you had a doctor?"

Amos admitted he hadn't.

"Have you got enough to eat?" Then Cate told him they were out of flour, but there were a few dried beans and enough potatoes to last a day or two. He suddenly stood up and went out the door, slamming it as he left.

The bishop lived just a block down the street. David knocked at the door and the bishop answered.

"My brother, Amos, is real sick with pneumonia, Bishop. Have you been to see him lately? His wife just had a baby. He needs a doctor. They're out of wood and need some money as well as something to eat."

The bishop shrugged his shoulders and said, "That's none of my business now. He's cut off from the Church."

"Well, then, we'll make it your business," said David, and grabbing him by his coat collar, he booted him all the way to Amos' cabin.

The Tithing Office provided wood and groceries and a doctor came to see the family. The Relief Society provided some extra baby clothes and some of the sisters took the washing home to do. Amos was obliged to accept the help, though unwillingly, and things began to look up for him and Cate. When David told his father about the episode, Jonathan told him he'd better go apologize to the bishop, but David refused.

As soon as Amos was well enough and for lack of anything better, he and Dave started freighting again, hauling provisions to Fort Boise from Salt Lake. They drove a ten-mule team. They often spent a night with the scattered settlers along the way and took provisions to them on order. They got many orders to buy supplies in Salt Lake and deliver them on their return trip to Boise.

As winter approached, the ward and stake authorities in Brigham City advised the men to find work close to home where they could look after their families. Freighting to the gentile towns was especially frowned upon.

David and Amos talked it over and decided they would make one more trip to Boise, fulfilling their promises to buy goods for the settlers, and then quit freighting for good. Amos' excommunication was not an isolated case. It happened often in those times. Sometimes a man didn't know what he was cut off for. If he went to the bishop or stake president and made things right, he was baptized and admitted to membership again. Some did and some didn't. It was a time when neither evil nor the appearance of it was tolerated, a time of fiery zeal. "All or Nothing" in the New Dispensation of the Fulness of Times.

In his present frame of mind, Amos wasn't above taking a drink when he and Cate went to the dances. Rules were very strict in this regard, especially when the dancers, with arms around waists, began swinging their partners more than once or otherwise going beyond what the bishop felt was "orderly conduct."

Amos' one extravagance was a pair of fancy leather boots for himself. Even in those days they were expensive. He could cut quite a swath on the dance floor in his "seven league boots"! The patience of the bishop eventually gave out, and Amos was barred from dancing anywhere in Brigham City or vicinity.

Increasing restrictions aroused rebellion and daring in Wright's breast. Cate tried to reason with him to no avail. Being a daredevil was one way to work out his frustration and resentment. He accepted a dare to ride a mule up the mill-race of the grist mill in town. This was a large wooden and metal open culvert, down which the water ran to turn the water wheel and thus furnish power for the mill. He not only rode up, but turned around and rode back down. Old-timers recounted this caper for years and said, "If there is anything dangerous to be done, Ame Wright will do it."

Force failed where Amos was concerned. His rebellious actions embarrassed Cate, but she loved him and couldn't blame him for feeling the way he did. He was unhappy and so was she. He had to have a job. In his present state of mind, Brigham City had nothing to offer. Two things he could do and get a job doing: freighting and mining. Both paid good wages. But it was a Hobson's choice. Both took him away from Cate. He couldn't ask her to live in such places as Butte or Virginia City. At least she had her Mother and Mary Jane in Brigham City. So again he kissed her and baby Silas goodbye and mounted his horse for Montana.

He loved to ride. Astride a pony he was free. Things looked different from the back of a horse. He could look farther and see more. A gun and blanket plus a loaf of bread or less, was all he needed. He could live off the land as he had learned to do from the Indians. Going alone was dangerous but Amos didn't fear danger. This trip was no exception.

He met a couple of riders about ten miles outside of Butte. He knew they were bad men and remembered seeing them in Virginia City. They had the trademark of desperadoes. They stopped and exchanged pleasantries and then rode on. Amos suspected they were up to mischief and might come back and try to rob him that night, but he'd be ready for them. Just outside the city, with his saddle for a pillow, Amos lay down, but not to sleep. There was plenty to think about to keep him awake. A couple of hours later his keen ear heard footsteps approaching. He reached for his gun and cocked it. The noise was loud enough to do what he intended it to do.

"Is that you Ame?" said a voice from the darkness. "We didn't mean you no harm." He kept quiet. The steps went away and Amos went to sleep.

Work in the mines was dirty work. Digging a tunnel hundreds of feet underground was dirty enough, but it was dirtier because of the kind of men he had to spend his days and evenings with. For a man who had been raised by women like Rebecca and Mary Jane, this was one kind of hell. Mining, to Amos, was a matter of passing thirty days of twenty-four hours, each as quickly as possible, collecting his pay and mailing all but enough for bed and board by postal money order to Mrs. Cate Wright, Brigham City, Utah.

Cate, at least, had baby Silas to love and care for. She counted the days between money orders. She took out barely enough to meet her needs, put the rest in a sock and hid it under the bedtick.

Cate was Amos' pole star and thoughts of her and their child drew him back at intervals in spite of the way he felt about Brigham City. On a July day in 1863, he surprised her by walking in, unannounced. He hugged her close to him and danced her around the little cabin. Fifteen-month-old Silas held out his arms to his father with a grin. It was good to be home!

Amos walked into Jonathan's office next day at the courthouse. After preliminary greetings, the talk gravitated to Indian troubles. "It looks like Colonel Connor finished off the Shoshones up on Bear River in January," said Amos, as he pulled up a chair for himself. "That was a massacre if there ever was one. Over three hundred men, women and children killed. They didn't have a chance."

"They asked for it, though," said Jonathan, leaning back in his squeaky swivel office chair. "You heard about what they did to the white emigrant train two years ago. About the same number of people were killed then. And they've been aggravating the Northern Utah settlers a good deal of late, stealing stock and begging all the time. I guess Connor thought he was doing a brave deed by his surprise attack," said Jonathan. "War is hell anyway you look at it."

"I can't help sympathizing with the Indians, though," rejoined Amos. "They can't be blamed for defending their land. People call the attack by the Shoshones a *massacre*, and the massacre by Connor, a *battle*. It all depends on whose ox is being gored. Connor was made a brigadier general right after that so he is the hero now. The Shoshone winter camp was entirely wiped out, and Chief Pocatello barely got away by swimming down the river underwater. Course I know old Pocatello is a mean hombre. He was in on the fighting at Salmon River and you can count on his being wherever there's trouble."

Jonathan nodded as he opened his desk drawer and pulled out a letter which he handed to Amos. "This is a copy of a letter which Charlotte's husband Alvin Nichols wrote to Governor Doty, the Supt. of Indian Affairs in Utah:

> I wish to inform you of the situation of the Indians of this vicinity and also what information I have relative to Pocatello and his band, a portion of them having been in this city lately, led by one George, consisting of nine lodges, bringing intelligence that they wish for peace and that Pocatello is willing to give ten horses to prove that he is sincere.
>
> He wishes to be at peace with the whites, and says the emigrants shall travel through the country without any molestation to them or their property by any of his men. Also he will be glad to meet with you and make peace but he is afraid to come to Salt Lake City lest he should meet any of the soldiers who, not understanding his business would kill him. They are in very destitute circumstances.
>
> There is also a band of Indians here consisting of about seven lodges who have remained, having no part in the late Indian difficulties, and who are in very destitute condition. They are almost naked and have never had anything done for them by the agency. They have always manifested a peaceful disposition and ought to be, in my opinion, relieved. This band is commonly known as Jake's band. I wish you would be so kind as to send me a note by return mail so that I can inform George, with regards to the matter. He wishes me to assist in bringing about peace, and you will much oblige,
>
> Your obedient and humble servant,
> Alvin Nichols. (ibid. p. 89)

Jonathan said it was this letter which made Governor Doty and General Connor decide to choose Brigham City as the place for signing the treaty, now only a few days away.

Amos folded the letter and handed it back to his father. "So

Alvin is in this thing, too. I'd forgotten he was in charge of Indian Affairs in this county." Then waiting a moment he added, "That happens to be why I'm here now. Governor Doty invited me to come for the signing of the treaty."

Jonathan looked surprised. "Well, how did you get mixed up in this thing?"

"That's a long story," replied Amos. "Will you excuse me a minute while I get a drink? It's pretty hot in here", and he wiped his forehead with the back of his hand.

Once again Amos settled himself in his chair, seemingly enjoying his father's curiosity. "Now, about this treaty business. I was working in the mines at Bannock City a couple of months ago when Shoshone Chief Snagg (a nephew of Sacajawea), and two other Indians came to town to give up a white child which it was alleged they had kidnapped. The whole town was excited over the issue, and since they knew I could speak Shoshone, they asked me to help settle the tempest. It turned out that the child was a half-breed boy and a member of the tribe. But that wasn't the end of the matter. While the three Indians were sitting peacefully in the street, a bunch of miners shot them down in cold blood.

"By pure luck I found out that Superintendent Doty happened to be in the neighborhood and I sent a messenger to get him to come help me out. He had been Superintendent of Indian Affairs for Utah before being appointed governor. Lincoln appointed him to the superintendent job in 1861, one of his first appointments. When he got there, he made an investigation and since the Indians were all murdered, I was the only witness for them. At the close of the investigation Doty said he couldn't do anything about arresting the murderers. There were no civil officers there, and no laws but those which had been made by the miners.

"When Doty found out I was from Brigham City, he suggested I go first with him to Fort Bridger, July 2 for a treaty signing between the United States and the Shoshone Nation. So I went. Washakie was there and was the first to sign. He is chief of about fifteen hundred Shoshones, assisted by six sub-chiefs. He is a very impressive Indian. Then Doty wanted me to come here for the treaty signing on July 30 in case I was needed. So that's how I got mixed up in this thing."

"Mighty interesting, my boy. Mighty interesting," grunted Jonathan as Amos brushed a fly off his nose.

"But, Father, the more I see of men, white or red, or any other color, the more I've come to believe that no man can be trusted to do what is right when it is to his interest to do what is wrong."

Jonathan pondered the statement. "If you could meet Charles C. Rich, you'd find your ideal man ... one who would do what's right under any circumstances. Brother Rich always acts from principle, never from prejudice. He has an unusual sense of justice and great moral courage. He is never afraid to take the part of those he thinks are in the right. I've met him a good many times and I know from my own experience that this is true."

"Where does this super-man live so I can see him and judge for myself?" inquired Amos.

"He is one of the twelve apostles, for one thing, prominent in civic affairs, as well, and has a large polygamous family. I just heard that Brother Brigham has asked him to head up a new settlement in Bear Lake Valley. I believe the first company has already left Utah by this time and they may be there by now."

""Well," replied Amos as he stood up ready to leave, "there's not much chance of my ever seeing him then, but I'll remember what you said. I still don't think any man can be trusted, except you of course, Father!"

Amos stayed around for the treaty signing in the Old Tithing Yard on First West Street, where he and Dave used to help distribute tithing hay and grain and other produce once a month.

It was quite a show. On the right, stood General Connor with a company of his uniformed "Black Coats" as the Indians called the soldiers. Seated at a small table in the center sat portly Governor Doty in charge of events. To the left stood Pocatello and his eight dejected, moth-eaten chiefs. In stark contrast, standing stiffly at attention were the bemedalled officers: a colonel, a captain and a first lieutenant, designated as witnesses. Lastly were three special interpreters. Amos recognized one of them as an old missionary companion from Salmon River days, John Barnard Jr. General Connor began to read the legal sounding treaty in a loud voice:

> Articles of agreement made at Box Elder, in Utah Territory, this 30th day of July, A.D. one thousand eight hundred and sixty-three, by and between the United States of America, represented by Brigadier-General P. Edward Connor, commanding the military district of Utah, and James Duane Doty, Governor and commissioner, and the northwestern bands of the Shoshonee Indians represented by their chiefs and warriors:

Then followed the henceforths, and heretos, and notwithstandings and thereupons. One of the interpreters repeated the reading in Shoshone, and it sounded as gobbledy-gookish as it did in English.

The Indians knew, as did their white captors, that this would be the end of the old free life for the Indians. It would be slavery described in high-sounding words. The treaty made it plain that "a firm and perpetual peace" was to exist from then on between them. That travelers through former Indian lands were not to be molested or harmed; and that the chiefs and warriors gave "full and free consent" to the agreements in the treaty. Further, that telegraph and overland stage lines had a right to continue across Indian lands without harm to either people or property. Also, that as soon as a railroad was built, a right-of-way must be allowed. The United States government promised to pay ten thousand dollars each year for twenty years to the Shoshones for the "inconvenience" of thus using their lands.

The signing came next. Alvin Nichols handed the pen first to the various white men and then to the Indians as each made his mark or signed on the dotted line.

"Taps," played by the trumpeter, signaled the end of the charade. It *was* taps for Pocatello and his band.

Chapter Ten
Bear Lake Valley

Brigham Young was a canny leader and always had his eye on possible new places for the Saints to colonize, both north and south. When the Homestead Act was passed by Congress in 1862, he recognized the opportunity it offered and quickly took advantage of it, before non-Mormons moved in ahead. By "proving up" on a tract of land, the Saints could get a quarter section and make a living without a big investment. No land surveys were made until 1871-72. The Bear Lake Valley was thought to lie in Utah territory.

Charles C. Rich was chosen to visit the valley and decide if it would be a good place to settle. If so, he was advised to have a meeting with Chief Washakie, whose tribe of Shoshones, together with Bannocks, claimed Bear Lake Valley as their own, and get permission to settle there if possible.

It was full of wild game and fish and the Indians did much summer hunting there. They also came to the valley after buffalo hunts to dress the hides. At regular periods they would hold a rendezvous with the Utes and various other tribes. They would trade their robes and furs for horses and other things. They also danced, played games and gambled. It was an important place to them.

When Washakie was approached, he surprisingly seemed willing to have the Mormons come there to live, provided they would reserve the lower area around the Lake for the exclusive use of the Indians. He had dealt with Brigham Young many times and trusted and liked him. President Rich promised that when the farmers began raising crops, they would share with the Indians, if in return the chiefs would do all they could to keep the Indians from molesting and stealing from the white men. Washakie frankly admitted he might not be able to control some of his "bad" Indians. "They are like white men, some bad, some good. If they steal your stock and we find out about it, we will send them back."

In the summer of 1863, Rich reported back to Brigham Young that he thought Bear Lake would be a good place to settle, in spite of its 6,000-foot elevation and cold climate. If he had seen the place in December, it might have made a difference.

Things moved fast after that. Brigham Young knew he needed a man who could operate under difficulties; one who would hang on. He and Charles C. Rich had a genuine affection and trust for each other. It must have been a test of faith for Brother Rich when he was asked to move his families to Bear Lake and take charge of the new colony. Respect for the authority of the priesthood gave him courage to go. Both men must have realized the enormous sacrifice of families whom they asked to live in that new frontier. But it was a call from the Lord through his servants. They were supposed to leave at once so they could prepare for the winter before snow fell.

Charles C. Rich had been a trailblazer long before in Missouri, Illinois and California. A big man physically and spiritually, he inspired faith in the men he chose for the skeleton crew to go ahead with him. The larger company of permanent settlers would follow. The men with him were a special breed who thrived on difficulties and danger. Barriers melted away before them as they chopped down trees and rolled boulders out of their path to make way for families to follow.

The trail led north past Cache Valley and Franklin to Idaho's Emigration Canyon with its evergreen and aspen forests bordering a clear mountain stream. Climbing eastward, scrub oak and maple, already touched by frost, spread a gold and red tapestry before them. As they reached the top of the divide, the beautiful Bear Lake Valley six thousand feet above sea level lay below. Gray-green sagebrush carpeted the valley floor wall-to-wall and the shimmering lake in the distance reflected a cloudless sky. The scouts entered the valley September 26, 1863, setting up headquarters at the present site of Paris, Idaho. They had jumped the first hurdle. There would be many more for the Saints who followed.

Bear Lake Valley stretched like a fish line with a piece of meat on the end. The line is Bear River and bait is Bear Lake itself.

Permanent settlers arrived during the next several weeks. Forty-eight men, forty women and about thirty children stayed in Bear Lake that first winter. Fortunately it was a mild one, for they had come to stay. Log cabins with dirt roofs sheltered them.

Like a fond parent hovering over the cradle of this baby settlement far from home, Brigham Young, along with Heber C. Kimball, made a visit as soon as the snow melted.

The place was alive with plowers, planters and fencers, assuring him that Charles C. Rich had chosen the right kind of pioneer people. Brother Brigham undoubtedly got the same impression Brother Rich's son Joseph had when he wrote, "What a country! Streams full of fish; the most beautiful lake on earth; wild game; grass up to a horse's belly; timber in the mountains, fine location for townsites, everything!"

"We cannot live without law. Be sure to say your prayers night and morning. If you stop praying you will forget God," counseled the Prophet. "Don't go alone to the canyon for timber. Build your cabins close together so you can defend yourselves. Keep your guns and ammunition dry and close at hand. Feed and clothe these Indian neighbors as freely as you can. Never turn them away hungry. Teach them to plow and plant and harvest. Be patient with them. They are children. If they steal, don't think you have to use your guns. Be just and quiet, firm and mild, generous and watchful. Learn to speak their language. Live the Golden Rule. What if you had been born with dark skin yourself?"

More than seven hundred people came to Bear Lake in 1864. There weren't any banks or jails, courts, saloons, or doctors. People kept their money in a sock if they had any and bartered their wheat, oats, potatoes, turnips, wood, poles, lumber or shingles with their neighbors. If ground squirrel, grasshopper or frost wiped them out, they shared what was left with their neighbor and said, "It'll be better next year and we'll try again."

They built strong corrals for their cattle to prevent Indian raids. When the fall harvest came, they furnished the Indians with fat beef and potatoes and didn't have to use guns. If late frosts damaged the crops and froze the wheat, they used it anyway. Each family had its own mill, a coffee mill, until a better grist mill could be built. Flour made from frozen wheat was dark and sticky and so was the bread, but they ate it. Peas always grew well. They could stand the frost. Potatoes came along in time to mix with the peas for a meal fit for Bear Lake kings.

Children and schools always went together from the first. The teacher collected his pay in produce, or money if there was any, from each family. School lasted only a couple of months, surprisingly turning out fine readers, spellers, and writers. A spelling book, a slate and one or two reading books took care of learning needs.

Snow was another problem. It came early and stayed late, confining the valley to "nine months winter and three months late fall." Bobsleds were used as much as wagons. Snowshoes were a must.

Fewer families came to settle the valley than were called. The sieve of fear shook out quite a few the first time and a good many came and left after a short trial run. President Young and Brother Rich called new families nearly every year at conference time with their names announced from the pulpit. When people got discouraged and told President Rich they wanted to leave, he smiled and wished them good luck, but he said he had been called by a prophet of God and was staying.

Chapter Eleven
The Ideal Man

Governor Doty talked to Amos a few minutes before leaving the Old Tithing Yard in Brigham City. He was planning another treaty signing sometime in October at Soda Springs, Idaho, and would be pleased to have Amos help out at that time. The governor invited him to travel with his party, and promised to keep in touch as to exact time and place. Amos thanked him and agreed. He said he could be reached there in Brigham City.

This meant he would have a couple of months before leaving, so he decided to try to pick up a job in Brigham until then. That would give him a pleasant break at home with Cate and baby Silas. Maybe he could haul some wood for the winter, too. It was painful however to be there after his excommunication, as he had no desire to mingle with old friends and associates. However, he did enjoy his visits with Father Jonathan and Mary Jane.

He had a letter from Governor Doty in early October saying they must be in Soda Springs on the fourteenth for the signing of the treaty, and he was to meet the governor's party at Hampton's Ford near Collinston. This he did, and the party arrived without incident at the Springs a day beforehand.

Soda Springs was quite a little settlement. After the Battle of Bear River in which about three or four hundred Bannocks and Shoshones were killed, Colonel Connor had been made a brigadier general, and in May of that year (1863) had established an army post in Soda Springs. The gold rush to Idaho had greatly increased the traffic on the Oregon Trail and the fort was needed to protect travelers from Indians. Along with his troops, this ambitious young officer brought 160 settlers from Utah. Bancroft says these were apostates from the Mormon Church known as Morrisites, and the town they founded became the Oneida County seat from 1864 to 1866. Rumor had it that Connor was there also to keep an eye on Rich's new Mormon settlement just begun in the lower Bear Lake Valley at a place called Paris.

Soda Springs got its name from a group of springs famous to
Oregon Trail travelers, most of whom stopped to try the acid taste
and effervescing gases of the waters. Earlier fur traders, often less
elegantly, called the place "Beer Springs", after one spring whose
waters tasted like Lager beer, only flat. Another called Steamboat
Springs made sounds exactly like a high-pressure steam engine.
(Historic Trails Marker at Soda Springs)

As usual, Amos absorbed all this information. He found out
the elevation was over six thousand feet and decided it would be a
poor place for settlement. That high and so far north would be no
good for farming.

The treaty signing was a rerun of the Box Elder affair.
However, this one was never officially ratified but remained in
effect for five years until the Great Treaty of 1868 was signed at
Ft. Bridger. Names of special interpreters appearing on the
document were Horace Wheat, Willis H. Boothe, and *Ames* R.
Wright. (See copy of treaty in Appendix)

He found that the little company of Mormons under the
leadership of Apostle Rich had arrived a few weeks before, near
the shores of Bear Lake about fifty miles south of Soda Springs.
His father's words about Charles C. Rich stuck in his memory and
he decided this would be a good time to pay him a visit. If such a
man existed as Jonathan described, he wanted to meet him.

He always enjoyed being in a saddle and even the monotonous rolling sagebrush country had a certain beauty about it.
Early frost had turned the scrub oak and maple into a gold and
red mosaic along the foothills.

After crossing Bear River and the swamps on either side,
Amos caught sight of the little Paris settlement of covered
wagons. Already a few log cabins were going up.

Like all other Latter-day Saints, those in Bear Lake felt the
need for a change from work even in those first busy days. They
had cleared a space for a dance floor and it was already tromped
solid. A dance was scheduled for the evening Amos arrived. He
was amazed and pleased to find his old chum Moroni Dunford
among the newcomers. As they chatted, Moroni told him about
the dance, and knowing how Amos liked to kick up his heels
suggested he stay.

"I don't think I'd better. They'd probably kick me out like they
did in Brigham City."

"No, you stick around with me and it'll be all right," reassured

Dunford.

With misgivings, Amos followed his friend that early evening and sat on a little grassy knoll watching people as they arrived. A full moon and a big bonfire lighted the area.

Presently, Amos nudged his companion and asked, "Who's that man over there?"

"Oh, that's President Rich," replied Moroni.

Amos watched carefully as Rich made the rounds of those present, shaking hands, laughing and talking as he went. He was over six feet tall and towered over the rest of the crowd. He looked to be fiftyish, heavyset; probably weighing over two hundred pounds, but well-proportioned and stately.

It wasn't long until the apostle came to where Amos and his friend were sitting. They stood up as he approached. Brother Rich shook hands and spoke to Moroni.

Then he reached out his hand to Amos, asking, "You're a stranger here?"

"My name's Wright." It appeared that Brother Rich was unaware he was a friend of Dunford. Then, surprisingly, the big man sat down and motioned Amos to sit by him. "Your name is Wright, eh? You don't happen to be any relation to Judge Wright from Brigham City, do you?"

"He's my father," and at once noticed it aroused interest in the older man.

"I've heard about you," he said.

Amos' heart skipped a beat, thinking the next thing he would hear would be, "You can get out of here; we don't want your kind in our community."

Instead, Brother Rich said, "I understand you speak the Shoshone language."

Amos swallowed hard and allowed he did.

"A man like you could be very useful in this country. I'm anxious to avoid trouble with the Indians in this vicinity, and have already met and talked to Chief Washakie and made some preliminary agreements with him but I need a good interpreter. Why don't you stick around a few days and maybe you can be a big help to me. How do you happen to be in this part of the country?"

Amos explained that he had been at Soda Springs at the treaty signing, and again he felt Brother Rich was impressed.

"I'm mighty glad to meet you. I know your father and respect him highly. If you're anything like him, I'd like to have you come to Bear Lake as one of our permanent settlers. Now, I'm sure you'll have a good time with these folks tonight, so make yourself acquainted and enjoy yourself. We have a good bunch of musicians. I always make sure we have a fiddler or two in a new settlement. They're indispensable. I'll get in touch with you tommorow and we'll try to see some of the Indians while you're here. Do you speak Bannock, too?"

Amos nodded. By this time, he could do no more than nod.

As soon as Brother Rich left, Amos whispered to Dunford, "Excuse me...I'll be back in a few minutes." He walked quickly toward a bunch of quaking aspen a few hundred yards away and in the darkness gave vent to his emotions in tears.

In the past year he had met nothing but criticism. He'd been cut off from the Church which he loved and knew was true. He'd been banished from his hometown dance halls and made to feel an outcast. Even most of his old friends gave him the cold shoulder. His companions the past year would as soon stab him as look at him.

In contrast, here was a man who treated him with special kindness and even intimated he might be useful in the community. There was a warmth and greatness about this man which was evident at once, and Amos' heart melted within him.

As soon as he regained his composure, he wiped his eyes and returned to the little group of dancers as he heard the fiddle start playing. His feet had springs on them that night for sure and his heart sang a song as he danced. From that moment when that big, great man appeared on the scene, Amos Wright all but worshipped Charles Coulsen Rich.

Next day he had a long talk with Brother Rich. Amos was electrified to recognize as they talked that his father's estimate of the man was correct. Here was one whom he could trust under any circumstance. Brother Rich questioned him exhaustively, first about his family; was he married? Any children? Then about the recent Soda Springs treaty; about Connor. What was his purpose in bringing the anti-Mormon families there? What kind of man was Doty? What would be the best way to proceed with the Indians in this area to insure peace? He asked him about Ft. Lemhi and was not satisfied with a quick reply. He probed for details, listening avidly, leaving no area unexplored. At length, he stood up to his over six-foot height and extended his big hand: "Brother Amos, this has been a most helpful interview. You could be very useful to me in dealing with the Indians. Would you consider bringing your family up here to settle? You don't need to give me an answer now. Think it over. Talk to your wife, then let me know what you decide. We need men like you!" Brother Rich clasped Amos' hand warmly, covering it with his other big one in a final evidence of friendship as the two men parted.

Amos had a lot to think about next morning. There were important decisions to make but they couldn't be made overnight. He couldn't afford to make a mistake. A skiff of snow covered his blankets and he shivered as he waited for the campfire to get going. This business of moving to Bear Lake would take a lot of thought. It seemed unreal and impossible after a night's sleep.

If I could just talk to Cate, it would help, he thought. She has such good sense, and talking to her always helps my thinking. She was pregnant again and the baby was due in two or three months ... that would make it about late January or early February. That meant he had to keep working so he could take care of her. He wouldn't let things happen this time like when little Silas was born. I'll write Cate a letter, he said to himself, but I won't say anything about Bear Lake; she'd just worry, and that can wait.

So it was back to the mines for him. This running around interpreting for treaties had been a nice change but it didn't pay much. No matter what happened, money was important and with two children he'd need more. He hoped the baby would be another boy. Cate chose Silas's name. This time he wanted to name the baby after his father ... maybe Jonathan Daniel ... Daniel was Cate's father's name.

The winter months dragged drearily on, but each month end Cate received a postal money order from Virginia City and the little hoard under the straw tick continued to grow. Amos worried about Cate's confinement, and wrote to her often, treasuring her replies. It was a happy day in early February, 1864, that word came about the baby. It *was* another boy! He wrote a long letter suggesting among other things that they name him Jonathan Daniel and that his father Jonathan bless the baby himself. He might be bitter about the Church, but things like naming his baby he still wanted done right.

Amos came back to Brigham City in June. He'd been away too long and he vowed he wouldn't let it happen again. Cate looked beautiful to him and he couldn't let her out of his sight. It took little Silas awhile to make up to this stranger but after a few days he shadowed Amos wherever he went. The first time he caught

sight of the baby lying in the cradle Mary Jane had loaned to
Cate, he slapped his knee and said, "By George, we picked the
right name for him. He's the spittin' image of a judge. Judge
Jonathan Daniel Wright!" He picked him up gingerly. He hadn't
handled a baby for a long time; and sat with him in Cate's little
rocking chair. From that moment on he was hooked. He'd never
felt like this before. The baby lay there looking up at him with
such a serious expression it was as if he were trying to say, "I
could tell you lots of things if I could talk." And the young father,
humbled, silently vowed he would try to be worthy of such a son.

Cate had fixed up the house while Amos was gone. There were
dotted swiss curtains at the window; hand-braided rugs on the
floors, and a pretty patchwork quilt on the bed. She had made a
woman's magic for sure and it all felt like "home sweet home" to
Mose.

One day while they were talking up a storm after dinner, he
told Cate about the Shoshone treaty at Soda Springs and about
the funny-tasting water. Then he described his visit to Paris and
meeting Charles Coulson Rich.

"He's a great man, Cate. I could feel it the minute I first saw
him. Besides, he made me feel so welcome ... like I amounted to
something, and that he needed me." Then he told her what
Brother Rich had proposed about moving to Bear Lake.

After what had happened the past two years, they both knew
they could never be happy living in this little town. "What do you
think, Cate?"

Intuition told her Amos would never feel different about the
Church as long as they stayed in Brigham City. She hoped he
would do whatever was asked of him by Church authorities even
now. She didn't dare think of how hard it would be to start
pioneering all over again. *She* could take it but how about the
babies? Wisely leaving the final decision with her husband, she
replied, "I'll go with you if you decide to go, Mose."

A few days later a letter arrived addressed to Mr. Amos R.
Wright from Salt Lake City. President Brigham Young, it said,
was calling a number of families to join the Bear Lake Valley
pioneers. Amos had been recommended by Apostle Charles C.
Rich. Would he be willing to go?

Amos probably didn't realize this was the most far-reaching
decision he would have to make in his life. It would irrevocably
determine the course of "his river" from then on, not only for
himself, but for Cate and their children, and their children's

children. Rebellious thoughts whispered, "I'm not good enough to belong to their church but they think I'm good enough to go to hell-and-gone to start another damn colony for them like I tried to do at Lemhi! I don't *have* to go just because Brigham asked me to! But I've got to get out of this town that goes by his name. I might as well go to Bear Lake, at least there's a decent man there named Rich. All right, I'll go! I'm going up there to be a Mormon bishop, by *G__!*"

With all their earthly belongings packed in a little spring wagon drawn by a skinny team, Amos and Cate, Pone, his sixteen-year-old brother, and their two little boys, Silas and Jonathan Daniel, headed north into the wilderness. It was slow traveling; the road was rutty and bumpy and uphill as the horses headed for the canyon. Sagebrush and rocks were everywhere at that point.

As they reached the top of the hill, the snow was melting and the road got muddier and muddier. The little wagon suddenly slid off the road into a mud bank and sank up to the hubs. Amos climbed down and tried digging them out. He shouted and swore at the horses as they struggled, but the wagon only sank deeper and deeper. He finally told Pone and Cate to stay in the wagon with the children and he'd walk ahead to see if he could find some help, which wasn't likely.

Just then he looked around and saw a couple of men coming up the road in an empty wagon driving a big fat team. He hurried back and told them he was stuck and asked them if they'd hitch on and pull him out. One of the men answered gruffly, "Vel, ve don't haf time now. Ve haf vork to do," and started to pull out around without stopping. Amos grabbed an axe in the back of his wagon and ran ahead of the team shouting, "You Danish s.o.b., you take that fat team and pull me out or I'll split that button on top of your cap right down the middle!" The driver was so surprised and startled, he hurriedly hitched on and pulled them out.

It was a long tiresome trip for Cate and the babies. Silas was only two-and-a-half and baby Jonathan Daniel, six months. When they finally got to Paris they tried to see Brother Rich. He was away for a few days so they camped out till he came back. Amos and Pone rode down around the south end of the lake to look over the country. He thought Laketown seemed a likely spot to settle because it was about as far south as the valley extended and might be a little warmer.

Brother and Sister Gilbert Weaver were living in one of the few log cabins at Paris and invited Cate and Amos to stay with them until they decided where they were going to settle. Everybody called them Gib and Sarah. Sister Weaver was very kindhearted and made a fuss over Silas and the baby and made Pone welcome. The Weavers had lived at Nauvoo where Gib was an expert plasterer on the interior of the temple. They moved to Provo, first, until Brother Brigham called them to settle in Cache Valley. He helped start the little town of Millville. Then he was called to come with Brother Rich to Bear Lake. They traveled with Brother Rich from Logan in September of 1863 with their two little girls. Gib later homesteaded some land a couple of miles north of Montpelier and built a cabin there.

When Brother Brigham and Heber C. Kimball visited the valley in May, Gib and Sarah invited the brethren to have breakfast with them. But when the visitors knocked at the door early next morning, Gib told them they would have to get their own breakfast. A new baby girl had arrived during the night and Sarah wasn't quite up to waiting on them. Brothers Young and Kimball came in and blessed the baby and named her Sarah Jennette. She was the first white child born in the valley.

Amos was waiting for Brother Rich who greeted him warmly.

"Well, Brother Wright, I'm very glad you decided to come to Bear Lake. Let's sit here on the ditch bank where we can talk. Now, where do you think you'd like to live?"

"Well, I've been down to Laketown and liked what I saw."

But Brother Rich apparently had been doing a little thinking himself on where Amos should locate. "I suggest you go up here about twelve or fifteen miles," he said, pointing north.

"President Young was out there when he was here in May and thought it looked like fine cattle country. Grass was up to a horse's belly. People had started calling it Clover because the wild clover was so thick, but President Young said it reminded him of his boyhood home in Vermont, so he called it Bennington, and the townsite five miles south, he called Montpelier. Why don't you ride out there and look the country over before you decide."

The two men shook hands and parted.

Next day Amos took Cate and the babies in the little spring wagon to Bennington. The twelve miles was a long trip, but she wanted to see for herself. It was late September. Indian summer had turned the willows and aspens to gold and the sun shone warm and bright. The sight that met their gaze as they stopped at the top of Bennington hill made them catch their breath. With Joe's Gap and Maple Canyon to their right, a sea of waving grass lay before them just waiting to be grazed off by a herd of cattle.

"I see what Brother Rich meant when he told me to look at this place before I decided on Laketown," Amos fairly gasped. "It's beautiful and this kind of feed grows wild!"

"Aye," breathed Cate, reverting to a Welsh expression. "We can get rich in a few years like my brothers down in Malad."

They talked enthusiastically on their way back to Paris about how they could build a house and start raising cattle. "There were only two or three cabins there, so we could have our pick of the land." Together, they built youthful air castles out of wishful thinking and imagination. They were all for starting at once until reality convinced them they'd better think of hard facts. The balmy days wouldn't last long and they'd have to find some shelter soon.

Brother Rich suggested they spend the winter on North Creek, later called Liberty, a few miles north of Paris. "There are a few families already up there," he said, "and they will be glad to have you join them. Ed Austin and his family are there. You'll like them."

But that first winter remained a nightmarish memory to Amos and Cate. They often wondered how they ever lived through it. They were glad Pone had insisted on coming with them. He idolized his big brother and tried to do everything *he* did, only more so. He chewed tobacco and swore and swaggered trying to make up for his five-feet-five-inch height. He learned Shoshone faster than Amos and could use all the words in the English dictionary and spell them besides. For the first time, he felt useful when he helped Amos dig a tunnel-like room in the side of a small bluff for their dugout shelter that winter, and cobbled up a slab door with leather hinges nailed to the frame. He had never got his share of mother loving or any other kind for that matter, and showed the effect.

Cate brought along the little three-legged cookstove she had used since the day she was married, and Amos made a hole in the dirt roof to put the stovepipe through. Each night, they moved the table and stools outside to make room for their buffalo robe beds on the dirt floor. They kept a shovel handy so they could dig themselves out when the wind drifted the snow deep against the door.

Ed Austin sold them a little Jersey cow called Beauty and

enough hay to last through the winter. Pone built a little brush windbreak for her and it was his job to milk her night and morning. Cate had bought two hundred pounds of high patent flour before she left Brigham City and paid for it out of her secret hoard in the sock. At least they could eat bread and milk. Brother Rich shared half a venison with them and assured them there was plenty more to be had by a man with a gun, and there were fish in all the streams. A creative woman like Cate could "make a magic" out of these basics, and she did.

It was dark and dreary in the dugout day after day. The men could get out long enough to split wood and hunt and fish, but Cate was tied day and night with the babies. J.D., as they called him, wasn't getting enough to eat from the breast and he caught a bad cold. Cate tried all the remedies she could think of, but she didn't have any mustard for a plaster nor onions for a poultice and the cough persisted and got worse. He cried most of two days and nights. Amos walked what floor there was to walk trying to comfort him. The baby's head was hot and feverish and he refused to nurse. Toward morning his breathing became shallow. A few gasps told the anxious watchers he was gone. Pneumonia had claimed another victim.

They would never forget that day. Grief, disappointment, heartache. Cate accused herself. "If I'd have done differently I could have saved him. I shouldn't have left Brigham City. He wouldn't have got sick there and, if so, there would have been a doctor."

Amos was inconsolable. There had been a special bond between him and this baby from the first. He found it was infinitely worse to lose this child; bone of his bone, than a baby brother or even his own mother Rebecca. Was this a judgment of God upon him for his rebellious actions and feelings the past couple of years? Whatever the reason, he would never let himself become so wrapped up in one of his children again.

Ed Austin made a little coffin and his wife Alnora Lane lined it with a white curtain. Pone and Amos took turns with a pick and shovel digging through two feet of frozen ground to make the tiny grave. They buried him in the new cemetery in Montpelier, their hearts as bleak as the gray sky overhead. This was one more evidence to Amos that nothing ever turned out right.

Ed Austin's kindness that first winter cemented a lifelong friendship between him and Amos. Ed was a small man, always carefully groomed and even in frontier days he dressed like a gentleman. To Amos, he was Mr. Integrity; another man cut after the pattern of Brother Rich, a man who "can't be bought."

Both he and Ed had been born in Illinois in 1840, came across the plains about the same time and settled in Cottonwood, though they didn't know each other then. It was strange that two men as different as they were would be drawn to each other so strongly. Ed was all spit-and-polish and Amos could care less for appearance. But when it came to the basics like honesty, loyalty and courage, they matched like two halves of the same arrow.

Then there was Joseph C. Rich, a son of his idol Charles C. Rich. Near the same age, his infectious spirit captivated Amos. He was a surveyor, budding lawyer, politician and writer, seemingly out of place in such harsh country. What others felt, he was able to put into words.

> We were all happy in those days. Coming from different parts of the country, we were cooperative strangers. Did not know each other's failings and were too poor, too honest, to lie about and slander one another. No class distinction. Hickory shirts and homemade pants reminded us we were all of the earth, earthy. Frost-bitten bread with a sucker from the lake was not calculated to make us very proud. We settled our differences by arbitration. If anyone was sick, the good mother who had raised eight or ten children usually knew what to do, so the death rate was low.

Thus, in the short space of six months, Amos found not only one ideal man in Bear Lake Valley, but three.

Chapter Twelve

War and Peace

Because of the agreement between President Rich and Washakie, the settlers in Bear Lake Valley felt obliged to share their hay and grain, vegetables and produce, and the Indians made the most of it. Old squaws, half-blind, would knock at the door, hold out a gunny sack and point first to the one answering the door and then to the sack, indicating, "Put something in it!''

Chief Pocatello was good at this game, his name meaning, "Give me another sack of flour and two beef." Young bucks often tried to bully the Saints with threatening looks and actions as they demanded whatever they thought they could get. The white women and children were usually at home alone and they had to learn to deal with the natives as best they could. Stealing was considered legal by the Indians if they could get away with it, which they often did.

In 1867 when the Indians came back to their fall rendezvous, they found that settlers had gone into their restricted hunting and campgrounds, had plowed, fenced, and planted crops, thus breaking the treaty Washakie had made with Presidents Young and Rich. The Indians were furious and began a war dance.

"Young and Rich lie again. We get even this time!'' Washakie promised to kill every white man, woman and child in the valley.

In record time, word of the trouble reached President Rich. He dispatched a messenger on a swift horse to tell Amos Wright to come at once. Amos was just finishing dinner. Cate saw the dust of a galloping horse about a mile down the road. Hurrying to the door, she watched the approaching rider. He fairly leaped off the horse and ran toward the cabin. Even before he reached the door, he shouted, "There's Indian trouble, Ame. Brother Rich wants you to come fast. Follow me!''

Cate turned pale. "Oh, Mose, do be careful." She was six months with her fourth child and easily upset. Now her heart pounded wildly. While Mose ran to saddle Toshats, she made a sandwich and slipped it into her husband's jacket pocket. There was no time for goodbyes and within minutes the two horsemen were galloping south, soon out of sight.

Cate gathered five-year-old Silas and toddler Winnie in her arms and tried to console them. Both sensed something was wrong. Now all she could do was wait and pray. It would be easier to be in the thick of things, than staying home, worrying and wondering.

At Paris, Amos slid off the horse and dashed into the house where Rich was waiting.

"Amos, there's a dangerous situation down at Round Valley. I need you. Washakie and his warriors are on the warpath and have threatened to kill all the settlers in the valley. They say we've broken our treaty by planting crops and fencing their hunting and campground. They've torn down the fences, trampled the crops, destroyed everything in sight. They're dancing, now. We've got to quiet them.

"Explain that most of the guilty ones aren't Mormons and we don't have control over them. You can use cattle and horses to bargain with, but don't promise more than you have to. Keep talking. Tell Washakie we'll make it right with him. Get them to give us another chance. Remind him how we've fed them and furnished them cattle ... but you know how to handle them better than I can tell you. I suggest you take a couple of men with you. Who do you want?"

Without a moment's hesitation, Amos requested Ira Nebeker and Ed Austin.

"Good. Ira is down at Laketown and I'll send a runner to pick up Austin at Liberty. Come, sit down and rest."

It seemed good to relax a few minutes. He knew he was lucky to have two such men to go with him. After living in a dugout next door to Ed Austin that winter on North Creek, he knew Ed would be a good man to have along. Ed understood and liked Indians.

Ira Nebeker, that broncobuster from Pony Express days, could still stick to a bucking pony like glue. A good man, too. The three had jokingly called themselves the "Three Musketeers" and their motto was "all for one and one for all."

Amos awoke with a start to the sound of Ed's voice saying, "Where's Mose? I'm ready to go!"

Brother Rich suggested a prayer before they left. The three men knelt together and it felt strange to Amos. He hadn't been on his knees for almost five years. The Apostle prayed like one man talking to another. He asked for wisdom and protection; that the hearts of the natives would be softened, and the Saints spared. By the time he was through, Amos had goose bumps all over him and a strange warm feeling in his chest. With a firm handclasp and a "God bless you," their leader bade the two young men goodbye.

"We'll pick up Ira in Laketown," said Amos as they mounted their horses and headed South. "This is dangerous business. Just don't act afraid. This could cost us our lives, but we can't back down now." At Laketown, Ira saddled up and was ready to go and the three of them headed for Round Valley a few miles away. "Remember now, no sign of fear and 'all for one and one for all.'"

A circle of tepees with smoke curling skyward and the wierd chanting of warriors greeted them. It was the war dance in the truest sense. A shower of arrows fell around them and a shot or two was fired. The three men rode swiftly into the circle and were pulled from their horses.

Amos opened his shirt wide, exposing his breast, and in Shoshone said, "We come to make peace, but if you don't want to listen, go ahead and shoot."

Nebeker felt the point of a knife pressing into his stomach as he looked into a scowling face. He stared back without flinching. The Indian finally dropped his knife, grunting, "Brave man."

Austin found himself lying on his back with a couple of men holding him spread-eagle fashion and starting to stick porcupine quills under his fingernails. He gritted his teeth.

Washakie strode into their midst. He was a hunk of a man; straight, bronzed, lean, muscles rippling as he walked. His hair hung in two braids in front with a single eagle feather stuck in the back. He said a few words which Amos understood. "Don't shoot now. Let the man up. Let *him* talk," nodding toward Amos. The Indians made a circle, some squatting, others cross-legged. To gain time, Amos asked Washakie why he wanted to fight. The chief launched into a diatribe in Shoshone and sign language against Young and Rich. "They talk with a forked tongue. They make promises and break them. They lie. They promised a hunting ground with no white men. Now we come back and find men and cabins and fences and plows. We get even! We kill all whites ... men, squaws, papooses!" The sub-chiefs chimed in amid a bedlam of chattering voices.

Amos had dealt many times with these people. He knew they had a different side if he could find it now. Keeping his voice steady and low-pitched, not showing anger or emotion, he began. "You have a right to fight. White men have taken your campground. But these land-jumpers are not Mormons. Young and Rich can't make them get off. They speak for Mormons only. If any Mormons are guilty, Young and Rich will punish them. They will talk to the land stealers and try to get them to move off but they can't make them get off."

There was heckling and objections, but always the trio stayed calm and low of speech.

"Did Young and Rich lie when they promised the Mormons would share their food and blankets with you?"

"Do you go hungry since the Mormons came?"

"When Sioux come and steal your horses do you kill Bannocks to get even?"

Amos settled back and waited. The argument got down "as thin as soup made by boiling the shadow of a pigeon that had starved to death." Finally, he said, "We have meat outside. Let's eat and then talk some more." Washakie's eyes glinted and he nodded. "You send two men. One stay here. My men will go, too. Don't try to get away. My men will shoot. Get meat." Amos raised his brows at Ed and Ira and they mounted their horses and went to get the meat.

Huge bonfires were built and allowed to burn down until only glowing coals remained. Huge slabs of beef were lugged in, cut in strips and stuck on pointed sticks to be roasted over the coals. The warriors fought among themselves for extra meat, tearing it with their teeth and devouring it half-cooked in huge gulps without chewing.

It was almost midnight by the time the feast was over. The Indians had quieted down and some were stretched out on the ground with their eyes closed. The talk was slower and quieter and the three friends took turns explaining, calming and cajoling, being careful never to show anxiety or fear. They sometimes replied with merely a lift of the eyebrow or a flick of the wrist.

At long last, Washakie said, "I need sleep. Wait till morning then we'll talk again." He set guards over the three men and the Indians drifted away to their own lodges. Amos, Ed and Ira took turns staying awake to be sure they weren't murdered as they slept. The night hours crept on ever so slowly. It was a deadly game of cat and mouse and a single false move could result in three scalps dangling from the belt of a warrior.

Three endless days and nights passed before Washakie agreed to give Young and Rich another chance. Amos promised there would be a specified number of horses and cattle provided as a settlement, and the Saints would furnish blankets besides. "But, if," said Washakie, "it ever happens again"... he drew his thumb graphically across his throat from ear to ear.

The peace pipe was lighted and Washakie stepped forward.

He took it and passed it through the four cardinal points: north, south, east and west, then to the sky and the earth. He took a long puff and handed it back to Shoogan who repeated the ritual. Amos, Ed and Ira solemnly followed suit.

Still surrounded by warriors, the Three Musketeers rode back to Paris to report to President Rich. The necessary booty was collected from the Saints and duly delivered to the Shoshones. The war was over, for a time at least. Wearily, Amos rode back to Bennington to catch up on three days and nights of punishing strain. He hadn't let Charles C. Rich down.

Cate ran out to meet him after he turned Toshats into the pasture. He took her in his arms and kissed her over and over, brushing her curly hair back from her face.

"Oh, Mose, thank God you came back safe! Daw! I've been praying ever since you left that you wouldn't get hurt. I couldn't stand that. Sit you down. I've got the boiler on so you can take a bath." Silas and Winnie clustered around for their share of loving as Cate got soap and a towel. The kitchen was steamy as she poured the hot water into the big galvanized tub.

He was too tired to eat after his bath. With a satisfied feeling in his insides, he sank into bed and drifted into a 'round-the-clock slumber.

Brother Rich realized this might be only a temporary respite. Any minor incident could inflame the Indians again, and he worried how he could prevent the outbreak from being repeated.

"There are a good many Indians in the Valley," he wrote to Brigham Young. "Bannocks, Shoshones and one small party of Pocatello's band. They all seem friendly at this time. The greatest trouble now is the begging and scarcity of provisions with us. We try to keep a good lookout and I have already notified the small settlements to be ready to move in when called on which I will do when I see the least sign of danger." (Arrington, *Charles Coulson Rich*, p. 268.)

Later, when it appeared that two tribes were going to battle in the midst of the Mormon settlers, Indian Agent Rich again intervened in an attempt at finding a peaceful solution. According to Rich family tradition, he consulted the chiefs of both tribes through his interpreter, Wright, and persuaded them to come to a conference or council meeting at Fish Haven. As each side presented its grievances, it became apparent that the villain was not the other tribe but, as usual, the white man. Rich agreed with them, and advised them never to do battle among themselves because it would only decrease their numbers. Then turning to the blue waters of Bear Lake, he asked his red brothers to watch the waves ripple the sand. As they kept coming toward them never ending, he explained that the white man would be the same; always coming in greater numbers with no hope of the good old days for the Indians. After this discouraging conclusion, Rich proposed a gigantic feast and the Indians finally agreed on a permanent peace. Cattle were butchered on the spot, a large circle was formed and again the peace pipe was smoked.

After the meal ended, Washakie, Rich and Amos climbed the

foothills overlooking the Lake and Fish Haven. The Indian Chief looked out over the scene below, speaking of its beauty and the love his people had for this land which had belonged to them for generations. Sadly, he asked the Mormon leader to talk to the Great White Father in Washington and see where the Shoshones could go. "If they tell us *where*, we will go." Then turning to President Rich and pointing toward the valley he said, "We give this land to you. Take care of it."

In 1868 the Uinta Wind River reservation in Wyoming was set aside for their use. Although the Shoshones were assigned to the reservation, they still made trips to the valley on an annual basis. Traveling in small bands, they set up their tepees near one of the towns to fish and hunt, bought and traded for supplies from the settlers and then moved on. Mary Ann Rich recorded in her journal:

> For several years they came about twice a year and we had to get a man who could talk to them to explain our right to live there. They thought we were intruding on their hunting ground and we had to furnish them with blankets, clothing, flour, and meat in order to keep peace with them. It took several beef every year to supply them, but it proved successful as we never had any real trouble with them after that.

Chapter Thirteen

Repentance

Ever since Amos met Apostle Charles C. Rich that first time at the bowery in Paris, he was sold on him. It was doubly good to find another man who couldn't be bought, and that it was his own father, Jonathan, who had recommended him in the first place. That was an anchor to hang on to. Brother Rich always called on him for counsel and help with Indian affairs. He was gratified that he had been able to settle the threatened war with the Shoshones at Laketown. The handclasp and word of approval he received when he returned was a rich reward and warmed him whenever he thought of it afterward. Of course, Amos belonged to a younger generation than Brother Rich so their friendship was like that between a disciple and his hero.

But when he met Joseph Coulson Rich, the eldest son of his idol, he knew he had a brother, and the feeling was mutual. He was a year older than Joseph; had been raised under similar conditions; taught the same principles from childhood by strong parents; and both had a rebellious streak that needed curbing. Joseph was an optimist and whatever he did, he did with enthusiasm. The two young men came to have a great influence on each other's thinking and actions. Whenever they got together they talked freely about nearly every subject that came up. They often took different sides just for the fun of it and it was hard to decide who got the better of the argument.

Amos' excommunication from the Church was one subject they avoided; Amos, because it was a tender spot, and Joseph, because he respected his friend's feelings. He'd heard the story through the gossip line. But one day it came up suddenly, and before they realized it, they were deep in an emotional free-for-all. Joseph was as enthusiastic and dogmatic about Mormonism as everything else he believed in and when Amos voiced his doubts and resentment, they were both off and going without restraint.

Amos recounted bitterly his unfair treatment at the hands of the Authorities in Brigham City. He did some exaggerating as he repeated the story, trying to make it look better. It was the first time he had talked about it to anyone except his father since it happened six years ago. He knew how Cate felt and couldn't bring himself to tell her outright of his bitterness knowing it would hurt her and he was afraid it would end up in a quarrel. So he built a wall around himself on the subject and tried to bury it, permanently. But when the dam broke, his feelings all came rushing out and it was Joseph who first realized the depth of his wound. Jonathan had tried to point out that there were always two sides to any story, which only enraged Amos because he thought his father was taking sides against him.

"What you need to do is repent," said Joseph.

"Repent! Who, *me*?"

"Yes, *you!*" said Joseph. "You must remember you aren't exactly perfect, but almost! You know what a terrible temper you've got. I know when you get that certain look in your eye I'd better get out of your way before something happens." Joseph laughed and Amos grinned in spite of himself. "You'd feel a lot better if you'd try to forget your grudges. How long has it been since you prayed?" And not waiting for Amos to answer, he went on. "I know ... a long, long time!" Joseph could see that Amos was getting angry, but he went right on.

"You'll never feel any better until you open up to the Lord. He knows your thoughts and he isn't pleased with your attitude. Don't you ever feel ashamed for what you did to Brother Snow? He was a lot smaller man than you and older, too. And besides, he is an apostle." Joseph ran his fingers through his hair and started pacing back and forth as he talked. "He must have had a million problems to worry about like my father has all the time. Cate could have gone to her mother or your father for help if she hadn't been so proud and independent. And, after all, they were the ones who should have helped her before she went to the bishop. It's easy to put the blame on somebody else."

He stopped and looked squarely at Amos. "What does Cate think about it? I'll bet she doesn't care a tinker's dam what happened that long ago. She just wishes you'd get this thing off your chest so you'd be the man she married six years ago, instead of a moody, silent fellow she is afraid to talk to. You know she has a testimony of the Gospel and you used to have one, too. Maybe you *were* treated unfairly, but everybody makes mistakes once in awhile...even you!"

Amos felt like punching his friend in the nose but instead he walked out of the room. He couldn't think of a comeback. What Joseph said was true. Joseph was sorry afterward for being so blunt but it was done now so there wasn't anything he could do. A few weeks later he bored in on Amos again.

"You know how much better you'd feel if you would repent? It would be like taking a good hot bath and using lots of soap from your head down to your toes. You'd come out feeling clean and fresh again; truly a new man. You've been traveling down the same stubborn path for years. It's time you turned around and went the other way. You're walking in the dark and the light hurts your eyes, so you haven't got what it takes to face up and admit you're wrong!"

Amos swore he'd never speak to that s.o.b. again and withdrew into one of his silent spells. Cate often grimly said, "Mose can sit and think without food and rest longer than any man I ever knew." Now, it was worse than ever.

"Is the Lord punishing me," Amos wondered. "Is that why little J.D. died?" He had doted so on that child. He still couldn't think of him without getting a lump in his throat. He worried about Cate. She was expecting again. She hadn't felt well ever since he left her alone to go to Laketown to meet Washakie and settle the Indian war. What if something happened to her or the baby she was carrying! He thought of Lois Moran occasionally, too, and wondered what their life might have been like if things hadn't happened the way they did. At that point, he was really feeling sorry for himself.

He tried to recall how he had felt before all these problems started. He remembered the wonderful feeling he had the day his father baptized him all those years ago. It was like Joseph said, clean and peaceful and new inside. Now, even the thought of praying was repugnant and he felt unworthy. "I don't think God would listen even if I did pray," he uttered half aloud. And so his thoughts went on and on and round and round. He determined to dismiss the whole thing from his mind. As long as he was working hard he could manage it, and he drove himself mercilessly as a result. But the minute he wasn't doing anything, the old merry-go-round started again. Even in the middle of the night he would wake up with a bad dream which always seemed to have something to do with Joseph's talk about repentance.

He purposely avoided his friend. It hurt to have the mirror flashed on himself the way he did it, especially when Amos had to admit it was the truth. But Joseph wasn't easily discouraged and seemed to make opportunities to see him. One day Joseph "just happened" to meet him. He was all excited.

"Father just got word that Brother Brigham and some other General Authorities are coming to Bear Lake in two weeks. My Mother is really tearing up the place getting ready for them. The visitors are all old men and it must be pretty hard on them to travel so far on bumpy roads. They must really care about us."

Mention of Brigham Young aroused Amos' resentment. *He* was to blame for getting him up here in this north pole country in the first place. He forgot all the help and kindnesses he'd done. "So what?" replied Amos.

"You can ride over to Paris on Toshats and be there for the meeting at 10 o'clock. I'll see that you get some dinner afterwards. There'll be loads of food and one more won't make any difference," urged Joseph.

"Well, I'll think about it and let you know," was his rather ungrateful reply. He was tempted more by the thought of a good meal than listening to some dry talk. He decided to go when Cate offered to do the chores that Sunday morning so he could get there on time. But he might have known. Joseph must have tipped Brigham off ahead of time. What did he talk about? Repentance! Bah!

The winters for several years in succession had been extremely hard; snow falling in November and staying on the ground until the following May. It was November again and cold weather already upon them. He'd never get over his resentment about the cold. He had decided the first time he came to Bear Lake he'd never live there if he could help it. Then came the call from President Young and here he was, in spite of his own wishes and good judgement and he didn't see any chance of getting out of it. He disliked farming. He did it because he had to survive and did it poorly as a result. He couldn't afford good tools or equipment so always had to make-do. He sold the best horses and cows he raised and got along with the scrubs. Many of the people he had to deal with were ignorant. He always said he'd rather deal with two villains than one fool. It had been the mistake of his life to move to Bear Lake. Nothing was right; everything was wrong.

Cate was expecting the first week in December. The weather would be even worse by then. He ought to know ahead of time so he could go for Sister Phelps, the midwife, but that was impossible. He was teased with the story about Alma Hayes of Georgetown who started out to get her one time but by the time they got back to his wife, the baby was nine months old! But people kept on having children just the same.

It was the 7th of December when Cate started having pains and told Amos he'd better go for Sister Phelps. He'd been up all night before taking care of the milk cow, Beauty, so the calf wouldn't freeze as soon as it was born. Acting, not exactly enthusiastically, he hitched up the mare to the cutter and started out, bundling up in his big sheepskin coat that Ed Austin had bought for him in St. Louis on one of his cattle dealing trips. He always wore a silk handkerchief tied over his head; a cap with ear flaps on it, and a pair of Cate's buckskin gloves to keep his hands from freezing. The wind was blowing hard as he left, and the clouds to the west looked threatening. It was five miles to Sister Phelps, so he'd better get going.

As usual, the old merry-go-round thoughts began, and the snow blew with the wind, cutting his face as he rode. This was worse than Pony Express. It was six o'clock when he left the cabin and already dark so he'd have to rely on the horse and his own sense of direction. He could make out Jed Merrill's fence, Jared Bullock's log cabin, and George Lindsay's, beyond. But after that he might as well have been blind. Time passed. The cold increased. Only a Bearlaker would understand what a December blizzard can do to sense of direction or visibility. He urged the mare on, hoping she knew more about where they were going then he did. He fumbled in his pocket to find his big watch with the hinged lid and tried to make out what time it was but he couldn't see even the hands. It didn't much matter since he had to admit he didn't know where he was. He was in a world of white, looking through smoke-covered glasses. There were at least eight hours of increasing darkness ahead and he knew Cate usually had a hard time with her babies. The mare stopped and whipping and yelling didn't get her started again. He finally made out the outline of a fence ahead and realized she couldn't go any farther. It seemed like he must have gone five miles already.

The baby just might be nine months old before he got back, if it got born at all, he thought in terror.

Maybe Joseph was right. Maybe he did need to repent! It was harder than ever for a stubborn man if he did it because he had to. But there was no other way he could go. It wasn't just *his* life he had to think of now, it was Cate's and the baby's. Bowing his head and closing his eyes, he began haltingly ... "Heavenly Father ... I need help. I don't deserve it, but it isn't for me I'm asking, but for Cate and the baby ... I'm sorry for what I've done that's wrong ... please forgive me."

It seemed to come easier after that and the words and thoughts tumbled out. "I went against the counsel of authority. I did a lot of things I knew were wrong when I was doing them. I lost my temper and abused Brother Snow. I haven't been as kind to Cate as I should have been. I quit praying. It all seemed so useless and hopeless. I nursed grudges. I haven't had anything to guide me for six years. It's all been dark and nothing seemed to really matter, anyhow. Things never turn out right, anymore. I try to put up a good front but it's no use. I'm more miserable than I've ever been before. This is hell!" Finally, he said, "If Thou wilt help me find the midwife and get back to Cate in time, I'll get Joseph to baptize me and I'll serve Thee all the rest of my life. In the name of Jesus Christ, Amen."

He climbed out of the cutter and waded in the snow over the horse's head. She was shivering, too. He turned her around and got back in. The mare started off slowly and he didn't try to guide her. The cold seeped through his sheepskin coat and up his back, numbing his brain. Time stopped, but the mare stumbled on. Then she whinnied. He pried his eyes open and caught a glimmer of light ahead ... or was it wishful thinking? Keeping his eyes focused on the spot again he sensed it could be a candle or lamp. A few minutes more and he was sure. The mare pricked up her ears and moved a little faster. He made out the outline of a cabin and a barn at the back. They'd make it now, but he still didn't know where he was.

Pounding on the door and calling out, "Is anybody home?" he heard footsteps. The door opened and Sister Phelps, holding a lamp overhead, peered into the darkness. "Come in, come in," she said, "Why, Brother Wright, is Cate in labor? "He nodded, and she went on; "I've been thinking about her all evening. Sit down and I'll make you a cup of tea," and she bustled around. "I'll be ready in a few minutes. My medicine case is right here."

As warmth slowly filtered into his bones, Amos asked himself, "How did the mare know where to go?" and suddenly he knew: the Lord had answered his prayer!

It was almost eleven o'clock. The wind had died down and Sister Phelps, all bundled up, climbed into the sleigh. She held a lantern to help see where they were going.

The mare knew now where she was headed, even without a lantern. It didn't take long to cover the miles this time and soon they were inside the cabin with the midwife taking over, confidently. Cate was cheered at seeing them. The pains had been bad ever since Mose left and it was now midnight. Sister Phelps got her to drink some herb tea she'd brought along. As Amos came in from stabling the horse he heard Cate's groans.

If he had done as Joseph wanted him to do, he'd have the priesthood again and could administer to her. Now all he could do was keep the fire roaring and wait and pray. At least he could do that again, and he did with all his heart and soul.

At ten minutes past one, the baby started to cry, and so did he. Sarah exclaimed, "Mose, it's a sweet little girl!" Cate's going to be all right now. You can go to bed and I'll see to everything." In the family Bible he later wrote: Adelaide, born December 8, 1867, 1:10 a.m.

Amos was a hundred and eighty degree man: an extremest. If things didn't work one way, he swung the needle all the way to the other side. If a little would do a little good, a lot would do a lot of good. He couldn't wait to see Joseph. All his friend had tried to tell him made sense now. It was like one of those trick pictures where you could see two different images, depending on what you were looking for.

The Lord had to let him get into such a tough spot he couldn't get out without help. And he found out he got what he asked for when he prayed with all his heart. He'd made a serious promise, though, that he'd work for the Lord the rest of his life to pay for saving not only his life but Cate's and baby Adelaide's. Well, he'd have to keep his word. The first thing would be to get Joseph to baptize him.

But it was winter, and a Bear Lake one at that. Unless they chopped a hole in the ice, there wasn't a place to do it and wouldn't be till spring. That's the way it had worked when he was eight years old and wanted to be baptized. He had to wait till June that time. He was afraid if he had to wait that long this time he might be out of the notion. He did talk it over the next time he saw Joseph. He was surprised how glad Joseph was. "You mean you really want to be baptized? And you want me to do it? Of course I will! But I never expected a stubborn son-of-a-gun like you to change your mind. I've been praying you'd finally decide it was right, but I didn't dream I'd have the chance to do it for you. When shall we do it?"

"The way I hate cold weather, I guess we'd better wait awhile. I got so cold the night I went after the midwife for Cate, the mere thought of cold water makes me shiver. But I do want it as soon as possible."

He decided not to say anything to Cate until he knew for sure when it would be. He didn't want to disappoint her and he still had his ups and downs about the whole thing. One day he knew it was what he wanted, and later he began to doubt again and wonder.

By the latter part of March, everything went wrong. He got a bad cold. A Danish neighbor came to collect a debt he said Amos owed him, which he had already paid. The children got on his nerves and he flew into a rage at something Cate said and stomped out of the house. The weather turned cold again after a few days of spring-like weather for a change.

Joseph rode out one day to see him and Amos told him he'd changed his mind. Joseph didn't argue but acted hurt and went back to town without staying to visit as he usually did. Mose felt miserable and Cate knew it, because he wouldn't talk to her and went into one of "his spells" as she called them.

Sunday afternoon, President Rich happened to be in Bennington for fast meeting. They didn't even have a branch at that time, but met in the homes of some of the members. He stopped when he saw Amos digging a ditch. Amos was embarrassed to be caught working on Sunday, but Brother Rich didn't seem to notice, and chatted about the weather and acted pleased to see him. Amos came over to the buggy as they visited, and later they both climbed on the rail fence and sat there talking. They got to talking about Indians and Brother Rich told him a lot of things he'd never known about the Book of Mormon and the prophecies about "the remnant of Jacob," who were the Indians. It was always a pleasure to talk to this great man and Amos felt especially honored to have him spend this time with him. Cate looked out of her little 'chinken" between two logs in the cabin and watched the two men. They sat there talking earnestly for over an hour. Finally, Brother Rich got back in his buggy and drove away.

Amos came in looking thoughtful. Cate waited for him to speak and finally he said something she couldn't believe. "Cate, I'm going to be baptized. Brother Rich said he'd tell Joseph to meet me in Paris next Thursday afternoon."

"Oh, Mose, I'm so glad!" was all she could say as the tears ran down her cheeks. "This is the happiest day of my life. I've waited and prayed so long. Thank God, Thank God!" That day was April 3, 1868.

Chapter Fourteen
A Decade of Doings

Things were looking up for Mose and Cate in more ways than one. Crops had been better the past year and the struggle for mere existence somehow seemed more encouraging. They had been married eight years, and were learning to understand each other better. Cate had always been undemonstrative. She didn't believe in "lalligagging" as she called it.

Then since his excommunication, there was always an area she sensed was "off limits" to her, and thus she didn't really know what Amos was thinking and feeling. She had prayed constantly that he would come back to the Church, but after six years she began to wonder if he ever would. And then when he did, their love and understanding for each other deepened perceptibly. There was a freedom of expression again between them which they hadn't known since their early marriage. They suddenly discovered they were "on the same team" and that things went better when they pulled together.

As for Amos, his commitment to serve the Lord made under threat of death to him and his loved ones, never left his consciousness, and directed his path as unerringly as a compass points north. And like all things he did and thought, halfway wasn't enough. There would come a time when Cate, as well as others, thought he was too dedicated to what he considered to be right.

Six years in Bear Lake Valley had made some changes for the better in day to day living. They now had a log house as good as most and better than some. Being among the first arrivals in Bennington they could choose a homesite without restrictions. After careful consideration they had picked a place near two springs, an upper and a lower one. The land lay level and gently sloped toward Bear River a mile to the West and extended eastward to the foothills. Old Baldy towered above, providing something for the Wrights and their children to look up to.

Amos wisely filed on the waters of Home Canyon. Land without water was like a man without a woman: pretty dry and unproductive.

They probably didn't fully appreciate the Homestead Act which made them a present of a quarter section of land just by filing on it, fencing it and plowing a few furrows around the edge. In addition to the homesite land, Amos also filed on a farm in Maple Canyon, about three miles northeast, nestled in a cove and protected from frosts. He and Cate still dreamed of having "cattle on a thousand hills."

David Lindsay and his wife came to Bennington the same time as Amos and Cate. The two couples liked each other. The Lindsays were about the same age as Cate and Amos but they didn't have any children. The four agreed to build a one-room cabin and live together for awhile. David was a good hunter, trapper and fisherman and Sister Lindsay was hungry for babies of her own, so adopted Silas and Winnie right away, thus giving Cate more free time which she made good use of. Amos had his hands full fencing, plowing and planting and if there was any time left over he went with David to trap.

Cate's practice at homemaking in Brigham City came in handy. A one-room cabin was a big step up from a dugout and with the things she brought with her from Brigham City it soon became a home instead of a house. Clothing was next to food in importance. Amos bought a couple of ewe lambs and from then on Cate clipped, washed, carded, spun the wool and knit stockings, mittens and caps for her family. She was a good seamstress, too, but she wasn't satisfied with making just socks and shirts, she created beautiful laces and quilted patchwork quilts from bits and pieces.

Beauty, the cow, and a flock of chickens became a source of income for thrifty Cate. The family benefited of course, but Sister Wright's yellow butter brought top price either in cash or barter, and she knew how to baby her hens into laying more eggs than any other woman in the valley. In this way Cate supplied the family with bacon and sometimes ham, sugar, salt, rice, beans, yards of calico, outing flannel and other materials.

She traded eggs, flour and butter for buckskin with the Indians. During long winter evenings she made mens' gloves, trimming the gauntlets with fringe. When spring came she had a nice box of gloves all ready to trade or sell to travelers as they followed the Oregon Trail. People were delighted to find they could buy such fine articles and were willing to pay a good price for them. One time Cate got a box of cube sugar and a couple yards of ribbon on a trade. Next Christmas, the little ones were surprised and delighted to find squares of "sugar candy" in their stockings, and the little girls were thrilled to have a bow of ribbon for their hair.

She was known widely for her beautiful quilting, and it was something to be proud of if young girls could learn to make buttonholes like Sister Catherine Wright.

Ira Nebeker's daughter described a typical Bear Lake home:

Family life was wholesome and pleasant in spite of the hardships because it was a religious adventure. Those first families developed the virtues of thrift, work, cooperation, integrity and neighborliness. The same hands that made candles to light the darkness of the first cabins, and taught their children to hang their clothing on the wooden pegs, later on provided rag carpets, clean coal oil lamps, an occasional shelf and after-sundown-curtains. There was always the woodbox by the stove so deep that one stood on his head when getting the last stick out. And a shelf at the back which held a pair of dull scissors, a shoe rag, a pair of forceps to pull teeth with, and a can of coarse salt. There was the bench for the wash basin, water bucket and dipper conveniently near, and the roller towel on the door. How those pioneer women must have blessed the man who invented nails, and the stove with a reservoir and fine salt. Whoever thought up the straw bed tick could be blessed, too. It smelled good when the straw was fresh at thrashing time, and smelled good if you reached in and stirred the straw. On Saturday, the day the lamp chimneys had to be washed, the house had to be swept with a broom that kicked up dust all over the place and it was then dusted with a rag. (Claire Nebeker Hulme, daughter of Ira Nebeker)

Five years of experience in pioneering was behind them and they'd survived the weather, Indians, and their own inadequacies. Amos would always resent the cold weather, love the Indians and downgrade his own potential. He loved to read and Cate often prodded him to put his book away so the work would get done faster. He would have made a better professor or judge than a farmer.

One time he was reading the *Deseret Weekly* and Cate saw him toss it on the table in disgust. "They must think people are fools to believe such a story!" he said.

"What story?" she asked.

"Why it says right here that there is a little box that can be hung on the wall of a house and that a wire can be stretched from it to another box in the next house, and that neighbors can talk to each other through these little boxes; just speak in an ordinary voice and be heard; or even in the next town! I've never heard of such a crazy thing!" But the idea fascinated him, nevertheless.

Brigham Young was anxious for the welfare of the Bear Lake settlers. Sensing the need of more families to strengthen the Saints already there, he issued a call in 1869 and again a year later for this purpose. A number came, and some new people moved into Bennington.

After the abandonment of the missionary settlement at Ft. Lemhi in 1858, President Young determined this would not happen again if he could help it. He came in June of 1869, traveling under discomfort and hardship. He called on the Saints to extend the road in Logan Canyon through to Bear Lake to improve communications and make it easier to haul logs for lumber as well as to bring hay and other supplies from Bear Lake.

He also suggested they put up a telegraph line.

So an expedition was formed to blaze the road through in the latter part of October that year and "missionary work" was done on the canyon roads every year from that time on. Arrangements had been made to put a ferry boat on Bear River for convenience of travel and communication between settlements in 1867.

He returned the following June, assessing present needs and giving counsel and advice. David R. Kimball was made stake president at that time and Wm. Budge acted as presiding bishop of the valley.

Conference was held every three months in Paris, a meeting Amos never missed. Seeing and hearing a General Authority from Salt Lake was a cherished occasion. He had a good laugh over J. Golden Kimball's remark that "any man who would live in Bear Lake for fifteen years would, without question, go to the Celestial Kingdom."

It was a chance, too, to see friends and exchange news and discuss crops and farming. Ed Austin lived at Liberty and Ira Nebeker was still at Laketown. The Three Musketeers always got together for at least a short visit and a few laughs. Ira and Ed were both overjoyed when they heard Amos had been baptized and their friendship was cemented even more firmly.

Austin's report as presiding elder was included in the minutes of the district April 2, 1868 as follows:

> The health of the people in the Valley is good and plowing will commence in a few days. Our stock has done well this winter. A good bridge is erected over Bear River west of Montpelier and Ovid. Breadstuff is scarce, and the people will have harder times in this respect than any season heretofore. The Indians are already returning from their buffalo expedition but as usual they are perfectly friendly.

Crops in the valley continued uncertain from year to year. Ground squirrels, grasshoppers and frost continued to be the farmer's worst enemies. The year 1866 had been a good one, but '67 was disastrous. Good crops didn't really come till 1874 and even the 1877 one was mediocre. It was no wonder people got discouraged. Quite a few families complained to President Rich, saying they wanted to leave. The winters were just too long and things weren't getting any better. They were sick of "nine months winter and three months summer" and southern Arizona with "nine months summer and three months suffocation" couldn't be as bad. President Rich always told them the decision was up to them, but as for him and his families, he intended to stay. A few went. Some came back later. But Brother Rich's attitude was a stabilizer for most of the pioneers, including the Wrights.

Cate often wished they'd go back to Brigham City now that Mose was a member of the Church again. But she knew that was wishful thinking as long as President Rich stayed in Bear Lake. So she kept all these things in her heart and made the best of whatever happened. The family was growing in number and in years. Silas was six and old enough to begin helping. Winnie, at three, was already showing her precocity and was considered by her parents to be the smartest little girl ever born. She *was* the first white child born in Bennington, and the second born in the valley. Addie, twelve months old, was frail and needed lots of care. But already she gave promise of beauty with her dark curly hair and brown eyes. Cate was "expecting" again in January and hoped it would be a boy. When the baby was born January 10, 1870 it was a boy, so one wish at least came true.

But Bear Lake was still isolated. Mail service between there and Cache Valley was irregular and by snowshoes in winter. But November 6, 1871 was a day long remembered. The wires of the Deseret Telegraph Company reached Paris at 4 p.m. bringing the people of the valley into constant communication with the world outside.

Charles C. Rich sent the first telegram to Salt Lake City saying:

"In view of our isolated situation, no people in the mountains can better appreciate telegraphic communication. We heartily congratulate you on the extension of the line and thank you for your labors in our behalf." (Ezra J. Poulsen, *Versatile Pioneer*, p. 274.)

Despite a bridge across Bear River near Montpelier, the river was a barrier for folks around Bennington and Georgetown. It was a treacherous stream especially in the spring, and the only way to cross was by fording either at Dingle or Pole Ford near the Buehler farm.

In those places, Texas longhorns were forced to sink or swim across. Men and Indians would get on the backs of the strong cattle and with sharp probes hustle them to the other side. Some drowned. In the spring, the river formed almost a lake from Bennington to Paris, including swamps and bogs.

Addie long remembered, whenever Brother Lindsay started on another trapping expedition across the river, he would say, "If

I can just make it across the main stream I'll be all right." She and Silas and Winnie would climb onto the shed roof so they could watch to see if he made it across.

One day during the winter, Brother and Sister Oakey started to drive their team and wagon over the ice. It broke and Brother Oakey climbed out of the wagon and tried to save the team by holding their heads out of the water. Sister Oakey ran screaming for help. Some of the men got there in time to save one horse. It was a cold day as usual and everybody stumbled afterward into Cate's house in wet clothes and icy shoes. She bustled around and found dry clothes for everybody; warmed them up with quantities of Brigham tea, baked a big pan of biscuits and made potato soup. By that time they could laugh about getting dunked in Bear River in February.

Schools were a problem, too. By the time Silas was old enough to go, the snow was so deep he couldn't make it to Ed Merrill's who was the schoolteacher that winter. So Cate turned teacher and piloted Silas and Phileman Lindsay through the alphabet and multiplication tables, and in a few weeks they were reading short words and sentences. Later, when the snow crusted, the boys joined the other children at Brother Merrill's.

"School" was held only a couple of months a year at first. Supplies were a spelling book, a slate and one or two reading books. Anyone who could master the fifth reader was considered educated. Penmanship and spelling were important and a good brand of writing was common. Later, when stake and wards were organized, each ward was to see that its people had a school. This was the responsibility of the bishopric under the direction of the stake officers. Bennington became School District N11. Two mills on the dollar were levied as a school tax, the minimum allowed by law. School was held in the meetinghouse, but the pupils paid so much per month tuition and the county paid a small amount to help out. At first, this was very small." ("History of Settlement of Bear Lake Valley," Russell Rich thesis (film).

Wm. Budge, the stake president, deplored hiring gentile teachers. At that time there were two non-Mormon teachers employed in the valley. He recommended that young men from Bear Lake be sent to the university to prepare for teaching. Some tension developed as to whether schools be Church controlled or not. Some communities included a few non-LDS families.

Thinking about this, Amos wished he could go to school. He felt increasingly hampered for lack of education. Taking stock of the books he owned, he found only the four Standard Works, and a rather large Webster's dictionary, which had belonged to his father. He subscribed to the *Deseret Weekly News* from Salt Lake and later to *The Improvement Era*. He determined to begin a self-improvement program.

Whenever he came upon a word, the meaning of which he didn't understand, he opened Webster and found out. He read and studied each of the four volumes of sacred scripture, making careful note of difficult words as well as learning more clearly Church doctrine. This had to be snatched at odd minutes during the day, or at night by candle or lamplight when it would have been easier to go to bed. At the end of a year, he recognized the effort was paying off and felt encouraged to continue. In this way he became somewhat of a scriptorian and never lacked for well-chosen words to express his thoughts. He was often asked to speak at Fourth of July celebrations and other special occasions, and was a favorite speaker at funerals.

One time he spoke before a congregation where some non-Mormons were present. When he started he said, "I cannot speak at length today. I've been sick and really shouldn't try to address you, but I will express a few thoughts." As he warmed to his subject he often emphasized his remarks with a loud shout or by striking the pulpit with his fist. He spoke for nearly an hour. The strangers were heard to say afterward, "If that's the way a sick Mormon talks, I'd like to hear a well one!" (Gwen Andersen, "My Grandfather Said.")

One day Winnie told a group of her friends that they could ask her what any word meant and she could tell them, and if she couldn't tell them right off, she would look it up in a book her father had at home. The children couldn't believe such a tall tale. No book could have *all* the words. So Winnie took them home and proudly showed them the first dictionary they had ever seen.

Amos later became the village schoolteacher. Many mornings little Winnie rode to school on her father's back as he waded through the waist-deep snow, with Silas tagging along trying already to follow in his father's footsteps. This was high adventure for the children. But they were afraid of "the teacher" because he seemed to expect them to set an example and demanded more of them than he did of the others.

A few years later there were enough pupils to warrant building a schoolhouse down next to Bennington hill. Amos continued as teacher and to carry the youngest one back and forth each day. But at first the children sat on a slab bench and held their slate on their lap when they tried to write. Amos, the teacher, sat in front of them, always with a book in his hand.

If the boys and girls got restless, he reached out and put his hand on their heads and straightened them out for a few minutes, meanwhile not taking his eyes off his book. They ducked behind each other, but he felt around till he found the noisy one. At other times he would put one foot up on a chair and stand there in deep thought, running his fingers through his beard and putting the ends in his mouth. This was a signal to the kids for "time out." They knew as long as he remained in this position, he was insensible to anything they were doing. But as soon as he put his foot down on the floor and stood up, they scurried back to the bench in nothing flat. He made up for lost time though and the children learned the three R's and obedience.

One day Silas found a patch of wild strawberries and began picking and eating them. When he had all he could hold, he took off his cap and picked till it was running over. Proudly he carried them home to Cate. She had just heard that the Brethren were coming for dinner next day and hadn't known what to feed them for dessert. Quickly she cleaned the berries and sent Silas back for more. She said it was an answer to prayer. Next day she served the usual fried fish, hot biscuits with plenty of her good butter, and skimmed a pan of milk for them to drink with thick cream to pour over wild strawberries, the meal was fit for kings.

Cate was a good manager and along with the other pioneer women, learned how to make do in many ways. Soap was made from scraps of fat and wood ashes. She made starch from potatoes. Candles were made from any fat they could find. Some families burned bear grease in a pan using a rag placed in it as a wick. They ate home-ground wheat mush, potatoes, fish, wild meat, cured pork and chipped beef and Mormon gravy made from grease, flour, milk and a vegetable tossed in if there was one. Lumpy-Dick was a pudding made with flour stirred into scalded milk, with a little sugar to sweeten if there was any. Fancy food was scarce but there were plenty of pigweed greens, thistles and sego bulbs. Clabbered milk was a favorite dish. With a little sugar or honey sprinkled over it they thought it tasted delicious!

It was always nip and tuck to make a dollar. Amos turned to freighting off and on, especially in the winter and sometimes was gone for weeks at a time. Cate hated this but made the best of what had to be.

It was late in the fall one year. The chores were done for the night and the tallow candle was lighted. Cate was singing "O, Willie Is It You Dear" to settle the children for the night.

All of a sudden they heard a shrill cry or howl. Silas rushed to open the door, but Cate was on her feet in an instant saying, "Don't open that door!" Pushing a large trunk against it and blowing out the candle, she whispered, "That was a bobcat … keep right still." The children undressed by the chimney light and got into their buffalo covers, but not before their mother gathered them around her and asked God to protect them.

Next morning they could see the tracks plainly in the snow. The bobcat had crawled onto the dirt roof of the chicken coop, scratched through the snow and dirt in one place, but the chickens were safe and Cate laughed in relief. Her chickens were part of their survival insurance.

"Father was away for a long time it seemed," recalled Addie. "Our provisions were about gone, including flour. We watched every day but Father didn't come. Mother told me I'd have to go to Sister Oakey's and borrow a pan of flour for supper. That seemed a long way and contrary like I was, I went to the flour bin and taking a big goose wing, began scraping flour out of the corners of the bin when it looked like there wasn't any. Believe it or not, we had flour for a week out of that "empty" bin. Then, oh, how happy we were to see Father with a big load of supplies … sugar, syrup, beans, and plenty of flour."

Hay was cut with a scythe and stacked in the shed. Blacky, the cow, furnished the milk, cream and butter, and Amos had a pair of oxen to do the heavy hauling. The family picked serviceberries and chokecherries every summer and dried them in the sun. People craved sweets and fruit and they were a treat when put in a pudding in the winter. Aside from gooseberries and rhubarb which made delicious pies but took too much sugar, that was all the fruit available until fruit trees began to bear in Utah.

Finally, there were plenty of apples growing in Cache Valley. They were dried and put in hundred-pound burlap sacks and hauled and sold to hungry Bear Lakers, and were they good! The first apple tree shoots were carried in on the back of a man wearing snowshoes in the winter and spring of 1865. These didn't grow. But by 1872, William Budge had fruit trees growing.

Ezra Phelps was the boy who ran from neighbor to neighbor with a greased rag dipped in mutton tallow to grease the dripping pans for bread baking. Then it was fish for every meal, as the children remembered, "but if you were hungry enough you ate it without complaining."

It was about twelve miles from Bennington to Paris, a trip that was usually planned ahead of time. But even with planning, things didn't always turn out as expected.

Amos often spoke of such a time:

"I was detained in Paris much against my will all one afternoon. I heard that Brother Rich was very sick and I went to see him and found him entirely alone. He asked me if I would be kind enough to administer to him. I told him I had had absolutely no experience. I didn't know what to do or what to say and I thought that was the greatest task I had ever been called upon to perform in my life. The idea of one so poorly informed and inexperienced to administer to an Apostle was more than I could imagine. But he said, 'no matter, I will tell you what to do and what to say.' I told him if he would do that, it would be easier.

"He said, 'Well here is some consecrated oil. You hold the priesthood, and in that authority anoint my head and afterward confirm it and say whatever the Spirit of God tells you to say, and if you do that it will be all right.' I followed his instructions and after I concluded, he told me that not very long before, some of the apostles had visited him and Joseph F. Smith was among the number, and 'you have repeated word for word what he said in his administration.' Then he commenced to enlarge upon the principles of the Gospel and he told me things I had never heard of in all my life. I knew him to be so truthful in everything else that I could not doubt him. And then he predicted certain things upon my head and they have came to pass and I have been blessed because of the circumstances which he said would occur to me and I asked him how I could learn these principles ... how I could know of these things for myself and he said, 'You will know it as I have known it and when it comes to you, no man can deprive you of it.'" (Gwen Andersen, "My Grandfather Said.")

This experience increased Amos' devotion to Charles C. Rich, and his testimony of the truthfulness of the Gospel of Jesus Christ. People often heard him say, "If any member of Brother Rich's family should do me an injury, I could forgive him in partial payment of the great debt I owe their father. Words cannot express my appreciation for his kindness to me, but I can testify that he influenced me at the turning point in my life. Therefore, I ask God to bless his descendants that they may have the same noble characteristics as Charles C. Rich had in such a large degree."

With the coming of warm weather Cate had a nagging homesickness. She needed her mother more than ever it seemed, but there was little hope of that. It was like wishing for the moon.

Amos must have sensed her feeling. He had to go to Logan, so asked if she'd like to go with him. Maybe her mother could come from Brigham and they could be together for a few days. The little spring wagon was greased and swept out, packed with food and bedding and the children bundled in a buffalo robe. It would be a long journey, but Cate wasn't worried as long as she was with Mose.

He seemed cheerful for a change and whistled as the horses trotted along the road. Sitting at his side, she was aware of his manly strength. She had seen him stand astride a two-hundred-pound sack of wheat or oats and hoist it onto a wagon in one swinging motion.

She loved his trim, muscled body and bulging biceps. He always insisted that she sleep with her head on his big thick upper arm, and it took a long time before she could get used to it without getting a crick in her neck. But it was worth it! The skin on his body where it was unexposed, was smooth and very white with little or no hair. She called him "Chief White Skin." His neck took a 17-inch collar. He stood five-feet eight-inches high and was well-proportioned, carrying himself with self-assurance; and he sat a horse better than any man she knew. His dark brown hair was wavy with reddish-gold tints which carried over in his soft, full beard. His eyes crinkled at the corners when he laughed. He was, indeed, a man.

The trip did them both good. They needed a change. Amos got his business taken care of and a few days with her mother gave Cate the lift she needed. They were both glad to head for Bear Lake and home again. She was full of news about her mother and Uncle David Evans who was getting rich raising cattle.

Cate tried to amuse the children by calling their attention to the Johnny jump-ups, sego lilies and Indian paintbrushes. All at once she spied a little calf lying under a sagebrush. "Oh look, Mose, it's a fine bally-face! Stop and let's load it in the back of the wagon. It's lost and will only die, anyhow. We'll take good care of it and we can soon have a whole herd of cattle and get rich like Uncle David."

Mose clucked to the horses and touched them with the buggy whip. "No, Cate. It doesn't belong to us. It would be stealing to take it. I'll have no part in such a thing." And Cate's sudden dream of cattle herds and wealth was squelched without further argument.

Cate was increasingly immersed in taking care of the children. Her health was usually good so a pregnancy didn't slow her down much. It was a good thing, too, because almost like clockwork, every two years she had another baby. John Wheeler was number six and was named in memory of Mose's mother, Rebecca Wheeler.

Brigham Young came to Bear Lake again in 1873. In the conference at Paris with Charles C. Rich at his side, he made a speech which had a lasting effect on the Saints in Bear Lake Valley, including Amos R. Wright.

> Brethren, if you will start here and operate together in farming, in making cheese, in herding sheep and cattle and every other kind of work, and get a factory here and a cooperative store, and operate together in sheep raising, store keeping, manufacturing and everything else, no matter what it is; when we can plant ourselves upon a foundation that cannot be broken up, we shall then proceed to arrange a family organization for which we are not yet quite prepared. You now, right here in this place, commence to carry on your business in a cooperative capacity. In every instance I could show every one of you what a great advantage would be gained in working together; I could reason it out here just how much advantage there is in cooperation in your lumbering and in your herding.
>
> We will make our own clothing, we will make our own fashions, we will do our own work. I can take fifty men who have not a cent, and if they will do as I would wish them to do, they would soon be worth their thousands, every one of them. We desire to go into this order. In it we would not lack means, we would always have something to sell, but seldom need to buy.
>
> Another thing I want to observe in all these settlements, and it is one of the simplest things in nature. I want you to be *united*. If we should build up and organize a community, we would have to do it on the principle of oneness, and it is one of the simplest things I know of. A city of 100,000 or a million people could be united into a perfect family, and they would work as beautifully together as the different parts of a carding machine work together. Why, we could organize millions into a family under the Order of Enoch." (Leonard Arrington, *Charles C. Rich*, p. 278.) (Preston Nibley, *Brigham Young the Man and His Work*, p. 282.)

Amos, listening to these words, recalled hearing about the United Order from his father, Jonathan. A revelation was given as a commandment from the Lord through the Prophet Joseph

Smith when the Saints were living in Kirtland, Ohio. He said the people tried then to make it work, but they were too selfish and had too much human weakness, so the Lord substituted an easier law called tithing.

Were Bear Lakers any better than those earlier Saints? Would they try it again? Amos looked around him at the bronzed faces of men and women listening intently to their leader, Brigham Young, with Charles C. Rich sitting on the stand behind him. They had all been through some hard times and tests already. They'd obeyed his call to come to this polar bear country; had stayed for almost a decade and proved it could be done. It hadn't been easy. It wasn't what they would have chosen. But most of them stayed. Why? Amos asked himself this hard question. He decided it all boiled down to *faith*. That was it! Like Paul said, "the substance of things hoped for, the evidence of things not seen." They trusted these leaders there before them. The people knew *they* wouldn't ask anything that they wouldn't do themselves or that couldn't be done. The Saints believed it was right because it was what the Lord wanted done. They were His servants. Brother Rich's integrity had been proven many times already.

Wisely, Brother Young merely planted a seed that day. He gave the people time to think and talk about it. It was the topic of conversation all over the valley from then on. "It won't work!" said the few weak and negative souls. "It *will* work, if we do our part!" said men like Ed Austin, Gib Weaver and Amos Wright. "Let's give it a try," was the concensus after months of pros and cons.

Early in 1873 Brother Bingham moved away from Bennington. Joseph W. Moore had come shortly before that from Fish Haven. Cate thought it wasn't just by chance that he came when he did. Anyhow, he was appointed to take charge of the Bennington Branch. He found a vacant house for the members to hold meetings in until a meetinghouse could be built. They took up donations and the men went to work and by fall, a small building with shingle roof and a pine lumber floor was finished which seemed mighty nice to everybody. The first Christmas program was held there on the 24th of December and each of the kids got a sack of horehound candy after squirming through a program of singing and recitations.

Mose was sustained as a ward teacher. This was the first time they'd had such a thing and the members loved it when a knock came on the door and he and Brother Lindsay stood there shaking the snow off their hats. They'd be invited in and the family would have a molasses candy pull. There would always be lots to talk about and the little ones had a chance to say a verse for the big folks. Then everybody would join in singing "Come All Ye Sons of God Who Have Received the Priesthood," and a prayer would be said. The time would go fast and everybody would enjoy this monthly visit.

And that wasn't all. A YMMIA ... Young Men's Mutual Improvement Association was organized, and Amos R. Wright was president. He put on some plays during the winter months and the young people loved it. At first they did some short skits made up by one of the Rich boys in Paris. But then they went on to big things like "As You Like It" and "Hamlet." Kids went around learning their parts out loud. "The quality of mercy is not strained," and "To be or not to be, that is the question!" They loved their president, too.

Then in the spring of 1874, Brigham Young, that doughty old man, just three years before he died, came back over the same bumpy roads and long hours of travel, to prove what caliber of men and women lived in the Bear Lake valley.

Most of the people came to stake conference in Paris that time, out of curiosity; and they weren't disappointed. President Young stood behind the pulpit and announced that the new emphasis of the Church was to be "The United Order." It was his goal to organize all communities along the lines he had described to them the year before. Then Brother Rich spoke and endorsed the idea, so the people voted for it unanimously.

Brother Young wisely allowed much leeway in the methods used. Rich, and Lorenzo Snow in Brigham City, chose the most conservative form based on cooperatives, which proved to be the most successful and lasted longer than the more communalistic ones at Orderville, Utah, and Sunset, Arizona.

As soon as Conference was over, Wilford Woodruff of the Council of the Twelve, and President Rich traveled around the valley, explaining and discussing United Order concepts. A branch was organized in each town with a president, vice-president, secretary and directors, whose collective duty was to see that the plan worked. They got to Bennington May 19th, 1874. Brother Moore was sustained as president, Dudley Merrill, vice president, and Amos R. Wright, secretary. Every man continued to own his own home, his land, and the tools of production, but the people's industry interests were pooled.

The United Order in whatever form, was serious business. In August 1875 a delegation of Church leaders from Salt Lake City came to Bear Lake to check on the progress of the new institution. John Taylor, Wilford Woodruff, George Q. Cannon and Charles Rich represented the Quorum of the Twelve. A large conference was held on Sunday, August 15th, and the Apostles spoke to the Saints regarding the United Order. After the rules were sustained by the members, the assembly adjourned to a stream, where George Q. Cannon rebaptized the local leaders including Rich and Budge, for a renewal of their covenants. This was a common practice while creating divisions of the United Order.

A co-op store in St. Charles netted its shareholders a good profit on their investment. A dairy co-op was started in Nounan with at times more than a thousand milk cows, which produced butter and cheese. Then a tannery was built and operated. Shoes and boots were later manufactured. A harness factory followed. A meat market next, then a shingle and planing mill. These were successful and the general community was benefited. This cooperative movement proved that large capital assets were not needed. A tin shop and a tailor shop also worked. A very successful co-op store in Paris was credited to the management of Wm. Budge and a man named Price. These enterprises supplied most of the immediate needs of the settlers, with a considerable number participating. With all this, there was no money in circulation. The co-ops issued scrip of various denominations. There was sawmill scrip and tannery scrip, and a considerable amount of bartering took place before an individual had the right kind of scrip to make an exchange.

There was a general clearing house for this money and when a person had sawmill scrip and wanted to buy a pair of boots, he would exchange his scrip for shoe department scrip with some person who needed lumber. A book published in 1884 on this subject said probably nowhere in the civilized world is cooperation carried on so successfully as it is among this "peculiar people." This institution has demonstrated that by judicious management, cooperative institutions can increase the wealth of a people. The citizens of moderate means and even the poor people can buy, sell and manufacture their own needs and share the profits among themselves. Monopolies do not become the tyrants of their customers. In 1878 the town of Paris reported the co-op had transacted the equivalent of $55,000 worth of business. The retail store, the dairy and the shoe shop carried the weight for the institution.

But all this Brother Rich considered as merely a step leading to a higher order of complete and harmonious unity. In his words, "the purpose of the co-ops was to establish confidence in each other that cannot be shaken." He believed the proper working of the cooperatives would lead to the abolition of poverty. "It is the purpose of the Lord to build up the poor."

"Whatever went on in Bear Lake during those years, Charles Rich was the man to whom the people turned for guidance. He was never a dogmatic theologian, but his handling of religious matters was done by kindness instead of harsh treatment. His aim was always to maintain peace as well as to help the people financially." (Leonard Arrington, *Charles C. Rich*, pp. 220-281.)

Sometimes things didn't work out peacefully, however. Amos had filed on a piece of land. The rule was that the land was to be fenced and that there must be at least six furrows plowed around the acreage filed on in order to receive legal title thereto. Cate had urged Mose to get the plowing done. They'd heard of claim jumpers even in the valley. He promised to do it as soon as the wheat was cut.

One morning she got up early to start the fire in the kitchen stove. Mose had gone to a meeting over at Liberty and she supposed he stayed with Ed Austin since he hadn't come home. She looked out the window and saw a team of horses hitched to a plow just pulling out of the field they'd filed on. There was a dark strip all the way around the edge, six furrows wide. She knew in a flash what had happened. Somebody had worked all night plowing the required strip and now would be able to get title to the land.

Grabbing Mose's overcoat, Cate put it on over her nightgown and ran out the door and across the field shouting, "Stop, stop!" The man driving the horses heard her and whipped the team to a trot, dragging the plow behind. She could see she'd never catch him. Breathless and exhausted she sank to the ground and sobbed out her frustration and anger. "That devil, I'd like to kill him and I will when I find out who he is!"

When Mose got home she took it out on him for not being there and for not getting the plowing done sooner. Now they'd lost their chance for more free land and her Welsh thrift was violated. She was pregnant again and that didn't help. It seemed she would never get rid of the hatred she had for that claim jumper. Why did she have to worry about such things anyway? Mose didn't seem to care about getting ahead. Since he was baptized, all he thought about was going to meetings and reading scriptures. And now she was going to have another baby. Six was more than she could look after alone. It didn't seem fair! Men got off a lot easier, anyhow. These and other rebellious thoughts made her days and nights miserable for her and the children and Mose stayed away as much as possible to avoid trouble.

When Bear Lake Valley was first settled, it was assumed to be in Utah. President Rich was a representative to the Utah Territorial Legislature for many years. Then a survey was made and it turned out that only the southern part of the valley was in Utah. Rich county was then set up. The northern end was in Idaho. So an act creating Bear Lake County passed the Idaho Legislature and was approved by the governor on January 5, 1875. Paris was made the county seat and three county commissioners were appointed. This would affect Amos in more ways than one as time went on.

Naturally his mind was much engrossed with such matters. He felt pleased to be named secretary of the United Order in Bennington, and was anxious to prove to President Rich that he was one hundred percent behind the authorities in this new project. The development about the Idaho legislature had possibilities also. Maybe he could represent the people one of these days. But he hurriedly put the thought out of his mind as seeming egotistical.

Cate felt neglected when he was gone so much and she had to do chores or see that Silas and Winnie did them. She was awkward and slow in her eighth month of pregnancy, couldn't find a comfortable position at night and so didn't get much sleep. June came and Amos had to go for Sister Phelps again. It was good weather at least and he made the trip without incident. It was another boy born the fourth of the month, and their seventh child, whose birthday was two years later to the day from John Wheeler's. They named him Frank Marion.

April Conference in Salt Lake was always an important occasion for all the Saints wherever they lived, Bear Lakers included. Though few of them went themselves, they depended on being represented by their Charles C. Rich. As a member of the Council of the Twelve, he would be there, they knew, even if he had to get there on showshoes and by hitchhiking of a kind. He made thirteen trips that way before the railroad changed everything. They knew, too, he would bring back important messages to the fifteen settlements in the valley. April 1875 was no exception. The United Order was still the most talked about and sometimes most controversial item of Church business considered, and Brother Rich returned with new ideas for further development.

Missionary calls were always announced over the pulpit in the tabernacle and relayed to those concerned through their local leaders or by the Deseret News Conference Report. Whichever way it came, Amos soon found out he was called, and *The Deseret News* of April 9, 1875 confirmed it:

"Elder George Q. Cannon read the names of the following persons to go on missions to the several countries named:... (A long list followed, but the only name he was interested in was)... AMOS WRIGHT, BEAR LAKE VALLEY ... TO THE LAMANITES."

He read it with mixed emotions. At least he wouldn't have to leave home. He would be working with people in spite of the traditions of their fathers. Those in authority were evidently aware of his capabilities and thought he could do some good. Did it follow, he wondered, that perhaps the Lord wanted him, too? The words of the blessing he received eighteen years before, echoed in his ears. Lorenzo Snow and Orson Hyde and Brother Richards had laid their hands on his head and told him, "Thy heart shall yearn for the salvation and redemption of the sons of the forest, and the Lamanites that behold in thee truth and light shall apply unto thee for instruction."

He had talked personally the year before with Elder Wilford Woodruff when he and President Rich had organized the United Order in Bennington. Brother Woodruff had seemed impressed when Rich recounted in his presence the part Amos had played in the Laketown Indian uprising years before. Maybe it wasn't just happenstance that he had been selected to do this job. President Rich set him apart for his new calling, and after that it was up to him.

From then on, the fields adjoining Amos' home in Bennington became a campground for a few weeks each summer when the Shoshones and Bannocks made their annual visit. They pitched their tepees and while their horses grazed on the lush meadow grass, the Indians sat around the campfire in the evenings and listened to their white brother tell them of things which stirred their hearts ... things which to some of them sounded strangely familiar, and which merged with stories their medicine men talked about.

Of course, they usually had a barbecue before they left, with meat furnished by Amos R. Wright, which might have had some influence on their coming and listening. They called him "Peah Tibo" which meant Big White Man, the same name they had given to his father, Jonathan, years before.

Relatives in Brigham City often asked Amos why in the world he stayed over in that Godforsaken part of the country. "Why don't you move back to civilization?" His thoughtful reply was always, "Well, first of all I was called to settle here. As long as Charles C. Rich can stand it, I can. This is good cattle country even if we have to feed three to six months of the year. We raise beautiful hay crops, and grass is always plentiful in the summertime. I can sell fat steers at a good price in the mines in Montana. I get cash for them so I can buy flour in Cache Valley if our wheat gets frozen. The soil is productive. We can raise good gardens even in the short growing season. Potatoes and carrots and cabbage are good winter vegetables and keep well when we store them in cellars. And since the United Order has been working so well, we have the necessities of life even without money and that way people don't worship it instead of God. What more can I ask? We live unitedly and peacefully together and our children aren't exposed to so many of the worldly influences. I still hate the cold winters, but one can't have everything!"

Ed Austin summed it up in one sentence: "We left the gold for the Gospel, and we've had no regrets, for it is worth more than all the gold of the Indies."

Chapter Fifteen
The Missionary

The Indians continued to come to Bennington every summer. They knew they were welcome to turn their horses into Peah Tibo's pasture. The squaws put up their tepees, stayed for a few days or a week, trading and bargaining for whatever they could get from the Saints nearby, then moved on and another band came. Many Shoshones and Bannocks knew Amos. If they hadn't met him, they had heard about him as the white man who talked straight. They knew, too, he was a "soft touch", but they said his squaw was sometimes harder to deal with. She thought these "children" were a nuisance with their constant begging, and stealing, too, if they had a chance.

One summer, an old woman named Susie got too sick to travel any further so she was left behind in a wigwam to die. Cate felt sorry for her and saw that she got something to eat every day. Susie stayed there alone all summer. Amos went to see her as often as he could. She was glad he could speak her language. She told him about her people long ago and some of the stories she heard when she was a little girl. In the fall she went to her happy hunting ground and Amos and Cate buried her, the white man's way.

A band of Bannocks took a fancy to a big fine cow, one of the best that Cate had. Amos gave it to them. As they drove it off, she hoped she would never see another Indian as long as she lived.

Another time, she had hung all the work shirts and socks on the wire fence to dry. It was late afternoon when she finished her large washing. It was almost dark when she happened to look out and see an old squaw taking the clothes off the fence and putting them in a flour sack. "Pikeway! Be off with you," cried Cate. The squaw went right on stuffing them in the sack. Cate picked up a rock as big as a baseball and threw it along the ground. It hit the old woman on the ankle and with a loud yell, she dropped the sack and made a fast getaway.

Amos knew he must gain the Indians' confidence before he tried to baptize them, so for the first and second year after his mission call, he made friends with them and explained the Gospel in simple words which he hoped they could understand.

One time in 1877, a band of Shoshones came up on the west side of Bear River and were going to cross over to Bennington. They found that the cable on the flat ferryboat was broken. A young buck swam across and told Amos about it. It was spring and the water was high. Amos waded in till he had to start swimming. When he reached the broken cable, he grabbed it in his teeth, swam and floated by turns till he reached the other side. When he got the cable mended, he took all the Indians across to the lower fields on the ferry and then went back and got their horses and tepees.

As soon as they made camp they began hauling loads of dried willows and haw bushes from the river bank. They made a big bonfire and danced and whooped all night and Amos was right in the middle of it all. Cate was worried. She took out the loose "chinken" from between the logs of the house to watch what was going on. "Daw! It's too good, he is, too good! Why don't he come home?" Silas and Winnie and Addie were so scared they all hid under a buffalo robe.

Amos decided next morning, it was time to start baptizing those who were ready. Standing in the cold water of Home Creek, he began with some of the leaders, hoping others would follow. Ed Austin and Brother Moore came over to help, and they took turns baptizing, recording and confirming. They baptized ten the first day and nobody else for a week or so until a new band arrived. By the end of the summer there were forty-five names in the little brown leather-backed notebook, with dates and other necessary information written in.

Some of the Indians' names had a vulgar interpretation. It didn't seem right to him to use that kind of name for such a sacred ordinance, so he substituted one of his favorite names like Silas or Adelaide or Catherine. The children thought it was fun to have their names given to an Indian man or woman.

There was a big barbecue the day the Indians left. Amos, Cate and the children followed them to Pole Ford afterward, to wave goodbye to their summer friends. The Indian women had made a cradle board for little Edgar Monroe who was just a year old. They were pleased and laughed and pointed at Cate and the baby on her back in the cradle board they had given her.

Brother Rich suggested that Amos take a trip down to the little Mormon village near Malad, named Washakie. About three hundred Shoshones and Bannock members of the Church were living there on land furnished by the Church, with a white man and his family as branch president to teach them how to farm. Amos went and when he returned he said the Indians were very unselfish and obedient and he believed they would be able to live the United Order better than their white brethren. As always, Brother Rich was interested, and encouraged Amos to continue his missionary work.

Stake conference was set for August 26 that year (1877) and, as usual, some changes were made. William Budge was made stake president, leaving President Rich more time for general supervising. Elder Wilford Woodruff had come to Bear Lake in mid-winter for a ground-breaking for a new woolen factory, February 4, as part of the United Order project. It was working out well, especially the dairy and cheese making over at Bern. President Young had called a family named Kunz, converts from Switzerland, to operate it. Crops, that summer, would be light because of grasshopper damage.

President Budge also announced that Bear Lakers were responding better than any of the three stakes on the temple fund. A call had been issued the year before for donations for a temple to be built in Logan. All the butter and egg tithing from Bear Lake had been put into this temple fund, and evidently the women in the valley knew how to get more eggs from their chickens, and butter from their cows than those in Cache Valley or Box Elder.

Cate determined to do even better in the future. She was surprised and pleased to hear her husband's name read out to be advanced to the office of a high priest, and the action was ratified by the congregation as he stood up. Well, he deserved it. He'd served the Lord for almost ten years since he was baptized and she was proud of her good looking husband.

Then, when Brother Rich began speaking, it seemed to Amos as if he was talking directly to him:

> I will say a few words on the subject of counsel. It never hurts anyone to obey the counsels of the servants of God, but we should never ask counsel unless we intend to receive it. You should never ask counsel when your mind is already made up concerning the thing you ask. If I were counseled to leave Bear Lake Valley I would leave. It is right for me, to be governed by counsel, and if it is right for me it is right for you also for this principle will apply to all. Now concerning marriage, it must be an important matter for God to teach and command obedience to it. What constitutes its importance? In the first place, a man cannot have an exaltation without a wife. It was some years before I learned the fact that I could not do much good without a wife and without posterity. I therefore concluded to marry.
>
> It is promised that the Saints shall be the richest of all people, and to realize this promise we must be guided by those placed to lead us. This is the principle of safety and success. Any other course will produce sorrow. In the name of Jesus Christ, Amen.

Amos was ordained after the meeting. President Budge congratulated him and said he was coming to Bennington the following Sunday, which set Amos to wondering what else was afoot.

He found out, when not only President Budge, but President Rich and President Hart, as well, all three of the stake presidency, walked into the meetinghouse the following Sunday.

In the few minutes before the meeting, Amos was told Bishop Moore would like him to be first counselor in the bishopric if he was willing. There wasn't time to say anything but yes. His name was therefore presented and approved unanimously, amid head nodding, smiles of approval and glances toward Cate and the children. Bishop Moore remarked that he had never been a good speaker himself, but now he, like Moses, would have an Aaron to speak for him. Again, Cate had reason for justifiable pride even though she knew she'd see even less of Amos from now on. The children enjoyed some added prestige, also. Now they could tell their friends their father was in the bishopric.

Amos was touched by this evidence of approval from the ward and stake leaders, especially when President Rich told him personally he was proud of his past service and knew he would add much to the progress of the Ward. Then he added, "Amos, you always follow counsel!"

"Well," replied Amos, "I had to learn it the hard way and I hope I'll never forget it."

When word reached Brigham City, Father Jonathan was naturally pleased and said Amos and Cate ought to make a trip to Salt Lake and be sealed in the Endowment House.

As usual, some of his relatives there asked if anything good could come out of that cold Bear Lake country, to which Amos replied by return mail: "Yes, plenty of good water and thousands of acres of land inviting the honest sons of toil to partake of her riches, rather than to squat around the old settled towns of Utah."

The idea of a trip to Utah naturally appealed to Cate. She could visit her Mother in Brigham City, and of course she had always hoped to be sealed to her husband. They wouldn't be able to take the children this time since only couples and not family sealings were performed in the Endowment House.

"Well, that's just one more reason for helping to get the Logan temple built as soon as possible," said Cate. "Then we can have the whole family sealed for eternity."

It took a lot of doing for Cate and Mose to arrange to leave the children and go to Salt Lake for the sealing ordinance. With Silas gone, it would be up to the girls to look after the little ones. Winnie was almost thirteen and Addie eleven, though she had never been very strong. Amos Jr. was ten, John eight and Frank four, so only he and baby Edgar would need much attention. Winnie felt the responsibility more than any since she was the oldest. She couldn't understand why at least *she* couldn't go along. Sister Lindsay promised to keep an eye on the children and told Cate not to worry.

They would have to go by horse and buggy as far as Brigham City, and then by train to Salt Lake. It would be the first time on a train for either of them so they looked forward to going even with the worry of leaving the children.

Mose had been to the Endowment House before, way back in 1857 and the memory of that trip came vividly to mind again. He hadn't thought of Lois Moran for years it seemed and her name was now just a tender memory. He couldn't remember much of anything that went on that day either. He was glad that things had turned out the way they did. Maybe the Lord had a hand in choosing Cate as his wife and companion for eternity, just as he had in choosing Rebecca for Jonathan. Cate was his intellectual equal. He recognized her good common sense and thrift as definite assets. Best of all she was a splendid mother for their children. Perhaps if he listened oftener to her counsel, they'd all be better off.

As they entered the House of the Lord that 28th day of June, 1878, Amos felt the Spirit of the Lord enfold him again. Every act and word was magnified as if he were looking through the three-dimensional sterepticon he'd seen at the Rich home one time. He found himself wiping tears of joy from his eyes as he glanced over at Cate on the other side of the room. He realized the truth of Brother Rich's words about being prepared to receive the words of the Lord. He was much better prepared this time after seventeen years of experience, than when he was only sixteen. In fact, he had forgotten most of what went on that day so long ago. But he would never forget this time.

Then he and Cate were kneeling across from each other at the sacred altar, sealed together as husband and wife for time and all eternity. Their eyes filled with tears as they kissed over the altar.

They were silent most of the way back on the train to Brigham City. There was so much to ponder and meditate upon. A deepened sense of union settled about them. With clasped hands they gazed from the window as the train chugged toward Brigham City.

On the right were the Wasatch Mountains, with green foothills and fenced fields of lucern and wheat. Flocks of white seagulls wheeled and lighted on plowed fields for an angleworm feast. On the left, the Great Salt Lake shimmered in the sun. Cate would have lots to tell the children when they got home.

Amos wondered what their lives would have been like if they had stayed in Utah. The farms looked well cared for and there were quite a lot of "doby" houses with fancy trimmings on the gables.

His reverie was interrupted by a long whooooooing whistle of the train announcing journey's end at Brigham City. He hoped there would be someone there to meet them. The conductor in his navy blue suit and fancy cap was waiting to help them down the steps. It was all quite like a storybook.

Amos' brother Brig was there with the horse and buggy and said he hadn't had to wait. The train was on time. There was much to talk about. Brig said Father Jonathan was very poorly with dropsy and confined most of the time to his bed after a stroke. Mary Jane and Caroline, his youngest wife from Denmark, took turns caring for him. Seth and Lorenzo, Brig's brothers, were in Arizona on a mission. They hadn't been heard from for some time. Amos told Brig he hadn't seen or heard from Pone for a long time, either. He lived with the Indians most of the time.

They noticed many changes as they drove up Forrest Street, new houses, trees grown and now arching over the road. Ahead was the courthouse, with a tower added, and the old familiar bell was hanging in the new tower. As if for their benefit, it chimed out the hour. What a sentimental journey. Brigham City had been home to both Cate and Mose in spite of unhappy memories. Strangely now, they seemed unimportant and far away and had lost their bitterness.

As they turned north on Main Street, there were other new buildings, and to the right, the Wasatch Mountains rose abruptly with Flat Bottom halfway up to the top. A mile or two further on they could see the old farmstead ahead. A big snowball bush hung in full blossom in the front yard, and pansies and delphiniums bloomed near the house. Some of Mary Jane's red geraniums and jack-in-the-pulpits peeked out from behind the lace curtains in the front window, as Mary Jane, herself, met them at the door with her beautiful smile.

"Mother!" said Amos holding her at arm's length to look at her, face lined and with touches of gray at the temples but the same shining eyes and spirit. As he took her in his arms, tears could not be restrained, but they were happy ones. She ushered them into the darkened bedroom where Jonathan's swollen body lay under white sheets. It was shocking to see his father's bloated face and dimmed eyes. Amos knelt by the bed as the two men silently embraced. Again, tears mingled as he heard Jonathan whisper, "My son, my beloved son, in whom I am well pleased."

Cate went to the kitchen to help Mary Jane, while father and son communed silently. Later, Jonathan said he'd like to give Amos a blessing. Amos propped his father with pillows so he could sit on the edge of the bed, and knelt to receive a Father's blessing. Jonathan's voice, weak and husky at first, strengthened as he continued:

Amos Russell Wright, by the authority of the Holy Priesthood vested in me, I place my hands upon your head and by virtue of the same I seal upon you a Father's blessing and dedicate and set you apart for the work of the ministry and I say unto you that the Eye of the Lord is upon you for good and thou hast been called of God to minister in the various offices of the Holy Priesthood. And inasmuch as you are faithful and your heart's desire is for righteousness, the light of the Holy Spirit of God shall always be at your command and the power thereof shall abundantly rest upon you and God will hear your prayers and grant the desires of your heart and therefore you will be clothed with the power of God and your words shall be like words of God, and the power of the Holy Spirit of Revelation shall be with and accompany you in the administration of all the duties you may be called to perform and act in. And the Power of God shall be made manifest in all your official acts. Therefore, go your way in peace and remember to put your trust in God and all necessary wisdom shall be given to you from time to time to enable you to officiate in all the duties you are called upon by virtue of your office and Priesthood in a manner that the Power of God will be made manifest in all your official acts and shall not fail. Be faithful and the spirit of God shall accompany you in all the duties and obligations of the Holy Priesthood. You shall live long and your name and that of your companion shall be had in honorable remembrance through your posterity to the latest generation.

"I seal upon you by virtue of the power and the authority of the Priesthood, in the name of Jesus Christ, Amen."

Then, a few months later, like Jacob of old, Jonathan, too, "waxed old and gathered up his feet into the bed and gave up the Ghost."

Chapter Sixteen
The Year of the Jubilee

Cate and Amos found the children in good shape when they returned from Salt Lake. The brief separation had been good for both. It was a breather for the parents, and proof by the young ones that they could get along alone for a time at least.

Winnie and Addie were grateful to shift back into low gear and let their mother take over, recognizing what a big job she seemed to do so easily. Baby Edgar Monroe nestled happily in his mother's arms and wouldn't let her out of his sight.

Cate's love for her children overflowed in a hundred small ways. She marveled how she could love them even more than before, but she did. When she discovered she was expecting number nine she was glad. She'd had a longer than usual vacation. Maybe this time it would be a girl. Four boys in a row was pretty strenuous. Girls were easier to raise, she thought. And this time it would be different. This child would be born under the covenant; hers and Mose's for eternity. The others would have to wait to be sealed in the temple as soon as it was built and dedicated. Well, they'd get that done too! It *was* a girl, born April 10, 1879. Mose insisted she be named for her mother, Catherine Jane Wright.

The usual summer work was always waiting for Amos. A small break had made him as ready as he'd ever be, to wrestle with being a farmer, short water supply, poor tools, and all the risks attendant on keeping the wolf from the door. At least he could think as he worked. He wondered about his father. He was thankful he'd seen him again. It might be the last time. He surely couldn't last much longer. *His* approval was basic, and now he had it in writing. He had made a copy of the blessing as soon as he got home, and was surprised how clearly he rememberd it. This he could turn to again and again for reassurance and comfort.

The Indians were already straggling into the valley. Last

summer he had neglected them as much as they would let him and had baptized only twelve. He'd do better as a missionary this time! A headline in the Millenial Star of December 15, 1879, verified his self-prophecy:

A MISSIONARY TO THE INDIANS: We have been gratified at receiving a letter from Bro. A.R. Wright written at Bennington, Bear Lake Valley, Idaho, U.S.A. dated Nov. 12, 1879. He is a missionary to the Indians, in that northern part. He says he has spent a profitable time among the Lamanites the past summer. In the neighborhood of sixty of them have been added to the Church by baptism during the season in that locality. Bro. Wright and all others engaged in teaching the Indians are employed in a very important department of this latter-day dispensation. Many precious promises according to the Book of Mormon are given by the Lord concerning that people. They are destined to perform a very conspicuous part in connection with the future building up of Zion. (Journal History, Church Archives).

Some welcome rains came in late August to supplement Home Canyon creek water. Amos laughingly said the Indians' sign of rain never failed: "Black all around and pouring down in the middle." Maybe he could stir up some enthusiasm for a reservoir for Bennington so they wouldn't always be short of water in late summer. He'd talk to Bishop Moore about that. He must do his share to help in the ward, too. He went in place of the bishop to stake priesthood meeting in Paris for November and reported, "Ward meetings poorly attended. Several Indian baptisms performed and some asked to be anointed and administered to for sickness."

It was the Year of the Jubilee, 1880! That meant the Church had been organized for fifty years. A circular to the Saints was issued by the First Presidency, asking them to relieve the worthy poor by cancelling their debts and lending seed grain to those in need. Special programs were conducted to memorialize half a century of growth and progress in the restored Church of Jesus Christ of Latter-day Saints.

It was a Jubilee, too, for the family when Silas announced he was going to get married. He was just eighteen and Ida Ellen Oakey was the bride. It was a June wedding. There would be a dance afterward for all ward members and other friends. Cate and Sister Oakey baked for days, so everybody would have plenty to eat. People brought gifts if they had any to give, and if not, they showered the young folks with potatoes, turnips, carrots and bottled fruit.

Jessie Dunn, who could play half a dozen instruments, was in charge of the music, but he found he had a broken fiddle string, and what was a dance without a fiddle? Two young fellows volunteered to ride horseback the thirty miles over the mountain to Franklin and get some new ones, so the dance could go on as scheduled. A few of Amos' special Indian friends showed up and watched the White men do their style of dancing, as well as loading up on pie and cake instead of dried buffalo meat and berries. They grinned with delight to see Peah Tibo and his squaw out on the dance floor keeping time to the music, the very best dancers of all.

Silas had been a good son, helping his parents willingly. "He built roads into the surrounding canyons and cleared and fenced the land as needed, besides working out both his and his father's assessment on the Logan Temple for three years. He was a good athlete; a fast runner, wrestler, and catcher on the Bennington baseball team. He never wore a mask, didn't have one, and got his nose broken as a result, but it healed without disfigurement.

"After he was married, he and a couple of other young men bought a threshing machine—the old horsepower kind, and did custom threshing for the farmers in the area. He was the "measurer." It took skill and stamina to measure up to a thousand bushels a day. The owners took their pay in toll grain and a job of a thousand bushels would yield eighty bushels in toll." (*Bear Lake Daughters of Utah Pioneers.*)

Just before Silas' wedding, Cate was asked to serve as Sister Vanorman's first counselor in Relief Society. And then, in late July, Brother Moore announced he was moving away. Amos, being first counselor in the bishopric, was appointed "acting bishop." As if that weren't enough, Brother Rich sent word a few weeks later he wanted to see him as soon as convenient.

Amos found the president in his office when he rode to Paris that hot day in August, 1880. He was naturally curious to know what Brother Rich had on his mind. Since he was "acting bishop" in Bennington, he supposed it might have something to do with that. He would find it another far more difficult test of his promise to the Lord to serve him unquestioningly.

He was greeted warmly by the big man, and Amos responded with his near-worship feeling, knowing beforehand he'd say yes, or thought he would, to anything he was asked to do.

Brother Rich seemed in no hurry as he motioned toward a comfortable chair, invited Amos to sit down, and made the usual comments about the weather. Then he began asking Amos about his experiences at Fort Lemhi in 1857 and '58; about the little group of Shoshones north of Brigham City, and just how successful that effort was in getting the Indians to adopt white men's farming methods.

To a willing listener, Amos could become a fascinating raconteur and this time was no exception.

"President Taylor," Brother Rich explained, "remembers the Lord's instruction to Joseph Smith to teach the Gospel to the Lamanites. Brother Brigham, too, remembered this commandment during his life. That is why he said, 'feed them, don't fight them.' You know first hand what happened at the Salmon River Mission, as you have told me. He considered that a failure, perhaps his fault.

"And now we are here in Bear Lake Valley for the same reasons, to extend the borders of Zion, and at the same time to show our love and concern for our Lamanite brothers. It is President Taylor's feeling that the best way to do it is to teach them the Gospel first; baptize them, and then having the spirit within them, they will more easily learn how to adopt our ways. You've been doing this very thing the past two or three years over there in Bennington and we think you've made a good start."

Then, looking Amos straight in the eye, he came to the point.

"Brother Amos, some of the Shoshones from Wind River in Wyoming, whom you have baptized here lately, want you to come over there and preach to the whole tribe, including Washakie. You speak the language and know how to explain the Gospel so they can understand. They think you could convert many more, and maybe the chief, himself. How do you feel about such an idea?"

Amos knew at once he wanted to do it. But thoughts of a wife and eight children to feed and look after made him hesitate. Brother Rich waited understandingly and then answered before Amos could ask. "You could go when you can arrange it and stay as long as it takes. You'll know when the time comes. As for a companion, that, too, is up to you. Find one, or go alone this time."

That raised another question and Amos voiced it.

"I guess you know there is some danger in such a mission. Since I've been baptizing these Indians, I've got the Indian agent on my trail. The former one, Mr. P., told my brother at Evanston, one day, if he ever got hold of me, he would put me in irons. The present agent has made similar threats. He considers our missionary work among the Indians as an insurrection against the government. You almost have to have their permission to take a deep breath.

"I think you know, too, that even Shoshones can still be murderers without much provocation, especially if you go on their hunting ground."

"Well, Brother Amos, suppose you think this over. Pray about it, and talk it over with Sister Wright. If you decide to go, let me give you a blessing before you leave."

Cate, naturally, thought it would be hard to keep things going without Amos, but maybe Silas would help, even though he was married.

"If you can just wait till the thrashing is done, we'll make out someway. You ought to leave before too long or you'll get snowbound."

Amos blessed Cate, silently, for her support.

Early September found Amos on his way with no idea how long he'd be gone. Cate was utterly amazed to see him back in a little over a month. A story of conversion, not unlike Ammon's *Book of Mormon* experience, unfolded.

This was no ordinary mission, and in answer to Amos' initial letter reporting the event, President Taylor wanted a detailed report. Amos was naturally pleased and filled nineteen pages before he was through writing.

Chapter Seventeen
Changing Times

Two weeks after Amos returned from his Wind River mission, he received word that his father, Jonathan, had passed away November 8, 1880. He was glad he had seen his father on the way home from Salt Lake so recently and received a blessing under his hands.

At the funeral which was held in the tabernacle in Brigham City, he saw most of his brothers and sisters, many of whom he hadn't seen in years. He was asked to speak at the funeral, one of the hardest tests he had ever had to pass, but somehow managed to get through without breaking down completely. He always said with disgust, he was half woman when it came to shedding tears.

As soon as he returned to Bear Lake he was shocked to hear that President Rich had had a stroke. The great man lingered for another three years before he passed away in 1883, but his active days of leadership were over. He had been the king-pin in Bear Lake Valley for twenty years and the ideal of many people, including Amos. With Father Jonathan gone now, the two "anchor men" who had most influenced his life were thus taken, leaving him thereafter to go it alone. His responsibilities as acting bishop were noticeably greater, and he could appreciate what Apostle Francis M. Lyman said at quarterly conference:

> A bishop should know all that is going on in his ward. I have always had great sympathy for a bishop. He is always the butt of everybody's jokes and criticism. He has to judge everybody and is the common enemy of all. The proper material for making bishops is scarce. It is a responsibility that very few desire and that nearly all shirk. We should support him, pray for him, and act in unison with him.

Well, he'd practically asked for the job with that blasphemous boast before leaving Brigham City nearly twenty years ago. But he didn't feel anywhere near as confident now as he did then. And when President John Taylor laid his hands on his head to ordain him as bishop of Bennington Ward, Bear Lake Stake of Zion, he suddenly felt bowed down with the weight on his shoulders. He knew it was an honor to have the President of the Church travel those many miles to perform the ordinance.

So it was a humble man who assumed his duties that August day of 1881, with a commitment to give the job the best that was in him. He chose two Davids, David Hunter and David Lindsay as counselors.

He was becoming immersed in politics, too. But, through it all, he maintained his interest in and love the for Indians. They continued to make his pasture a grazing ground for their ponies. When people protested that he was being imposed on, he simply would say, "They saved my life many times. I can never repay them for their kindesses to me."

Old Sam, his squaw and boy, Hugh, were regular summer visitors. Hugh wore overalls and a jacket instead of the usual buckskin. He wanted to be like the white boys in Bennington and when he saw some of them combing their hair, he tried to do the same thing with a borrowed comb, but his thick, black locks were so matted he soon gave it up. Old Sam caught a bad cold and decided to cure it. He dug a hole two or three feet deep by the side of Home Canyon Creek and put in a few cobblestones. Then he built a fire in the hole till the stones were hot and then scraped the fire all out. He climbed into the hole and sprinkled a bucket of water over the rocks so they started to steam, after covering the hole with a buffalo robe. This would make him sweat and he stayed there as long as he could stand it. He jumped out and into the cold water for awhile, then he wrapped himself in the buffalo robe again and laid in his tepee until he was cured.

The Indians did a lot of trading at Ed Burgoyne's store in Montpelier. They brought their furs and pelts to trade for everything from tobacco to matches. Sometimes his wife, Mary Ann, helped out in the store when Ed was away. She knew how to bargain with the Indians as well as Ed himself, and got the name of "Wino" or good squaw. Four or five of them came in one day, wanting to trade for some flour. She figured out the worth of their pelts and gave them fifty pounds of flour in exchange. One buck thought it wasn't enough and raised his whip to hit her. She ran for the axe behind the counter and chased him out of the store. The other Indians laughed and called him a squaw man.

The store was a wonderland for children. They begged to go when their mothers went to trade on Saturday. Back of the counter were gunnysacks full of peanuts. Big bunches of bananas hung from a hook on the ceiling. There were glass jars full of mints and stick candy. Women traded butter and eggs for whatever they needed, like dress goods, soap, sugar, Doan's liver pills, or asifetida which smelled so bad it was supposed to drive away germs when hung on a string around a sick person's neck.

One February day Amos happened to be in the store when a smart-looking drummer came in to sell a bill of goods to Burgoyne. He began asking questions about the Mormons. Ed couldn't answer them very well so he said, "Wait a minute, there's a man here who can tell you anything you want to know," pointing to Amos. He had on his sheepskin coat which Ed Austin had bought for him, with a bandana tied over his ears and a cap over that. The drummer naturally wasn't much impressed, at first, but after an hour or so he changed his mind. When he left, he told Ed he'd learned more in that conversation with Bishop Wright than he'd dreamed was possible.

Sugar sold for a dollar thirty-five a pound and tea was seven dollars. Boys brought their squirrel tails in and collected two and a half cents each as bounty and Ed settled with the county later on. Men liked to hang around the potbellied stove on cold winter afternoons and swap stories while their wives traded butter and eggs for anything they took a fancy to. Cate was in the store one day and met Sister VanOrman, the Relief Society President. Cate was her first counselor. "Oh, Sister Wright, did you know the Merrills are quarantined for diphtheria? Their little three-year-old is real bad and they don't know whether he can pull through or not. The family is doing all right, so far, but they may need help later on."

Cate worried about the terrible news all that day and the next. Diphtheria was a most dreaded disease. Children especially seemed unable to survive when the suspicious white membrane appeared in the patient's throat. She prayed that her own loved ones would be spared.

That night Amos came in looking troubled. "The little Merrill boy died an hour ago. Sister Merrill is down in bed too. Someone will have to go in and prepare the body for burial and help the family. Sister VanOrman can't go." Cate waited for the next words and guessed what they would be. How could she go and maybe bring the dread disease back to her own children? Amos waited, knowing Cate was trying to decide what to do. Then, with tears in her eyes, she looked at him and said, "Aye, Mose, I'll go."

Prayerfully, she prepared an extra set of clothing for herself. Taking some soap and a towel along, she left them in the barn before going to the afflicted home. There she waited on the sick ones and washed and dressed the dead child. In a tiny coffin made by another neighbor, he was carried away to the graveyard. After Cate cooked up some stew and did the washing, she returned to her own family.

Calling to Winnie to bring her a pan of hot water, she waited outside for it and then took it to the barn. There she stripped off her clothes, took a sponge bath and washed her hair. She put on the clean clothes and only then did she venture inside her own house. She anxiously counted the incubation period day by day, fearing the worst, but none of the family took diphtheria.

A little later, however, things didn't turn out so well. Charles Elmer was the tenth child born to Amos and Cate, August 25, 1881. Eleven months later, he too, was dead in spite of all his parents could do to save him. The girls always remembered their Mother's grief, blaming herself for not knowing what to do. Such

experiences increased Amos' sensitivity to other people's grief. He
was called upon both as bishop, and to talk at funerals all over the
valley. He knew how to sway people's emotions because he truly
cared. Their sorrow became his sorrow. Like Father Jonathan
before him, he never turned down a call to serve.

He did say no to Annie Weaver one time. She was a chronic
hypochondriac and sent word to the bishop she was sick and
wanted to be administered to. When he arrived, she was sitting at
the table with a big plate of food in front of her. He said anybody
with that kind of an appetite didn't need a blessing.

The coming of the railroad made the biggest changes. "The
Union Pacific began a branch line from Wyoming through to
Oregon—the Oregon Short Line. It reached the eastern boundary
of Idaho in June 1882. Construction continued the next two years,
with 540 miles built in Idaho; 45 in Bear Lake County. This
brought money to the valley. Workers were paid in cash. Silas
helped get out logs from Home Canyon to make ties, noted for
their good quality. The first train came through Montpelier on the
24th of July, 1882. The first telephone system between there and
Paris was built the same year. Thus, the New Era dawned."
(Russell Rich Thesis)

Freight and cattle shipping became good business. Mail
service, "outside" goods, new settlers, jobs etc. provided the yeast
for the bread of so-called progress. With it came what Amos ever
after referred to as "the depot element" with its inevitable
accompaniment: liquor, tobacco and saloons.

Montpelier soon became the largest settlement in the valley
with a good many gentiles as merchants, buyers of town real
estate, despite the counsel of President Budge against selling to
them. Chances to make some real money was heady stuff for
people who had been forced before to rely on barter. Even the
Saints welcomed the chance to buy a ticket to Salt Lake and
conference for eight dollars. They came home feeling like world
travelers, no longer shut in by isolation walls.

In 1881 a gentile purchased some land and built a saloon in
Paris. Counsel from Church leaders said, "We should shun the
saloon and let it severely alone." The bishops and their counselors
were advised to visit the Saints in their homes, urging a
community action against the saloon. But after 1882 it was
always possible to buy liquor somewhere along the tracks in
Montpelier. Tullidge said, "up to the advent of the railroad, the
morality of the people was strictly in accord with the teaching of

their religion." Till the last few years, jails didn't exist and there was no need for any. One man was excommunicated for selling liquor but he said he objected to being cut off from the Church for selling liquor for "medicinal purposes" or keeping a drugstore.

Amos got the contract to carry the mail from Montpelier to Bennington, riding back and forth each day on a horse. Then he became the postmaster and devoured the papers and pamphlets which came through the office before they were delivered to their addresses.

He worked out a plan after he became bishop to make things work more smoothly in the ward. "Deacons served two at a time as janitors for the meetinghouse for two weeks at a time, serving whatever shows, dances or any Church activity was held. They were given a free ticket to these. The Church was heated by a wood stove. They sawed and split large logs which were donated by the men of the ward for fuel. Then they carried it in the Church and built and cared for the fires, swept and dusted. They went in a group and sawed wood for the widows. Once each month they visited the entire Ward to collect fast offerings for the widows. They received meat, flour, potatoes and fruit." (Charles Coulson Rich, Leonard Arrington, p. 278.)

Amos tried to keep in mind his own rebellious youth as he presided at the dances each week, but knowing the dangers inherent in greater freedom between the sexes, he, along with leaders from General Authorities down, counseled against round dancing. Liquor of course was taboo, but again "the depot element" crept in as relentlessly as a glacier grinding down a mountain and had to be opposed constantly. Gang fights between town bullies were common and were sometimes settled out back of the meetinghouse between dances.

Amos encouraged wholesome entertainment. Home talent road shows, minstrels, comedy skits and plays furnished relaxation from the steady grind of farm work. Dancing was always the favorite and furnished the main discussion at stake priesthood meetings for twenty years. Responsibility for conduct at dances was the bishop's and he was "damned if he did and damned if he didn't" as respect for parental and Church authority diminished in the New Era.

"The spirit of dance was in the air. People danced a jig on the street and women danced around the stove in the kitchen. At mealtime such expressions were used as 'please swing the fried fish around to this corner, please cross the hotcakes to the couple

on the left and promenade the mince pie to the right-hand lady.'"
(Russell Rich Thesis)

Rules for dances were recorded in the stake priesthood minutes. January 3, 1880:

> For dancing assemblies in the Bear Lake Stake of Zion. Our dances shall be conducted under the dictation of the bishop who will be held responsible for the manner in which dances are conducted in their respective wards. Our dances shall be commenced and closed with prayer and shall not be continued later than 12 o'clock. We will not practice waltzes or other round dances in our assemblies. Persons dancing out of turn shall be considered violators of good order and may be requested to retire and if persisted in, may be ejected. We will not use liquor in our assemblies nor suffer any person inebriated to participate in the dance. Swinging with one arm around the lady's waist shall not be permitted in our assemblies. To swing a lady more than once against her will shall be considered ungentlemanly. To swing more than twice under any circumstances shall be considered disorderly and if persisted in, the offender may be requested to retire and, if necessary, may be ejected. Dances gotten up to make money will not be countenanced unless specially ordered by the presidency or bishops. The above rules were adopted by unanimous vote. (Stake Priesthood Minutes N1, Nov. 1877 to Dec. 1890 LDS Archives)

Nobody enjoyed a good quadrille or French Four more than the bishop himself. Whenever he decided to swing a partner, an announcement was made: "Ladies and Gentlemen, the next dance will have only one set on the floor. Bishop Wright will be dancing." There was usually room for two sets at a time.

The ward was still in debt for part of the cost of the meetinghouse, so a character ball was planned for the 24th of July. The sisters scrounged everything available for costumes for weeks ahead. Real money was charged for tickets, but anybody who didn't have enough could substitute anything from livestock to garden vegetables. Everybody in the ward turned out and the judges had a hard time deciding who deserved some of the prizes. Harl Weaver and his wife Addie came as George and Martha Washington, so there was no doubt who won first prize. Needless to say, the debt was wiped out and the meetinghouse duly dedicated.

Private parties continued to be popular. Games were played after supper and carpets, if any, were rolled back as the fiddle tuned up for dancing. The babies were put to bed on the floor or any nook available and slept through it all.

John Dunn moved to Bennington in 1868. He taught dancing

to all the young folks. He played the violin. He would walk among the dancers as he played counting time and if someone was out of step he would tap them with the violin bow and never miss a count. Daniel Burbank was the floor manager and caller and Ella Perkins played the organ. Charge was ten cents for admission each night. Jessie Dunn moved to Bennington in July 1876 and was skilled in music and dramatics. With people like this, the ward was well-fixed for wholesome entertainment. (Bear Lake Daughters of Pioneers)

By the fall of 1884, the Church lost control of dances. A dancehall was built by L.D.S. members in east Montpelier and run free of bishop dictation. They promised to close at twelve o'clock and prohibit liquor. This held until the 1900's. For many years there was no saloon in Bear Lake Valley. There was one in Soda Springs, 40 miles north, but it was pressured out of business. The brethren wondered where liquor was coming from. Then under questioning, the mailman confessed he had been bringing it in. During the early years, no L.D.S. member opened a saloon, but would get liquor and "carefully" sell it out.

"The railroad was responsible also for the downfall of the cooperatives. The tannery could not compete with outside leather goods. Shoe and harness business went with it. By the end of the century most of the mercantile and manufacturing co-ops had either been bought up by private individuals or had gone out of business. The co-op stores closed up and Bear Lake reverted to a solely agricultural community. Bear Lake was a literal theocracy for twenty-two years. It served the people well and although they were not wealthy, they were contented and prosperous." (Russell Rich Thesis)

These subtle changes came gradually; not many people realized what was taking place. A few with vision saw, and did what they could to prepare for what was ahead. Even Bear Lakers, still semi-isolated as they were, were made conscious of anti-Mormon activities, political and otherwise.

"At a stake conference in April 1882, President Budge, recognizing the weakening of cooperatives in the valley, counseled the Saints to 'do our trading with ZCMI in Salt Lake City or it's branch stores or else send cash for our supplies. This would insure a united action among the people. It was voted that we sustain only the ZCMI stores or those of our brethren who obtain their goods from the East, or the Evanston merchants who have always been friendly.'" (Stake Records, Bear Lake, Church

Historical Archives).

As Amos read everything that came under his eye, he decided perhaps he could do some good by getting into politics. He had always maintained that the office should seek the man, not the other way about. But friends like Joseph C. Rich, Ed Austin and Ira Nebeker urged him to run as a representative from the county. He was surprised and pleased to be elected in 1882 along with H. S. Woolley and C. E. Robinson.

"The Idaho Territorial Legislature of 1875 had created Bear Lake County. This also changed things, politically. Paris was the county seat and provided for three county commissioners. Before that, allegiance was to Utah with President Rich as representative. "In 1880, Pres. William Budge was elected a member of the Territorial Council. John B. Neil, an avowed anti-Mormon was governor. He was sent out from the East by Pres. Rutherford B. Hayes, and was determined to get anti-Mormon legislation passed before the session closed." (Poulsen, *Versatile Pioneer Joseph C. Rich.*)

Cate was elated that her husband was "gradually coming into national prominence" as she laughingly put it, and proceeded to Ed Burgoyne's to get some suitable clothes for him when he went to Boise. She went to her sugar bowl where she kept the butter and egg money. This wouldn't be enough, but it would help. His suit might do if she could find the right kind of shirt, and some good-looking shoes, instead of moccasins or boots. Anything to take away that Indian look. She found some really handsome shoes. They looked like slippers, in fact. No tops to lace, and the clerk said they were made out of "patent" leather. They were all shiny black. She gasped when she heard the price, but no matter, Amos should have the best. The shirts all looked pretty ordinary. Realizing Cate was on a spending spree for a change, the clerk brought out a shirt that *was* a shirt. Stiff white pleats all down the front. That was something like it! "Wrap it up," she said without asking how much.

She couldn't wait to get home and have Mose try her treasures on. She could just see how distinguished he'd look; as good as President Budge any day. Even better, though she might be prejudiced. She waited until after supper and the smaller children were in bed. Laying the two packages on the table, she told him to guess what was inside. Amos entered into the game good-naturedly, guessing it might be a dozen eggs or a stovepipe hat. Cate said he was getting warm anyhow, wishing she had thought of a hat. When the paper was off he took one look and went over to his easy chair by the fire without saying a word. "Oh, Mose, I want you to be the best-dressed man in the legislature. Come on, try them on. I'll get your coat for you. The clerk says those patent leather shoes are the very latest thing. You won't ever have to shine them. And I'll keep the shirt washed and starched as good as new."

He went into "one of his spells" then and wouldn't say a word; just sat there with that far-away look in his eye. Maybe it was a mistake that he ever got into politics at all. Would it make him neglect his priesthood duties. If so, he'd resign. He abhorred a pompous man and he'd seen a good many. Vanity could be a disease and grow if you weren't careful. All kinds of evil could come like bribery and misappropriation of funds. Finally he said, "Cate, I wasn't elected because I wear fine clothes. They don't expect that of me in the first place, and if they do they're mistaken. They'll have to take me as I am. It's just plain vanity on your part. Take the stuff back to Burgoyne!" And with that, he buried himself in the paper.

Cate was mad. "Now, Mose, you can't be so stubborn. After I tried so hard to please you. Come on, try this shirt on anyhow," and she started to cry. Wearied with the nagging, he purposely slipped his arms in the wrong way so the pleats were in the back and delivered his ultimatum: "All right, if I have to wear a board, I'll wear it up my back!"

For the eleventh time in twenty-two years, Cate entered the valley of shadow to bring forth a child, another girl whom they named Elizabeth, not named for anybody in particular but that she looked like a little queen. Her birthday fell on November 30, 1883. Cate's life was immersed daily in the multitude of small details and irritations which only a mother of eleven could comprehend. Fortunately her health was good and the children were seldom sick except Addie, who was always frail.

While Amos wrestled against poverty and Indian ignorance; worried about ward members, in addition to those of his own family; dreamed up plans to improve life for the Saints temporally and spiritually, all the while trying to keep from any act which would make him unworthy of the spirit, he seldom talked to Cate about all these things constantly preying on his mind. There was little chance with so many children demanding attention. He depended on her, of course, but took her help for granted.

Cate had made a covenant when she was married, and again

over the temple altar to be a faithful wife under all circumstances. This she felt she had done so far. She served dutifully in Relief Society when some women with smaller families said they didn't have time.

Amos' disgust at the new clothes still rankled her and she often found it impossible to understand the strange man she had married. She respected his wisdom because others did and because he earned it. But why, for instance, couldn't he move to Malad as she had suggested many times. Her rich Evans brothers would have helped him to make some real money for a change. They had started from scratch and were now wealthy cattle ranchers. They had nice houses, elegant furniture and the women even had a hired girl.

There was a part of Mose that Cate had never known and maybe never would. He paid little attention to the smaller children. That had to be her job. His was to provide, and he realized he didn't do a very good job of it, hard as he tried. But with Cate's thrift and know-how, they were at last accumulating a few of the things which made life easier.

Amos had title to two farms, one in Maple Field and the other south of the house, extending from the foothills to Bear River. They were out of debt in spite of their large family. Perhaps they were about over the hump and for the rest of their lives, they could just coast.

Chapter Eighteen
Liahona

At forty-four, Amos had reached the prime of life. Now he was old enough to comprehend to his own satisfaction *who* he was, *why* he was here on earth, and *where* he was going. He had discovered by his own experience that the restored Gospel of Jesus Christ was true and that the principles, if strictly obeyed, brought him inward peace of mind. This, he knew, did not mean that "he had it made" by any means. But by following the guidelines and enduring to the end, he could make his life acceptable to God. It was upon this foundation that his future choices would be made. And though he didn't yet know it, the most crucial decision of his life, here and hereafter, would have to be made in the coming year 1885.

As early as 1882 when the Edmunds Act passed Congress, Amos sensed the coming storm, then no bigger than a man's hand. The nub of the difficulty was the Church doctrine of plurality of wives, commonly known as polygamy. This, of course, was nothing new to him, having lived through one generation of that form of family life. But perhaps because of this knowledge, he hoped this time it would blow over and that he would not be again directly involved.

In the early days of the Church and by command of God, Joseph Smith himself practiced and taught this principle to some of his trusted friends, among them Amos' own father, Jonathan Calkins Wright. Not until 1852, however, was it publicly announced to the world and accepted as doctrine by the members of the Church. Orson Pratt, the apostle, was chosen to make the announcement, which he did in big words and long sentences. What he was saying, was that marriage was God's way of preserving the human race, just as he told Adam and Eve after he married them in the beginning, that they should "multiply and replenish the earth."

Now a better, but more difficult, system had again been revealed. It was not new, but like the Gospel itself, was a restoration of something very old, and sacred. Abraham, Isaac, and Jacob successfully lived it, likewise under God's direction. It was a very selective system. Only men designated by a prophet of God as worthy, were eligible. But those so selected could accept or reject it as they desired. The hazards were great on the face of it. Not only would they have to assume full responsibility for another family, or two, or three, with all the problems that presupposed, but by so doing, they would incur the wrath and persecution of society as a whole.

Thus, only men and women of great courage and faith would ever consider such a thing. Weaklings and undesirables would automatically fall through the sieve. Anyone who would desire it unworthily would do so to his own condemnation. As a result, few qualified. As a final deterrent, enemy threats already promised to grind the Mormons and their Church to powder.

It was at a monthly stake priesthood meeting in Paris that

Brother Budge suggested to Amos the desirability of taking another wife and raising a second family. Twice before, he had been approached on the subject by General Authorities, but had done nothing about it. He and Cate had eleven children. They already knew what poverty tasted like from first-hand experience. Surely, this sacrifice would not be required of them. But here it was in front of him as big as a mountain.

Amos said he'd think about it, and he thought about it whether he wanted to or not. It was there the last waking moment at night and the first thing in the morning. He didn't have the courage to mention it to Cate.

He was always working on the "what-if" puzzle. What-if he did do it? His thoughts trailed off in mind-boggling impossibilities. What if he refused? Again he ran into a Chinese wall with no possible solution.

As always, his first recourse was to prayer. It seemed this time the heavens were brass and only the echo of his own words and thoughts came back to him. He read the Old Testament about Abraham, Isaac and Jacob again and again. Reading *about* Sarah and Hagar and Leah and Rachel sounded reasonable and not too difficult, but it was a different matter when he substituted the names of Amos and Cate and some unknown female. No wonder the other religions had sidetracked the Old Testament as unnecessary. That was much more convenient.

Then he turned to his former priesthood blessings, the one he received while on his mission at Ft. Lemhi, the other one from Father Jonathan given on his deathbed. There was no indication in either that such a thing was expected of him. He breathed a sigh of relief. Maybe his calling as an Indian missionary would take him off the hook. But then it occurred to him, he had never had an official patriarchal blessing. Maybe that would give him the guidance he needed. But that would involve an expensive trip to Salt Lake and an appointment with John Smith, the Patriarch to the Church. Miserable days and nights and weeks of indecision followed. Since by this action he might find a solution, he determined to go. It occurred to him he might kill two birds at once. April Conference was just around the corner and he could get his patriarchal blessing at the same time. So he packed his little grip, said goodbye to Cate and the family, and boarded the train at 'Pelier and was on his way.

To Cate and the family it was a relief to have him go. He had been so silent and moody and impossible to understand all this time. They would now be able to act natural for a change.

It was still cold in Bear Lake the first of April. It would have been an April Fool's joke if it was ever any different. Amos would never be reconciled to cold weather under any circumstances, and in his present frame of mind, he hated it. He had to admit it was nice just to sit in the red plush seat and look out of the train window at the passing scenery; quite a change from snowshoes, ox team, horseback or wagon. The train stopped at every little settlement and only took a few hours to get to Salt Lake.

He didn't have any relatives to stay with, so got a place at a rooming house near the depot. Next morning, he went to the patriarch's office. He found he would have to wait till tomorrow, the fifth, to see Brother Smith. That would work out fine. He'd go to conference in the meantime and stay over Sunday, the sixth, when conference would be over. He could go to the temple grounds and see how the temple was coming along, too. It was taking a lot longer to finish than the Logan Temple. Dedication for that one was set for May 17, only about six weeks away. He hoped he'd have a chance to be there.

He was tired after being in conference all day and went back to his room. He decided to fast for two reasons: so he would be in the right spirit for the blessing on the morrow, and to save the price of two meals. The room was small and dark but better than he was used to at home. It was noisy all night with trains clanging back and forth in the railroad yard across the street so he didn't get much sleep. This city life wasn't for him, he was sure of that.

He had to wait next morning for Brother Smith to get to his office even though he hadn't arrived, himself, until 7:30. These city folks sure wasted most of the day. The patriarch finally came and was very kind and cordial. He asked Amos about his home life, where he lived; said he knew President Budge and Gib Weaver. After asking Amos if he had a testimony of the Gospel, he called a young man in with a notebook and a pencil in his hand, who sat down at a table and began making squiggles on the paper. The patriarch then laid his hands on Amos' head and began slowly:

Brother Amos Russell Wright, in the name of Jesus of Nazareth, I place my hands upon thy head and pronounce and seal a blessing upon thee as the Spirit shall direct. Thou art of the house of Israel, numbered with the sons of Zion and notwithstanding thy life has been a changed one, the hand of the Lord has been over you for good.

His eye has been upon thee from thy birth. He has many times delivered thee from thine enemies and warded off the shafts of the Adversary which have been hurled at thee by false friends and in thy journeyings, and also in thine associations at home and abroad. He has preserved thy life to fulfill a mission wherein His name shall be glorified. Thou hast been called and chosen to be an instrument in the hands of God among thy fellowmen.

Thy mission is among the House of Israel. It is thy lot to assist in gathering those who have been scattered. Thou hast already traveled much for the Gospel's sake and have encountered perils by land and water and the wicked have sought thy life. Thy guardian Angel has delivered thee. Thou hast found friends among strangers who have defended thee and turned aside the anger of the ignorant; for the Lord knoweth the secrets of thy heart. He is pleased with thine integrity, and thou shalt verily receive thy reward. And I say unto thee, continue firm; seek diligently to know the will of the Lord and thy mind will continue to expand. The eyes of thine understanding shall be opened and thou shalt see and understand things as they are.

It is thy duty as an Elder in Israel to be a peacemaker among thine associates; that peace may reign in thy circle. The gift of healing is also thine, through prayer and faith it is thy privilege also to prophecy when necessary.

Therefore, reflect upon the past, present, and future, and listen to the whisperings of the Spirit which cometh from our Father in Heaven, and thou shalt have the gift of discernment hereafter to a greater extent than thou hast in the past and as you grow in years thou shalt grow in knowledge, and the closer you live unto the Lord, the more His Spirit will rest upon thee, and the Angel who has watched over thee in the past, if necessary will confer with thee as with a familiar friend and thou shalt be warned of danger by dreams of the night.

Thy duties will be made known by visions of the day and inasmuch as thou wilt listen to the promptings of the monitor within thee, thy pathway shall be made clear and thou shalt have power over evil and unclean spirits, and evil and designing persons shall not deceive thee. And so long as thou art in the discharge of thy duty, no power shall prevail against thee, and thou shalt fulfill thy mission and secure unto thyself an inheritance among those who have fought the good fight, kept the faith and won the prize.

Thou shalt yet see many changes and behold the arm of the Lord made bare in behalf of His people. Thou art of the blood of Joseph through the loins of Ephraim, and entitled to the blessings of Abraham, Isaac and Jacob, with the gifts and privileges promised unto the Fathers in Israel, and thy name shall be handed down with

thy posterity in honorable remembrance from generation to generation. Therefore, be upon thy guard, and it shall be well with thee
both here and hereafter. Thou shalt not lack for the comforts of life.
Thou shalt feed the hungry, clothe the naked and comfort the hearts
of the fatherless. And thy days and years shall be according to thy
faith and desires of thy heart.

It is thy privilege and duty also to be a savior in thy father's
house, for there are those who are wayward and do not realize their
position and thou art the legal heir to this privilege; therefore be
prudent. Seek unto the Lord for wisdom and His Spirit shall direct
thy course and give thee power and influence among the people
wheresoever thou shalt sojourn.

Amos, these are thy blessings, gifts and privileges and also more
thou shalt have where necessary, and if thou wilt ask the Father in
faith; and I seal thee up to Eternal life to come forth in the morning of
the first resurrection with many of thy kindred and friends, even so,
Amen.

Brother Smith told Amos he would send a copy of the blessing
to him in Bennington in a few days. Amos thanked the patriarch
with tears in his eyes, and left. He would want to read this
blessing many times later, to be sure he understood the true
meaning from each line.

Conference was full of highlights and inspiration. The choir
and big pipe organ gave him goose bumps. They even made the
hymns sound grand and soul-stirring. They sang one of his
favorites, "O My Father" and the tears seeped from between his
closed lids as he listened. Only once, was mention made about
polygamy and that by Apostle George Teasdale:

Another evidence of the divinity of this work is the peace that
reigns in the families of the Saints. Even in what is called polygamy,
while it is difficult for persons in the world to get along with one wife,
and even among us, it will be found that there is more trouble in
monogamous families than among those who have received the
celestial law of marriage. This is accounted for by the fact that this
people come here for the love of God, and they try to claim the
blessings promised to those who seek first the Kingdom of God and
His righteousness. (L.D.S. Historical Archives, *Deseret Semi-Weekly
News*, April 8, 1884, p. 2.)

Being under the sound of the voice of the General Authorities
bathed his spirit in a warm glow, and difficult problems seemed to
be clearer by the time conference was over.

On the train going home he was lost in thought. He tried to
recall any reference in the blessing to the problem he was faced
with. There was that place where it mentioned he was entitled to

the blessings of Abraham, Isaac and Jacob. Did that mean he didn't have to earn them even if he was entitled to them? Then there was that sentence where it said, "inasmuch as thou wilt listen to the promptings of the monitor within thee, thy pathway shall be made clear." That alone was worth coming for. If he didn't know yet, he *would* know.

The usual spring work of plowing and planting relieved his mind somewhat. It was good to use muscle and brawn for a change. Then at the monthly priesthood meeting in May, President Budge outlined a tree-planting program for the whole valley, and encouraged the bishops to get it going in their respective wards. He recommended especially a tree called "Balm of Gilead", said it would grow in high, cold climates. "Well," thought Amos, "I could use a little balm of Gilead right now." He planted one of the trees on the south side of his house.

It was time for quarterly stake conference before he had time to turn around. Joseph F. Smith and A.H. Cannon were to be the conference visitors from Salt Lake. He had special reverence for Apostle Joseph F.

As he rode his horse toward Paris that twelve miles in the early spring morning, he noticed the greening grain fields, yet untouched by frost. Maybe there would be a good crop this year. The air was brisk and his buckskin coat felt comfortable. It was good to be alive! It would be fun to see Ed Austin and Ira Nebeker as usual. President Budge was a man whom he respected and admired though he had never felt the degree of warmth and closeness that existed between him and President Rich. He felt a pang of loneliness at the thought of him. What a great man he had been! He was a splendid pattern for one's life and he would never be able to repay him for his understanding kindness. He would always be grateful, too, for his friendship with President Rich's son, Joseph, who had baptized him in 1868. But Joseph had fallen on evil times himself. A Church court had recently excommunicated him. There had been a long period of drifting away, difficulties with Church authorities and personal troubles. "What a tragedy!" thought Amos.

People were arriving from all directions in buggies, wagons, on horseback or afoot. Greeting friends and neighbors was always a joy, and they were all one big family in the valley. President Budge saw him at the door and shook hands, asking him to come to the stand and give the benediction at the close of the morning meeting. The visitors also shook hands with him as he made his way to the stand. Well, things were going well today, so far, and his heart swelled within him in gratitude.

The speakers were aware of the growing spirit of persecution, and encouraged the Saints to calmness and continued righteous living. The effect of the Edmunds law was mentioned, and the people were counseled to vote at the coming fall elections, if they were allowed to do so. President Cannon's words fell bullet-like on Amos' ears. "We cannot ignore the principle of plural marriage with impunity!" Then, as if to emphasize the message, Joseph F. Smith continued. "Speaking of plural marriage, we want every man to do what he knows to be right. Those who have been married in the House of the Lord, have covenanted to keep the whole law and if they don't do so, they are covenant breakers." Amos found it difficult at the close of the meeting to make his legs walk as far as the pulpit, or his voice to speak a few words of benediction, but he somehow managed to do so.

Well, he had gotten his answer. Now the rest was up to him. He'd have to talk to Cate as soon as he could bring himself to mention it. Meantime he would be going to Logan for the temple dedication in a few days, so there wouldn't be time till after that. Anything to postpone it.

The Saints in northern Utah and southern Idaho had looked forward to this day for the proverbial seven years. On this May 17, 1884, their hearts were melted with gratitude and thanksgiving as their eyes beheld the magnificent fortress-like castle on the hill overlooking Cache Valley. Wilford Woodruff had prophesied twenty years earlier there would be a temple built on this spot.

For many, the sight of the temple was the first glimpse of the results of their scrimping and saving and widows' mites. Gifts known as "labor donations" made up of muscle and brawn and strength, of time away from their own fields and farms, formed the basis of what now stood before them in beautiful reality. Other contributions such as livestock, merchandise, farm produce and cash had been offered unselfishly by generous hearts, to bring to pass this great result.

Bear Lake Stake's share, Amos remembered, was twenty-eight men and six teams, which seemed like a lot. Each man stayed a month and was replaced by another one so everybody had a chance to help. When Amos' turn came, he didn't see how he could leave home that long, since he had just been put in the bishopric. So Silas said he would go in his place. He was only sixteen but he was strong and husky. He was lucky to be alive about three weeks later. The men were cutting and hauling timber and one of the big trees fell crooked and Silas and two other men were in the way. He was hurt the worst, but after a few days off, he went back to work again as if nothing had happened. Sometimes it was hard to get enough men to work when they were needed most.

What pleased Amos most was to find out that a good many of his Indian friends had volunteered to help on the building. They mixed mortar and plaster, slacked lime and did other odd jobs and felt it was an honor to be allowed to work on the House of the Lord.

As Amos entered the sacred building, the same mantle of warmth enveloped him as he felt when he and Cate went to the Endowment House together. His eyes tried to take in everything, the soft hand-woven carpets; the intricately carved woodwork and gold-leaf plaster; staircases like an endless spiral stretching up, up, up with no evident support; and arching ceilings lifting his soul to the God who created him and whom he worshipped. Truly, this *was* the House of the Lord!

He and his two dear friends, Ira and Ed, were ushered upstairs together to the fourth floor Assembly room, which could seat fifteen hundred people. Amos looked upward to the thirty-foot ceiling; to the tall narrow, arched windows on the north and south sides of the room, and to the elevated platform at the east end with three pulpits with armchairs behind, reserved for officers of the Melchizedek Priesthood. Then his eyes swept to the far end where a duplicate set of pulpits on a slightly lower dias were provided for the Aaronic Priesthood officers. Down in the body of the assembly room where the three of them sat together, were the swivel chairs which could be turned to face whichever priesthood group was presiding and speaking.

They were each handed a program, on the back of which was printed the remarks of President Brigham Young made seven years before when the site of the temple was dedicated. This spiritual giant was now gone.

> We have dedicated this spot of ground upon which we expect to erect a temple in which to administer the ordinances of the House of God. Into this house, when it is completed, we expect to enter to enjoy the blessings of the Priesthood and receive our anointings, our endowments and our sealings. From the architect, to the boy who

carries the drinking water, to the men that work on the building, we wish them to understand that wages are entirely out of the question. We are going to build a House for ourselves and we shall expect the brethren and sisters, neighborhood after neighborhood, ward after ward, to turn out their proportion of men to come here and labor as they shall be notified by the proper authorities.

We can carry this temple forward with our labor without any burden to ourselves if our hearts are in the work, and we will be blessed abundantly in doing so. We will be better off in our temporal affairs when it is completed than when we commenced, and than we would be if we did not build it.

I feel to bless you according to the power and keys of the Holy Priesthood bestowed upon me and my brethren with me, heart and hand, and all the Saints feel to say 'Amen.'

Brethren and sisters, awake and lay these things to heart. *Seek the Lord to know His mind and will and when you ascertain it, also have the will to do it.* God bless you. Amen. (Talmage, *The House of the Lord*, pp. 217-19.)

Amos recognized again that those last words were especially for him. A hush fell over the crowded assembly as President Taylor and his counselors, George Q. Cannon and Joseph F. Smith, took their places at the east end of the room. He wasn't sure whether the music came from another room or from heaven itself. The climax came when the nearly two thousand Saints at a signal, stood and shouted three times as with one voice: "Hosanna! Hosanna! Hosanna! to God and the Lamb! Amen! Amen! Amen!"

The Three Muskateers, a little older and a little wiser, and much more humble, were again pledging "all for one and one for all," only in a more sacred and spiritual way than ever before.

Chapter Nineteen
The Gift of Tongues

Apostle George Teasdale spoke in stake priesthood meeting in August. The words burned deep and unforgettably. "We must all understand fully the covenant. It is fallacy for people to suppose that they will be saved in the Celestial Kingdom of God and that their union will be perpetuated throughout eternity provided they are sealed by the Lord's anointed over the altar and they still ignore the principle of plural marriage. They might just as well have been married 'until death do us part.' We cannot officiate for our dead if we are disobedient. Our acts will be null and void. We must be honest with ourselves and with God." (Paris Idaho Stake Minutes, Melchizedek Priesthood. LDS Archives)

It was Fall again and the calendar said October, 1884. Mail was always the high point of Amos' day and now more so than ever since he agreed to be mailman. As he jogged along on his horse toward Bennington, having picked up the mail sack from the daily train in Montpelier, he thought of the difference between Pony Express days, and this leisurely ride each day. Until the railroad came through two years ago, they were lucky to get a weekly post.

It was exciting to sort through the letters and packages and papers when he dumped the sack on the table in the little post office in Bennington, especially when he spied something addressed to him. But even if there wasn't anything, he could always skim through the headlines of any newspaper he found in the pile. The printed word held a fascination for him which he couldn't resist. It represented a world of wonder and adventure, a window to the outside, beyond Joe's Gap, Old Baldy, and the closed-in hills of Bear Lake Valley. But he recognized headlines heavy with evil portents of the future for him and his family and the Bear Lake Saints.

But today was his lucky day, for there was a letter postmarked Logan, Utah, and addressed to Mr. Amos R. Wright. Leaving the rest of the mail to be sorted later, he tore open the envelope. He didn't recognize the flowing Spencerian handwriting, so he glanced at the signature at the bottom of the page. *Moses Thatcher*, Quorum of the Twelve Apostles. His heart skipped a beat as he recognized this was no ordinary letter.

Dear Brother Wright:

This will inform you that I and a party of six Elders will be leaving Logan on Friday, Oct. 17th, to go on a brief mission to the Wind River Agency, Wyoming Territory, having been directed by President John Taylor to visit Chief Washakie and determine the best way to help him and his tribe now that many of them have been baptized.

Brother Jim Brown, a Lamanite from the Malad Washakie Farm has promised to join us at Paris on Sunday, the 19th. Will you arrange to meet our party at Montpelier Canyon, four miles above town on Monday morning and proceed with us to Wind River? We will probably be gone three weeks or a month. You will need a pack horse in addition to a saddle pony, together with bedding, camp outfit and food to last that long.

Please reply as soon as possible to confirm the receipt of this letter. President Taylor specified that you be asked to go with this party as Interpreter, if at all possible since the success of this mission will depend on effective communication with the Indians.

Your brother in the Gospel,
Moses Thatcher, Quorum of the Twelve.

Amos glanced at the calendar. It was already the ninth. There'd be barely time to reply and get ready to go. Most of the harvesting was done. He'd have to get Johnny to carry the mail and maybe Winnie or Addie could distribute it.

Cate would see to the chores with the help of the boys. He'd have to ride Toshats, who wasn't as spry as he used to be. He didn't have a pack animal. Maybe Brother Phelps would let him take one of his. His counselors would have to take over in the Ward till he got back. He was naturally pleased that President Taylor wanted him to go as interpreter. It was always good to feel needed, and especially by the President of the Church.

The election was coming up in November and he would be running as representative from Bear Lake County again. He ought to be back by then, if possible. It would be shaving things pretty close, but he couldn't help it if he wasn't back, so no use worrying.

Cate took the news without comment and planned a wash day for the sixteenth. No, that wouldn't work, that was a Sunday. She'd have to wash on Saturday that week so Mose would have some clean clothes. She could bake bread the same day and send that and some of her good, aged cheese along which he was so fond of, and maybe some smoked ham and whatever else he needed. She could tell he was excited and glad to be going.

Amos sighted the party at the rendezvous at Montpelier Canyon without difficulty. Brother Thatcher explained the plan. "You and James will be going directly to the Agency. I have bought some presents for Washakie, some shirts, shawls, handkerchiefs, etc., so you can put them on your pack animal, along with grain for the horses and your camp gear. The rest of us will go to Star Valley to look it over as a possible future settlement for the Saints, and then meet you there in ten days, or not more than twelve. It may be dangerous to be seen by the agent or the soldiers, so be careful. I suggest you call a meeting with Washakie and the leading men of the tribe. I understand you baptized over 300 of them four years ago. Find out how they feel about reservation living by now, and about the Gospel. Explain our desire to help them. Propose to them a system something like the Malad-Washakie colony, where they could learn to farm instead of leading their old nomadic life. If some of the chiefs want to come back with you, I'll meet with them then. Follow the guidance of the spirit and then be prepared to report to me." They agreed on a place to meet ten days later.

Amos explained that there were two routes to the agency. "There is an Indian trail through the Wind River Mountains about 180 miles from here. The other goes by way of Lander Road, Green River and South Pass, which is about 240 miles." Brother Thatcher thought the short route would be best, provided the trail wasn't obscured by snow, but to use their best judgment.

The weather had cleared after the storms of Sunday and Monday, so the two men shook hands and Amos and Jim waved goodbye to the rest of the party.

All went well the first day, but things started to happen the morning after. Jim had a hard time catching his horse. He managed to get the saddle on after the pony did a lot of snorting and kicking. But the minute Jim hit the saddle the horse was off like a shot, kicking and bucking like a wild zebra. Jim would have hit the ground after the first jolt, but as he tumbled off, his left foot caught in the stirrup and the horse dragged him over fallen timber, rocks and gullies, scattering his gun and personal belongings everywhere. Amos finally caught the horse and released Jim, who by then was badly bruised and in no shape to travel. It took a couple of hours to recover the scattered articles and persuade the injured Indian to try to ride again. The horse seemed to have calmed down by then, and they finally got started, with Jim barely able to sit in the saddle.

They hadn't gone more than a couple of miles when the pack horse showed signs of giving out. He wasn't heavily loaded, but he got slower and slower and finally laid down in the trail and refused to move. After trying everything they could think of to get him going again, they finally gave up and cached the pack, consisting of camp outfit, grain and most of their bedding. They left the animal looking more dead than alive. It would soon be dark and hard to follow the trail so they decided to take the longer route southeast of Star Valley and keep riding even though they couldn't see much. They soon realized they were completely lost and had to wait for daylight before finding the road again.

That many misfortunes in a row couldn't "just happen," and by this time Amos was sure it was "the devil himself, bigger than a mountain." But that wasn't the end. At Piney, near Green River, Amos' horse took sick. They stopped at a lonely cabin whose owner agreed to look after Jim's injuries, and doctor him and the sick horse, while Amos took Jim's horse and went on alone. He strapped the Indian gifts and one blanket behind and put a hunk of cheese in his pocket and took off.

As soon as he got his feet in the stirrups he realized he was on the hurricane deck of a cayuse pony. His experience with express broncos saved him from a fate similar to Jim's, as the ornery critter tried every way to get rid of his rider, but without success. After about a dozen bucks and thirty miles hard riding, he began to calm down. Amos felt sorry for the beast in spite of his meanness and thought he'd stop long enough to give him a drink and a chance to graze. He unsaddled and hobbled him with a makeshift rope and turned him loose, while he stretched out on the hard ground and fell asleep at once.

He awoke with a start wondering where he was. He didn't know how long he had slept but the horse was nowhere in sight. After an hour or two of fruitless searching he decided the horse must have broken the rope hobble and never stopped running. Tying the bundle of presents for Washakie on his back, and leaving the saddle behind, he took off afoot and walked for what seemed an eternity, resting only when he was completely spent.

Climbing up a knoll, he saw smoke drifting out of a tepee. He was so glad to see a sign of life he began to walk toward it. He stopped in his tracks when he heard a voice within him say: "Don't go that way, those are enemies." He turned around not daring to go on.

He estimated he traveled about forty miles, which seemed more like a hundred, before he came to a lone Indian lodge. The owner let him take a horse, and have a bite to eat. He thankfully proceeded via South Pass till he reached the agency at two o'clock in the morning. He found he'd been on the way for seven days and nights.

He managed to get in touch with Tabonashier and Ohata without arousing the suspicion of anyone at the agency. They ministered tenderly to Amos' blistered feet and shrunken stomach and laid him on their best buffalo robes for a day and a night and a day. They told him they were first and second counselors to Washakie; that Washakie had gone on a two-month hunting trip in the Owl-Creek Mountains. The back-packed presents would have to await his return.

What a devilish trip it had been. A pure nightmare all the way. This was a complete switch from his mission four years earlier. It didn't make sense and he wondered what he'd done wrong. There was no time to lose if he got back in time to meet Brother Thatcher. Tosha called together twelve other leading men for a council meeting and the fifteen Indians sat cross-legged in a circle awaiting Amos' pleasure.

He opened the meeting with prayer, asking that good might come from their being together; that their tongues might be loosed; that they would have a meeting of minds and find a solution to their problems. The Shoshone words flowed freely from his lips as he prayed. A quiet peace settled over the group as Amos explained the purpose of his visit.

"President Taylor, the Mormon Chief, has sent me to give a message to Washakie, but since he is gone, I'll tell you and then you can tell him when he gets back.

"First, I'd like to hear what is on your minds and what you have been doing since I was here four years ago. I have thought of you often since then and wished I could talk to you again. I am glad to see you have made Washakie your president, and 'Tabby' first counselor and Ohata second counselor. You also have twelve councilmen. That is good. President Taylor will be pleased when I tell him. You couldn't have done this four years ago before you were baptized and some of you received the priesthood. You know it has changed the way you think and feel. Isn't that true?" The Indians nodded. "But sometimes you let the bad spirit get back inside and then you think and feel like you did before you joined the Church. This sometimes happens to me, too. But I can get the good feeling again when I tell the Lord I'm sorry for what I've done wrong, and ask him to let his holy spirit return. So can you."

Then Amos told them what happened to him on his way to the agency. "But I knew I must get here and see and talk to you so I could bring you President Taylor's words. The good Spirit is here with us now and we will understand what each other says. Now it is your turn to talk."

Tabonishier began. "What Peah Tibo says is true. When I have the good spirit I feel good inside. If Wright could stay with us and tell us more, it would help. Since you were here before, some of us have dreams. Our Fathers, way back, tell us the Book of Mormon is true, that Joseph Smith is a good medicine man. Washakie knows this, too. But now the bad spirit has come again.

"Last summer sixteen Crow Chiefs came to see Washakie. Washin-don and the Indian Agent made them move from their Rose Bud country to the Big Horn. They don't like that. That was their home for many years. Now they are what you say: homesick. Washin-don gives them beans and rice but they like elk and buffalo and fish. They can't hunt off the reservation when the agent says no, or the soldiers will put them in jail, and beat them. The Crows came to ask Washakie to let the Shoshones fight Washin-don; fight all whites. We can't win. But it is better, we think, to fight and die than do what Washin-don and the Agent and soldiers say."

"'Tabby' stopped talking a minute, but he wasn't through. Then he began again. "The Shoshones feel like the Crows. Now we have to do what Washin-don and the agent says. We want to do like the Crows say: fight, *even if we die*. That is better than this way. But Washakie says no. He showed the Crows a picture of his white friend, Brigham Young. Washakie told us he was a Mormon Chief. He talked straight. Wright is a Mormon. He talks straight. Brigham Young is dead, now. Taylor is Peah Tibo for the Mormons. Washakie said, 'I will ask Taylor what to do. Wait till Taylor tells us. Then we will do what he says.' So the Crows went back to the Big Horn to wait."

Amos watched the faces of the men sitting in the circle. His heart went out to these dark-skinned brethren and he could not restrain his tears as he listened. They were saying in their tongue what all men have said from the beginning and which Patrick Henry said for Americans, "Give me liberty or give me death."

Then Ohata spoke. "What 'Tabby' says is straight. Washakie says 'Don't fight. There is a better way. Wait till Taylor says what to do.' But Washakie sometimes wants to fight, too. He fought once himself. The agent and soldiers made him mad. A soldier captain wanted to buy land from Washakie. He wanted to have reservation land for a cattle ground. He said he would give Washakie money. Washakie said, 'No, this land is Washin-don's, not mine.' The soldier kept after him. 'You sell me land, I will give you money.' One day the soldier saw Washakie in the post-trading store and asked again. Washakie said, 'Give me whiskey and I'll talk about it.' The captain told the trader to bring out five bottles. He did. Washakie took the cork out of one and drank all of the whiskey at once. Then he threw the empty bottle and broke all four full ones, and the whiskey ran on the floor. Washakie took his pistol out and pointed it at the soldier captain. 'You want everything the Indian has. I am an old man and would as soon die now as any time. Bring your soldiers and I will kill them all!' Then he hit the soldier over the head with his gun, aimed it at him and drove him out of the store. The agent and Washin-don didn't bother Washakie. They knew the old man meant what he said and would do it."

It was Tasha's turn next. "Why won't the Mormons help us fight the other white men? Gentiles, you call them? They are your enemies, too. They hate you and would kill you if they could. You are cowards not to fight back. They drove you Mormons out of your homes and you had to come here. They killed your chiefs Joseph and Hyrum. Now you say 'don't fight.' Tell us why!"

Amos realized after hearing the Indians' story, why he had to get to the agency when he did. No wonder he had met all that opposition. Well, he made it and now he would try to see that they understood the message he had for them. A wrong word or impression could light a torch that would ignite the pent-up hatred of these people into a war nothing could stop. The Crows were even more volatile. Such a war would wipe out all the good feelings that Brigham Young had built up so carefully in the past thirty-seven years and the Indians with it. The whites would be massacred before help could arrive. Bear Lake Valley would probably be attacked first.

With a prayer in his heart, he began. "Thank you for telling me about the Crows and Utes and Washakie. I needed to know. You have told me you are waiting to know what President Taylor says, and that you will do what he tells Washakie to do. He has sent me to carry his word. I am his messenger. He says, 'Don't fight now, even if they treat you like prisoners and slaves. Wait. Be patient. Trust Taylor's word. He is wise because he speaks for God. Someday God will fight your battles for you. You are not strong enough to win now, and he doesn't want you to die. He wants you to live, even if you think there is nothing to live for. You are his children and he loves you.

"There is a better way for you now. I will tell you. Mormons know how to plow land, plant seeds and grow food. They know how to grow cows instead of buffalo and deer. They will show you how. President Taylor will buy land near the reservation. He will send Mormons like me to teach you to work. Then you can have better than beans and rice to eat and you won't have to be afraid of the agent and the soldiers and Washindon. Some Shoshones and Bannocks are already doing this down by Bear River. They like it. You can go down and see for yourselves and they will tell you that it is good. They call their camp, Washakie, after your chief."

"We can't go off the reservation," said Ohata. "The agent says no, Washin-don says no. It would take too long to learn how to live like white men. We would starve while we were learning. If we can't fight we will have to starve or all move onto our Mormon friends and they wouldn't like that!"

"You ask why Mormons won't fight other white men? They are our brothers, like you are my brothers. The Great Spirit, Jesus Christ, tells us it is wrong to fight and kill. He says, 'Love your enemies. Do good to them and pray for them instead of killing them.' If that sounds too hard to understand, then just believe that President Taylor speaks straight, because he speaks for God and that is what he says. Will you all promise to tell Washakie what I have said when he comes back? Tell him fighting is the wrong way." They nodded. "Will you promise that you will not go to war against the whites? President Taylor sent me to tell you not to."

He waited. Finally, he said, "All who will promise this, raise your right hand and say, yes."

One at a time, and slowly, the hands went up, all but one, and they solemnly nodded their heads and said "ess."

"Thank you. I know you talk straight and I can trust you to keep your word. I must go now. Another Mormon chief is waiting for me in Star Valley. If any of you want to see and talk to him, I will take you with me now. He will tell you the same things I have said."

"We can't leave the reservation this time of year without making the agent mad. We will meet your chief next Spring at Green River and have a long talk," said Tosha, speaking for the others. Amos explained he could not promise that Chief Thatcher could come then, "But President Taylor will not forget you and will send someone to help you." Amos asked "Tabby" to offer a prayer before they parted. The first counselor said a simple prayer in Shoshone as he had been taught, and the meeting was over. Amos had done everything he could think of to change their minds and hearts from war to peace. He would report to Brother Thatcher when he got to Star Valley.

The Indians gave him a good horse to ride home on, and said he could keep it till someone called for it next summer at Bennington. They also gave him some dried elk meat and some berries to eat when he got hungry. The squaws and papooses came out of their tepees to wave goodbye to Peah Tibo Wright and he waved back.

When he got to Piney he found Jim feeling much better. His horse, Toshats, seemed to be all right again, too. Jim rode him and the two met Brother Thatcher's party as agreed. They also found the pack horse on the road and after giving him a dose of Jamaica Ginger, which Jim's "doctor" gave him, he was able to carry the cache they had left, all the way back to Bennington with no trouble at all. They never did see old "Buckaroo" again.

Brother Thatcher listened carefully as Amos recounted his strange story, making notes so he would remember, and promised to write a report to President Taylor as soon as he returned to Logan. This he did in a nine-page letter, just as Amos had told it to him.

As the party rode toward Bear Lake, Amos had time to ponder the strange events just past. Those horses acting the way they did, reminded him of Father Jonathan's experience on his way to see Joseph Smith at Nauvoo. What if he'd given up and gone back home without seeing the Prophet? And what if he, himself, hadn't kept going till he delivered President Taylor's message? Would the Indians fight or keep their word? The voice of the patriarch in Salt Lake came into his mind: "It is thy duty as an Elder in Israel to be a peacemaker among thine associates, that peace may reign in thy circle." Amos marveled. How did President Taylor know the Indians were on the verge of war? A wave of emotion swept over him at the thought of these adopted children of his. Speaking their tongue was a gift to be grateful for, simple as that might seem. He would always love them, no matter what.

Chapter Twenty
The Test Oath Act

"The election campaign of 1880 in Idaho produced a number of anti-Mormon rumors and tales that foreshadowed more bitter things to come. Crude attempts to stir up anti-Mormon feeling were made, and thus influence the coming election. On October 6, the Oneida anti-Mormons formed an 'Independent Party' convention at Malad. They said they would support any candidate who would be independent, apparently meaning independent of the Mormons. Its platform declared that the new party would 'fight to the bitter end, by all honorable means, the efforts of any religious sect to trail a free people in the dust at the wheels of a priestly chariot.'" (Blackfoot (Idaho) Register, Oct. 9, 1880.)

This was an indication of the aims and methods to be used with great success later in the anti-Mormon movement. The two issues used most successfully against the L.D.S. Church were the accusation that it told its members how to vote, thus dominating political matters in the territory, and by practicing polygamy they were a disgrace to a Christian nation.

When the 1880 Idaho Legislature met December 13, Governor John B. Neil proposed that a law be passed so that Idaho could do under its own law, what it could not do under the Federal Anti-Bigamy law: That is allow officers to arrest and have convicted in the court, any person preaching or favoring the doctrine of plural marriage. The law, he said, should specify that evidence of cohabitation (actually living together) could be accepted as proof of a polygamous marriage.

The year of 1880 was an important date for another reason. Frederick Thomas Dubois came to Idaho at that time and skillfully conducted a vendetta against what he claimed was undue political influence by the Mormon Church. He was young; a recent graduate of Yale University, and though claiming no political ambitions, his actions belied the claim. He was soon appointed as United States Marshal for Idaho. This gave him his chance to build an anti-Mormon organization.

By 1882 this was a well-oiled machine, with Dubois as the clever operator. Passage of the Edmunds Act, March 23, 1882, gave him the tool by which he could destroy Mormon political strength in Idaho. As U.S. Marshal he made many more arrests and convictions than did his predecessor, but he could not or did not by the Edmunds law alone, force the Mormons to give up plural marriage, or make them desert the Democratic Party.

Destruction of polygamy as a moral evil was not his real objective, as he admitted in writing. What he really wanted was to make the Democrats a minority party in Idaho. Then, sponsored by the Republicans, gain statehood for Idaho, thus placing the state under that party's control.

He said he didn't hate the Mormons. What he did hate was the fact that they were so united and that the Church had the power to dictate how and what its members did under the guise of religion.

His words on the subject were:

> Those of us who understood the situation were not nearly so much opposed to polygamy as we were to the political domination of the Church. We realized however, that we could not make those who did not come actually in contact with it, understand what this political domination meant. We made use of polygamy in consequence, as our great weapon of offense and to gain recruits to our standard. There was a universal detestation of polygamy, and inasmuch as the Mormons openly defended it, we were given a very effective weapon with which to attack. (Grenville H. Gibbs, "Mormonism in Idaho Politics, 1880-1890," *Utah Historical Quarterly*, vol. XXI, no. 4, October 1953, pp. 294-5.)

At the 1882 election a man could not be prevented from voting unless he had been convicted of polygamy. Only a few voters were kept away from the polls as a result. Bear Lake County, being almost 100 percent Mormon, could keep on sending Mormons to the legislature, which they did until a way was found to disfranchise all of them. By 1884 the anti-Mormon campaign was working smoothly and effectively.

Dubois and his deputies relentlessly chased "polygs" and "co-habs" and used any and all means to arouse anti-Mormon sentiment. Bingham County, a new voting district, was strongly anti-Mormon. Fees and expense account padding played a big influence in finding "sympathetic" witnesses. This, in brief, was the condition which Amos faced when he returned from his Wind River mission in October 1884.

In the months just past, he had a series of spiritual experiences which had moved him deeply and increased his faith that God lived and was mindful of him. He knew his prayers had been answered many times and that he had often been protected from danger. Now he was about to be plunged into a bitter political arena with no holds barred; a totally telestial experience. The rules were stacked against him and he had little chance of winning. Should he give up without further effort? Politics could be dirty business. Maybe he should clear out while there was still time.

Then he remembered the "what-if game" he often played by himself. What-if he hadn't kept going when he was having such a bad time getting to Wind River? What-if he had refused to go on a mission to Fort Lemhi? What-if he had said no when he was called to settle in Bear Lake? He'd see this thing through. Win or lose!

He got back from Wyoming a few days before the election. He made a speech to an enthusiastic crowd in "Pelier" the night before the second Tuesday in November 1884. When the polls closed next evening he and William N.B. Shepherd were elected as representatives from Bear Lake County and James E. Hart was a member of the council or senate of the territorial legislature.

By this time the fight against the Mormons was at its height. Oneida County included most of the southwestern part of the territory and had elected four delegates who were either Mormons or friendly to them. The opposition party was badly beaten at the polls, but the Mormons held that William B. Thews, auditor and recorder for the county, while working late in his office on the night of November 26, was set upon by a bunch of anti-Mormon office seekers, among them being Harkness, Smith and Bennett. They held a gun on him while they forced him to make out a set of election certificates for all the candidates of their party.

The anti-Mormons said they didn't use any force. "Mr. Thews," they swore "was asleep at his desk when they knocked at his locked office door. So one of them climbed through the transom, unlocked the door and let the others in. There was no difficulty in getting Mr. Thews to make out the certificates since it was obvious, they said, that they had won the election fair and square."

Consequently, there were two sets of delegates to the territorial legislature who appeared and claimed seats. The "Anti's" of the Democrats joined the Republicans in the house and seated the anti-Mormon party from Oneida County. This unfair proceeding gave the anti-Mormon party a large working majority so that during the whole of the session, every measure designed to injure the Mormons politically, and otherwise, passed the legislature easily. There were only three Mormons in the House, including W.C. Martindale of Cassia County and the two from Bear Lake County. James Hart was in the Senate.

These were some of the issues which Amos faced as he left Bennington in mid-winter to attend the 1884-85 session of the legislature in Boise. He arrived December 7 and the House met the next day. After preliminary formalities in which he and his friend W.N.B. Shepherd participated, "Kentucky" Smith introduced what later became the Idaho Test Oath Act. This was more extreme by far than the Edmunds Law. It provided that any qualified voter could challenge the right of a person offering to vote, and such person was then required to sign the oath included in the Act, if he still wanted to vote. The Test Oath was as follows:

You do solemnly swear or affirm that you are a male citizen of the United States over the age of twenty-one years; that you have actually resided in this territory for four months last past; and in this county thirty days; that you are not a bigamist or polygamist; that you are not a member of any order, organization or association which teaches, advises, counsels or encourages its members, devotees, or any other person, to commit the crime of bigamy or polygamy, or any other crime defined by law, as a duty arising or resulting from membership in such order, organization or association, or which practices bigamy or polygamy or plural or celestial marriage, as a doctrinal rite of such organization; that you do not, either publicly or privately or in any manner whatever, teach, advise or encourage any person to commit the crime of bigamy or polygamy, or any crime defined by law, either as a religious duty or otherwise; that you regard the Constitution of the United States and the laws thereof and of this territory as interpreted by the courts, as the supreme law of the land, the teachings of any order, organization or association to the contrary notwithstanding, and that you have not previously voted at this election so help you God. (Land of the Sky Blue Water, Russell R. Rich p. 146)

Just before the vote on the bill was taken in the Senate, James E. Hart, the council's youngest member and the delegate from Bear Lake County, received permission to speak.

"Gentlemen," he said. "I propose an amendment to the bill before the council, which is to read as follows: 'You do solemnly swear that you are not a bigamist or a polygamist or that you do not cohabit with any other woman who is not your wife.'"

Upon hearing this motion, Judge Brierley of Alturas County jumped to the floor and shouted: "My G..., gentlemen, we can't accept Hart's proposal. That would disfranchise all of us!"

Hart replied: "No. It wouldn't disfranchise all of us. I married a good, pure Mormon girl in a place that I consider sacred, where we promised to be true to each other and, so help me God, I intend to do just that."

Judge Brierley thus admitted the lawmakers' guilt but the amendment was rejected. The Anti-Mormon Commission in Utah got around the difficulty by using the words: "that you do not cohabit with any other woman in the marriage relationship."

The United States Supreme Court ruled in April 1885, that it was legal to exclude Mormons from serving on polygamy trials and unlawful co-habitation, because they would naturally be biased. The method of selecting jurors by Dubois which had been questioned as unconstitutional was also upheld. Dubois hoped that Mormons wouldn't even try to vote in the 1886 election in defiance of the Test Oath law.

An example of his skill as a Mormon-hunter is the story he told of what happened in the winter of 1885. A group of his deputies was sent to Paris, Idaho, across the high mountains from Oxford through deep snow. They got there early one morning. Seven or eight arrests were made and all the men convicted. The Mormons had such a good warning system worked out that it was very hard to catch the wanted men, but this method worked.

Dubois boasted that his juries "would convict Jesus Christ." He was called before Judge Morgan, but explained he only meant that any polygamist who was caught would be convicted, even Jesus Christ himself. The Judge accepted his explanation.

Each evening after the session was over, the four out-numbered Mormons got together and talked about what had happened that day and what they could do next.

"We need to be heard, but that's next to impossible," said

Hart. "It was a miracle that I got the floor at all. They simply ignored me when I asked to be recognized. Of course, it's no wonder. They were afraid of what I might say. My proposed amendment really threw them into a tizzy."

Shepherd said he had an idea. "Why don't we get Amos here to give a speech? Ask for permission to speak just before the third reading of the bill. That will be coming up in a few days. He could at least present our side and it might do some good. We can't just sit on our hands."

"I don't think they'd let us talk. We wouldn't have a chance," said Martindale.

"At least we can try," answered Shepherd.

Accordingly, the four men went to the speaker's office early next morning before the regular session began. They had to cool their heels for an hour or so, as the clerk kept putting them off saying Mr. Baldwin was busy in a meeting. Finally, he let them in just as a group of anti-Mormons came out of the office.

"Your Honor, Mr. Baldwin, we have a petition to present if you would give us a few minutes of your time," said Hart. "All right, but make it brief. It's almost time to convene the session." The "Anti's" pricked up their ears at this and hung around. "We would like permission for Mr. Wright here to speak before the third reading of the Test Oath bill. Would you agree to recognize him at that time?"

"That would be out of order I'm afraid," said Baldwin curtly. "But I'll consider it and let you know later."

One of the hangers-on laughed and said, "Ah, why not let that country clod give us a speech. It would liven things up a little and mebbe we'd find out how to get us another wife or two, ha ha ha!," and the group joined in the raucous laughter.

"Yes," said another mocker, "We might as well be fair about this thing. Give 'em enough rope and they'll hang themselves anyhow. Come on, George tell 'em yes and we'll get set for some fun for a change. This legislatin' business gets pretty dull most of the time, you've said so yourself." So under pressure from his friends, Baldwin agreed.

Amos went to work organizing what he wanted to say. A small library was available which helped. He didn't usually use any notes, but he wrote an outline this time. Maybe he was a country clod, but he might surprise them. He recalled how Cate had begged him to dress up when he was first elected in 1882. Well, he'd *dress* like a clod.

When he met his friends the morning, he was wearing a plaid shirt, no tie, everyday pants, a beaded belt and moccasins. It was the last day of January 1885, and he said a silent prayer for help, knowing he'd need it.

A group of rowdy men ran up behind him. "There he is, that s.o.b. in the plaid shirt. He looks like he's got a dozen wives, now don't he!" Then pointing their loaded revolvers at him, one of them shouted, "This is what you'll get if you dare make a speech against the Test Oath."

Amos looked at them and replied quietly, "Go ahead. But I intend to defend my people so long as I have a breath left in my body." His manner, as much as what he said, seemed to cow them and they put up their guns and disappeared down the hall.

Mr. Baldwin tapped the gavel three times to bring the session to order. Amos felt strangely calm despite his encounter with the rabble, and when the speaker recognized him, he stood and surveyed the hostile House as he began to speak.

"Mr. Speaker, Gentlemen: We are about to vote on a proposal to take away some of the Constitutional rights of a large body of citizens of this territory. You know them as Mormons. You have lived among them for years and know them to be law-abiding and patriotic citizens of this great Republic. As such, they expect to be protected in their liberty and Constitutional rights.

"The founders of the Republic were afraid of *parties of the people* as much as they were of a king. Madison said in 1788, 'Wherever there is an interest and power to do wrong, wrong will generally be done, and just as likely by a *powerful and interested party* as by a powerful and interested prince.'

"Our ancestors, called Pilgrims, fled to America because they were persecuted for their religious beliefs. They set up a government of free men so they could worship God according to the dictates of their own conscience. Strangely today some of their descendants have become religious persecutors themselves.

"Article I of the Bill of Rights states: 'Congress shall make no law respecting an establishment of religion, or prohibiting the free exercise thereof.' Mormons believe the Constitution under which they live was established by God, by the hands of wise men whom he raised up unto this very purpose. Its Founders acknowledged his hand as they met to write that document, sentence by sentence.

"The Courts of the United States up to this time have quite clearly established that if a law takes for granted that a person is guilty, it implies that he is disloyal if he will not take an oath swearing he is loyal. Thus, it judges that person guilty with no hearing before a court, and is a bill of attainder and so is unconstitutional. We contend that denying a man the right to vote because of what he might have done in the past and making him swear he didn't do it before he can vote or hold office, is a bill of attainder.

"The Constitution also says, 'No ex-post-facto law shall be passed.' An act is ex-post-facto when it makes a crime out of what was not a crime when it was done, or when it makes the crime greater than it was when committed, or when it inflicts a greater punishment than was lawful at the time the crime was done; or when it changes the rules of evidence in order to secure a conviction; or when it in effect deprives the accused of some protection to which he had become entitled.

"The Framers of the Constitution saw how unjust such punishment was, so they put in not only one prohibition but two, against bills of attainder. One was to curb the national government and the other was to prevent a state government from doing the same thing. Jefferson wrote, 'The tyranny of the *legislatures* is the most formidable dread at present and will be for many years.'

"The statements I have just cited are mere words and sentences until they are applied to people or against men and women. And when those people include me, they become either my shield and helmet if interpreted as the Founding Fathers intended, or an arrow pointed at my heart if used wrongly or unfairly.

"Who are these Mormon people? Where did they come from? What is their history? Why is this issue before us today?

"Like the Pilgrim Fathers, they are liberty-loving men and women and they came from every state in the Union and from Northern Europe. For half a century they have left well-established homes to gather together to worship God according to the dictates of their own conscience; to live unitedly under a leader whom they recognize as a Prophet of God. Americans are a Christian people who claim to believe the Bible. The Children of Israel worshipped the same God the Mormons believe in, and looked to prophets for guidance in their daily lives. The Mormon's prophet was Joseph Smith. He declared he received a vision in which he saw God the Father and His Son Jesus Christ and talked with them face to face as I am talking to you. He wanted to know which of all the churches he should join. The Lord told him not to join any of them, but to wait and he would later be given authority to establish a church exactly like the one Jesus Christ organized when he lived on the earth. Thus it would be a restoration of Christ's own church by authority received directly from him.

"From the moment Joseph Smith told about his vision, he was hounded, ridiculed and hated. But strangely, there were many people who joined the new Church as soon as it was set up, saying they knew it was true and demonstrated it by flocking to a gathering place so they could live under the direction and influence of this righteous leader. Kirtland, Ohio was the first gathering place. Persecution continued.

"Missouri was their next temporary home, but an order of the governor a few years later threatened their lives by extermination. The murders, house-burnings, robberies, rapes, drivings, whippings and jailings suffered by these people have never been fully told. The Crusades and the Inquisition of European history were mere preludes to what happened in our own America between 1820 and 1847.

"My father, Jonathan C. Wright, like thousands of others from America and northern Europe, was one of those early Mormons. He came from Illinois. He heard about this man Joseph Smith with his new doctrine, and went to Nauvoo to find out for himself. He did find out. He found out that Joseph Smith was a true prophet, as real as Isaiah or Moses.

"Father had been a Methodist minister making a decent living for himself and family. Why would he be so foolish as to join the Mormons? Mormon priests didn't get paid for what they did. Yet he took his wife and three children to cast his lot with the Saints. In a few months after he was baptized, he went on a mission to preach this wonderful news to others. Converts began calling one another brother and sister like one big family, which they were: the descendants of Abraham, Isaac and Jacob and the children of Israel.

"My parents got to Nauvoo about the time the temple was being built. It was made of white stone taken from a quarry nearby and it cost a million dollars. They called it The House of the Lord. The city had been a swamp at first but the men drained it and named it Nauvoo the Beautiful. In a few years it became just that: a city of beautiful homes and parks and the next largest town in Illinois. Visitors marveled that it was so peaceful. There were no jails, no courts, no policemen, no saloons, no houses of prostitution. They asked Joseph Smith how he governed his people so well. He replied, 'I teach them correct principles and they govern themselves.'

"I was four years old when the Prophet and his brother Hyrum were murdered by a mob called soldiers. I can still see the white faces of these martyrs lying in their black velvet caskets, as Father lifted me up so I could look at them. From then on *I* was part of the story. We had to leave Nauvoo in the middle of winter and drove our ox-teams across the wide Mississippi on the ice. The weather was cold enough to freeze the river. Our enemies believed this would be the end of Mormonism now our leaders were dead. But another Prophet-leader named Brigham Young was raised up to guide us across the forbidding dry plains to a wilderness Zion in Utah.

"On the way my mother and three brothers died of exposure. Enroute, Brigham Young induced five hundred Mormon men to volunteer as soldiers in the Mexican War. They called it the Mormon Battalion which loyally served a country which had driven them out of the United States.

"The valley which Brigham Young said was 'the place' was a desert land which nobody else wanted. Even the Indians found more desirable locations. Many Saints died on the way from exposure, hunger and disease, but we found the place we believed God had prepared for us. Here we hoped at last to be free from persecution and to enjoy the liberty which American citizens had a right to expect.

"The Pioneers built a series of settlements both north and south of Salt Lake City. At the same time they began to build temples and tabernacles and meetinghouses and schools and universities and theaters, along with fences and homes and farms. All this to them was part of building the Kingdom of God on the earth. They taught their children love of country and patriotism and reverence for the flag of the United States of America, and to live in peace and harmony under the Constitution. They believed this was a land choice above all other lands. The 4th of July was being celebrated by them ten years after their arrival in the valley, when word reached Brigham Young that a 2500-man army of the United States was already enroute to Utah by order of President Buchanan. The Mormons had been accused of disobeying the laws of the country, resisting the appointed officials and destroying the court and civil records, without even having been given a chance to answer the charges against them.

"This time they did not propose supinely to surrender without resistance, knowing the charges against them were utterly false. But it was a different kind of resistance. Brigham Young proposed a scorched-earth policy. The Saints were called from all the outlying settlements to the north, to gather south of Salt Lake. They came again by ox-team, bringing their food supplies and camping equipment to last for an indefinite time. A man was left at each settlement with orders to burn houses, farms and crops if the army continued to advance. Meantime, to delay the army, scouts harassed the soldiers and burned wagon trains and supplies and ran off the cattle and horses. They were directed to avoid taking life if possible. By that time the expedition came to be known as 'Buchanan's Blunder' and the President finally sent a proclamation to Utah forgiving the Mormons, and as agreed, the army marched silently and peacefully through the streets of Salt Lake and made camp beyond the Great Salt Lake. The Saints returned to their abandoned farms and homes and villages, having won a bloodless victory.

"I have lived through these experiences myself and know whereof I speak. I walked and drove an ox-team and wagon across the plains to Utah when I was ten years old. I saw Salt Lake grow from nothing to the beautiful city it now has become. I came with my wife and two small children to Bear Lake Valley in response to a call from this same prophet-leader Brigham Young, and have endured a quarter of a century of hardship, of cold and sometimes hunger, to establish a home for me and my family. I did this, as did all faithful Latter-day Saints, because I knew it was right and true. I did it to obey what I had been taught by my father and mother and a Prophet who spoke for God. Since coming to attend this session of the legislature, I received word that two of my brothers, Seth and Lorenzo Wright have been killed by a band of Apache Indians while trying to recover cattle stolen from peaceful Mormon settlers in Arizona. They went south to make homes in the desert, as I went north, and sacrificed their lives in the process. So far my life has been spared as I have dealt with the Shoshones and Bannocks here in the north. Brigham Young's motto, 'feed them, don't fight them' has been followed with good results. The Saints are peace-loving, law-abiding, home-and-community-building people and have been since 1830.

"As to why this issue is before us now with such emotional

impact, perhaps you can answer better than I can try to tell you. Search your hearts and listen to what you hear.

"These are the people against whom this Test Oath bill is directed and who will be denied the right to vote, hold public office, or serve on a jury if it becomes law, unless they deny their religious beliefs which are as dear to them as life itself. The victims of this crusade are not criminals nor law-breakers. The men who have accepted plural marriage as a part of their religious obligations are among the most honorable men of the Latter-day Saint communities and regarded as men of honesty and good character. The women involved in this marriage system are not low-class or of brutal natures, but chaste in thought, speech, and action; refined in manners, mothers of children whom they love and care for; women who are truly queens in their own homes.

"By united effort we have built a society where the poor and needy are provided for, where families are raised and loved and cared for and where the stranger is not turned away. Surely you who have seen first hand, what we stand for will never allow such an infamous bill to become law. I appeal to your honor, your fairness, your sense of right and justice as you prepare to cast your vote. The Latter-day Saints whom I represent in this honorable body, protest this action with every fiber of their being and plead with you to search your hearts before God, that right may prevail. I thank you."

Silence hung over all as Amos sat down. A few nose-blowings and eye-wipings were evident. Nobody applauded.

The third reading of the Test Oath was then made, followed by a vote to accept or reject it. If accepted, it would be sent to the floor for final action. When the votes were counted there were seventeen ayes and seven nays, which indicated that four non-Mormons had voted with the losers. This was remarkable considering the tense and bitter situation. A young lawyer named James H. Hawley approached Amos at the close of the session and asked him where he got his education. Extending his hand he said, "That was the greatest oration I have heard in my life. Although I was risking my political career, I voted against the bill a few minutes ago." Others who heard the speech told him privately they agreed with him but didn't dare change their vote. James H. Hawley later became governor of Idaho. He was one of the best friends the Mormon people ever had in Idaho. He also remained a life-long friend of Amos Wright, always calling to see him when he came to Bear Lake Valley.

The delegates cleared out of the legislative chamber and Amos was left alone. He sat down in the chair he had occupied during the session. He was glad to have time to think and try to assess the results of his speech and of the overwhelming vote in favor of the bill after its third reading.

Fred Dubois had planned well, and so far his plan was working. The final passage of the bill was inevitable. Amos' effort to sway the delegates was a failure. But at least he had tried. Would possibly some long-range good come from what he had said? Joseph Smith declared, "Truth will cut its own way." The knife seemed pretty dull at present. He shifted himself in the padded chair and tried to part the curtains of the future.

With this law on the books, no Mormon could be elected to the legislature. Bear Lake would be unrepresented. This would be his last trip to Boise. He looked around the room. It had been a learning experience at least and learning experiences were often painful. What a disappointing bunch of men these were! How could good government come out of such an assembly? With Dubois and his henchmen in the saddle, they would successfully petition for Idaho's statehood under Republican sponsorship, and that party would come to power, which was what Dubois wanted. The Democrats, by the absence of Mormon votes, would be reduced to a minority, guaranteeing success to the Dubois plan.

No Mormon who was a true Saint would forfeit his membership in the Church to get a chance to vote, precious as that franchise was. Should the Saints continue to fight for that right even under the present circumstances? At this point there wasn't a chance of success. He suddenly thought of the Shoshones and their desire to fight for their freedom even in the face of death. He had told them, Wait! Don't fight. Give the Lord a chance. It made a difference when the shoe was on the other foot! Advice was easier to give than to take.

His mind switched then to his own problem; one which had been put on the back of the stove far too long. Should he take a plural wife? With the country on fire against polygamy, the idea seemed even more ridiculous. But he knew now he couldn't temporize or postpone a decision any longer. He'd have to face up to that mountain without further delay.

Amos pulled himself out of his daydream and his padded armchair, and walked out of the legislative hall for the last time.

The Test Oath Act was passed and became law by February 3,

1885. A plan was worked out with the consent of Church leaders whereby shortly before an election, a voter could officially have his name taken from the Church records. He could then subscribe to the Test Oath Act, vote and later be rebaptized. But this smacked of being devious and only a few tried it. One faithful member said, "I left my homeland across the ocean, left friends and loved ones. Now I have been deprived of my right to vote in my new country. I can live without voting, but I can't live without my religion. Even for a few days, I will not have my name taken from the records of the Church."

The Test Oath Act kept all members of the L.D.S. Church from voting or holding office for nearly ten years. It disfranchised a fourth of the people, almost 25,000, in the territory.

Back in Bear Lake again, Amos went to stake conference. Apostle Heber J. Grant was the Salt Lake visitor. His words were summarized by the stake clerk:

> Apostle Grant felt grateful for the Edmunds law because it brought to light those who are astride the fence and he felt glad when their true characters are known. Such men when they get in a corner are willing to bow down to Baal. There is no safe course for the Latter-day Saints only in the strict discharge of their duty no matter how unpleasant it may be. The rulers of the Nation have trampled down the Constitution, have wrested from this people all their rights and privileges guaranteed to by that sacred instrument. Our would-be reformers will be judged out of their own mouths. Those who will break their covenants and discard their wives are called 'manly Mormons'. We should be careful how we talk, through carelessness we often betray our brethren. Apostle Grant said it would be a hard matter to get gentlemen to put the law in force against the L.D.S. They get disreputable characters to carry on their work. (Minutes of Stake Conference in Bear Lake Stake, L.D.S. Archives)

Amos wondered how he might act under the circumstances. If he adopted the principle of plural marraige, he undoubtedly would have to face this problem himself. If so, he resolved he would remember Brother Grant's words.

Reaction to the legislative session in Boise was immediate, and picked up intensity as the year advanced. An item appeared in the *Deseret News* from Paris, Idaho, August 5, 1885 as follows:

> A mass meeting was held here today which was the largest and most enthusiastic political gathering that has ever been held in Bear Lake County. The large new Court House was fitted up for the occasion and was filled to overflowing, many having to stand in the corridor.

The meeting was called by the Territorial Central Committee for the purpose of expressing dissatisfaction at the present condition of affairs as they exist in Bear Lake County, caused by the unjust and unconstitutional "Test Oath Bill" which was passed by the Idaho Legislature at its last session.

The speakers at the occasion were *Amos R. Wright*, E.A. Williams, Joseph C. Rich, Wm. Walter Hogue, James Athay and R.S. Spence.

The speakers dwelt largely upon the anarchy that prevails in the county, on account of the Test Oath law that disfranchises all persons belonging to the Mormon Church. The District Court sat last week. A grand jury could not be obtained as there are not sufficient non-Mormons in the county and the Mormons all being disfranchised, it was found impossible to investigate crime, or put a stop to the lawlessness that is being perpetrated under existing circumstances.

The article continued in the wordy style of that day, which evidenced the aroused feelings of the people of Bear Lake Valley:

We are in a deplorable condition in this county. Thieves and vagabonds are plying their nefarious vocations with impunity and the law is powerless to protect life and liberty and property. Every right guaranteed to us by the Constitution of our country has been ruthlessly taken from us and our lives and property left to the march of the lawless lawbreakers without any protection or redress. The infamy of this test oath is more apparent when it is understood that one out of every thirty whom it has disfranchised and left unprotected, have broken no law and why should twenty-nine innocent persons be made to suffer for one that may or may not be guilty?

A committee of five persons were appointed by the chair to make a statement of grievances and draft a petition to President Cleveland to be circulated through the county for signatures asking him to grant us relief by removing those odious and unscrupulous partisans who have labored so diligently and successfully in bringing about the reign of misrule and anarchy that prevails at present, and appoint in their stead honest Democrats who will administer the law without fear or favor, etc.

STATEMENT AND PETITION

That the Republican Party of this Territory headed by Republican Federal Office holders entered into a conspiracy last fall to defraud the people at the polls; and by ballot-box stuffing, bribery and other corrupt methods, did steal the last Territorial Legislature and thereby made it Republican. The government of this County represented by a majority which cast four hundred and one democratic votes, is to be turned over to the rule of an insignificant minority, represented by seven Republican voters." (*Journal History*,

L.D.S. Historical Archives, Church Office Building, Salt Lake City)

Chapter Twenty-one
Decision

It was early March 1885, shortly after Amos returned from the legislature that President Budge sent word he wanted to see him. He rode his horse the twelve cold miles to Paris. Spring never came that early to Bear Lake, so he bundled up as usual in his old sheepskin coat with a bandana handkerchief tied over his head and a cap with earflaps over that. Cate knew he would be late getting back and the days were still short. She purposely delayed supper. The children were hungry and impatient when they had to wait. Those still at home ranged in age from eighteen to two. Silas and Winnie were already married and Cate and Amos were proud grandparents of three. There was grown-up Addie, and then four rambunctious boys: Russ, John, Frank and Edgar. Then came Catherine and baby Elizabeth, 'Libby' still in a highchair.

Finally, they heard their father stomping the snow off outside. When he opened the door his breath hung on the air like a fog and there were little icicles on his beard.

Cate dished up the stew and poured milk into the mugs. There was a big plate of homemade bread in the middle of the table, yellow butter in the butter dish, and some buffalo berry jam Addie had made last summer. The chairs were turned away from the table which meant everybody knelt down for evening prayer, thus purposely delaying the chance to begin eating, as the boys thought. At long last their father's prayer ended and it was time to eat. The stew bowl had to be refilled two or three times and the bread plate was always empty before everybody was satisfied.

Cate's curiosity couldn't wait any longer and she said, "Well, Mose, what did Brother Budge want to see you about?" She was used to getting a noncommittal answer. Being a bishop's wife didn't mean she knew all that was going on, by a long ways. In fact she was most always the last one to know. Part of a bishop's job was to keep things to himself. After a long pause Amos replied, "He says I should take another wife." A silence settled over the group.

"What did you say?" asked Cate.

"I told him I was having a hard time providing for the wife and family I already had and I didn't know anybody that would have me. He said he could arrange for a Danish or a German girl."

Cate rebelled at the mere thought. She wouldn't stand for that. The children giggled as they remembered Brother Edlefsen's new wife with her 'vells' and 'disses' and 'dats.'

"What did you say then?" persisted Cate.

"I told him I'd see what I could do about it myself," said Amos with finality as if closing the subject. But the subject wasn't closed in the minds of any of the family. It was a serious problem they faced that night around the supper table, not just for Amos and Cate but for every child as well. Little clouds no bigger than a man's hand, appeared on the horizon of each one's thinking, different in size depending on his individual personality. None of them were scarcely aware of it at first, but time and circumstances changed their lives from that day on.

While Cate and Addie cleared the table and washed the dishes, Amos tried to read the paper by the light of the coal oil lamp on the table, but his mind wandered as his eyes merely scanned the page. I wonder if I *could* find a woman who would have me? I'm only forty-five, and I don't *feel* old! I never have any trouble getting somebody to dance with me. And with that he got up and walked over to the cracked looking glass above the washstand. He hadn't really looked at himself for a long time.

His broad forehead was unlined. Blue eyes looked from under straight brows, with little crinkles at the corners when he smiled. His nose was straight and well-formed, and his ears lay flat against his head. His face was oval and his dark brown hair showed glints of gold and auburn. His moustache and beard were thick and curly and covered all but his lips, but his cheeks were cleanshaven. His beard also covered his square jaw, but others recognized it was there and treated him accordingly. He straightened his broad shoulders and there was a trace of a satisfied smile around his mouth as he turned back to his chair and his paper.

After the children were all in bed and asleep, so they thought, Amos and Cate returned to the subject neither of them could forget. Addie pretended sleep but her ears were wide awake. Amos began. "I'm sure you realize what a trial it would be to both of us. We're just beginning to get a few things around us after scrimping and saving all these years. I've been thinking about this matter ever since Brother Budge first spoke to me about it almost a year ago. It seemed so impossible and unreal. Even though my father lived this principle I never could imagine myself doing it. I've kept putting it out of my mind, but now I can't put it off any longer."

Cate drew her rocker closer and they spoke in whispers so as not to disturb the children. "What if you refuse? What will happen?" asked Cate.

"I suppose I might be released as a bishop sooner or later, but many prominent men in the Church have only one wife. They must have been advised to do what I've been asked to do. I know some women who refuse to let their husbands take another wife. Brother Budge told me it was a privilege to be given this opportunity. He explained that only certain men were so chosen: those who qualified spiritually and who were men of principle and integrity." He paused a moment before he could bring himself to ask, "How do you really feel about this Cate?"

She didn't answer for a long minute. "If the Church and those in authority require this of us, then we must obey," she said quietly.

"Then you will give your consent?" he asked anxiously.

"I know it will be hard, but I know it is right," she replied.

"Thanks, Cate," said Amos.

"Have you thought of anyone yet?" asked Cate cautiously.

"No. I've never brought myself to consider such a thing. Who do you think would make a good wife for me, one you could like and get along with?"

"I think that will have to be your choice unless it is someone I couldn't accept at all," replied Cate.

"How about fasting tomorrow then? We must have the Lord's help and approval."

Cate nodded and they both knelt by the side of the bed as they humbly and tearfully talked to God.

"Our Father in Heaven," Amos began, "We kneel before thee this night, to thank thee for thy goodness to us. We thank thee for our children and for each other; that we are well and have enough to eat and to wear and that we have a shelter from the cold. We now need thy guidance more than ever before. I have been counseled by Brother Budge to take another wife. We thank thee that we are united in this decision to follow his counsel and that of the General Authorities. Our hearts quail at the problems and difficulties which lie ahead. We need wisdom. Help me to find a companion whom thou wouldst approve of, as well as Cate. We know we will be persecuted. Give us courage to stand it and to endure to the end. In the name of thy son, Jesus Christ, Amen."

Silently, and with tears, they climbed into bed and clung to each other for strength and comfort. Sleep didn't come for either of them as they tried to push aside the dark curtains which hid the future. Cate's what-if fears multiplied alarmingly. What-if he'll love another wife more than me? Will I be second best from now on? What-if I have to share the things I've worked so hard to get? What-if I don't like her? What-if she is younger and prettier than I am? and on and on it went as sleep was banished and she stared wide-eyed into the night.

Amos, too, was pondering how to proceed. Now that he had Cate's consent, he almost wished she hadn't agreed so readily, then the responsibility would be on her hands. Was she glad to hand him over to another woman? Who would this "other woman" be? Since his marriage to Cate, any such idea had never been born in his mind. Would the Lord point her out to him? Should he look further than here in Bear Lake Valley? Should he look for a woman near his own age? The reason for plural wives was to raise up a righteous seed. She would thus need to be younger than he was, and here he was, back to the place he started from, who would have him?

He began mind-searching for any likely young woman who would be desirable or even acceptable. Thoughts of a girl from the "old country" repulsed him. There were the Lindsays and the Cranes and the Perkinses. They all had girls in their teens and twenties. There was Gib and Sarah Weaver's girls, a whole flock of them. He never could remember their names. Maybe he'd look the field over more closely next Sunday. Whomever he chose, he'd have to get her father's permission first and then hers. It all seemed so complicated and impossible. Now that he thought of it, too, these girls were all popular with the young fellows. They wouldn't even give him a second thought.

At this point he was aware of Cate's quiet regular breathing beside him. At least she was able to go to sleep at last. What an anchor she had always been for him. He loved her with a deep trusting love. He depended on her. He needed her and she never failed him. She wasn't demonstrative, none of her family were. He was naturally so, but after twenty years, he had adopted her attitude: quiet acceptance and trust with a minimum of outward expression.

Pre-dawn light was creeping through the one little window, but still sleep eluded him. How would he ever be able to provide for another wife, let alone more children? The wolf was never more than a few paces from his door as it was. A crop failure was always disastrous. Maybe another woman wouldn't be a good manager like Cate. That would complicate things even more. But if they were doing what the Lord wanted them to do, surely the way would open. A quiet peace crept over him then, and sleep came on padded feet an hour or two before dawn.

Sunday morning as Amos sat on the stand, he looked over the congregation with a new purpose and a new vision, from a different pair of spectacles. It was amazing the things he saw, especially the unmarried girls as they came in. Hon Crane's girls were there, and the Lindsay daughters and the Perkins girls. There were Gib and Sarah Weaver with their seven girls in a row.

When meeting was over there were always a dozen things he had to attend to and people with problems. Gib Weaver was waiting to see him. He wanted to know about the water rights on the land he was proving up on. Amos tried to give a helpful answer, but just then it occurred to him maybe this was the time to ask him about one of his daughters.

"Gib, there's something I need to ask you. The authorities tell me I'd better find a plural wife. Would you be willing to let one of your girls marry me?" The surprised look on Gib's face made him wish he hadn't said anything.

It seemed a long time before Gib replied. Then with a sudden relieved look, he laughed and said, "Sure! You can have one, *if* you can get her to say yes, ha! ha! ha!"

So Gib didn't think he had a chance, eh? He was probably right, but at least he had made a start. Now he'd have to trust to luck and any sense he had left. This was the most embarrassing thing he'd ever done. He tried to recall how he had managed when he asked Cate to marry him, but couldn't even remember. Anyhow, he was twenty-one then and she was nineteen and that made a big difference. He wished his father were still alive. Maybe *he* could tell him what to do. After all, he had had seven wives.

A dance was scheduled for the following Saturday night. Maybe he'd think of something by then. Most of the young people went to the dances in groups; a bunch of girls together and the boys together. Then when they got there and the music started, they began to dance and by the end of the evening, went home two by two after a boy got up nerve enough to ask a girl if he could take her home. It would look all right for him to be there. After all, he was the bishop and in charge of all the dances.

He took extra pains before he left for the dance that night. He shaved carefully, washed his hair and beard; wiped his shoes off with a rag and put on a clean shirt under his best coat. He needed all the bolstering he could get. He decided he'd rather face two cantankerous sessions of the legislature than what he was trying to do now. What-if the Weaver girls didn't come? He'd already got Gib's consent, so he'd have to try one of them or start all over again and that was no good.

Bennington was noted for its good musicians, and good music made a good dance. It was the last of March and still dancing weather. People were too busy after mid-April to dance, so there would be a good crowd. The married folks came and parked their babies on a bench to sleep while they danced. For about the last five years the bishops had instructions to ease up a little on the strict rules about waltzes and two-steps. Otherwise the young people would go in to 'Pelier where there were no restrictions at all.

Amos stood at the door where he could greet everybody who came in. His heart gave a jump when he caught sight of the Weaver girls. He shook hands and welcomed them, meanwhile giving them a special looking over. The one who looked oldest had blonde hair and blue eyes, but he couldn't remember her name. Well, that didn't matter he guessed, so, putting on a smile, he asked her for the dance. It was a quadrille and when he walked out on the floor with his partner, the caller announced: "Only one set this time, the Bishop is going to dance!" People were used to that. Amos loved to cut some extra capers and there wasn't room for much of that if there were two sets. This time though he felt his face go red. The girl was a good dancer and he let himself go and had a good time in spite of what was on his mind.

As the dance went on, he asked her for a waltz and later on they did a two-step together. She *was* a good dancer, and nice looking besides. As they kept time to the swinging rhythm, he got up courage to say, "Can I walk you home after the dance, Dora?" She gave him a startled look and then began giggling. "Oh, thanks, Bishop Wright, but I'm going home with Jim Crane, and my name's Evaline. That's Dora over there!"

Well that finished it for that evening. He swore he'd never try such a thing again, no matter what President Budge said or thought. When he got home Cate noticed he was extra quiet and thoughtful and asked him what was wrong. He mumbled something about not feeling well and went to bed. Next morning when Cate ventured to ask him if he'd decided who to marry, he said he'd decided to forget the whole blasted thing for awhile.

He had to make a trip to 'Pelier to get some flour for Cate so he took the wagon. Spring was in the air for a change and he caught himself whistling. The meadowlarks were lilting and the winter wheat was beginning to green up in the fields along the road.

He got the flour at Burgoyne's store and splurged a nickel for horehound candy to munch, on the way back to Bennington. He picked up the sack of mail, threw it in the back of the wagon and started home. The team trotted along in the new harness he had managed to get on a trade a few days ago, and for a change it felt good just to be alive.

Just then he noticed a smallish woman walking along the road ahead and pulled up to offer a ride. A young girl looked up at him with flashing dark eyes. He could have sworn it was Lois Moran herself, and the very sight of her set his heart to thumping.

"Are you going to Bennington?" he asked.

"Yes," she replied. "I missed my ride and started walking."

He helped her onto the spring seat beside him and noticed her dark wavy hair under her bonnet. She started talking gaily about the fun she had had in Montpelier. He knew she was one of the Weaver girls but wasn't about to make the same mistake twice, calling her by the wrong name. So he listened and laughed with her as they rode along.

"You're Gib Weaver's daughter, aren't you? I never can keep all you sisters straight. I'm always getting the wrong name on the right girl." And they both laughed.

"I'm Martha Loella," she said simply, and then added, "Yes, people are always getting us mixed up. There's Evaline, she's the oldest. Then Sarah and Alice and me and Dora and Catherine. We call her Kitty, and Ida is the baby girl, but Hought is the real baby of the whole family."

It seemed only a few minutes till they got to her place. She smiled her thanks, jumped down from the wagon and ran into the house, dark curls bouncing as she went.

He whistled the rest of the way home and all the while he

unharnessed and fed the horses. Loella, Martha Loella. A beautiful name for a beautiful girl. Maybe this thing would work out after all, and she *did* remind him of Lois Moran.

Amos looked up the ward records and found out she was sixteen. There it was. Martha Loella Weaver, born July 8, 1868, Millville, Utah, daughter of Gilbert and Sarah Conover Weaver. Yes, he remembered Gib and Sarah had left Bear Lake a few years after they came in 1863. They thought Millville was a better place to raise a family. But then things changed and they moved back to good old Bear Lake after all.

Hummmmmm sixteen, and he was forty-five! And he had thought it was preposterous that his father fell in love with Lois Moran when he was forty-nine and she was fifteen. He smiled grimly. History seemed to have a way of repeating itself. But he pulled himself up suddenly. "This is ridiculous. She'd never be willing to marry me! Look what happened at the dance with her sister, and she wasn't half as pretty as Loella."

He caught himself thinking of her often. He visualized her beautiful face with the saucy black eyes and dark wavy hair making a perfect frame for a lovely picture. He even prayed about her. Surely it wasn't wrong to feel this way if he was going to marry her. But what-if she wouldn't be willing? What-if she laughed at him like Alice had? His dread of polygamy evaporated suddenly and in its place was the dread he wouldn't get this girl. He couldn't tell Cate about her until he asked Loella herself, or Cate would laugh at him, too. So he suffered silently with this sweet new pain. What a mass of contradictions he discovered himself to be. And he thought he knew himself so well.

He tried to formulate a plan so he could decide if Loella was the right one, and how to get a chance to ask her if she'd marry him. Nothing seemed right. Then a simple little thing happened to help him make up his mind.

After church, Cate told Addie to look after eighteen-month-old Libby. Addie put her down for a minute, turned her back and the toddler made straight for a puddle of mud and fell down in it. And who was it that ran to pick her up and comfort her cries? Martha Loella Weaver. Soon the child was happy again, but Loella's new dress was ruined and as muddy as the baby's, though she didn't seem to mind.

Amos saw this little drama, and remembered the words he'd read about Samuel looking for a king and what the Lord said to him, "but the Lord looketh on the heart." If she had a tender heart, as well as being so lovely to look at, surely he couldn't go wrong. Now the problem remained, how to get a chance to ask her if she'd marry him.

Tuesday evening he was supposed to check on the young folks at Mutual. They were having a short dance after classes. Before time to go he poured some water out of the teakettle into the washbasin and lathered his hair and beard. There was so much suds he had to get another basinful of water to rinse it in. As he combed his hair a little later, he decided to part it on the opposite side for a change, but when he looked in the glass, he combed it back the usual way. It was getting late, so he hurried off to the meetinghouse. Cate watched the performance out of the corner of her eye, without comment.

Loella was there with the rest of the young folks. Sight of her now set his heart zigzagging. A couple of boys were teasing her and one of them began singing a little ditty he'd made up:

"There's Lell Weaver, the heart-smashing girl,
You'd really think so if you saw her curls.
She rolls them up a week at a stretch
Till first thing you know, an old man she'll ketch."

As if this reminded her of something, Loella caught sight of Amos and ran over to him. "Bishop Wright, I need to talk to you."

"All right, why don't we dance and you can tell me your problem." Putting his arm around her waist for a waltz was pure heaven. He couldn't think of anything to say. He was as tongue-tied as a sixteen-year-old boy, instead of a 45-year-old man with a wife and eleven children. Then she said something that changed everything.

"Bishop Wright, do you think it would be right for a girl to marry a man a lot older than she is? My sisters have been talking about it and say they would never do it when there are so many good-looking boys their own age. But I told them I thought it would be an honor to marry a fine older man who held the priesthood. You're the bishop, what do you think?'

"How would you like to marry *me*, Loella? The Lord wants me to have another wife, and I've fallen in love with you." She looked at him in wonderment and said, "I'll ask my Father when I get home and let you know." It was as simple as that. She had opened the way, and he knew it was right.

Gib was naturally upset when his daughter told him what had happened. He had felt so sure such a thing could never occur in his family that he gave his consent when Amos asked him. And

now the sky had fallen on him and his favorite daughter, Loella.
Sarah, too, was perturbed. They prayed about it and finally told
Loella the decision was up to her, hoping, of course, she'd say no.

But Loella said yes, and told Amos next time she saw him at
church. Tears came to his eyes and he could only hold her hand a
moment and murmur "Bless you, my dear!" It was all so fantastic
he couldn't believe it was happening to him. Now he could tell
Cate and the uncertainty would be over at least.

A chance to talk to Cate didn't come till they got to bed that
night. How should he say what he had to say? Well, he might as
well just say it and have it over with. "Cate, I've decided who I
want to have for another wife."

She had been waiting for this and dreading it at the same
time. "Who is she?" she asked.

"Gib Weaver's daughter, Martha Loella. She is sixteen, and
says she'll marry me. I know it is right from the way things
worked out."

There was a long silence. "If that's your choice I'll go along
with it. She's a nice girl." That was all she said, but her thoughts
went on and on. "She's so young! She's pretty. Why couldn't he
have chosen an old maid so I wouldn't have this fear of losing
him? How could she be willing to marry Mose when she is so
popular? She could have any boy she looked at! But I told him he
should be the one to choose, so I have to keep my promise." Tears
fell silently onto her pillow. She mustn't reveal her feelings. By
morning she might be able to face up to this thing and maybe it
wouldn't seem so bad. She was grateful for darkness.

What would the children say? What would they think? This
girl was just the age of her Addie. Would the boys be willing to
accept such a thing? They'd all have to learn to share. Maybe that
would be the hardest part for them, and for her. Never mind, the
important thing was that she *knew* it was a commandment. The
Lord wanted them to do this and the authorities told them so and
that was final. Whatever else happened, no matter how hard, that
would make her able to do it. Many other women had done it and
lived through it. Amos' own mother Rebecca for instance. She had
heard how Emma Smith had found the commandment impossible
to comply with, and thus came under condemnation. Well, she
couldn't let that happen to her. This was her trial and she'd have
to bear it. Why did the Lord ask such a sacrifice? What if she now
refused to give her consent? She'd already agreed, only then it
wasn't so real as now. He had made the choice and chosen a

beautiful sixteen-year-old girl, twenty-five years younger than she was. "Oh, Heavenly Father, help me, help me, help me! I want to do what is right!"

Amos felt guiltily happy. Things had worked out so easily when he expected it to be hard. It seemed as if his sacrifice of Lois Moran to his father all those years ago was now being rewarded in a miraculous way. This unbelievable singing in his heart took him back to his youth. He tried to remember the pain he felt when he discovered Lois was already married, but he couldn't. All he knew now was that he was happy, that he felt young again and that things were right for him. He wondered what the next step ought to be. He couldn't afford a ring for Loella. Maybe some little piece of jewelry would do.

Next time he went to Burgoyne's store he looked in the showcase and saw a pretty brooch marked $4.50. That was a lot more than he had. Cate handled what money that came in, and most of it was her own earnings and savings from butter and eggs. That night he talked to Cate about it.

"I think I ought to get some kind of a gift for Loella. I can't afford a ring. I saw a little brooch down at Burgoyne's that might do but I haven't any money."

Cate went over to the cupboard and reached for the sugar bowl she used for a bank. She dumped out a handful of coins, counted out the amount, and handed it to Amos. He was so grateful he kissed her on top of her head, a language she understood. Anything more than that she called "laligagging."

Amos decided he'd better talk to Gib and Sarah again. He rode over on his horse, and, as always, was deep in thought all the way. He felt he was being swept along by "his river" again, and strangely this time he wasn't fighting the current. It was exhilarating just to float. Gib and Sarah greeted him solemnly. He noticed Sarah's eyes were bloodshot. She said the girls had taken Loella to Burgoyne's to get a gift for her.

They invited him in and as he sat down he said, "I thought I'd better talk things over again with you folks. I believe I can understand how you feel about letting Loella marry an old man like I seem to be, when he has a wife and children already. Maybe forty-five seems old to you, but I really don't feel old. I'm just getting my second wind." Amos stood up. He couldn't just sit quietly and talk. He needed action as well. Putting his hands in his pockets, he began pacing the floor as he talked.

Gib and Sarah sat hand in hand on the little love seat, seeking strength from each other.

"You know some of the things we'll be facing as well as I do," he continued. "More poverty for one thing. There'll be two families now to share what one had before. Then, Dubois is hounding polygamists harder every day. I'll be high on his list and Loella will probably have to go underground. I'll have to depend on you to help us out. We may as well face what's ahead of us, and I know, and you know it won't be easy. All I can say is, I never would have thought of such a thing if the authorities hadn't kept after me. Brother Budge has been urging me for over a year and every time the visitors from Salt Lake came, they talked about it and said we weren't keeping our temple covenants if we didn't obey this principle. I've fasted and prayed a good many times about it and concluded it is right. I feel good about it now. Cate gave her consent and encouraged me to go ahead, and I know my prayers have been answered. I give you my word that I will love and protect Loella as long as I live, and I'll never be able to repay you for your kindness and understanding."

Tears were flowing now as Gib and Sarah battled their emotions. They respected Amos as a friend and as their bishop. They had tried over and over to unravel this knotty problem, sometimes alone and sometimes together. Was it selfishness to shrink from what they saw would happen if their beloved Loella took this step? Was it disobedience? Would they be at fault if they stood in her way? Would they regret it to the end of their days if they allowed her to marry Amos? Gib took out his wrinkled handerchief and blew his nose.

"Well, Brother Wright, you know how hard this is for us. Will you give us another day or two to decide? We'll do some more fasting and praying and then we'll let you know." Sarah couldn't talk for weeping. The three of them embraced one another in turn and Amos left.

Nothing much got done during those unreal days. Both Amos and Cate went around in a daze, going through motions while their thoughts stayed on the merry-go-round of doubts and wonderings. Yet, through it all, they both knew they would go through with it however it turned out. They would play it by ear and pray for the right answers and wisdom to make the right choices as the needs arose.

Gib saw Amos after meeting the following Sunday. "We give our consent, Bishop. We can't seem to oppose it. God bless you and her. You'll both need all the blessings you can get!"

Amos went over to the Weaver's house that afternoon and took the little brooch for Loella. She seemed surprised and pleased. They talked over a date for the wedding and decided on a week from Friday, which the calendar said was May 6, 1885. Amos said he'd arrange for them to get to Logan the day before.

Cate made sure Amos had clean clothes ready, such as they were. He had never worn the fancy shirt and new coat she bought him to go to the legislature in. Maybe he'd change his mind now. He was such a stubborn mule! She decided to put the shirt in his grip without saying anything. That way he wouldn't have any choice. She went to Burgoyne's and got him a new pair of shoes with elastic in the sides. These new "congress gaiters" just slipped on and didn't need any lacing. She'd see he looked decent this time if she had anything to say about it. After that, he would be Loella's problem.

Amos got ready to leave, next morning early, before the rest of the family was up. He was full of exuberance. Cate hustled around putting up a box lunch for them and preparing his usual two eggs and a bowl of mush with cream and sugar. She noticed with surprise that he was wearing his new coat and the fancy shirt she had tucked in his grip for him to find later. Miracles had already begun to happen.

They both realized this was the end of a long chapter in their lives and the beginning of a new one. Yet they were committed to it by their own choice. Amos poured some thick cream over his oatmeal and sprinkled it generously with sugar. Between bites, he spoke, almost as if he were thinking aloud.

"We'll be trying to live a celestial law in a telestial world, and that will be the test. But the Lord evidently thinks we can do it. He's giving us a chance and we'll do our best not to let him down. We've proved we can trust each other and him. and we've never considered quitting." Then pouring one last spoonful of cream to top it off with, he pushed away from the table. Taking Cate in his arms he said, "I promise you I'll give this thing all I've got. How about you?"

"Aye, Mose," was all she could say, as she clung to him wordlessly. Then, as if ashamed for giving way to tears, she pushed away saying, "Be off with ye now!"

As he drove down the road in the buggy with Old Bird between the shaves, she watched through her little "chinken" window between the logs. "Oh, Mose," she whispered, "it's too hard, it is ... too hard ... don't forget your little mourning dove."

Loella was waiting for him when he arrived. Gib and Sarah and the girls were putting on a brave front as she ran out to meet him. She was always beautiful but this morning he thought she looked like an angel. He noticed she was wearing the little brooch he had given her and he gathered her into his arms impulsively and kissed her on the cheek.

She ran from one to the other of her sisters, kissing and hugging them excitedly. They all hurried back into the house before their tears broke loose, and stood at the window waving goodbye.

Alice was the first to break the silence. "Did you notice that Brother Wright was wearing white kid gloves? He'll need them to handle that situation!"

Sarah nodded. "Lell will need us more than ever, too. Your Father and I gave our consent because we couldn't say no to the Lord."

Amos asked Gib if he would please go with them to 'Pelier to meet the train and then bring the horse and buggy back, till they returned day after tomorrow. All three climbed into the little buggy and Gib held Loella on his lap. There wasn't room any other way and he was glad of the chance to hold his darling for a few minutes before losing her. Probably he would feel this way no matter who she married, but it seemed harder under the circumstances. And yet he and Sarah were convinced there was no other alternative, and they too had made the difficult choice.

There were a few other passengers waiting when they got to the depot. Amos bought two tickets to Logan and return. The train was on time. It was always exciting to hear the long mournful who-oo-oo-ooh as the train approached and the big black giant came grinding down the track with steam spurting out of each side as the brakes were applied. Then the bell began to clang, and the conductor came down the steps and put a little step stool on the ground for the passengers to use as they climbed aboard. A couple of passengers got off, lugging heavy satchels. Gib gave Loella a last quick hug. Amos helped her up the steps and he followed. They found two empty seats on the side where they could wave to Gib as the train began its chug, chug, chugging motion ahead, off into the great world beyond Bear Lake Valley.

This was Loella's first trip on a train. There was so much to take in all at once. She ran her hand over the soft red plush of the car seat. There were more seats just like this one, ahead and behind, with an aisle between and more of the same on the other side. There was a shelf above where Amos put their satchels, the lunch box and his overcoat. He had her sit next to the window so she could look out as the train picked up speed. She marveled how the fields melted away almost before she had time to glimpse them, seeming to be moving while she sat still. Surely this was a new world she was seeing for the first time, and there was much more to come.

The conductor, with his stiff round blue cap and shiny visor, was suddenly standing there smiling at them saying, "Tickets, please." Amos reached in his coat pocket and handed them to him. The conductor scribbled something on a little red card and tucked it in the window shade above Loella's head. Amos asked him when they'd get to Logan and he said, "two thirty five." She couldn't believe they could get there so soon. When they came by team and wagon, the trip had taken two whole days. She was full of questions about everything, and Amos delighted in her childlike wonderment. He drank in her every word and movement, trying to anticipate her slightest wish. Her beauty would always amaze and fascinate him, and now she was to be his for eternity. The thought was more than he could comprehend at the moment.

Together, they watched the moving panorama of sagebrush flats, rolling green hills and approaching canyon. The quaking aspens were shivering in their pale green dresses newly-donned, it seemed, for this special day. Now the train was rushing between dark evergreens like uniformed soldiers guarding their path, and a moment later they glimpsed patches of scrub oak and maple not yet in leaf. The sky was softly blue with a few white clouds scudding by.

Amos broke the spell by asking if she was hungry. *He* was and he knew there'd be something special which Cate had provided. His heart went out in gratitude to her. She had always been so dependable, so strong and unfailing. He reached over and turned the seat ahead so it faced them, much to Loella's astonishment. That way they had a place to put the lunch box. He let her open the box so he could watch her pretty little hands as they deftly untied the string and lifted the lid. She exclaimed with delight at sight of Cate's homemade bread with roast beef tucked between the slices. And there were deviled eggs and pickles and finally two pieces of Amos' favorite chocolate cake. It was a double feast for him as he relished the cake and watched the child-woman at his side daintily satisfy her hunger at the same time.

How could he be so blessed? She would be his to guard and protect against harm and danger from this day forward. And there *would* be danger, with the world seemingly arrayed against them as they made covenants on the morrow, which would flaunt tradition and challenge preconceived morals. But he shut out these solemn thoughts to enjoy the delight of the present, as they ate and laughed and partook of soul manna together.

President Budge had offered to write to his sister who lived in Logan. He said he was sure she would be glad to give them a place to stay overnight. Her house was near the temple and it would be an easy walk over there next morning. He gave Amos careful directions so "they couldn't miss it."

It seemed only a few moments until the conductor came through the car announcing, "Next station is Logan," and everybody began pulling down luggage and coats and checking to see they hadn't left anything. Loella felt so helpless, yet safe, with this big man at her side, who seemed to know all the answers even before she asked. She instinctively waited for him to take the lead as they made their way out and down the steps. The conductor stood there smiling and ready to help if needed. There were people waiting to greet the arrivals and others ready to get on the train heading for Brigham or Ogden or Salt Lake. What a wondrous way to get where you wanted to go, if you had the desire, and the money of course!

It was quite a walk from the depot that May day as they followed Brother Budge's directions. Straight ahead and rising above them was the gray stone fortress-like building where they would be tomorrow. Loella was excited and a little scared. It looked like a fairy castle and she was going inside with her prince who would carry her clear to the top of the winding staircase in the temple she'd heard so much about. She would be wearing the long white dress that Evaline and Dora had made for her. It had white ribbon bows down the front and long puffed sleeves. She ventured a look at Brother Wright and thought how handsome he looked in his new suit. He felt her gaze and squeezed her hand.

It was uphill now, and Amos took her arm. She got goose pimples at his touch. Tomorrow he would be her husband! She wondered what she should call him. He had always been "Bishop" or Brother Wright to her, but maybe he'd want her to call him Amos or Mose. She had heard Sister Wright call him Mose, and she liked that. It seemed warm and intimate. Well, she'd find out.

Amos took out the paper with the directions Brother Budge had given him, and like he said, "they couldn't miss it."

They were greeted kindly by Brother Budge's sister and her family. Her house was nice inside with wood floors, a woven rag carpet and colored curtains at the windows. The Home Comfort range gave out a cheerful glow which was welcome even in early May. There was lots to talk about, too.

Logan was growing ever since the temple was started. Now they were talking about having a college up on the hill, too. It was mostly in the planning stage so far, but people knew how important it was for their children to go to school. That would mean more taxes and work, of course.

A sudden thought jumped in Loella's mind. "Maybe one of my sons will go to that school some day!" And then she squelched it as being impossible and almost immodest when she wasn't even married yet. But she would be by this time tomorrow, and the thought gave her a nice warm feeling.

Amos asked Sister Budge if she remembered a prophecy that President Heber C. Kimball made when the Salt Lake Temple was started. He said, that when its walls reached the square, the powers of evil would rage and the Saints would suffer persecution. They "reached the square" in November 1882, eight months after the Edmunds Law was passed by Congress. "We know what has happened ever since," said Amos, "and Heber C. Kimball was a true prophet."

Her bed that night was soft with a feather bed-tick underneath and a down-filled quilt to cover her. Such luxury was beyond her fondest dreams. Maybe this *was* all a dream and she'd wake up in her own straw-tick bed with two other sisters crowded together to keep one another warm. But it wasn't a dream when she woke early next morning and saw the light filtering in at the east window. This was *the day, her* day; the day that would change her from a girl to a wife. Only her imagination could part that curtain to give her even a glimpse of what lay ahead, and it was well she couldn't see. The words of the song suddenly came to mind: "Lead kindly light amid the encircling gloom, one step enough for me." But this day couldn't be gloomy, it would be happy and glorious. She was going to the House of the Lord to be married to a man who honored his priesthood; and they would be sealed for time and all eternity. She had heard these words as long as she could remember, but today they took on special significance and were meant just for her. It would take years to even partly comprehend their full meaning.

Men and women in white greeted them at the door of the temple. A soft glowing warmth enveloped them as they entered the sacred precincts and they were guided and directed at every step. Words, instructions, concepts, ordinances, covenants! Passing from room to room each portrayed by oil painted murals, man's journey from his pre-existence, through mortality and on to celestial life. It was more than a sixteen-going-on-seventeen-year-old girl's mind could encompass in one morning. By the time they reached the intimate high-ceilinged sealing room, it was all a mingling of awe and unreality for Loella. Amos had been through the temple a number of times and each time his mind was able to grasp a few new concepts. He realized he would never run out of new things to learn and understand in that sacred place.

White tatted lace covered the altar in the center of the room, with a place for kneeling at each side. Plate glass mirrors all the way around the room reflected a crystal chandelier hanging from the ceiling. This really was a fairy castle thought Loella.

The temple president dressed in white, showed them where to kneel, Amos on the right and Loella across from him, their clasped hands resting on the altar, and looking into each other's eyes. He explained to them the sacredness of the covenants they were about to make and that he held authority to marry them by the power of the Melchizedek Priesthood, not only for time, but for all eternity; that through their faithfulness they would come forth in the morning of the first resurrection to inherit thrones, principalities, powers and eternal life as husband and wife with their families, forever and forever. And across the altar they gave each other their first kiss.

Chapter Twenty-two
Another Mission

Amos realized that from now on as a polygamist, he would be among the hunted men of the Church. He explained to Loella on the way back from Logan, the need for caution now that they were married. Dubois marshals were everywhere. They kept their ears to the ground for suspects. Every conviction meant money in their pocket, and they weren't particular how they went about catching their prey. He thought perhaps the best way would be for her to continue to live with her family for the present. He said he would talk to her father about it, and promised to see her as often as he could without arousing suspicion. "We'll have to proceed cautiously a step at a time." He also warned Cate and the family and asked them to help him avoid arrests by never telling anybody where he was or answering any questions about him. Thus his family immediately felt the results of his marriage to Loella, and there would be much more to come.

A few days after he got back from Logan, Amos saw a man on horseback riding down the lane. He suspected who it might be and ran out the back door and down into the willows by the lower spring. The man knocked and Cate answered.

"I'm looking for Amos R. Wright," he said gruffly.

"He's not here," said Cate truthfully. He pushed past her and searched the two rooms. Coming back he handed her an official-looking paper.

"Give this to your husband and tell him we'll be back."

When Amos came back in the house awhile later, Cate handed him the paper and said, "What do you have to say to that? He wouldn't believe me when I told him you weren't here, so he searched the house."

Amos unfolded the paper and saw that it was a warrant for his arrest signed by David D. Wright. So, his brother was living up to his threats and wasn't wasting any time, either. Well, he'd have to be extra careful from now on.

Upon his return he was immediately swamped with problems connected with the bishopric. Brother Budge needed more men to work on the tabernacle at Paris. The pretentious building had been started a year ago, and after the first enthusiasm had worn off, it was hard to get men to leave their own affairs to go twelve miles and work for the Lord, even if it would be a beautiful place of worship.

Roads in the valley were a constant headache. Snow and ice in the winter, and mud or dust in the summer. Getting men to pay poll tax in cash or work in lieu thereof, took a special brand of tact and persuasion. This was really a job for the county officers, but the line between civil law and the Church wasn't clearly defined, so the bishop was often involved in disputes and efforts to keep the roads from becoming impassable.

Now, as never before, Amos felt the weight of the world on his shoulders. What could he do to provide a home for Loella? He couldn't expect Gib and Sarah to keep her now she belonged to him. At this point he didn't think it would be wise to ask Cate and the children to let her come to live with them. They would soon feel the pinch of sharing the little there was to share. His new role as a fugitive from the law was a weight he'd never carried before as Fear became his unwelcome companion. Coupled with that, he felt the injustice of it when he was merely obeying a command of God.

Then there was the threat posed by Montpelier, as a railroad town only five miles away, with all the evils that went with it. The "depot element" as he came to call it, brought pool halls and saloons temptingly near, to beckon the Bennington boys. The parents of some of these boys openly boasted about their policy of letting their children choose for themselves. Thus Amos sensed the threat to his own sons. The bishops were commended by the stake brethren for discouraging gambling and drinking, but it was a never-ending worry and an added wight to the total responsibilities resting on him.

In the same priesthood meeting in Paris, President Budge told of another source of irritation in the valley. A Presbyterian minister named Boyce had arrived a few months ago and at his request was very liberally allowed to hold meetings in some of the wards. But when he began to malign Church leaders and Joseph Smith and insinuate against the character of local members, President Budge advised bishops to refuse him the use of meetinghouses unless he made a public apology.

Finally, President Budge spoke about the subject now upper-most in Amos' mind. "We have had peace for a short time from the marshals. There are about one hundred fifty indictments for men accused of co-habitation whom they have not found. They are determined to arrest them and are planning a special session in the near future to carry on the work of prosecution. We are proud of our brothers from Bear Lake in the course they have taken and we should help and comfort all those concerned." (Bear Lake Stake Priesthood records, LDS Historical Archives)

Meantime, events were shaping up unbeknownst to Amos, which would have far-reaching consequences upon his life in the near future, as well as that of his wives and children. John Taylor, then President of the Church, wrote a letter to Lorenzo Snow in Brigham City, dated July 2, 1885:

> Our attention has been called to the condition of the Indians and the necessity of laboring among them in teaching them the principles of the Gospel ... I laid before the Council with great plainness the necessity for this, showing to them that when we raised up branches among the Whites, we did not neglect them and leave them to themselves, but considered it our duty to furnish them with Elders and other officers to instruct them in their religion and to maintain the organization established among them.

> I have felt greatly impressed to have you, Brother Lorenzo, visit the various tribes to which you can get access in accordance with the appointment which was made for yourself, Bro. F. D. Richards and Bro. Moses Thatcher at the time of which I speak, November 1882. (Whitney, Later Leaves of the Life of Lorenzo Snow, pp. 19-20.)

Elder Snow was further informed that he could choose his company to assist in the work, but Elder Taylor suggested the name of Amos Wright as an excellent prospect since he was full of zeal and was familiar with the Shoshones and their language. The letter stated that the Indians were being prepared to receive the truth through dreams and visions; a number of them, including Chief Washakie, had already been baptized into the Church. Washakie, President Taylor felt, was willing to be taught as well as to have his people taught.

Taylor and Snow by experience, had learned to proceed with caution on all fronts as well as that of polygamy. Every move they made was viewed by the enemy with suspicion, and twisted to appear sinister.

President Snow replied to Elder Taylor's letter outlining in detail a plan to carry out the wishes of the president regarding the

Shoshone Indians in Wyoming, suggesting the names of five
other brethren to accompany him. He said he hoped to keep this
affair quiet at least until he returned. He enclosed a clipping from
the Salt Lake Tribune dated two years before, to illustrate what he
meant.

> Apostle Snow of Brigham City has been looking after the Indians
> up north. He has been around the agencies in Idaho, notably that of
> Ross Fork, accompanied by one of his Bishops as interpreter and has
> visited the various camps for some purpose.
>
> It is well known that the Mormons sell ammunition and guns to
> Indians, and that they class these Red Men as the Battle Axes of the
> Lord who are ready to do the bidding of the Priesthood.
>
> "Would it not be well for the Government to make inquiry into the
> cause of these visits by Apostle Snow, and learn what mischief he
> might be concocting in the interest of the Mormon Church?

Brother Snow further indicated that the company appointed
to the Wind River Reservation was being outfitted, and would be
ready to leave on the 24th of September. He had a few qualms
about writing to Amos at Bennington, but President Taylor had
specifically mentioned his name as the one to go. He had many
times regretted the unfortunate episode between himself and
Brother Wright in Brigham City over twenty years ago. He
recognized that his own quick temper had been partly responsible
for Amos' excommunication. He had been relieved when he heard
from his counselor, Jonathan C. Wright, that his son Amos had
been baptized again and had at length become a bishop.

In due time, however, he received a reply from Amos, agreeing
to meet the Snow party at Montpelier on the 26th. Likewise,
Brother Snow received a letter from the First Presidency approv-
ing his suggestions relative to the way missionary work should be
carried on among the Lamanites. They suggested that Chief
Washakie should be visited when the missionaries got to the
reservation, asking for his cooperation. Later the Indian brethren
should be ordained to the priesthood when found worthy and as
directed by the Holy Spirit.

Amos was surprised to hear from President Snow. It was a
kindly, warm letter and was the first time he had ever heard from
the apostle since their altercation in Brigham City. It pleased
him, too, to know that President Taylor had confidence in him
that he go with President Snow to Wind River.

It would be hard to get everything done before he left. He'd try
to get the thrashing and haying over by then and Cate and the

boys could manage after that. The boys were getting older now
and could do the chores. He might be gone a month and he hated
to leave Loella that long. She depended on him so much these
days and got lonesome when he couldn't visit her often. She said
she knew he'd come whenever there was a storm, because nobody
else would venture out in that kind of weather.

Amos met President Snow and his party at Montpelier as
agreed. The old man, now seventy-two years old, left his family in
Brigham City, at three a.m. to set out on this short-term mission
to the Indians on the Wind River Reservation in Wyoming.
Accompanying him were Bishops Madsen and Zundel, counselor
May and Elder James Brown, and an L.D.S. Indian. President
Snow wrote an account of the trip in his own quaint manner and
sent it to President Taylor and the Council of the Twelve:

Saturday 26th I arrived at Bear Lake and was here joined by
Bishop Amos Wright. Our outfit consisted of two wagons, one
carriage, three span of horses and two riding animals. We performed
the trip in three weeks and one day, including two days and a half
spent at the Reservation, holding council with Indian Chiefs,
making inquiries and searching the most suitable places for purchase and location of land, with your instructions.

The trip proved a pleasant one and through a kind Providence we
returned without harm or accident to ourselves, animals or vehicles.
Still we all felt we had been too late in starting and were liable and in
danger of being snowed up among the mountains. In fact a few days
before we arrived at Hams Fork the snow had fallen covering the
country round to the depth of three to four inches, and on our return,
the next day after leaving South Pass, we encountered a heavy storm
which covered with snow the mountains we had passed in our
outward journey, rendering it necessary to take our course more
southward.

They traveled a total of six hundred forty miles, going and
returning. They got to Wind River on Sunday October 3rd, and
camped just outside of Lander, eleven miles from the Agency.

Monday morning Amos and Bishop Zundel went to the
agency to invite Washakie and some of his head men as well as
the Arapahoe chiefs, to a meeting with President Snow the next
day at his camp. Amos and Bishop Zundel came back that
afternoon saying Washakie had gone on a hunting trip and would
be gone about two months, and he didn't want to be sent for, as he
needed a rest. He said his head chief could take care of any
business that came up. The head chief talked to them very kindly
and said he would come to the meeting next day. He also promised

to notify the Arapahoe chief and other leading men.

Brothers Madsen and May went on an exploring trip covering about twenty-five miles, looking for possible farms and ranches to settle the Indians on. They inquired about prices, water privileges, markets, etc. and brought back detailed figures.

Next morning two of Washakie's principle chiefs arrived at President Snow's camp. The Arapahoe chief didn't show up. They said a band of Sioux had just arrived on a trading expedition. President Snow continues:

> We invited the Chiefs to our tent, which while entering, they doffed their hats very politely and took seats which had been prepared for the occasion. A desultory conversation was carried on through Brothers Wright and Brown, while Bishop Madsen laid the cloth in the center of our little group, and spread upon it in great abundance the luxuries of our camp: venison, ham, pork and beans, hot potatoes and cakes, bread, butter and honey, with a few sardine boxes brightening the scene. Occasional furtive and penetrating glances from the eyes of our dusky visitors toward these preparations, accompanied with smiles of approval, could not quite escape our observation. Dinner being announced, Indian Brown asked a lengthy blessing in the Shoshone language, listened to by the Chiefs with reverential feelings. Dinner over, we seated ourselves in a circle and began our conference which held between two and three hours of which the following is a brief review.

Amos interpreted for this long meeting. Brother Snow was pleased and surprised how well Amos understood and could speak Shoshone. His written report continues:

> We are sent by President John Taylor, to tell you again what you have been told before that he is your friend, and all the Mormon people are also your friends and your brethren. President Taylor would be glad to know what you wish him to do for you, and how you think he can do you the most good.
>
> The Chiefs replied, they knew President Taylor and the Mormons were their friends, and they would like to visit Pres. Taylor but the Agent was unwilling to permit them to go from the Reservation so far as Salt Lake City. They said they were very poor, that their rations were delivered to them every Saturday, but insufficient to last more than three or four days, and every Fall the Government gave them a few blankets and some clothing in part payment for their lands sold to the United States which was now, they believed, nearly paid according to the terms of the agreement. A few of their people, they said, were furnished with wagons, plows, and other farming implements but very little was done. Some cultivated one or two acres apiece.

When President Snow asked the Indians if they would like to own their own houses, have plenty of food and clothing and send their children to school, they said, yes, they would. Then he asked them if they would be willing to work for those things like the white man does. They said, yes, but wanted to know how to do it.

Amos told them about the Shoshones who lived down in Washakie Ward under Bishop Zundel. He said President Taylor had bought several thousand acres of land and these Indians were living there with plenty to eat and clothes to wear etc. They said they knew that was true because some of their people had been down to visit at Washakie Ward.

I now asked the Chiefs if they would like Bishop Wright and Elder Brown to be with them this winter, to teach them the Gospel, and would they take good care of them? Yes, they answered. How could it be done, we asked. They replied, it would be necessary to come *"slyly"* and if the soldiers got after them they must *"run"*.

After indulging, to some length, in this line of questions and answers, I commenced another subject: explained how the Angel appeared to Joseph Smith and told him about their fathers and the promises made to their children, the authority given to Joseph Smith which he gave to others to baptize, lay hands on for the Holy Spirit, and Bishop Wright had received this authority, by whom their people had been baptized. Therefore they could have the Holy Spirit if they would do right, be humble and prayerful and it would be in their hearts and minds telling them how to do and act, etc. etc. using the most simple language I could command, to which they listened with a degree of interest that surprised us.

Though they have good warm hearts they are extremely ignorant, and to do them permanent good one must be armed with much patience and perseverance. These two Chiefs were Elders and have received their endowments.

Brother Snow suggested in his report to President Taylor that Bishop Amos Wright be appointed president of the Shoshones and Arapahoes on the Wind River Reservation, with Elder James Brown his counselor. That as soon as their family matters could be arranged, they take the train to Rawlins, on the Union Pacific; from there, the stage to Lander City, four miles from the reservation.

Some four years ago Bishop Wright baptized Washakie, his family of seventeen members, also three hundred of his Indians— this he did within about ten days and immediately left. Some twenty or thirty cases of marvelous healing of the sick occurred during this time through his administration.

These converts have been left since then without much care or instructions and are as ignorant of the Gospel as wandering babes in the woods. These Chiefs have expressed a wish that these Elders should visit their people and teach the principles of the Gospel, and their wants would be supplied. These Brethren have expressed their willingness to undertake this mission immediately if sanctioned by your counsel.

Bishop Wright is poor, and in rather embarrassed circumstances, and will need assistance. He thinks if he had two or three cows and a small house built on a quarter section near Bennington so he could hold it, and after awhile secure a title, his family might support themselves. If you see proper, Pres. Budge could be authorized to look after his family, and report to you their circumstances and what assistance will be required.

Another matter I wish to mention; Brother Wright has been an active member of the Legislative Assembly at Boise, Idaho, and stirred the wrath of the anti-Mormons. His brother, David, has sworn out a warrant against him for co-habitation, and there is no man in Bear Lake Valley, except Pres. Budge, so liable for arrest and the penitentiary. And though he can feel at home, comfortable and happy in a tent under a blanket beside an Indian, he will scarcely relish, so well, six months in a penitentiary with a fine of $400. and costs to liquidate.

I think it wisdom he be off as soon as possible. He says it will cost nothing for the Indian Brown on the train to Rawlins. The distance from there, by stage to the Reservation is 150 miles. Junius Wells, I think, can give the cost of stage fare. There are four companies of U.S. troops stationed near the Agency, half of them are Negroes, partly for their accommodation the stage route, I believe, is kept open through the winter.

If these Brethren do not go by the way above indicated, two-thirds of the year must pass before they can reach the field of their mission as the month of June will be as early as can be undertaken with safety over the mountains and deserts by other conveyance.

With kind regards and praying for your peace and safety,
Your Brother in the New and Everlasting Gospel
    LORENZO SNOW.
(L.D.S. Archives, Salt Lake City)

On the return journey, Amos had a long talk with President Snow when they happened to be alone. The president seemed anxious to hear about Amos' life after he left Brigham City, and of his relationship with President Rich. Then Amos told him about Cate and his family, and confided to him his recent marriage to Loella. Brother Snow then recounted some of his own experiences as a polygamist and gave Amos encouragement and wise counsel. He told Amos about the time when the Prophet

Joseph explained celestial and plural marriage to him when he was living in Nauvoo shortly after he received the revelation. "I know he told me the truth and that he was a prophet of God."

Brother Snow spoke lovingly of Father Jonathan C. Wright, and of his dedicated service as his first counselor in the Box Elder Stake. It was at this point that Brother Snow stopped for a moment, put his hands up to his eyes as if he were praying. Then, looking Amos squarely in the face, he continued:

"Brother Amos, can you forgive me for what happened in Brigham City? I realize I didn't treat you fairly and I know you were badly hurt. I had no idea Cate was suffering as she was that winter you were gone, but I'm not trying to excuse myself. Tears stood in his eyes as he spoke.

"It was my fault, Brother Snow," said Amos. "I've been ashamed of my actions ever since, but it took me six years to make up my mind to be baptized again. That was six years of hell for me. My priesthood means more than anything else in my life, and I pray I may never lose it again. Brother Rich and his son Joseph were the ones who saved me from my own stubbornness and pride." The two men embraced, and from that moment, mutual repentance cemented their friendship for the rest of their lives.

Chapter Twenty-three
Interlude

A few days after reaching home, Amos wrote to President Snow:

Bennington Idaho
October 22, 1885

Lorenzo Snow ... Dear Brother:

According to your request I write you a line or two to inform you of my safe arrival at home, hoping that the remainder of your trip was as pleasant to you as the other part was to me. As soon as I got to the top of the hill from where I left you, I turned to the right and struck the Indian trail to Smith's Fork where I arrived shortly after noon. Then coming on that afternoon to Thomas Fork, stayed overnight and came on home next day in time to take dinner with the folks.

I found my family all well but my affairs otherwise somewhat disarranged. In consequence of which I am very anxious to know at your earliest convenience what the intention of the President is concerning me, as my position at present is an awkward one.

Yours Ever, A. R. Wright.

After ten days of anxious waiting, a letter came from Brother Snow.

Brigham City, Utah
Nov. 1, 1885

Dear Brother Wright:

I received yesterday from Pres. Taylor and Cannon a reply to my communication of Oct. 22, descriptive of our Mission to the Wind River Reservation. They were pleased with the report.

They inform me that they have appointed you to take charge of the Indian Mission at the Wind River Reservation, with Elder James Brown as your assistant. I feel truly glad and thankful that you have been chosen to take the Presidency of this important mission, and feel assured that you are the right man in the right place, and you will be greatly blessed and do a good work that will prove lasting in its results and which will redound to your honor and glory. You will nourish and strengthen the good seed, which heretofore you have sown in the hearts of so many of our Lamanite Brethren, inasmuch as it will, in time to come, bring forth fruit in rich abundance to the glory of God and the increase of His Kingdom.

If times prove favorable it is quite possible that I may meet you somewhere in the neighborhood of the Reservation next Spring, as early as the roads and weather will permit.

I am pleased that Pres. Taylor has directed Pres. Budge to look after your family and, I suppose, your other matters. If bonds and imprisonment should overtake Pres. Budge, while I am unmolested, anything I can do for yourself or family I shall feel much pleasure in doing. Please keep me posted in regard to your journey, labors, situation, wants, and so on, as I think no one will take a deeper interest in your welfare and success in your mission than myself; and please remember anything I can do for you "behind the throne" I shall do gladly.

Your financial condition and circumstances have been fully represented and I trust, have been or will be responded to generously. Now Brother Amos, let me remind you what, no doubt your own experience has taught you, viz: that when you begin your labors with our Lamanite Brethren, the necessity of patience ... do not try to do too much in too short a time. Consider that all eternity is before you, and that you are teaching theology by commencing with the Alphabet, and instructing only Primaries. (L.D.S. Church Historical Archives)

Amos read and reread the letter with mixed emotions. He was pleased and humbled by President Snow's intimate message and concern. If his family and Loella could be taken care of financially while he was gone, at least that worry would be removed from his list of responsibilities. By this time he was well aware of what was ahead of him on the reservation, but he would cope with that when he got there. Brother Brown, the half-blood, was "a willing child" and necessary because missionaries were to go "two by two," but it would be easier to go without him.

Loella told him she was pregnant and would be expecting a child sometime in the spring, possibly February or March. He hoped Gib and Sarah would be willing to take care of her while he was gone. He could pay them with the money the Church would provide. Cate and the family would probably fare better under this plan than if he were at home. One last advantage occurred to him: the marshals would have a hard time catching him if he were three hundred miles away. Obedience and respect for authority precluded any doubt about going. It was merely when and how. Even how long wasn't considered.

Cate was especially solicitous of him those last few days and he was deeply grateful. The test was even greater for her, he felt, than for him. She motioned him into a chair. "Sit you down!" Then pointing her finger at him for emphasis she said, "Now, Mose, you take care of yourself. You aren't as young as you think you are and you know what rheumatism can do to you!"

Amos grinned as he stood up and imitated her serious finger pointing. "It's you I'm worried about, Cate. You might break your leg or fall in the ditch. Don't be like you were when we were first married. You wouldn't let anybody know how bad off you really were."

"Ah, well, if you insist," she replied, laughing.

And then, seriously, he went on. "Be sure to let Brother Budge know if you need help. He'll take care of things for you. Brother Snow told me he had no idea how much you suffered that winter in Brigham City while I was gone up at Portage herding cattle. He asked me to forgive him for what happened all those years ago. We both wept and made up. That was worth waiting for, believe me."

A little later he put on his coat and said, "I've got to see Loella before I go. I'm taking a chance but there's no moon tonight and it's as dark as it can get."

"So you be thinkin' of your darlin', are you?" said Cate wistfully, as he went out the door.

That last night with Loella was precious. She clung to him like a frightened child. "Oh Brother Wright, I'll miss you so much! I get so lonesome even in a few days if you don't come. How can I stand to have you gone so long!" She patted his cheek and kissed him fondly. "How long will you be gone this time? Surely you'll be back by February."

He drew her close and tried to comfort her. "I can't tell you how long it will be. I have to wait until I'm released. But I'll write to you often and pray for you every hour I'm gone."

Her expression changed. "I'm scared, too. Will the marshals try to arrest me, too?"

"I don't think so, darling, but nobody knows what they might do. You'll be safe here with Gib and Sarah. I couldn't leave if I didn't know that."

"It's different here, now, though," she went on, running her finger down his nose. "Mother and Father and the girls are good to me but you are the one I want and need."

His love for her was all-enveloping. It amazed him that she could move him so strongly . . . a combination of pain and ecstasy. She was so trusting and depended on him so completely. At times he felt almost like a father to her. But it was dangerous to stay longer.

Brother Snow had arranged transportation for him by train as far as Kemmerer, and by stagecoach from there on. It was too late in the season to risk riding a horse. Brother Budge assured him again that he would see that his loved ones were provided for.

It was already winter the morning thirteen-year-old Johnny drove him to the depot. He was silent most of the way, lost in thought as was his wont, seemingly unaware of his son at his side or of anything else. Then he boarded the train, waved to Jonny from the window, and the train pulled out of the station.

Chapter Twenty-four
Love Letters

That there are letters to scrutinize is the wonder and marvel. Few people of that day knew how to write even if they had the desire. To scrounge paper and ink and a quill pen on an Indian reservation in Wyoming Territory in 1885 was a major miracle.

Happily, Amos' half-breed friend George Terry worked at the agency and no doubt provided the paper and ink. Some of the letters bear the printed heading, UNITED STATES INDIAN SERVICE. Others are written on 8 x 10 lined paper. Every quarter-inch of space is used on both sides of the page. Margins and paragraphs are dispensed with in the interest of paper economy. Often the signature is written up the right hand side of the last page on the very edge. Thanks, then, to Amos R. Wright that they were written at all. But to his child-wife to whom they were written is offered wondering gratitude for their preservation through near a century. Their fragile, yellowed pages bear mute evidence of her love for her absent husband as she was driven, in her written words, "from pillow to post."

Writing letters was difficult for Loella. Her school days were few. She no doubt was in awe of Amos, her former schoolteacher's ability, which may account for his urging her to write more often.

He speaks of writing to Cate, but, unfortunately, research failed to find any letters.

Choice of the alias signature *"T. Benton"* carries significant irony. He was a bitter Mormon-hating senator from Missouri. Amos dared not use his own name for fear of identification and arrest.

It was late December before Amos arrived at his destination and found the time to write to Loella. He asked only for the news and sought her daily prayers.

At first, the letters were infrequent, three to four weeks apart.

He spoke generally of the weather, his health, conversions of the Indians, and passed the time of day as if he had been at her side.

By January 14, 1886, when Amos penned his second letter to Loella, he had received but one letter himself from home, and that not from her.

On February 1, when a letter finally arrived from Loella, Amos was ecstatic with joy and answered it immediately. He suffered extensively from lack of decent food, poor accommodations, and the seemingly insurmountable distance between the Indians he could preach the gospel to. All of these things, he assured her, were unbearable, but not nearly so unbearable as the lack of word from home.

Love for Loella burst from every line he wrote. Tenderness shone through as he poured out his innermost feelings of love and concern for her welfare. But it was Cate's daughter, Addie, who sent the news of the birth of Loella's and Amos' firstborn.

Words of love for his wife were overshadowed only by the reassurance and love he expressed for their new little daughter. He went on at length about what barbarians boys are, expounding on the lovely and precious qualities of a girl.

His letters to Loella became more frequent and urgent, as by May 1, two exceptionally long months had gone by without a single word from her. He was beside himself for some word from his beloved, and offered to do anything short of "deserting my post assigned me by the Priesthood of God," to see her.

His position in a letter of May 5 could not have been pled more successfully by any senator, orator, theologian, lawyer or judge. "I can't believe you have throwed me away on account of some ones talk or persuasion without giving me a hearing or a chance to defend myself or even say goodbye to me.

"Well, Lel, you was good to me and I pray God with the fervency of my soul to bless and prosper you anyhow, even if you don't think of me now anymore."

The next day, desperate that he was, Amos wrote to Sarah Weaver.

"I am ever uneasy all the time about Loella. It is two months since I had a line from her. I have written five letters to her but have had no answer. I am afraid my poor Girl is laying in her grave. If this is so, for goodness sake why wont no one tell me about it."

Two days later, Amos received the long-looked-for letter from Loella just before he posted the letter to her mother.

In his final love letter to this beloved young woman, he poured out heart and soul. "Oh My God Loella I never was so thankful since I breathed the breath of life as I am tonight to hear thank Heaven that you are alive. Yesterday I rode all day as hard as I could go without eating a bite till after sundown, then I wrote to your mother to tell me for the Lord sake if you was dead... I have prayed for you every day. I shall never forget you. We shall yet have a home and be happy together so God bless you and take care of you. To this end is my prayer and blessing for you. *T. Benton.*"

Then, at the bottom of the letter, a post script, "This is the letter I sent to the Office yesterday. You mustn't tell anybody about it only your Ma. I wonder if you think I am such a fool as to trust you to the care of an Indian even for ten seconds. I thought you knew my style of joking and would understand me. *Injin Hell* I'd like to see one touch you while I am alive." (See letters in appendix)

Chapter Twenty-five

A Fugitive

Amos received a letter from President Taylor in late May. There was no return address on it and the postmark was blurred so he couldn't make out where it was from. This indicated that he, too, was on the underground because of the Edmunds Act! "I have decided to release you and Brother Brown from this mission," he wrote. "You need to get home to put in your crops and look after your families." He praised and thanked them for their labor the past winter under such trying circumstances. He enclosed a three-year-old clipping from the *Deseret News* dated April 6, 1882. It was part of President Taylor's talk at Conference about the Edmunds Act. Amos remembered reading it at the time, but it was more meaningful now since it applied directly to him this time:

We do not wish to place ourselves in a state of antagonism, nor act defiantly towards this government. We will fulfill the letter, so far as practicable, of that unjust, inhuman, oppressive and unconstitutional law, so far as we can without violating principle.

We shall abide all constitutional law, as we always have done, but while we are God-fearing and law-abiding, and respect all honorable men and officers, we are no craven serfs, and have not learned to lick the feet of oppressors, nor to bow in base submission to unreasonable clamor. We will contend inch by inch, legally and constitutionally, for our rights as American citizens. We need have no fears, no trembling in our knees about these attempts to deprive us of our God-given and constitutional liberties. God will take care of His people if we will only do right. (Preston Nibley, *The Presidents of the Church*, pp. 116-17.)

President Taylor also informed Amos of Brother Snow's arrest and conviction six months earlier and that he was still serving sentence in the penitentiary. In addition, he told him about a mass meeting of over two thousand women which was held in the Salt Lake Theater March 6, 1886, representing the wives, mothers, sisters and daughters of the whole territory of Utah. They protested against the way the anti-polygamy laws were being enforced. "Many men—hundreds in fact, and among them some of the first citizens of the community have gone into exile rather than to submit to this injustice." (CHC Vol. VI p. 120)

His letter closed by blessing Amos and counseling him to follow the whisperings of the Spirit.

So now he could go home! A flood of emotions swept over him at the thought. How heavenly to be with his loved ones again. The miles that lay between couldn't keep him away from them now. What was ahead? What would he do if he were captured? Brother Taylor's letter would be a guide and comfort to him whatever happened. He'd face it as it came.

When he told the Indians he was leaving, he was surprised at their reaction. He called a meeting that evening. There was a full moon and the picture was permanently imprinted on his memory of those dear, brown children of his, sitting in a circle around him listening in love and trust to his every word. They spoke about the "good spirit" which Peah-Tibo always brought with him. Of the many things he had taught them; of their gratitude to him. They said they would try to remember what he told them and to do what he said. But they would miss him and would pray for him to come back again. They loaned him a good horse to ride home on.

As he and Brother Brown prepared to leave next morning, a group of them including squaws and children, gathered to say

goodbye. Little rivulets ran down brown cheeks as they wordlessly expressed their grief. Washakie, himself, was there as a
mark of respect and affection. His old Mother Hanabi gave the
elders a buckskin sack full of dried elk meat to eat on the way
home. Amos had told her about his new baby papoose whom he
had never seen yet, and she tucked a pair of tiny moccasins in his
hand to take to her. Amos' eyes became a fountain of tears.

Five days later he timed his arrival at Cate's just after dark.
He knew he would be a prize captive for any deputy from now on.
His wavy, brown hair under a slouch hat hung almost to his
shoulders. His beard had grown as much as his hair, and he was
wearing a buckskin shirt and pants, with moccasins on his feet.
Cate was startled when he walked in.

"Daw! I thought you were a ghost, an Indian ghost. I'll never
get used to your surprises."

The children gathered about him in admiring wonder. Addie
was nineteen and as tall as her mother and beautiful with her
dark, curly hair and brown eyes. Russell was man-size at sixteen
and Johnny was almost as tall as his big brother. Frank and Ed
were husky boys, forever wrestling and scuffling to prove which
one was stronger. Seven-year-old Catherine led toddler Libby
toward Amos, but she started to cry at the strange looking man,
and ran to Cate for protection.

"She's a smart one, she is," laughed Cate. Libby was past two
and Cate was expecting again.

"You're just in time for supper, Mose. Frank and Ed went to
the river today and caught a big mess of suckers. You'll have to be
careful you don't get a bone in your throat. Here, let me pour some
water for you to wash and then we're ready."

The chairs were turned away from the table as usual for
family prayer, and as they knelt together, Amos told the Lord how
grateful he was to be at home with his family again.

The boys were starving as usual. Addie poured the milk and
took a big panful of Cate's biscuits out of the oven. The fish were
crispy brown and there was a whole platter full, besides hashed
brown potatoes.

Amos broke open a biscuit and spread butter on it. This is the
first time I've sat down to a table since the day I left." And
looking at the boys he added, "I hope you never have to live the
way I do whenever I'm with Indians."

The boys were always somewhat awed by their father. His
word was law. They preferred the easier-going discipline of Cate

when he was gone. Amos' hard-hitting enforcement was often literal. Yet they respected him and sensed he was right even though they resented it.

At the end of the meal Addie brought on a special treat. "I must have known you were coming, Father. I made rice pudding and that's your favorite." Amos smiled as he spooned out a big helping. "You're a good girl, Addie. You'll make a fine wife for the right kind of a man." An aura of contentment and well-being settled about him.

After the children had gone to bed, Cate heated a boiler full of water and brought in the galvanized tub. Homemade soap and a washrag were his tools as he knelt at the side of the tub and lathered his long thick locks and dunked his head again and again in the glorious warm water. It was better still when he sat down in the tub with his legs hanging over the side. The warmth flowed about him as he luxuriated in its delicious comfort. Cate carefully poured additional hot water from the teakettle to keep the temperature right and scrubbed his back with the soapy rag. A warm bath. What a luxury! Finally, he sank into a feather bed with clean, soft sheet blankets and one of Cate's handmade quilts on top. He was home ... what a change, what a change!

He couldn't remember where he was for a minute when he awoke the next morning. Then he remembered. There was work to be done. The crops must be taken care of and irrigating started. His bishop responsibilities settled heavily about him, and thoughts of Loella filtered into his mind. He must see her at the earliest moment and he prayed for a storm so the deputies wouldn't be on the watch.

While Cate made pancakes for his breakfast, he glanced through the pile of *Deseret News* she'd saved for him. Among them was an old one dated February a year ago. It contained a speech made by President Taylor in the Tabernacle ... his last before he went into exile:

> I will tell you what you will see by and by. You will see trouble, trouble, trouble enough in these United States. And as I have said before, I say today, I tell you in the name of God, woe to them that fight against Zion, for God will fight against *them*. (Nibley, *Presidents of the Church*, p. 117.)

Well, there was plenty of trouble already and they'd need God more than ever. In the meantime, there wasn't time to sit and worry. Things would happen no matter what. He felt a strong urge to see Loella. He was a dual person now. Each wife supplied

a different need. Cate was the solid strength he had learned to
rely on. He counted on her mature judgment. She managed
things. There was always a degree of organization in her home
despite the poor accommodations available. She took care un-
complainingly of even the little they had. He long ago had left the
care and discipline of the small children entirely in her hands.
That wasn't his department. Building the morning fire, milking
cows, tending chickens and such chores also fell to Cate, unless
she could get the boys to do them for her. That seemed like
women's work to him. His father thought so, too. He and Cate had
never talked about it, it just seemed the natural way. He wasn't
afraid of work. Only farming wasn't his first love by any means.
He did it because it had to be done.

A sudden thunderstorm next evening provided the opportunity for him to ride over to Gib Weaver's. Even before he
reached the front gate, the door flew open and Loella threw
herself into his arms, their tears mingling with the falling rain,
accompanied by flashes of lightning and the roll of thunder. "Oh,
Brother Wright, I've been so lonesome and you've been gone so
long ... I'm so glad you're back. Don't leave me again. I need
you!" He was overwhelmed by her relief and joy at sight of him.
He had been far from sure that this girl-woman would still be
waiting for him, either alive or dead, and now she was here in his
arms. They hurried into the house for greetings with Gib and
Sarah and the girls. "Come see the baby," said Loella, guiding
him toward the cradle. Through his tears he saw a blond, curly-
headed blue-eyed baby smiling up at him. His heart went out to
her, immediately, as she held out her tiny hands to him to be
taken. He kissed her and held her in the crook of his arm as he felt
in his pocket and pulled out the tiny, beaded moccasins which
Hanabi had given him. Together he and Loella put them on the
baby's feet, and tied the buckskin laces. "They just fit!" Amos felt
a dual affection for dear old Hanabi, the donor, and this tiny
miracle in his arms, his own three-month-old daughter whom he
was now seeing and holding for the first time and with whom he
would always have a very tender relationship.

The great hearts of Gib and Sarah and their daughters
willingly agreed to have Loella continue to stay with them until
Amos could arrange a place for her. At this point there wasn't any
alternative. Where else could she go? Her presence in Cate's home
at this time was unthinkable. It would be a dead giveaway. He
assured Loella he would come to see her as often as possible

without arousing suspicion. Her trusting helplessness aroused his deep tenderness and desire to protect her. His inability to do so under the circumstances, left a haunting physical ache in his heart, which would remain for the almost two more years she stayed under her parents' roof.

He was relieved to find that Idaho polygamists were not being hunted so relentlessly as they had been when he left. At a stake priesthood meeting in Paris, President Budge said, "We have had peace for a short time. There are about a hundred and fifty indictments for men whom they have not found and they will no doubt hold a special session next month to carry on the work of 'grinding.' We are proud of our brothers who have gone from Bear Lake in the course they have taken and we should help and comfort all those concerned." (Bear Lake Stake Priesthood minutes, LDS Archives, May 1, 1886)

He was no doubt referring to the polygamists who had been arrested and were standing trial in Blackfoot. The usual procedure was to plead not guilty, the idea being that a Mormon polygamist did not consider himself guilty under the law of the Lord given through Joseph Smith, and that this law was higher than the law of the land, which they hoped and expected would eventually be declared unconstitutional by the United States Supreme Court.

A defense fund was set up in Bear Lake to which each ward and individuals contributed. This was used to pay defense lawyers and assist needy polygamous families when the head of the family was arrested or standing trial. Church leaders, local and general, did all they could to get a judicial ruling against the Test Oath.

The Idaho polygamists had been given a reprieve for at least three reasons. Since Fred Dubois was running for Congress from Idaho, he was giving most of his attention to the campaign. He resigned as U.S. Marshal and his successor was not appointed until September 1, 1886. It took some time for the new officer to get organized, and by the spring of 1887, lack of funds prevented new Idaho indictments and convictions. At the same time, the U.S. Supreme Court ruled on February 7 that polygamists could not be sentenced repeatedly for each day of "unlawful cohabitation" and ten men from Idaho who had been convicted under that ruling were released March 19.

One night he was awakened by Cate. "I'm sorry to have to wake you up Mose, but I think you'll have to go for Sister Ipsen.

My pains have started and you'd better hurry." He went, and a short time after the midwife got there, Cate gave birth to her twelfth and last child, a little girl. Amos later inscribed the record along with that of his other children in his family Bible: "Frances Wright, born August 16, 1886, Bennington, Idaho." They called her Fanny. There was just five months difference between her and Loella's baby Nelly, which was prime evidence of co-habitation.

By the end of 1886, Church leaders, because of continued harassment and additional laws, had discontinued encouraging any of its members to take plural wives, though no official change of policy was announced. The anti-Mormons in Idaho did not want the Mormons to give up polygamy because it was such an effective tool against them politically. But a new blow against the Church fell, when the Edmunds-Tucker Act was passed by Congress March 3, 1887, without President Cleveland's signature.

This law was much more severe than the Edmunds law of 1882. It was designed to destroy the Church politically and economically. The national sponsors reasoned that if they could succeed in this aim, the Church would have to give up the practice of plural marriage. The attorney general was directed officially to dissolve the Church of Jesus Christ of Latter-day Saints as a legal corporation. The law confiscated all its property over $50,000 to the United States. The Perpetual Emigrating Fund was thus escheated and the Nauvoo Legion was disbanded.

The law also provided that all witnesses had to attend court trials conducted against polygamists and that a legal wife could testify against her husband. Of course the Idaho Test Act prevented any Mormon in Idaho from serving on any jury or from voting. Mormon influence in public schools was also weakened and a new test oath was added to election rules under the Edmunds-Tucker law. Finally it stated that all children would be disinherited if born of plural marriages more than one year after the act was passed.

When Amos heard about this he knew that polygamy raids by themselves couldn't make him or any Mormon polygamist give up plural marriage. But the legal campaign in the courts had and would continue to drive the Church leaders underground. This would, among other things, spell disaster to the successful United Order cooperatives in Bear Lake and elsewhere, for without Church leaders to direct them, they could not operate effectively. Up to this point, however, instead of destroying Church government in Bear Lake, the Test Oath had forced the Saints to depend even more on it. They continued to use church courts, church schools, stake priesthood and other Church-governing organizations. Now with the property of the Church taken over by the government and the other punitive rulings in this latest law, the only hope the Saints had was that the supreme court of the United States would declare these laws unconstitutional. But it had now been demonstrated that religious liberty in the United States did not extend far enough to protect some of the Mormon's most vital political, economic, social and theological doctrines.

A cause for much excitement occurred when President Budge was arrested in Ogden, Utah, June 2, 1887. No charges were filed or a warrant issued against him. Announcement was made in stake priesthood meeting that Brother Budge had been thus arrested. "It is very difficult for us to accept the situation peaceably but we are commanded to do so and we should humble ourselves before the Lord and purify our hearts and lives." (June 3, 1887, Priesthood Minutes, LDS Archives)

"Inability to secure more than one witness against Wm. Budge, after failure to subpoena a substantial number of others, ruined the case against him. None of Budge's plural wives could be found to testify against him. Even an open venire jury was in a poor position to convict after the disreputable single witness, Mathew Thompson, upon whose testimony numerous indictments had been based, turned out to be a perjurer." (*Anti-Mormonism in Idaho*, p. 110)

Later that same year it was widely speculated that the Saints might all go into exile again as they had done when they left Nauvoo forty years earlier. Charles Ora Card had established a haven for Idaho polygamists at Cardston, Alberta, but only a few Bear Lakers or other Saints took advantage of it.

When Amos read of President John Taylor's death at Kaysville, Utah, July 25, 1887, he mourned the loss of this great man as a personal friend. He had ordained Amos as a bishop six years ago, making the long trip from Salt Lake to do it. He had written to suggest that Amos write and send to him the detailed report about his remarkable Shoshone Indian mission in 1880 when he baptized Chief Washakie and over three hundred of his tribesmen. Brother Taylor had named Amos to accompany Apostle Moses Thatcher on his visit to the Wind River Agency as interpreter in 1884, and had corresponded and counseled and comforted him during his 1885-86 mission.

President Taylor was known as "The Champion of Liberty" and was beloved by many outside of the Church. He had been in hiding for over two years and denied the comforts of home, though lovingly ministered to by friends. He was in his seventy-ninth year at the time of his death, caused in part at least by being denied the comforts of home life. His funeral was held in a capacity-filled Salt Lake Tabernacle, July 29, 1887.

As late as December 1887, stake priesthood records show that Ed Austin and Amos were still vocally opposed to round dancing in the wards. Ed was bishop at Liberty and the two bishops worked out a system to persuade their ward members to stay within Church rules. If Ed felt his ward was slipping in this respect, he invited Bishop Wright to come to Liberty and give a strong talk about the evils of round dancing. Amos reciprocated and Ed Austin gave the Bennington members a lacing on the same subject. They felt the indirect approach might be more effective.

Addie was a popular girl in Bennington at twenty. Her father was anxious that she marry a good man. Brother Ream was much bedaddled over Amos' beautiful daughter and approached him about her as a possible plural wife. Addie vividly recalled the scene between her parents at the time they were deciding what to do about polygamy, and thus wasn't anxious to try it herself. Since the Church was not encouraging it, Amos didn't press the matter. Horace Weaver was a nice young fellow who was courting Addie. Like most fathers, Amos was a little skeptical about him. He came to dinner one night and Amos invited him to offer family prayer. Horace gave such a good one that Amos didn't offer any further objections from then on. Addie and Horace Weaver were married in Bennington by her father, January 1, 1888. They later went to Logan and were sealed in the temple there.

With the possibility of arrest by deputies considerably lessened for the past year or more, Amos decided to move Loella nearer to him. He bought a log house from John Jameson and moved it onto the farm near Cate's. Loella was overjoyed to have a home of her own, at last. Sarah and the girls helped fix it up as best they could, and at long last Gib and Sarah turned their daughter over to the care of her husband.

The hunt for "polygs" and "co-habs" resumed shortly after Loella got settled in Bennington.

Evading the marshals became a serio-comic game for the polygamists in the valley. The people in Paris had a way of discovering when the marshals were coming. They could always be spotted when they came in on the train to Montpelier. A boy was always lounging around whenever the train arrived, and when he saw them head for the livery stable to get mounts to ride to Paris, he headed for the telephone. After they crossed Bear River, he cranked the phone once to call Woolley Brothers' store in Paris. That was the only phone in town. Someone always slept in the store to answer the call. Then the polygamists in the town would be notified. A man with a tin horn went up and down the street blowing it, which was the signal that the deputies were coming. This gave the fugitives time to run for the nearby hills or other secret hiding places. Two Church leaders hid in the tower of the big tabernacle which was being built. One time the deputies caught eight brethren at once. One was caught because he stopped to change his trousers in the middle of the night, after having in his haste, put them on back to front.

Each man had a place of retreat set up ahead of time. One man tried various hiding places. First, he hid in the attic of his house, but that wasn't satisfactory. He then dug a hole under the bedroom. The trap door was covered by a large box full of clothing. As a result, when search was made, they didn't find the hiding place. The marshals were after him for seven years before they finally caught him. It was a grim game of hide and seek and many stories were exchanged over the supper tables about escapes and captures. (*Land of the Sky Blue Water*)

Amos' brother Dave had been hired as a deputy, and he boasted he would turn his brother in as readily as any other polygamist. Amos had to go to 'Pelier one day. He left before daylight to avoid being seen; got his errand done and was on his way back to Bennington. Suddenly, he heard pounding hoofs behind him and veered his saddle-less horse toward the first farmstead he came to; he seldom used a saddle in those days. Jumping off in the yard near the barn, he pulled off the bridle, taking it with him. Spying a hayrack half full of hay nearby, he quickly crawled into the hay leaving just room enough for his nose so he could breathe. He heard the marshals ride into the yard shouting, "I'm sure he went in here somewhere. We'll get the son of a gun this time."

They proceeded to scour the premises including the house where a frightened woman insisted she hadn't seen anybody. While one man searched the house in spite of the woman's protests, Amos muffled a sneeze as best he could. A moment later he felt a hand reach under the hay and give his chin whiskers a jerk.

"You old rascal, I knew you were there. It's a good thing I was the one to find you."

Just then the other man came out of the house and the mighty United States Marshal Dave Wright, Amos' brother, called out, "I guess he slipped through our fingers this time. He's nowhere around." They rode off cursing their bad luck.

The Mormon Crusade not only produced stories about polygamy, but people sometimes broke into unliterary verse about it. President Budge's counselor in the stake presidency, William H. Hart, was no exception:

> The Anti-Mormon hosts seem going mad.
> Their case is desperate—their symptoms bad.
> Convulsed with venomed spleen and Christian hate
> They're rushing wildly to their dismal fate.
> The storm is culminating fast and furious
> To know the ultimatum some are curious.
> Just to listen to the secret angel tell
> "The Lord Controls the Storm, and all is well.'"
> Then fight ye angry fiends, as best ye may
> And fortify yourselves against the day
> That's stealing on you like a thief tomorrow.
> The day of vengeance, and your day of sorrow!
> The sign of truth and liberty must come
> And Saints from every land be gathered home
> Then "hold the fort" till Christ shall come again
> And with the royal Priesthood rule and reign.
>
> (*Land of Sky Blue Water*)

Monthly stake priesthood meeting in Paris was a "must" for Amos. The family often chided him half in jest, half seriously, that the world would stop rotating if he missed a priesthood meeting. He wasn't taking any chances, anyway.

In April, 1888, President Taylor had been dead for nine months and the first presidency had not been reorganized. The Council of the Twelve with Wilford Woodruff as president, was thus the presiding authority for the Church.

As usual, Amos rode his horse to Paris for the April meeting. When he got there, President Budge asked him if he would make a few remarks to the brethren assembled. The stake clerk summarized them as follows:

> We are living in a time when we are measurably left to ourselves and it is absolutely necessary that we enjoy the companionship of

the Holy Ghost. If we lose this spirit we will fall away if we do not take a course to have it renewed. It is a time calculated to try and prove men whether they love the truth above all else. The Lord says woe unto the unbelievers and he is sending them strong delusions as is manifest by many people placing their faith in miracles. Such ones reject the Gospel and God's curse attends them." (Bear Lake Stake Priesthood minutes April 7, 1888, L.D.S. Archives.)

A few weeks later Cate wasn't feeling very well so Amos decided to sleep in the house instead of in his hideout, so he could look after her. They were awake most of the night and just got to sleep before the sun came up. They were suddenly aroused by the dog barking. Cate got up and took the little chinken from between the two logs of the house which she used as her lookout, and saw two men on horses galloping toward the house. There wasn't time for Mose to get away this time. They were pounding on the door before she could get dressed and she went to answer in her nightgown.

"Come on, open up!" they shouted. "We know you're here this time." Cate opened the door a crack and tried to keep them from coming in by assuring them her husband would be there in a minute. He walked to the door buttoning his shirt as he went. The minute they caught sight of him they pushed the door wide open and grabbed him quickly and pulled him outside.

"If you'll wait a few minutes I'll go and get my horse," he said quietly.

"Oh no, you don't. We'll go with you. We don't let a slippery Indian out of our sight now we've got him," and they followed him across the road into the field laughing and cursing alternately while he caught Peanuts. Amos could tell they'd been drinking and their vile language disgusted him. He put a rope around the horse's neck and took off the hobbles. Leading the animal toward the house he stopped and called to Cate. She came to the door and he said, "Will you please bring my wallet?" She disappeared and came back in a few minutes. "I can't find it." "It's there, look again," he called back. As they waited impatiently the deputies slid off their horses and rolled a cigarette, bantering Amos meanwhile. "They told us we'd have to be mighty tough to catch old Ame Wright, and here he surrendered without a struggle. This'll be a feather in our cap by G—!" said Hodgson, waving his cigarette insolently toward Amos.

Again, Cate came to the door. "Mose, it isn't there, I can't find it." The marshals looked toward the house as she spoke. Quick as a flash Amos made a running jump onto Peanut's back, giving him a whack on the rump with the hobbles in his hand, and was off like a streak down the road toward Maple Field. As soon as the deputies saw what was happening, they pulled their pistols and started shooting. Amos rode like an Indian, lying close to the horse's neck and throwing himself alternately from one side of the horse's back to the other as he rode. The pony kicked up a lot of dust, making it hard to draw an accurate bead on him, but they fired away nevertheless. His captors had lost a good deal of time, and now mounted hurriedly and gave chase. Cate stood in the cabin door shouting, "Go it, Mose, go it! They can't catch you!!" Saying a prayer for him she strained her eyes until he was a mere speck in the distance speeding toward Maple Canyon, with the two riders still trailing behind. If he could reach the canyon he'd have a chance to escape. She realized he knew every inch of that mountain and was a clever Indian at concealing his tracks.

Late that afternoon she spied the two deputies returning. They were both riding one horse and leading the other one which was limping badly. They turned south on the road to Montpelier so she pretty well knew Mose had got away. She still worried that they might have hit him when they first began shooting there in the yard, but they couldn't have hurt him too bad or he couldn't have stayed on Peanuts and kept riding.

About ten o'clock that night there came a knock on her door and it was Brother George Lindsay. He and his wife lived in a little cabin up Maple Canyon. "I thought I'd better come and tell you Ame's all right, so you wouldn't worry. One of the bullets made a hole clean through the brim of his hat and the marshals about stepped on him a couple of times after they started tracking him on foot. His horse finally gave out, so Ame and the pony hid in a little secret cave he knew about, and the marshals had to give up the search. He said to tell you not to worry and he would be home in a few days after he was sure the deputies had left Montpelier. We gave him something to eat and we'll look after him, that's for sure." Cate thanked him and he left.

Amos came back a few nights later. Cate was learning not to be surprised at anything these days. Again she put on the wash boiler and repeated the business of getting him scrubbed up before he got into bed. It was easier to wash *him* than her bedding.

Next morning he shaved, put on some clean clothes and said he was going to Paris.

"What for?" asked Cate.

"I'm going to get the deed fixed up to the Maple Canyon farm so Loella will have some land if anything happens to me, and then I'm going to give myself up."

"But why give yourself up when you just got away from the marshals?"

"This business of hiding around in a free country goes against my grain. Besides, I wasn't about to take it when a couple of drunk devils joshed me about being so easy to catch. President Taylor said we weren't to lick anybody's boots," and he brought his fist down on the table with a bang. "President Snow gave himself up; President Taylor went into exile mainly hoping it would cut down on the persecution of the rest of us. I showed those devils they couldn't catch me, and now I'm ready to give myself up voluntarily. It will be simpler for all of us if I turn myself in, have a trial and if I'm convicted, pay the fine and get it over with. But I'll fight every step of the way!"

"But how will you pay a fine? You haven't got any money."

"Well, we'll take care of that when we have to. I've got to see Loella before I go. She can't stay here now, but I've made some arrangements for her, it's probably best you don't know anything about that in case you should have to testify against me. Goodbye, Cate, and God bless you."

Chapter Twenty-six

On the Underground

Loella was five or six months pregnant again and Amos didn't want to let her stay alone in the little cabin across the road from Cate. He got Loella's sister, Alice, to come and stay with her. What he was about to do now would make a difference in their plans.

When he walked in, two-year-old Nelly came running to meet him saying, "Pa-Pa-Pa!" He swept her into his arms and kissed her again and again. She was his blonde beauty and Loella thought the child looked like her father.

"Oh, Brother Wright," said Loella. "I'm so thankful you got away from the marshals. I woke up when I heard the shots that morning and saw you riding down the road ahead of them. I prayed you'd get away safely."

He pulled her down on his lap. "Yes, I was lucky I guess. But, my dear girl, I'm afraid things won't be any better for awhile, and maybe they will be worse. I'm going to give myself up. There's no use playing cat and mouse any longer. But I've got a plan for you," he said, running his fingers through her wavy hair.

"I talked to Brother Osmond while I was staying at George Lindsay's. He says he has a cabin over in Elk Valley, about twenty-five miles east of Montpelier. If you can ride a horse, you can go over there and stay until my trial comes up. He says nobody could find you there. You can't stay with your folks now because if the deputies find you there they'll make you testify against me."

"But what will I do? Nelly can't stand to ride a horse twenty-five miles!" said Loella.

"You're right, honey. We'll have to ask your mother to keep her while you're gone. She couldn't go that far."

Loella burst into tears. "Oh, Brother Wright, I can't leave my baby!"

"I'm afraid you will have to," he said, drawing her closer and wiping her tears away. "I've wondered if your cousins Riley and Henry Weaver would be willing to take you to Elk Valley and stay with you. I'll talk to them right away and let you know what they say.

"What if I get sick while I'm way back there in the woods? I'm expecting my baby in November, you know."

"We'll have to take that chance and rely on the Lord," said Amos. "Our enemies are heartless. They don't care what happens to you or your baby. If they catch you and make you appear as a witness, now, I wouldn't have a chance to stay out of jail, and then I couldn't take care of you, either. I'll give you a blessing and things will work out all right."

"How will I know when it's time to come back again?"

Amos shook his head. "I just don't know, dear."

Loella looked at him trustingly. "All right Brother ... I mean Mose. I'll do anything you say." She had wanted to call him Mose ever since they were married but didn't quite have the courage before. He looked pleased and hugged her.

He laid his hands on her head and promised her she would be

protected and return safely among other things. He walked down
the path and she watched him through the little window as he
mounted his horse and rode away. She was only half a person
when he was away it seemed.

Later that day, Henry and Riley Weaver, her two cousins
whom she knew like brothers, came to tell her they'd be ready to
leave early next morning with horses and a pack outfit. Henry
was sixteen and Riley fourteen. Then Sarah and Gib came a little
later to take little Nelly with them. At least Loella knew they
would take good care of her while she was gone. She waved bye-
bye through her tears as Gib carried her out to the buggy and
drove away. All Loella could do now was pray. At least she would
have God to talk to.

The twenty-five miles seemed like a hundred. Loella wasn't an
outdoors girl. She never liked riding horses. And being six months
pregnant, the saddle was anything but comfortable. The boys
were very considerate and stopped often to let her rest. Henry told
her he promised Brother Wright he would pose as her husband if
the deputies should find them. "But I don't think even deputies
would go into the wilds like this to hunt a man or a woman, either.
So don't worry, Loell, we'll take good care of you."

It took two days travel to reach the cabin. Through brush and
trees, over fallen logs, up hills and down hollows they went. Her
face and arms were scratched and she ached all over. There
wasn't even a trail to follow. Henry spread a buffalo robe on the
ground that night and covered her with blankets. She was warm
enough, but it was a hard bed, and she didn't get much sleep.

Another long day was almost gone when they reached the
little cabin. She wondered how the boys ever found the tiny one-
room hut with not even a window in it. They tied a rope across one
end of the room and hung a blanket over it, to make a little
privacy for Loella, cut some evergreen branches to put on the dirt
floor, covered them with a buffalo robe, and made her a somewhat
comfortable bed. She helped the boys unpack the things and put
them on the one shelf inside. Henry made a fire outside and
showed Loella how to make sourdough biscuits and cook them in
a bake kettle on the hot coals. A little stream nearby furnished
them with water and the thick-growing lodgepole pines provided
protective shelter from the prying eyes of deputies.

But it was a waiting game. With so little to do, Loella's
thoughts returned continually to her baby Nelly,to Mose; to her
own little cabin in Bennington; and memories of her home with

Gib and Sarah. Had she made a terrible mistake to become a plural wife? She thought of her sisters at home. They seemed happy and free to do what they wanted to do. She knew they pitied her and she didn't want their pity even if she needed it. If she could just have Nelly with her she wouldn't be so lonely. She felt the baby she was carrying move inside her. Would she love it as much as her firstborn? If Mose could be with her, she wouldn't be so scared and worried. He seemed so strong and confident and she was weak and dependent.

Such thoughts were only temporary, and her usual cheerful disposition overcame them. The boys played mumbletypeg with her and let her beat them, and they played tick-tack-toe on the ground, using a stick for a pencil. She took short walks marking the trees as she went so she wouldn't get lost.

The ground was carpeted with pine needles and the trees grew so close together that very little sun filtered through. One day she found a bunch of trilliums growing at the foot of a large cedar, and a little further on some dogtooth violets. She took a bouquet back to the boys.

She wondered how long she would have to stay in this lonely place. How would she know when it was time to leave? One day when she was alone she knelt down and prayed. "Heavenly Father, I need to know when it is time to leave. Don't make me stay till we get snowed in. Keep me well so I'll be able to ride the horse. Please give me a sign so I'll know when. If you will send just a little skiff of snow, I'll know it's time to go. Thanks. In the name of Jesus Christ, Amen." A calm peacefulness settled over her as she returned to the little cabin.

Riley made a calendar out of birch bark and used a piece of charcoal from the bonfire to check each day off. The days and weeks dragged by. On the morning of the fifth of October, Loella awakened to a skiff of snow on the ground. "Today is the day we must leave," she excitedly exclaimed.

"How do you know?" asked Henry.

She told them of her agreement with the Lord. The boys looked at each other, wondering if they should believe, but she seemed so sure, they decided to do as she said. Packing up their few belongings and saddling the horses, they helped Loella climb on by standing on a big log. The horses made tracks in the snow as they started but they hadn't gone far when there wasn't any snow at all, and by the time they got to Afton, Wyoming, the ground was dry and dusty.

They stopped by the edge of the trail to let Loella rest. She slid off the horse and sat down with her back against a tree, closing her eyes wearily. She must have dozed for awhile, but was awakened by the sound of a horse galloping toward her. She opened her eyes and cried out, "Mose!" She was so awkward she couldn't get up but in a moment her husband was kneeling beside her kissing her and saying, "Darling, how did you know it was time to come out?" And without waiting for her to reply he went on, "I just got out of court day before yesterday and have been riding steadily ever since. I didn't know whether I could find you or not, but I asked the Lord to help me and he did!"

Loella told him about the skiff of snow sign, and they both marveled. Henry and Riley couldn't believe the way things had worked out, either.

"How's my baby?" asked Loella.

"She's wonderful and the folks are spoiling her terribly."

"What happened in Blackfoot? Did they hold your trial?"

"They postponed it until June when the next district court convenes. They subpoenaed Silas, Addie and Johnny and Gib as witnesses. We all went down together. Gib was worried about having to testify. He knew if he told the truth he would have to admit his daughter was married to me. If he lied he would have all sorts of explaining to do, such as accounting for the birth of a child to his daughter, besides risking a penalty for perjury. He asked me what he should do. I said, 'Let's pray about it.' Just before the trial, we went into an empty room and I asked that Gib wouldn't have to testify. They didn't call on him at all. I plead 'not guilty' and then they postponed the case for six months. The witnesses were supposed to get paid three dollars a day for the time they were there, but they offered to apply it on my fine. Oh, I forgot to tell you that my brother Dave was on the grand jury hearing my case. He didn't look at me as far as I could tell, and I didn't get a chance to talk to him afterward. Maybe he didn't want to talk anyway."

"Where can we go now? Can I go back to my own house?" asked Loella.

"I'm afraid it won't be safe," said Amos, lifting Loella into the saddle. "They'd love to have you for a witness, especially right now. We'll figure something out, though, so don't worry. It's time we got started. It's still a long way to Bennington. We'll take you to Gib and Sarah's first so you can see the baby and we'll play it by ear from then on."

The journey went surprisingly well for Loella, then, despite her discomfort. Having Mose with her again made all the difference. She was so anxious to get home she wouldn't stop as often as Amos wanted her to. "I'm all right dear, don't worry. I can't wait to see Nelly."

The baby had changed and learned some new words and Sarah had taught her a cute little song with hand motions to go with it. Loella was beside herself with joy to have her child in her arms again. "Oh, Mother, I'll never be able to repay you for taking care of her all this time," and she kissed the child again and again.

Sarah insisted on Loella staying with them for a few days, at least, until Amos could find out what was best to do.

"I'll see the midwife right away," he said. "Let's see, when are you due?"

"I think about the first of November, though I'm not sure, of course."

He returned next day. "I talked to Sister Ipsen. She said it would probably be safer to have you go somewhere else to have your baby. The deputies are everywhere, and somebody is sure to talk. She suggested Sister Tippets over at Georgetown. I know her. She's a wonderful midwife. She took her training in Salt Lake from Dr. Shipp and she's the best there is. I'll try to get word to her, somehow."   A few nights later Loella awakened with pains in her stomach and the gnawing fear of how to get word to Mose. She toughed it out till morning and then Gib went to tell him. By the time he got there, the pains had subsided. A false alarm.

"If they don't start again till this evening," said Amos, "we'd better wait so nobody will see us leave. I haven't talked to Sister Tippets, but we'll have to take a chance. Get your things ready and I'll call for you after supper.

"Do I have to leave Nelly with Mother again?"

"Yes, I'll take care of her, dear," said Sarah quickly, not waiting for Mose to answer.

Loella was ready and waiting when Amos drove up in the bobsleigh with old Rock and Bird in the harness. He tucked her in with a hot brick at her feet. The wind wasn't blowing, thank goodness, so they should make the ten or twelve miles without any trouble.

It was midnight when Amos knocked on Sister Tippets' door in Georgetown. She answered the door, sleepily, holding a candle and clutching her robe about her with the other hand.

"Sister Tippets, do you remember me? 'm Amos Wright from Bennington. My wife, Loella, is ready to deliver a child, and we need your help. May we come in?"

"Why bless your hearts, of course you can! Bring her in and I'll build up the fire." From that moment, Amos' anxiety and Loella's fears evaporated as dear Jeanette Tippets took over. She seemed to know exactly what to do and proceeded to do it.

"We didn't dare wait any longer to come," explained Amos. "She's on the underground you know."

"Now don't you worry a minute. She can stay here with me as long as necessary. I'll make a bed down on the floor for both of you till morning and then we'll decide what to do."

Amos unhitched the horses and tied them to the wagon box where they could munch the hay he brought along. Next morning he left for Bennington, knowing his dear Loell was in good hands, and danger of the deputies finding her were very slim.

Loella gave birth to another little girl November 2, 1888, and both Mose and Loella decided to name her Jeanette Tippets, after the ministering angel who took them in unannounced. Loella stayed with her for two weeks and was treated like a queen. The baby had dark, curly hair and eyes that would undoubtedly be brown. She was a beautiful child. Loella's heart was magically drawn to this baby. No question now about loving her as much as Nelly. Her heart had suddenly stretched to include them both.

A kind neighbor offered to let Loella stay with them for a month or two. After that, others fell in love with this beautiful young woman. She was welcomed into four or five homes in turn, until after the next term of court was called in June. People had learned to be very discreet and close-mouthed about such matters. The deputies didn't have a chance around Georgetown Saints.

Meanwhile, the same court routine went on at Blackfoot as it had six months earlier. Amos, accompanied by Gib and Addie and Silas and Johnny took the train June 28, 1889. The interminable waiting, the senseless form and mummery, and finally the decision to again postpone the case until November, left Amos frustrated and boiling inside, but having to appear calm and respectful to the judge and jury. He was treated as a number and a name and with a mocking manner that burned his soul. He caught sight of Dave sitting in the jury box again and this time there was a flicker of acknowledgment, but that was all. Dave knew better than to expose his feelings. He would be dismissed at once as a juror if they suspected he was anything but anti-Mormon. Being a deputy marshal wasn't all it was cracked up to be.

Amos found a place for Loella at Liberty. His dear friend Ed Austin volunteered to look after her. Ed was a polygamist, himself, and under indictment the same as Amos, so he couldn't take Loella into his home but he found a place for her. She stayed there a few weeks.

The *Deseret Weekly* published the news of Wilford Woodruff being sustained as President of the Church, July 10, 1889. He was eighty-three, an old man and people wondered how he could take on all the responsibilities necessary, but like the others had done before him, he did.

November 1889 came at long last, and for the third time Amos and his subpoenaed witnesses made the trip on the train to Blackfoot. Ed Austin and Brother Hart were there for the same purpose as he was, so at least he was in good company. He decided to plead guilty this time, hoping to get it over with. This made any further delay unnecessary. The jury declared him guilty and judgment would be announced next day. Next day came and he was fined two hundred dollars or six months in jail.

Amos' heart sank. Where would he get $200? He had spent a year and a half waiting to be sentenced or released. His family had contributed everything they could get hold of to cover his expenses, but it wasn't enough. Cate was having a hard time even taking care of day to day expenses. Going to jail would be the last straw, but there was no alternative.

The sheriff slipped a pair of handcuffs on him and took him out the back door. They each mounted a horse to ride to the jail and started down the road. They had gone only a little way when Amos heard another horse galloping toward them. The rider pulled up alongside him, all but his eyes covered with a bandana handkerchief. It was nearly dusk.

"Here," the masked man said, stuffing an envelope in Amos' hand. "Pay your fine and tell those s.o.b.'s to go to hell," whereat he galloped off into the distance. The eyes and voice were unmistakable. Dave, his brother, his accuser and member of the grand jury which declared him guilty, had somehow got enough money together to pay his fine. Amos wept as the sheriff wonderingly took the money and said, "You're free. Go home and don't come back." (See Notes at end of Chapter 26)

As he rode home on the train from Blackfoot, he wondered

what he could do about Loella now. It would still be unsafe for her
to stay with Gib and Sarah, especially since she was expecting
again. He couldn't risk another arrest. Maybe he'd see somebody
at stake conference who could help him out.

Stake conference was held Nov. 9 in Paris with the tabernacle
also being dedicated. The place was packed. Five years of labor
and love had gone into that beautiful building, to say nothing of
money. It had cost $50,000 and it was the largest and finest
church building in Idaho. As Amos sat there and gazed at the
great hand-hewn doors and looked up at the intricately carved
ceiling designed by a shipbuilder, he marveled that such beauty
could be produced by the little group of hard-working farmers in
Bear Lake Valley. It was a symbol of the great cause to which
they were dedicated: building the Kingdom of God on the earth.
Brother James E. Hart, who had just returned from Blackfoot,
too, where he was fined $300, spoke at the conference:

"The Idaho Test Oath has been deemed constitutional by the
Supreme Court. I believe the ultimate result will be to strengthen
instead of weakening the Kingdom of God, but it is an outrage!"
(Stake Priesthood minutes, Bear Lake Stake, LDS Archives)

Amos was called on to give the benediction. As usual, after the
meeting he visited with his friends, among them Ira Nebeker. Ira
asked about Loella and where she was. Amos told him she was at
Gib's and Sarah's but couldn't stay there, nor did he dare let her
stay in her own little house in Bennington.

"Why don't you bring her down to Laketown for awhile? We'd
love to have her and the children and you know we'll take good
care of them."

Tears stood in Amos' eyes as he shook his dear friend's hand.
"That's mighty kind of you, Ira. You know Loella is expecting in
February and Nettie is only a year old. That would be a big order
to take on in addition to your own family. But with persecution
the worst it's ever been, I don't know what we'll do."

"Now don't you worry, Mose. We'll take care of your family
and glad to do it. Bring them down right away and let them stay
as long as they need to."

Amos drove Loella and the two little girls in a bobsleigh to
Laketown one night the following week. They stayed all winter.
The Nebekers were the salt of the earth, and opened their home
and hearts to the wayfarers. Living in other people's homes, no
matter how welcome, wasn't easy, either, and took all the virtues
attributed to Saints to do it.

Loella was homesick, especially at Christmas time when Mose didn't come down to see her. A Bear Lake Christmas in 1889 wasn't much as to gifts, but there was a world of love and happiness. Nelly, though only four, never forgot the wonderful time she had and the little rocking chair the Nebeker Santa Claus brought for her.

February 2, 1890, at Laketown, Idaho, Loella gave birth to her third daughter in less than five years. She had lived only a month of that time in her own house. She named the baby Mary Ellen after Ira Nebeker's wife, another angel to match Sarah Weaver and Jeanette Tipetts.

Amos knew he couldn't wait any longer to relieve the Nebeker's from the responsibility of caring for his family, but he still didn't have any place to take them, and it was risky to move them in a Bear Lake winter. But by early April he decided something had to be done. Sarah and Gib told him to bring Loella back home to them even if there was a chance the deputies would find her there. Winter hadn't retired by any means, so it was a tossup whether to take the bobsleigh or the wagon. He took the wagon. Rock and Bird was the only team of horses and Bird was an ornery critter. You never knew what she might do in a pinch.

Amos drove to Laketown one night. He'd forgotten how to travel in the daytime. The weather looked threatening but it was April so it couldn't be too bad, he hoped.

Loella was overjoyed to see him again and anxious to leave. Next morning it was snowing and the wind was rising. It looked like a regular Bear Laker. The Nebekers thought it was foolish to start out, but Amos said it was a blessing because no deputy would venture out in that kind of weather. They decided to risk it.

Loella and the three little ones bundled up in quilts in the bottom of the wagon box and Amos sat up on the spring seat in his old reliable sheepskin coat. The horses knew they were heading for home so Amos didn't have to apply the whip and they made good time as far as Paris. The visibility was zero by then and he decided it would be best to give the horses their heads since they were probably smarter than he was under the circumstances. There had been a warm spell the week before. The ice in Bear River had melted and the slough on both sides of the river was two or three feet deep. The water had overrun the road in a number of places so it was hard to tell which was road or which was slough.

A mud hen suddenly flew up in front of old Bird and startled her. She shied, pulling Rock to the right and the next minute the wheels sank up to the hubs in mud and water. The horses lunged forward, breaking the tug on the left side and tipping the wagon box over into the slough, with Loella and the babies landing in two feet of water.

Amos let go of the reins to catch himself. The horses frantically kicked, broke loose from the wagon and disappeared down the road, dragging the rest of the harness with them. The children screamed and Loella and Amos managed to pull them out of the water and back onto the road. Loella clutched two-month-old Mary to her breast and managed to keep her from getting as wet as the others.

"What shall we do, Mose? We'll die or freeze to death!" And she, too, became hysterical.

"You stay here and I'll go back toward Paris," he yelled over the children's screams and the roaring wind. "There's a house back there a ways. I'll try to find my way and get some help. You'll have to hold out till I get back. Keep the children's feet and legs in the water so they won't freeze," and he staggered off in the opposite direction fighting the wind.

The three of them sat in the mud at the edge of the road, the little girls' stockinged feet and legs dangling in the water. They screamed till they couldn't scream any longer. Loella's clothes were frozen so stiff she could hardly pull them away from her breast so the baby could nurse. She finally succeeded and tried to hold the baby to her breast with one arm, and keep Nelly's and Nettie's legs in the water with the other.

It was over an hour before Amos and a German farmer returned with horses and a wagon and quilts to wrap the sufferers in and take them back to his house.

"Vell, Vell, das ist schade!" said the fat, motherly woman who ran out to help carry them inside. "Ve vill vix dem soon now." More cold water was used to peel off the frozen clothing, and gradually warm water was added. Their stomachs were warmed with ginger tea, and at last they were dry, clothed, and tucked in bed to recover from their dreadful exposure.

The storm was over in a couple of hours. Sister Voss prepared pea soup and kuchen and fussed over Loella and the children like a mother hen. She made a warm bed in the bottom of the wagon box and Amos carried Loella and the children out and wrapped them in quilts and a buffalo robe. Brother Voss went along to drive his team and Amos sat on the spring seat beside him.

"I'll go vid you, Brudder Wright, and den I come back vid my horses and vagon."

It was eight o'clock that night when they arrived at Gib's and Sarah's. The children were surprisingly well-off by that time, but when Amos carried Loella into the house, she fainted dead away. Smelling salts and prayer finally revived her and after a few days of complete rest, she miraculously recovered from the ordeal.

The final straw broke the camel's back when the supreme court, May 18, 1890, declared that the Edmunds-Tucker Act was constitutional "as pertaining to the confiscation of Church property." The long-awaited decision of that legal body came with devastating force and wiped out further hope for the Saints. What would they do next?

Chapter Twenty-seven

The Manifesto

Amos first came under the influence of plural wives as a boy of seven. He lived sixty-eight years of his life, either as a son or husband in that environment. Mary Jane was his second mother and he loved her as much as he did his own. He loved Lois Moran, too, but in a different way. "Aunt" Caroline Olsen was Father Jonathan's sixth wife who lived in Brigham City a few blocks away from Mary Jane.

Amos married Loella Weaver in 1885, twenty-seven years and eleven children after he wed Catherine Roberts and just a year before the Church stopped advocating plural marriage. Loella and Cate lived across the road from each other in Bennington for twenty-four years. After the Manifesto, Amos continued to provide for Cate and their children as long as they were at home, but he spent most of his time at Loella's.

Only two of Jonathan's thirty-four children chose plural marriage for themselves. Amos and Charlotte, the two eldest, became "second generation" polygamists. Third generation Addie might have become a plural wife but she chose otherwise because she knew ahead of time how hard it was to live. Amos knew, too, but he realized the Lord wanted him to take another wife so he obeyed.

By the spring of 1890 when Loella came back to her father's home from Laketown, she was about at the end of her rope—physically, spiritually and mentally. The pressure had been so intense for the past five years it is a wonder her sanity was saved. Marriage, even under favorable circumstances, is a test of unselfishness. She wondered if she had taken on more than she could manage.

Cate's hurdle, so far, had been in consenting to her husband's marrying a young beautiful woman as his second wife. But her test wasn't over yet.

Amos was humiliated in having to ask Loella's parents to take care of their daughter for six years after he married her. Their test was to do it cheerfully and lovingly. To a man with the sense of independence and pride which Amos had, it was humbling to have to leave Loella in Georgetown for six months staying with strangers, and to accept the offer of his friend, Ira Nebeker, to take care of his family all one winter. What made it far worse was having his wife and three little girls thrown into a swamp in a Bear Lake blizzard and thus threatened with death, when he was sitting in the driver's seat.

Should he curse Joseph Smith for starting this thing, and the Lord for commanding it? Was Satan bent on destroying his wife and children? Could he put the blame on Father Jonathan for setting the example for him to follow? Or was he a fool with nobody to blame but himself? If he had waited just one more year before marrying Loella, the plural wife practice would have been discontinued and he'd have escaped the terrible test. How much misery and persecution could or would he take? Was there a way out? He could get on his horse, keep riding, change his name and get lost. He could commit suicide, or deny his belief in Mormonism and plural marriage.

Deep thinker that he was, Amos undoubtedly considered these alternatives. Yet, it must have been a shock to him and other faithful Saints when they heard and read President Wilford Woodruff's declaration in general conference in Salt Lake City, October 6, 1890:

> As President of the Church of Jesus Christ of Latter-day Saints, I do hereby in the most solemn manner declare, that inasmuch as laws have been enacted by Congress forbidding plural marriages, which

laws have been pronounced constitutional by the court of last resort,
I hereby declare my intention to submit to those laws, and to use my
influence with the members of the Church over which I preside to
have them do likewise. And I now publicly declare that my advice to
the Latter-day Saints is to refrain from contracting any marriage
forbidden by the law of the land.

After the Manifesto had been read to the conference, President
Lorenzo Snow offered the following:

I move, that, recognizing Wilford Woodruff as the President of
the Church of Jesus Christ of Latter-day Saints, and the only man on
the earth at the present time who holds the keys of the sealing
ordinances, we consider him fully authorized to issue the manifesto
which has been read in our hearing and which is dated Sept. 24, 1890,
and that as a Church in General Conference assembled, we accept
his declaration concerning plural marriages as authoritative and
binding.

The vote to sustain the foregoing motion was unanimous.
(Sjodahl and Smith, *Doctrine & Dovenants Commentary*, pp. 836-
37.)

Amos knew if he had been there himself, he'd have raised his
hand and voted as all the other Saints did, because he knew it was
right and for no other reason. He didn't argue with the Lord or his
authorized servant. It was this very thing which had so puzzled
and enraged the enemies of the Church and which continued to do
so. It was expressed by the United States District Attorney in
Utah in anger before the court:

They (the Latter-day Saints) are not obeying the law of the land
at all, but the counsel of the head of the church. The law of the land,
with all its mighty power, and the terrible pressure it was enabled to
bring with its iron heel upon this people crushing them to powder,
was unable to bring about what this man did in an hour in the
assembled conference of this people. They were willing to go to
prison; I doubt not some of them were willing to go to the gallows, to
the tomb of the martyr, before they would have yielded one single
iota.

And such was the truth in the case. The Saints in this matter
of surrendering the practice of plural marriage obeyed God, not
man. (CHC Vol. VI p. 227) The eyes of the nation and even the
world were on the Mormons.

The Mormon image for almost a century had been pro-
gressively bad, painted by sensationalists bent on lining their
own pockets. They wrote about plural wives running away from
brutal husbands; slaves in a harem of horrors. It sounded

credible. Few people knew any real Mormons, and besides, it was exciting reading. Americans and the world in general believed what they read and started a crusade to free mankind from the results of such "barbarism."

Amos recalled his fishing experiences at Ft. Lemhi when the silver salmon swarmed up the river each spring. They innocently nosed through the trap set by the Indians and found themselves being beaten with clubs and thrown out on the bank to die at the hands of their captors. Would the Lord provide an escape for the Saints,which had not been forthcoming for mere fish? Answers to these and other questions did not come immediately. Amos and others like him would long wrestle with these problems as part of their test.

He and Loella and her parents faced the new situation together as they sat around the stove at Gib's and Sarah's. "Well, folks," said Amos, stroking his beard thoughtfully, "it's hard for me to know what will be the outcome of this action. Can you have patience a little longer and keep Loella and the children again till we see what happens?

"Sure, she can stay," said Gib, nodding his head. "It's been a long, hard row to hoe, but there's been a lot of happiness tucked in between. We've learned to love little Nelly and Nettie and baby Mary. Loell has been a brave girl and she's learned to be unselfish and patient, living here with us in our poor quarters."

"None of us wanted to get into this thing." Sarah wiped a tear away as she spoke. "I know I was afraid at first and worried that Loella wasn't old enough to get married, let alone go through what she's had to, but I must admit she surprised all of us," and she reached over and kissed her daughter on the cheek.

"Does the Manifesto mean that you will have to give me and the children up, now? What will happen to us?" asked Loella.

"I don't think that is what it means, but if it does, I'll never do it, be sure of that," replied Amos.

"Can I move back to Bennington then, Mose? There's nothing I want more than to be in my own home once more. Please let me go!"

"Well, my girl, we'll have to wait awhile longer to see if things settle down now. I promise you it won't be one minute longer than is necessary. We must wait for counsel from the authorities, whatever it may be," he said with finality. It was a year before counsel came. Amos attended Cache Stake Conference at Logan, Utah, Nov. 1, 1891, and found solace and comfort in the words of

President Wilford Woodruff and others:

I have had some revelations of late and I will tell you what the Lord has said to me, that there are many members of the Church throughout Zion who are sorely tried in their hearts because of the Manifesto.

The Lord has commanded me to ask the Latter-day Saints a question, and that if they would listen to what I said to them and answer the question put to them, by the spirit and power of God they would all answer alike.

Which is the wisest course for the Latter-day Saints to pursue: to continue to attempt to practice plural marriage, with the laws of the nation against it and the opposition of sixty millions of people, and at the cost of the loss of all the temples and the stopping of all the ordinances therein, both for the living and the dead, and the imprisonment of the First Presidency and Twelve and the heads of families in the Church, and the confiscation of personal property of the people (all of which themselves would stop the practice)? Or after doing and suffering what we have through our adherence to this principle to cease the practice and submit to the law, and through doing so leave the Prophets, Apostles and fathers home, so that they can instruct the people and attend to the duties of the Church, and also leave the temples in the hands of the Saints, so that they can attend to the ordinances of the Gospel, both for the living and the dead?

I saw exactly what would come to pass if there was not something done. I have had this spirit upon me for a long time. But I want to say this: I should have let all the temples go out of our hands; I should have gone to prison myself, and let every man go there, had not the God of Heaven commanded me to do what I did do; and when the hour came that I was commanded to do that, it was all clear to me. I went before the Lord, and I wrote what He told me to write. I laid it before my brethren, such strong men as Brother George Q. Cannon, Brother Joseph F. Smith and the Twelve Apostles. I might as well undertake to turn an army with banners out of its course as to turn them out of the course that they considered to be right. These men agreed with me and ten thousand Latter-day Saints also agreed with me. Why? Because they were moved upon by the Spirit of God and by the revelations of Jesus Christ to do it. (*Deseret Weekly*, Nov. 14, 1891, Vol. 43, No. 21, pages 659-660 L.D.S. Archives)

President George Q. Cannon, 1st counselor in the first presidency also spoke, following President Woodruff:

I know that President Woodruff has been led by inspiration. The word of the Lord has come to us through that man to cease this practice. This principle, in many instances, has been abused. This is evidenced by the fact that some, because the law encourages it, have forsaken their wives who have been true and faithful to them. How mean and cowardly it is to take this course. Such men will not be worthy of wives in eternity. The Lord will judge us. He knows the motives that actuate us.

There will be men who never had a wife, and again men who have had but one wife, who will enter into the Celestial Kingdom of our God. President Woodruff said that is true, and some who have had several wives will not. God knew our hearts and the opportunities we have had of obeying his commandments, and will judge us accordingly. I say this for the consolation of the Saints. The Lord knows our sacrifices and sufferings and has accepted our offering.

No man who has a plurality of wives is required to break his covenants. He should feed, clothe and support them and educate their children. (Ibid.)

"Well," thought Amos at the close of the meeting, "now I have received my counsel I know what to do. I'll move Loell back to Bennington and I hope we can begin to live like American citizens for a change."

This he did, but the old, nagging questions kept coming back whenever he woke up in the night, and then sleep was out of the question. In 1885 the Church strongly advocated plural marriage. A year later a stillness on the subject fell over the Church leaders and by 1890 they made a hundred and eighty-degree switch when President Woodruff issued the Manifesto making plural marriage unlawful and a sin. It seemed like an on-again, off-again policy just to placate the government when it applied the persecution pressure hard enough, and left him and others, like the fish at Ft. Lemhi, caught in a trap with no escape possible.

He wrestled silently with this idea for eight years before he got a satisfactory answer and it was Lorenzo Snow as President of the Church who gave an explanation which laid Amos' inner war at rest. At a special conference held at St. George, Utah, in May, 1899, Brother Snow spoke and his words were printed in the *Deseret Weekly News* where Amos read them:

The Lord has determined in his heart that He will try us until He knows what he can do with us. He tried His son Jesus. Thousands of years before He came upon the earth, the Father had watched His course and knew that He could depend upon Him when the salvation of worlds should be at stake; and He was not disappointed.

So in regard to ourselves. He will try us, and continue to try us in order that He may place us in the highest positions in life and put upon us the most sacred responsibilities.

When we were placed in certain circumstances with our wives

and children, and the nation was pursuing us with the intention of destroying us, the Lord opened our way in a manner that we never expected. Very few, indeed, thought our deliverance would come in the way which the Lord saw proper to bring it. A sacrifice had to be made—a greater one than had ever been made before. The Church, itself, depended upon the Saints acting in a wise and prudent manner, and making the sacrifice that was required at that time.

The word of the Lord came to President Woodruff. When that Manifesto was issued, you knew what it meant. Some were alarmed. They thought the Church would go to pieces; thought they were breaking their covenants; thought the Lord had withdrawn from them. But that Manifesto was issued by the command of the Lord; and the Saints humbled themselves before the Lord and bowed to the requirement.

The heavens rejoiced and God smiled upon us. He blessed His people, and delivered us from our enemies, and they were brought to shame and disgrace. They thought to destroy the Latter-day Saints, but they failed in their attempt. Nevertheless, we had to make the sacrifice, and it was right that we should. The Lord could have delivered us in some other way, had He so wished; but He knew best, and that was the course He required us to pursue and the sacrifice He desired us to make. We made it, and He has blessed us wonderfully from that time to the present. He has given us power among the nations, and in various ways the people have been raised in the estimation of the world. Men of great wisdom have looked upon us, though they may have been silent, and they have honored the course we have taken. The Lord required that of us. "My Kingdom Shall Roll Forth," *Readings in Church History*, pp. 70-71.

Thus, the practice of plural marriage in the Church, clung to by Church leaders and members like Amos, was abandoned. Latter-day Saints were not responsible for its introduction nor for its stoppage. The Lord commanded its practice.

In the face of the sentiment of ages, and in opposition to the teachings of their own traditions, many of the Saints obeyed the commandment. For about half a century they continued the practice. They defended it in the public press, proclaimed it from the pulpit, debated it on the platform and practiced it in their lives notwithstanding fines and imprisonments and exile. A whole generation had been born and grown to manhood and womanhood in this marriage system, and the affections of family ties were entwined with it.

Then under the pressure of suffering brought upon the people through the laws of the United States, the President of the Church proclaimed its discontinuation and the people with sorrowful hearts submitted to it, and there the matter rests.

If the labors and sufferings of the Church of Christ for this principle have done nothing more, this much at least has been accomplished: The Saints have borne testimony to the truth, and it is for God to vindicate His law in his own time and in His own way. (CHC Vol. VI p. 226.)

Chapter Twenty-eight
The Storm

When persecution kept Amos in a series of crises and Loella was on the underground for six years, things, by comparison, rocked along fairly well for Cate and her family. The Church, in an unusual move, had given Amos enough money to support his large family and provide for his own bare necessities while on the Wind River missions. The need for his services at that time evidently demanded this action. Under Cate's frugal eye and hand, the money was spread effectively so that the family did not suffer, and may even have fared better than when Amos was at home. In fact, the boys in later years said they were quite relieved when their father was gone. They discovered they could get by on less effort under Cate's guidance and, naturally, they liked it that way.

Silas and Addie had always been obedient children. It seemed to be in their blood. They trusted their parents from the first and accepted their example and word without question. When they were grown, the same thought-patterns continued. Therefore, they accepted this strange new doctrine as something which had to be met as part of life.

Winnie had a mind of her own from the first. Her keen intellect had to know for itself and until she found out, she wasn't about to take someone else's word for it. But she had married and had her own life and family by the time her father married that little girl who was barely as old as her younger sister, Addie. Russ was fifteen, John, thirteen and Frank, eleven. To them fell the hard work on the farm. Traditionally, boys chafed under the firm hands of their fathers in that time. Now they felt doubly put upon.

Amos often left them to do the work when he had duties with the Church, looking after others' needs. But this time he was off chasing after a young girl; someone they knew but didn't ever see because she was hiding! They saw their mother's troubled looks and sensed her sadness at the turn of events. Then another blow! Off went their father on another mission for the Church, leaving everything to them for months.

The Church! Their father pressured them incessantly to set a good example because he was the Bishop. The Church took him away and left them with all the work to do. And now it encouraged him to break up the family, taking up with a girl less than half his age. Worst of all, the fruits of their hard work would go to support that girl and her brood. They suspicioned she was already expecting. The shame of it all!

When Amos returned from his 1885 mission, the boys had grown considerably. They seemed more unmanageable than ever. With his mind preoccupied with the mission experiences and with his new young "illegal" family to care for on the underground, he simply couldn't tolerate any hint of rebelliousness. He'd made them see that obedience and sacrifice was the first law of heaven, even if they hated it.

When they were teen-agers, John was smaller than his brothers and resented it. He had to make up for it by outsmarting them, and he often did. He couldn't lift as much as Frank and Russ so he figured out ways to be somewhere else when lifting had to be done. When he got a little older he decided to get some land of his own and be his own boss. He asked his father about it. "You'd make a better barber than a farmer," said Amos, bluntly. John felt squelched and thought his father was just being mean. He acknowledged years later that his father was right and that it was good advice. They didn't talk the same language but neither one knew it at the time.

Russ was the oldest and set the pattern for Frank and John. They found out they could play their mother against "the Old Man" as they thought of him, but didn't call him. Cate could see their side and helped them out in subtle ways that he didn't know about. They managed to do things their way instead of his. And when he came back, they all sort of braced themselves for what they knew was coming, and it came.

Amos knew nothing of the "soft approach" in discipline, especially with his own boys. If telling didn't work, stronger methods followed in quick succession. People believed then that "children should be seen and not heard." "Spare the rod and spoil the child" was a truism from the Bible itself. Didn't Brigham Young say "break their backs if you have to!" So Amos' boys got the rod treatment and if they resented it and were sassy, they got another round. Force and fear were locked in the struggle. Wives and mothers were expected to listen to the counsel of their husbands, though often they didn't.

Amos told Russ he couldn't go to the dance one night because he lied and Amos found him out. Russ swore and went anyway. His father was waiting for him in the barn when he got back. He had a strap in his hand and laid it on. The harder he whipped, the more Russ fought. They finally quit because it was a draw. Russ was eighteen by then and strong. They were both exhausted physically and emotionally. But that wasn't the end. Russ resolved he'd get even and a few days later he got his chance.

Amos got after him for taking Toshats to ride without asking him. He had needed the pony urgently, and Toshats was not supposed to be used by anybody else. Russ slyly put a few yards between himself and his father before answering. Then he let out a stream of cursing including all the evil words he'd ever heard, including those which implied that his father was immoral for having more than one wife. The effect was electric. Russ was ready to run. But Amos didn't move. He just stood there looking at Russ with a sort of pity in his eyes as he quietly replied, "Russell, my boy, those words just cost you your life." Frank was there and heard it and it gave him goose bumps. He told Cate about it and the word passed along to others of the family but they soon forgot about it, though they would recall it later.

Things went from bad to worse. It seemed as if everything was stacked against him. This game between father and sons was for real now. Only he wasn't playing for the same stakes his boys were, and his boys sometimes added dirty tricks to the game. He was trying to save them from inevitable disaster. What one couldn't think of, the others could, and took delight in seeming him suffer.

Even Cate seemed sometimes to side with the boys against him and told him so in actions and harsh words. This hurt worst of all. Couldn't she see where it was leading? His authority was being undermined and without that, he was stripped of power to act as a father, and being a father meant everything to him. The evil game went on, as tensions mounted.

Cate asked Winnie to come over. Then, together with the three boys, (Edgar was still too young to take much part) they held a family council and decided to appeal to the one thing they knew Amos would have to listen to, stake leaders. Since he was the bishop, they went to President Budge. A high council court was called and the adult family were there. This was a far cry from a civil court. It had functioned well ever since the Church was organized. In most cases the two parties were able to come to a satisfactory agreement; a meeting of minds and hearts, which involved sincere repentance and forgiveness on both sides. Bitter enemies often became fast friends afterward. The Lord was the Supreme Court Justice, to whom they appealed. Those who thus accepted him were usually willing to abide by his decision through his earthly servants in the spirit of peace and love.

Those present included the stake presidency and twelve councilors. Six councilors were assigned to represent the accusers and six, the accused. The stake president acted as judge. The court opened with prayer. The men were Amos' longtime associates and friends.

Accusations were sharp and bitter and covered a wide range of subjects. The boys complained their father was cruel and unreasonable, touchy and domineering. Many cases were cited for proof. The accused said practically nothing. What could he say? How could he explain what was in his heart? They wouldn't understand if he tried to tell them. He felt that right was being violated and the outcome would be inevitable. What was right to him meant something entirely different to them, so it was no use. Their weapons of ridicule, sarcasm and suspicion wounded his spirit far worse than a physical blow. He put his head in his hands and wept. The court, after deliberation, determined to take no severe action. Afterward, President Budge quietly and sadly reproved Amos for his harshness and recommended he try to get along without coming to blows and that his family try to be more obedient and cooperative with their father.

Amos couldn't wait for the closing prayer. He had to get out. He hurried to where his horse was tied, climbed on and galloped all the way back to Cate's house, the steam of wounded pride boiling up as he went. Striding into his little bedroom, he pulled the enlarged portrait of himself from the wall and made for the woodpile. He grabbed the axe and pulverized his likeness on the chopping block. His frenzy was unabated. Back into the house he went, heading for Cate's pantry where she kept the filled milk pans while the cream rose. One by one he picked them off the shelf, spilling half the contents as he went, dumped it all out into the dooryard and threw the pans after it.

When the madness subsided he was ashamed, but pride kept him from admitting it and the events of the unhappy episode continued to churn his insides. He nourished his wounds and an armistice of sorts was the best either side achieved. Ever after he refused to have his picture taken if he knew about it and and his determination to keep his boys from going astray as *he* had done, solidified within him.

"Why," he asked himself, "is there so much contention in my family? I obey the Lord's every wish. Why don't my wives and children obey me?" This was the root of sorrow which he chewed on, with no nourishment to be had from it.

Russell had a chance for a job near Boise and went to work for the summer. He came home in about six weeks with typhoid fever, contracted from a polluted well. Dr. Hoover prescribed a liquid diet, cool baths to decrease the fever, plenty of water to drink and complete bed rest.

Cate was soon exhausted with the constant vigil. Amos took turns every other night, sitting up with the patient and trying to follow doctor's directions. Sleep wasn't a problem for him. He *couldn't* sleep under any circumstances. There was too much to think and wonder about. Would Russ pull through? Could he exercise his priesthood rightfully in behalf of his son in his present state of mind? Russ hadn't asked to be administered to and probably would refuse if the idea were suggested to him. Amos prayed that Russ would ask.

How much soul-stretching and agony could a human being take? He had been sure that he was making the right decision when he married Loella and still believed it, with only a sliver of a doubt now and then when the screws were turned ever tighter. His Dutch heritage came to his rescue at such times and made him hang on. Prayer continued to be his only source of comfort, and sometimes he didn't get much of that, but he kept praying.

One thing he knew for sure which nothing could take from him: His priesthood was his most precious possession. He'd been without it for six years and discovered what hell really was. When it was restored by those who held the divine authority to restore it, he knew an unspeakable relief and peace which remained through all that had happened since. *This, he knew.* Now he understood Brother Rich's words to him. "You'll know it as I know it and nothing can take it from you as long as you keep the commandments to the best of your ability."

Typhoid fever is a lingering illness. There are ups and downs, and the watchers hope and pray the latest *down* is the last one and the latest *up* will continue. The patient floats from one to the other in a semiconscious haze of weakness and not caring. Russ had no appetite while the fever raged, and food had to be forced on him. Liquid was emphasized by Hoover as he explained that the intestines were a mass of open sores and any roughage would irritate them even more.

But, one morning, Russ opened his eyes after a restful night. The fever was gone, even below normal for a change. He was hungry! Cate hovered over him in anxiety now turned to hope. He drank some warm gruel avidly and asked for more. His body at last was winning the germ battle and cried out for the food-ammunition long withheld. The doctor came and looked relieved.

"He'll pull through, now. Only remember, no solid food till I give the word!"

A few days later, Amos came in from the field to see how Russ was doing. He found him groaning with pain which nothing seemed to relieve. Cate admitted she'd given in to Russ' pleading. "He wanted some pickles so bad I couldn't say no. I thought just one wouldn't hurt him; maybe that's what's the matter," and her eyes turned pleadingly toward Amos. "Won't you administer to him?"

He laid his hands on his boy's head and said words, just words. That's all that would come this time, hard as he tried. Russ passed away a few hours later after intense suffering and a return of the high fever.

Friends and relatives rallied around. One of Amos' counselors in the bishopric conducted the funeral and made burial arrangements. The family was overwhelmed with grief and Cate was inconsolable. All were subdued in mind and spirit for many, many days and months, even years.

Unfortunately, the estrangement between their father on the one hand and John and Frank on the other, persisted until even after he was gone. At times they "got along," but at others, there were moments of conflict and bitterness. As the younger family grew, they sensed the conflict and some of the hard feelings were transferred to them. Seldom were love and warmth expressed between these two older boys and members of the second family. An example of the situation occurred about 1905.

One day Amos took Loella's boys, Coulsen and Conover, with

him to Maple Field for the day. They took a jug of milk along and gathered watercress from a spring for their lunch. By quitting time they were pretty tired and hungry. As they neared the house they saw Loella standing at the gate. She motioned them to stop.

"You can't come in," she said pointing to a yellow sign tacked by the door. "We're quarantined for smallpox."

"Who's got it?" cried Amos in alarm.

"Nobody. Frank came by and put up the sign this afternoon."

"Oh, I see," said Amos, clenching his fists. "I'll have to see what I can do."

Frank had been elected sheriff a few weeks earlier. Amos had electioneered in his behalf. Unhooking the tugs from the wagon and turning the horses into the corral with their harness still on, Amos took the two boys with him to a thick clump of willows east of the house. Taking off his hat and telling the boys to do likewise, they knelt on the damp ground and he began to pray. He asked the Lord to forgive those who had willfully wronged him and pled for wisdom and patience to know what to do. He and the boys camped out in the meadow and slept in the barn for three weeks. None of the family had smallpox.

It appears that Amos usually engendered either strong love and respect or strong antipathy among his children. Even in the second family, the two younger boys, Amos and Rue, viewed their father only as a stern, cantankerous and even cruel old man. They felt strongly that polygamy was the source of much hardship and that their beloved mother was tricked into it and trapped, thereafter.

Chapter Twenty-nine
Plural Wives

As Amos' daughter Loella said many years later: "They had more to bear than was anticipated by the three of them: Father, Cate and Loella. Even the children had to learn to be unselfish and banish jealousy from their natures; to cultivate love and respect for one another and, above all, to have tolerance and charity. I think we all did fairly well considering the great and noble and absolutely self-effacing principle involved.

"Father's idea was to have a righteous seed to bear his name. At one time he told Mother in my presence that he did not have one to lose and if he did not have to forfeit one of his family he would be more than paid for the sacrifice and the economic distress experienced by the two large families. I believe we all did the best we knew how to do. (Loella Jacobsen Simms)

At long last, Loella was going to live in her own home. The few things she had accumulated before, had all been taken away from the little log cabin, so she had to start all over again. Sarah and Gib shared some of their hard-earned possessions with her for the second time.

The house sat on an opposite corner of the ten acres from Cate's home, and a little ditch ran beside the house which furnished wash-water for household use. It was a two-room log cabin chinked with mud, with willows covered with mud for a roof, later replaced by shingles. To the east, rose Mt. Baldy with Joe's Gap to the south of it. Bennington Hill cut off the view to the south, with Montpelier, five miles further on. Bear River meandered about a mile to the west with wide sloughs on both sides filled with marsh grass and cattails. During spring run-off, the whole area became a veritable lake. Amos and a few of the earliest settlers built their cabins about a mile south of what later became Bennington because they were close to an upper and a lower spring for drinking water.

The full impact of polygamy began to be evident when Loella moved back to Bennington after the Manifesto.

Shortly after Loella became a neighbor to Cate, the weather suddenly turned cold and she didn't have enough quilts to keep the family warm. She used coats and rugs and a buffalo robe, instead. Amos thought of Cate's trunk filled with warm bedding.

"Let's go over and see if Cate will let us have a couple of quilts. She has so many she can't use all of them."

They went together the next morning. Amos broached the subject. Cate was surprised but without a word went to her trunk and picked out two brightly-colored hand-quilted ones and laid them in Loella's lap. Loella was delighted to receive such bounty for the asking. Gaily, she unfolded one and put it around Amos' head and shoulders, and did the same with the other one for herself. Putting her arm around her husband's waist, she laughingly waltzed him around the room and out the door. Cate watched them as they happily walked arm in arm across the road and disappeared into their own little dove-cote.

It seemed so heavenly to Amos and Loella to be released from fear and caution as their constant companions, that they were unaware of anyone else in their bright new world. Loella was even more beautiful at twenty-two and was always young-at-heart. Thus it was that Cate took to calling her "your darlin'" when she spoke of Loella to Mose, and he didn't correct her.

It was out of this world to go to a dance, openly together, and let the music sift into their hearts again. Loella had had so little romance in her young life. The past six years had provided no room for such frivolity. Her happiness was contagious and Amos relived his young manhood days buck-and-winging at the ward dances, to their heart's content. Sundays were exciting, too. Loella could go to meeting sure of being greeted warmly by the Bennington Saints. Of course, on any special occasion, Cate sat by Mose and she took a back seat.

Amos was again immersed in the ever-present fight with the survival wolf as well as looking after his ward flock. He had been bishop for ten years and the problems were always with him in one form or another. He was active in Republican politics, having followed President Budge's lead in choosing that party after the People's party of former days was dissolved. Funerals and holidays demanded Amos' talent as a sympathetic speaker or orator as the situation called for. His thirst for knowledge led him constantly to the written word, the scriptures, the daily paper and Literary Digest, accompanied by a pocket dictionary as his interpreter.

A patriotic oration was always part of the Fourth of July celebration, which the young ones squirmed or slept through. So when Amos was asked to do the honors, he determined that wouldn't happen. The day of the Fourth suddenly turned cold with a wind from the north, and the festive atmosphere was chilled. Amos delighted the audience by appearing in his sheep-skin overcoat, cap and gloves. As he warmed to his subject about liberty and justice for all, he did a striptease by shedding his winter garments one by one and standing finally in a beaded buckskin costume complete with moccasins. Donning a feathered headdress, he launched into a Shoshone war dance accompanied by a genuine Indian drummer hired for the occasion, and the crowd went wild, as they joined him in war whoops and shouts of approval, ending up with a salute to Old Glory.

Whenever a death occurred in the valley, the bereaved family turned instinctively to Bishop Wright as comforter and sympathetic friend. He knew how to say and do what was needed to heal hearts and administer hope to sagging spirits. His message carried the conviction of sincerity and truth. Amos Wright was integrity personified.

He often went to Burgoyne's store and loaded his wagon with beans, bacon, flour, and other supplies, paying for them with his own money, and adding whatever had been donated as fast offerings. When anyone asked him where he was going he replied, "That's a secret." Those in need said the bishop came in answer to prayer.

In harmony with the spirit of the Manifesto, he and Cate agreed that he would henceforth live at Loella's, but take some of his meals with her, meanwhile providing for her and the unmarried children of the first family.

Cate's three youngest daughters, Catherine, Libby and Fanny, early showed special musical talents. A new organ stood in the front room and the girls sang and played, accompanied by mandolin and harmonica. Many happy hours were spent this way and Cate's home became a mecca for young folks' socials as time went on. Nelly, Nettie and Mary grew up as playmates of their half sisters, though that term was seldom used. They started to call Cate, "Aunt Cate" but she said she would rather be called Mrs. Wright, or Sister Wright.

Loella was pregnant again. Nelly was five, Nettie three and Mary two. The little girls came to her one day and with Nelly as spokesman, asked if they could have a baby brother. "I think maybe you can," replied Loella. And true to her promise, she gave birth to her first man-child, March 18, 1893.

The little girls had been hustled over to Gib's and Sarah's beforehand and when they returned next day they marveled to see the tiny baby lying by their mother's side. He looked like a little red, wrinkled doll but they loved him immediately and were told his name was William. He died a few days later. Loella's hectic life previous to his birth may have been responsible for his frail body which, though perfectly formed, lacked the strength to keep his spirit alive within it. The children were heartbroken and never forgot this first encounter with death and always carried the memory of his tiny body lying in the little coffin which was later taken to the graveyard below Mt. Baldy. Each Decoration Day, thereafter, they gathered wildflowers to lay on his grave.

The years which followed could have been counted by twos for Loella, each time marked by the birth of another child. Whenever her baby was a little over a year old and weaned, Mose would say, "Now, Loell, you are well and strong again, and we can't hold off any longer. We covenanted to raise a righteous posterity and we dare not break our promise to the Lord." The older children were never told that a new baby was coming, but they came to recognize the sign when their mother began wearing her Mother Hubbard dress.

Nelly recalled years later how they felt:

When I was nine, my two sisters younger than I, talked about how we'd like to have another brother. We decided to ask Mother about it. She said we might have one any time now.

On a very cold day, the 18th of March, we were having a Bear Lake blizzard. Father said, 'Bundle up good, little girls. We're going to Grandma's.' I didn't know how babies were born, but I thought maybe this was the time our brother would come. When we got to Grandma's we were hugged and kissed and petted. We loved going to Grandma's. We stayed overnight.

A lady named Staples was a midwife and Father took her back home with him. The next day, Father came to get us. Sure enough, he said we had another baby brother. When we got home we stood by Mother's bed where she was lying and saw a blonde, curly-haired baby lying beside her and we thought he was beautiful. Father was proud, too. He'd waited a long time for a son by his second wife, and this new brother was born a year to the day after William. Father said, "I'm going to name him for a great man, my friend Apostle Rich." He did, and gave him the whole thing, Charles Coulsen Rich Wright, only we started to call him Coulsie and later, Couls. He was the apple of Father's eye.

After that, we had another brother and we loved him, too. Coulsen was a Wright in looks and build, but Conover looked like our beautiful Mother and we called him 'Laughing Boy'. The two boys were two years apart and learned to do the chores and farm work together.

Alnora Lane, called Norey or Nona and named after Ed Austin's wife, was born October 16, 1898. Amos Weaver, was named by Loella May 27, 1901, of the new century, while his father was on his last official mission to the Wind River Shoshones. Harriet was next, November 28, 1903, and called Hattie. Another boy, Arunah Caesar, shortened to Rue, was born March 1, 1906. Even then at age sixty-six, Amos was proud to father a child and bragged a little when he wrote the news to daughter Nelly in Arizona after her marriage, saying: "He (Rue) is the twenty-second child of your steady-going old Father that still seems to be on deck when it comes to actual service."

Loella went to Brigham City for the birth of Virginia, May 9, 1908, because of a flare-up in Idaho of the old polygamy persecution. And last of the twelve children was Ruth Esther who arrived February 19, 1911. At that time Amos was seventy-one years old and Loella was forty-three. He had fathered twelve sons and twelve daughters, a dozen in each family.

These years were full ones for Mose and Loella. The mere matter of feeding, clothing, and keeping the family clean and healthy was a full-time job for both of them in a two-room cabin with a wood-burning stove which constantly deposited soot and grime on walls and ceiling. Hungry children demanded the skill of a baker making bread three times a week. Monday was always washday. The little boys lugged buckets half full of water from the ditch outside, which was all they could carry. The boiler went onto the stove immediately after breakfast so the water would be hot at the right time. The big galvanized tub, which served as Saturday night bathtub, was taken off its big nail outside of the house, and placed on a bench with the washboard inside the tub and a big square bar of homemade soap ready for the scrubbing to begin. The clothes were sorted and Loella showed the little girls how to soap and then rub the clothes on the washboard even when they had to stand on a stool to reach the board. They took turns scrubbing, though Loella often had to do it over when they were through, but they were learning. The "whites" were always boiled for a spell in the soapy, boiler water to which a dash of lye was added for whitening, and then 'rensed' in two waters, wrung as dry as possible and hung on the clothesline to whip dry in the wind. It was an all-day job at least once a week.

Loella disliked outside work. Her sisters had always done that while she did the housework, but now, like the little red hen, she had to do it herself, or it didn't get done. Chickens always scared her, especially setting hens, and it seemed as if her hens never laid as many eggs as Cate's did. Often she sent Nelly over to Mrs. Wright's to "borrow" an egg or two or three, and they seldom got paid back. Amos expected Loella to milk the cow or cows twice a day until Coulsie and Conover were big enough to do it. Cate had always done it; that was women's work. But Loella hated the job and sometimes forgot it entirely either by chance or design. The calves were always getting over the fence into Cate's pasture where her cows, with full udders, soon got sucked dry. This didn't improve family relations though Cate tried to hold her tongue. Her children saw what was happening and voiced disapproval. It took a month of summers before Loella learned the trick of producing green peas and new potatoes by the Fourth of July, and late frosts didn't help any.

In between times, however, were moments and hours in the evening after supper when what happened was etched on the memory of the growing Loella children. Mose was a great joker, actor and storyteller. He could make the people he told about come alive, and the children listened with lanterns on their ears as he told about David and Goliath, Nephi and Sam and Laman and Lemuel, always pointing out the moral of the story, of the bad guys and the good guys. Loella came under the spell, too, as she sat in her little armless rocking chair nursing the baby and learning along with the little ones. She never tired of hearing Mose's dramatizations. He made them different and exciting. The finale was always an Indian war dance which the children soon imitated as they shuffled their tiny feet like their big "Shoshone" Father.

Amos was keenly aware of the need to begin early to teach proper ideals to his second family. Like all parents, he had made some bad mistakes the first time around and determined not to repeat them now he had a second chance. This was harder than he imagined, since each of his twenty-four were individuals and there was no set formula which worked in all cases. But he never missed an opportunity to point out the need for good playmates.

One autumn day as Nelly and her father were digging potatoes in the fall, flocks of crows settled nearby to pick angleworms out of the freshly dug earth. Later, a pair of redbirds alighted where the crows had been. Amos stopped a moment to wipe the sweat from his forehead and said,

"You see, Nelly, redbirds never fly with crows. And remember, you are a redbird."

He told her about her great-grandmother, Catherine Fox, who was a princess, which made Nelly decide then and there that she would be one, too. Whenever her father brought a gunnysack full of childrens' shoes from Burgoyne's store, she always looked for slippers like a princess would wear, but they were always sturdy, hard-toed shoes which she tearfully wore because there was nothing better.

"We knew Father liked to have our hair clean and shining and neatly braided in two braids down our back. Hattie had long, thick braids which curled naturally when it was unbraided. Father often called her to him as he sat down after supper and unbraided her shining locks and ran his fingers through the silky strands as her hair spread in waves over her shoulders.

"He liked to have us keep our skin white and soft, too, so we always wore a sunbonnet when we went outside, and if he ever saw us running barefooted, he always told us to go put our shoes on, admonishing that "girls should wear shoes so their feet won't get tough and hard like papooses."

When Coulsie was four years old, Amos showed him how to stand on a box so he could lift the harness onto the horses' backs and fasten all the intricate hooks and buckles that had to be done to harness them properly. The reins must be straightened, too, because Amos couldn't abide a crooked rein and would even stop the team to get down and straighten it before he could go on.

Loella spent many hours at the sewing machine making the children's clothes. She was a good seamstress and in later years made a little extra money by sewing for other people. Coulsen loved to sit by the foot pedal and watch his mother's feet rock back and forth to make the machine hum. He always asked for the scraps of material that were too small to be of use to her. These he stacked in a neat pile and pretended they were buffalo robes and deer hides for a make-believe Indian tepee.

Bowser was the family dog. He watched over Coulsen and Conover like a guardian angel and went everywhere they did. Loella didn't worry about them when she knew the dog was along. The three of them were out in the lane one day when Frank came riding by on his horse. He always carried a quirt with him. When he saw Bowser, he snapped his quirt at the dog, making him run, howling across the road. Frank laughed and sicked his own dog, Smut, on the frightened Bowser. The two dogs started fighting as the little boys watched in terror.

"Kill him, Smut, kill him!" shouted Frank. Bowser was old and didn't have a chance against the young Smut. Within minutes the poor old fellow lay gasping with his throat torn open, while Frank rode nonchalantly down the lane and the little boys ran home to tearfully tell what had happened.

One day Loella stopped on the way from Bennington and picked a bouquet of wild roses. She put them in a tumbler in the middle of the table at supper time. When Mose saw them, he went outside and came back with a piece of sagebrush in his hand. He put it in a tin can and set it beside Loella's roses. "You are the roses and I am the sagebrush," he said with a grin.

In spite of herself, Loella always felt inadequate around Cate. Sister Wright seemed so capable in every way. She was first counselor to Sister Vanorman in Relief Society, and was recognized as the bishop's wife whenever there was a public doings of any importance. Cate's washing hung on the line at the regular time each Monday, much earlier than Loella's. Her butter and eggs brought the best price at the store and at bazaars. She could sew up a dress in jig time and it looked nice and fit the wearer. Her blue sunbonnet was starched and fresh whenever she went outside, and her aprons were the same. She had a trunkful of gayly-colored patchwork quilts for the beds, and her house was beautified with knitted and crocheted doilies and scarves. Loella seldom went to Cate's house herself when she could send the little girls instead.

The meetinghouse was now built on the new townsite almost a mile north of the Wright homestead. It wasn't often that Loella could get away long enough to go to church. The children were still young and it was a hassel to get them ready to go, and it was too far for them to walk, anyway.

One Saturday, her sister Alice came to stay with her overnight and offered to stay with the children while Loella went to church. Mose usually went early to priesthood meeting. It was a lovely June day, so she started early to walk. About half a mile later she heard a wagon coming but didn't turn around to see who it was. As it passed her, she recognized Mose and Sister Wright sitting on the spring seat together and the young folks in the wagon box behind. She hesitated a minute, expecting Mose to stop and pick her up. But the horses jogged right on and neither he nor Sister Wright looked in her direction as they passed. She felt completely demolished and didn't know whether to sit down and cry or to turn around and go back home. Why hadn't he stopped? Was it Mose or Sister Wright who was to blame? Hot tears ran down her cheeks and onto her only Sunday dress unheeded, as she walked on determined not to let either of them know how hurt she was.

Perhaps it would have comforted her had she been able to understand how Cate suffered at being supplanted by a pretty young woman openly adored by their husband. Having to share so many material things with the second family which she had scrimped and saved to get, was a trial which was custom-made for her thrifty soul. She constantly caught herself comparing herself with Loella, always, it seemed, coming off second best in her appraisal, and then feeling guiltily sorry for herself before she was able to throw off the uncomfortable and unhappy thoughts.

Bennington always had a big time on the 17th of March. That was the date the Relief Society was organized by the Prophet Joseph Smith. Everybody celebrated: fathers, mothers, and children. There was always a dance at night. Cate was in the presidency so, naturally, she was going. She got ready early and waited for Mose and Loell to pick her up. She heard a team and wagon going past the house and looked out just as they drove by without stopping.

She had to be there, so she put on her coat and knitted fascinator and started to walk. It was almost a mile to the meetinghouse. There was plenty of time to ponder exactly what she'd say when she chastised Mose for leaving her. She was hot inside and cold outside by the time she got there.

There was a big crowd as always and she managed to find a seat right behind where Mose was sitting. Loell was sitting with her folks. Amos didn't see her come in. He and Brother Smart had their heads together telling each other how terrible it was to try to get along with two wives who were jealous of each other. She couldn't help hearing what they said and got angrier and angrier, finally leaving in a huff. Winnie followed her out and Cate said she wanted to go home, so George drove her back.

One day Amos aired his feelings to Cate, hoping to get some sympathy. "It seems I never can make the money stretch enough to cover both families these days, no matter how hard I try."

Cate was sitting in her favorite rocker. She crossed one knee over the other and started bobbing her foot up and down, which she always did when she was perturbed or upset. "That's what you bargained for, Mose Wright," was her reply, and that closed the subject.

Loella needed some calico and thread at Burgoyne's and gingerly approached her husband one morning. "Mose, I have to get a few things at the store. Could I take Old Rock and the single buggy today?" Amos thoughtfully scratched his ear and allowed she could. Gladly she got the work done up and told Nelly and Nettie to watch the babies and she wouldn't be gone long. She had a hard time putting the bridle on the horse and getting him backed into the shaves but, finally, she got him all hitched up and felt quite proud of herself. Just then, Sister Wright came down the path from her house in her usual starched apron and sunbonnet manner.

"Where are you going, Loell?" she asked in her quick Welsh accent.

"Mose said I could take the horse and buggy and go to Burgoyne's."

"I'm going there myself, today, and I can't put it off."

Loella wasn't one to guard her tongue and was about to spill out her feelings, but managed to say, quietly, "I'll go down in the field and ask Mose what we should do." It never occurred to either of them that they might go together.

She hurried out in the field and told him the problem. He tied the reins to the plow, and without a word, followed Loella back to the corral. Cate was there waiting. He didn't look at either wife as he quickly unhitched Old Rock and turned him out into the pasture. "Neither of you can go if you can't agree," he observed Solomon-like, and returned to his plowing.

After that episode, things seemed to pile one atop another for Loella. Nothing went right. Amos was cross and criticized her for not having meals ready like Cate did. The children's noise and constant demands shattered her ability to cope. One of the babies was sick and kept her up every night for a week and Mose slept right through it all. Then she found out she was pregnant again. As she sat in her little rocking chair at two o'clock one morning with Hattie in her arms, she wondered when all this would end.

"I'm so disgustingly healthy there's no chance of dying, I guess," she muttered to herself. "Mose is the stubbornest man; a real Dutchman, especially on some subjects. I don't blame Cate for giving up on him. I thought I could get him to dress up once in awhile, but I haven't had any better luck. I started out wrong!"

Later that day, her muttering picked up again as she was mixing the usual batch of bread to be ready for dinner.

"I started out wrong! I thought he was St. Peter himself and never questioned anything he said or did. But I'm finding out he makes a few mistakes himself, but now it's too late to change him. He either clams up and leaves the room or puts on a show making fun of me, and that's something I can't take!" With that, she took it out on the bread she was kneading and ended with punches intended for Mose.

"If I ask him to do something around the house, he says, 'That's woman's work.' But if Brother Budge raises his eyebrow, Mose is right there lapping up crumbs for him. If he thinks I'm going to toady to him every time he crooks his little finger, he's mistaken. I've had it and I don't even care about covenants this time. I'll bake this darn bread for the last time and then I'm leaving!"

Gib and Sarah had sensed her low spirits and took Nelly and Nettie home with them for a spell. Coulsie and Conover went each day with Mose as he plowed and planted.

Putting on her sunbonnet and taking the baby in her arms, she told Mary to carry the bundle she had tied up, and started down the lane toward Bennington hill and the Weaver farmstead a couple of miles beyond. Her square chin was set determinedly but the tears couldn't be shut off and she cried unashamedly as she trudged along in the midday sun carrying heavy year-old Hattie in her arms. She was leaving! She couldn't and wouldn't take it any longer. He'd have to get along, somehow. He could go back to Sister Wright. Loella was oblivious to anything but her own inner way as she reviewed why she was doing what she was doing, not caring what might happen.

Suddenly, she heard Sister Wright's voice behind her. "It's pretty hot for this time of year, isn't it?" And taking Hattie out of Loella's arms, she began cheerfully talking about the new baby calf old Bossy had had in the night and now there would be more milk for both families. The two women walked along together till they got to the top of the hill where the little ditch ran down to Loella's house. A willow tree on the ditch bank offered welcome shade.

"Let's sit here and rest for a spell," said Cate. "You're hot and so am I and this baby is heavy." She took off the baby's moccasins and let her feet hang in the cool water and Hattie gurgled with delight. Mary played contentedly by herself making mud pies.

The conversation was one-sided for some time, but gradually Loella overcame her black mood and the wives talked woman-talk about recipes, ways to do what needed doing in a better and easier way as the shadows lengthened unheeded. Finally, Cate wiped the baby's feet and legs on her starched apron, put the little moccasins back on, and handed her to Loella.

"My goodness, it's most suppertime. We'd best be getting home. Everybody will be starved." The younger woman settled Hattie astraddle her hip, Mary took Sister Wright's hand, and the little group started back down the hill. Loella had waded through her 'slough of despond', and now, her burden lightened with the help of her understanding sister-wife, returned to home, husband

and children as if nothing had happened.

Chapter Thirty
Another Indian Mission

Amos received a letter from President Lorenzo Snow, who was still in charge of the Northern Indian missionary work. The letter, dated about the first of September, 1901, from Brigham City, Utah, asked if he would consider going on another mission to the Shoshone Indians in Wyoming. He said they had requested that Amos return to teach them more about the gospel.

Amos' reply was written in the wordy style of the times, using ten words when five would say it better. He was conscious of writing to an important man whom he admired and respected. It was embarrassing to admit to President Snow that he didn't have any money, and the apostle strongly hinted that Amos might need help, if he decided to go.

Thus, at age sixty-one, Amos was again called on a mission to Wind River, Wyoming. To him, the Gospel of Jesus Christ as taught by Mormonism had been tested in the crucible of his own experience over many years, and his entire existence was a part of it.

It is unusual that the brethren sent him five hundred and eighty-five dollars expense money, but they must have felt he was the only man capable and willing to go on that difficult mission. That much money would probably meet the needs of both families and still supply him and his companion with a camp outfit and horses.

Loella valued her love letters from Amos sufficiently to save all of them. But still, she had a hard time keeping up with his desire to hear from her. Her letters were read and reread, worn with unfolding and folding and rereading long before he came back to Bennington.

The children would anxiously gather around Loella while she read the eagerly-received letters and made various remarks about what Amos said. It seemed quite proper to them that he should be gone "doing the Lord's work."

Grandfather Weaver and Loella's brothers came often, helping a good deal with provisions.

Living conditions on this mission apparently were not so primitive as in 1885-86, but Amos still lived with and about in the same circumstances as the Indians. The Indians had largely ceased to live wholly by the chase, but had settled down somewhat and established more permanent homes.

Thirteen-year-old Nettie suffered a serious accident while she was staying with Aunt Kitty. She pried a carpet tack loose and it flipped into her eye. Extent of the damage was hard to determine, but she couldn't see. Loella sent the news to Amos, but, he did not fully realize at that time how serious it was.

Loella never questioned the propriety of her being left with the family. She seemed to accept it as her part in the great scheme of things.

With Amos no longer under the ban of "no proselyting" by the Mormons among the Indians, he camped within about a mile of the government post. He enjoyed good health in spite of, or because of, his rough living conditions. He did not complain much, but continued to mention his privations and his ability to cope with them as though he got some satisfaction from it.

When Amos found a man he could respect and trust, his love bubbled up like a flowing well. This was his feeling for Ed Austin. Ed's son, Torrey, said, "Our family used to refer to them as 'David and Jonathan' of Bible lore. We believed either one would have given his life for the other if need be. Whenever Bishop Wright came to Liberty to stay overnight, he and Father occupied the same bed and no matter what time of night it was, those two men would be talking, and they always seemed much refreshed next morning. They were different in personal habits as day and night. Father was given to polish and liked to exhibit his best in clothes, horses, carriages, etc., while Brother Wright, so long as he was clean, didn't give a hang for polish. I don't believe I ever saw him with a necktie on in my life."

Letters to Ed described in detail the conditions at the Indian reservation, all confidential, naturally. (See copy of letter in appendix.)

Jim Joshua was Amos' Indian companion and was known as the "White Indian." The Shoshones had great confidence in the power of the priesthood in administering to the sick, and as a result, practically all administrations by the elders were followed by immediate healings.

About dusk one evening, Amos was asked by an Indian to come at once, with his companion to an Indian's tent because a squaw was very sick. She was so bad the messenger feared she would not live to be blessed unless the elders hurried. Elder Wright, at once, got Jim and they rushed to the aid of the sick squaw. As usual, she recovered immediately after the blessing.

"The Lord has been kind to you, Sister," said Amos, as they sat by her bed. "He has healed you. You now suffer no pain. To show your gratitude to the Lord, I suggest you stay in bed and rest. Do not try to get up tonight, and do not go to the Wolf Dance across the river."

The Indian sister lay quietly in bed for a short time, but she kept thinking about the Wolf Dance and wanting to go. About midnight Elder Wright was awakened by the same Indian messenger who had come before.

"Come, hurry! The squaw is dying," pleaded the Indian. Amos reached over and woke Jim and explained what was wanted, as Jim rubbed his eyes and yawned.

"I happen to know," said Jim, "that she didn't mind what you told her. She got up and went to the Wolf Dance. I don't think we should go, but if you say we should, I'll go."

Amos thought that was good sense and told the messenger they wouldn't go, as he turned over and went back to sleep. The Indian returned to the bedside of the sick squaw and before long, she passed away.

The Relief Society President in Bennington wrote to Amos asking him to write a message to be read at the annual March seventeenth Birthday Celebration, since he could not be there in person. She said they would like to exhibit his picture at that time to honor him as bishop, under whose priesthood authority the society operated. He was so surprised and pleased that he responded immediately to the request. He even wondered if Cate might have suggested the idea, since she was first counselor.

In his letter he told the sisters that Joseph the Prophet had issued a Magna Charta for the emancipation of all women in

1842, as he said, "I now turn the key in your behalf in the name of the Lord, and this Society shall rejoice and knowledge and intelligence shall flow down from this time henceforth."

Amos explained that "neither the man nor the woman is without each other in the Lord," And that there is a Mother as well as a Father in Heaven, though that idea is ridiculed by "the world." Our Heavenly Mother earned her exalted position as did our Heavenly Father, by keeping the solemn covenants made at the marriage altar in the temple. Great blessings follow obedience and are withheld by disobedience. He reminded the sisters of their fortunate condition in contrast to the Indian women he saw every day on the reservation.

Yesterday, I went into a field and saw several men and women plowing. Without exception the women walked and trudged along all day, driving the team while the men held the plow. When mealtime arrived, instead of being allowed the privilege of performing the duties of wife and mother in the house, she was compelled to first water and take care of the stock. And when that was over and she went in to work and wait on her Lord and Master, if she sits down at all, it is by the door and the coldest place in the lodge.

But this feature of trial and servitude for life is a very tame affair compared to the impositions and outrages that are heaped upon her, of such a criminal character that I forbear to mention them and from which her sex affords her no protection, being reduced to this almost heart-rending condition and degradation, all because of a departure from those great, glorious and eternal truths with which you Sisters are familiar.

"The Womens' Relief Society," Amos continued, recognizes the inherent differences between men and women and provides specific training, temporal and spiritual, to help the sisters reach their highest divine destiny. By so doing, they become queens and priestesses to their husbands in the celestial kingdom."

In a letter to Loella, he mentioned that the Relief Society was going to put his photograph in the hall. "I didn't think any one in the world thought that much of me. It was more honor than I ever expected to receive in this life or possibly in any other."

When President Budge heard about Nettie's eye accident he wrote a sympathetic letter to Amos and followed it up by asking Nancy Pugmire, who was M.I.A. Stake President and a daughter of Charles C. Rich, to organize every ward in the stake and raise money to pay for an operation. Dances, concerts and dinners were held in every ward. Seventy-five dollars was raised, which paid train fare for Loella and Nettie to Salt Lake, as well as $15 doctor's fee for removing a cataract which had formed because of the accident. But Nettie's sight was never restored.

Baby Amos was almost a year old and still nursing. Loella took him from the breast and left him with Nellie and Grandma Weaver, who weaned him while she was gone. When she came back, she put a weasel skin on her breast so Amos wouldn't want to nurse. Evidently, the baby wasn't named before his father left on his mission. Loella wrote, asking what she should do about it and Amos replied, "It doesn't matter what you name him, just so he grows up to be a good man." So she had him blessed and named Amos Weaver.

Amos was outraged when he found out what she had done. After the tragic experience with his older son, Amos Russell, he couldn't bear to have another son named Amos. He was so hard on little Amos as he grew up, that the boy finally left the valley, vowing he would never return, and he didn't.

The children, always and forever, it seemed, were having little accidents. Coulsie had had an accident with his toe. Loella thought it was broken, but discovered later, it was frozen. A frozen toe didn't seem especially serious, but when it refused to heal, Loella took him to Dr. Hoover who said the foot and perhaps the leg would have to be amputated. She couldn't bear to have it done, so she put it off and it eventually got well.

Later, the boys were wading in a stream of water and Coulsie stepped on a plank with a rusty nail in it. The nail ran into his foot, going through the instep and coming out through the top. There were no men around, but finally Loella's cousin came along and pulled the nail out. It made an ugly sore for a long time, and it was hard to know why it wasn't infected. It, too, was let go, and it finally healed.

Another time, Coulsen was harrowing some ground near the house. He had three head of horses hitched to the harrow, one of which he was riding. Old Rock got scared and started to run, throwing him to the ground. The sharp teeth of the harrow ran over his body, bruising him badly and cutting a deep gash in the back of his head. They considered it a miracle that he wasn't killed, and always carried the scar to prove it.

The Journal History of May 23, 1902, in the L.D.S. Church Archives says: "A letter was written today to Bishop A.R. Wright releasing him and his Indian associates, James Joshua and wife, from their labours on the Shoshone Reservation."

Amos' first reaction was pure relief. He had served honorably and now was released the same way. For a man over sixty, the conditions he'd lived in for six months were unbearable, but he'd borne them. He had held regular meetings with the Indians, though sometimes he wondered if they understood even the simplest things he told them. He taught them doctrine as well as how to mend a harness, make sourdough biscuits, plant potatoes, and anything else that could make their lives more liveable.

His Indian companion, Jim Joshua, was like a child, and for one who enjoyed being with men like Charles C. Rich and William Budge, only the spirit of Christ within Amos made life endurable. He hoped this was the last time he would be called, but knew if he were called again, he'd go.

As his Indian pony jogged along the trail, homeward bound, he breathed deep drafts of gratitude. But he realized, too, there would be problems waiting for him as great as those he had left behind. He was still bishop and his counselors would be relieved to turn things over to him again. There was spring plowing and planting to do. He had cashed the $200 check he received from Salt Lake and spent it a dozen times in his head. He patted his bulging pocket to assure himself he still had the money, and settled his mind on buying a Studebaker wagon.

Then there was Cate and Loella. He was always in the middle of a volcano which could erupt unexpectedly and he knew his own boiling point was low. Loella respected Cate, but resented her. Cate had learned to restrain her quick emotions, but it always hurt to know that Loella was younger, prettier, and Mose's darlin'.

Maybe this time he'd try a new angle. He'd go see Cate first and show her he really loved her. Loell could wait, she already knew.

It was spring again and snowdrops and wild crocus already peeked out from the edge of the melting snow. His pony sensed the urgency of getting home and Amos didn't hold him back. At last he caught a glimpse of smoke drifting out of the two chimneys in the cabins where his heart lived. Coulsie came running to meet him.

Amos slid off the horse, caught his little boy under the arms and tossed him high in the air and then hugged him hard.

"Turn the pony into the pasture and from now on, he's yours." Coulsen was too surprised and excited to say more than, "Mine?" He ran to tell his mother the good news. "Father's home and he gave me his pony!"

As usual, when he returned from Wind River, Amos' hair was long and hung in curls which he tied with a shoestring at the nape of his neck. He was wearing a wide-brimmed hat, a buckskin shirt and pants, a beaded belt and moccasins.

He turned in at Cate's and stayed for supper. But even before he ate, he went through the scrubbing-up process he always followed after he had been living with the Indians. He first washed himself all over with kerosene and soaked his hair and beard in it. Then came the hot, soapy-water bath and clean clothes. Finally, he had one of the girls comb his hair with a fine-toothed comb to remove any possible vermin. Only then did he feel fit to associate with his loved ones.

All evening and into the night, Loella sat by the window in her little rocking chair, rocking and waiting, and waiting.

"Why doesn't he come? I can't wait to have him pick me up and swing me around and kiss me all over. Maybe Cate won't let him leave. I know he wants to come. But maybe he's changed his mind. He's been gone a long time. Maybe he found someone else, maybe a pretty Indian girl younger than me. Oh, he wouldn't do that! Would he? Well, I won't give him up, anyway. Cate can't have him all to herself. Even if he wanted to quit me, I'd dog his footsteps and make him so miserable he couldn't stand it. Maybe when he does come, I'll run away from him. He'll have to chase me a little, maybe. I'll show him he can't do this to me. Why doesn't he come? *Why doesn't he come?*"

But Mose didn't come that night, nor next morning. After he'd had breakfast with Cate he went over to Winnie's and played with the children and they were goggle-eyed at his appearance. He stopped in at Silas' and repeated the process. He felt like a kid again, himself.

At long last, he walked into Loella's house, caught her in his arms and whirled her around as he kissed her eyes and ears and neck and lips. Then holding her at arm's length he said with a twinkle in his eye, "You're my favorite wife, Loell!"

Chapter Thirty-one
Amos the Man

In 1898, quite a number of families (56 persons) had moved away from Bennington which made quite a hole in the ward population. They were discouraged because of lack of irrigation water. Most of them went to the Big Hole in Wyoming or to Canada.

The Saints in Idaho had finally regained their franchise to vote and hold office in civil affairs, and though Idaho's constitution still contained the anti-Mormon Test Oath, it also guaranteed "perfect toleration of religious sentiment." Anti-Mormons gradually accepted the Mormon Manifesto, ending plural marriage as genuine, and seemed willing to forget that they still believed in celestial marriage in heaven. Thus ended the 1800's and the twentieth century was ushered in with ringing bells and tooting horns.

The new century seemed to inspire old men to have visions and young men to dream dreams. This happened to John Perkins of Montpelier and Isaac Speirs of Bennington when they got their heads together and volunteered to wire Bennington houses for electricity in 1906. The main line ran just above town from "Pelier" to "Sody." They canvassed the town and got enough subscribes to make it worthwhile. Course it cost money and some folks thought they'd just as soon keep on with kerosene lamps. After all, this new gadget might not work.

A day and hour was set for the lights to go on all over town at the same time. A single, green wire hung from the ceiling in each house, with a fifty-watt bulb at the end. That was the magic made by the two dreamers, mixed with enough faith to believe it could happen. The switch was thrown at seven-thirty. That was dark enough to make the sudden light seem brighter, and suddenly the homes in little Bennington were bathed in light. The days of smelly kerosene lamps and lanterns, smoky lamp chimneys and

matches, were gone. Light was there in place of darkness each
evening at dusk when the power came on, and it lasted until ten
o'clock, when all decent people were ready for bed, anyway.

About the same time, J.G. Merrill, a well-to-do and venture-
some Benningtonite, decided to have the first telephone put in.
That took more faith and an unheard-of amount of money, but he
did it and it was the talk and marvel of the town for months to
come. W.H. Speirs followed with a toll phone so the neighbors
could use it in case of sickness or death. That was a comfort. At
least they could get Dr. Hoover if things got bad enough.

Sickness always came in batches, especially when measles or
whooping cough broke out. It was a big help after Dr. Clayton
Hoover moved to Montpelier in 1891 and hung out his shingle. He
owned the Hoover Drug Store and people could buy the simple
remedies known and used by them. People learned to trust
Hoover. He never refused a call and drove his one-horse rig
through wind, rain or snow all over the valley. People often put off
calling him too long because it cost money, but he was a valuable
addition to the life of the community.

Amos and Ed Austin continued their close friendship and
when Ed was called on a mission, Amos missed him. A letter to
Ed contains some of their familiar banter and news exchange.

...Say, Ed, who in the deuce put that picture of yours in the
paper. If you were as devoid of intelligence as that makes you appear,
then your Mission would be a failure.

So far as climate is concerned, you ought to be thankful you're
not here. The papers say we had 33 below shortly after you left. The
Register said 48. It certainly seemed dangerous to be out, though I
did stand it for twelve miles one day without a coat and if it had been
any colder, I suppose I should have forgotten my shirt.

We had a fair number at Priesthood meeting last time. Pres.
Budge ordered all the dance nonsense discussed at the previous
meeting, struck out of the minutes altogether.

Returning from his latest and last mission in June 1901, Amos
was again immersed in being father, bishop and civic leader. He
had twenty-one children, ranging in age from a baby in arms to a
man forty-four years old. He would yet father three more children,
making a double dozen. He had been bishop of Bennington Ward
for twenty-one years, which would stretch to thirty before he was
honorably released. It was too long. Over so many years,
personality clashes were inevitable and enthusiasm waned as
ward activities settled into routine. Amos therefore worked harder

than ever to make it successful. Some people hated him. Many loved him. A few almost worshipped him. All respected him. His image was either black or white, never gray.

He was an idealist. Only perfect was good enough. One critic said, "The only thing predictable about Amos Wright is that he is unpredictable!" Words used to describe him included: eccentric, controversial, misunderstood, rock of Gibralter, unchangeable, contradictory, honest, Abe Lincolnish, inspiring, pessimistic, cruel, orator, stubborn, courageous, unusual, man of faith, fanatical, tender, Ibn Saudish, emotionally unstable, man of character, and many others. He tried to live up to his Wright name; if a thing wasn't right it was wrong.

Because of his unusualness, he often made news. But experience made him wary of reporters. "If they would get it right and print the truth I wouldn't mind, but they always twist things around, therefore I won't give the newspapers anything."

His contempt for style, "following a multitude to do evil" as he expressed it, branded him as eccentric. He wore clothes to cover his nakedness and for comfort. He was a poor man and the kind he wore didn't cost much. He was himself and didn't feel obliged to impress people by the way he dressed. Indian clothes or white man's clothes were equally satisfactory to him.

One day, his son-in-law came to see him, wearing a blue double-breasted shirt with two rows of white buttons down the front. Amos asked him where he got it.

"In Sody," (short for Soda Springs). "Don't you like it?"

"No," said Amos. "It's too much like the Gentiles." Soda Springs was a "Gentile" town.

But Amos liked to visit with Gentiles. Cate said she could always tell when Mose had been visiting at a Gentile wagon emigrant camp because he would be good-natured for several days.

He was invited to be the principal speaker at an unveiling ceremony to be held in the stake tabernacle in Brigham City. Portraits by Ramsey, a well-known Utah artist, of Lorenzo Snow, Jonathan C. Wright, and Samuel Smith were being hung on the walls of the building. These men had been a long-time stake presidency and President Snow had afterward become President of the Church. All three were then dead.

The request overwhelmed Amos. He felt unequal to the task as he always considered himself an uneducated man. "I can't do it," he told Cate.

"Why can't you? Of course you can!"

His real reason for refusing, was fear he would break down when he saw Father Jonathan's picture. He always said he was half woman when it came to emotions. Finally, after continued urging, he decided to go, and boarded the train for Brigham City, wearing his customary cotton pants, a plaid shirt and no tie. A delegation of officials including his brother Brig, met him at the depot. The meeting was scheduled for the next morning at ten o'clock, so he went home with Brig.

He was surprised to see a number of his relatives there who had come for the special occasion. They were proud of Amos as an orator, but wanted him to look the part, also, so they had pooled their money and bought him a new suit of clothes and all the fixins, as a surprise, and laid it on his bed before he got there.

Next morning when they called Amos for breakfast, he wasn't there, which threw them into a tizzy wondering what had happened to him. The new suit was lying untouched where they had put it the day before. Ten o'clock came and the tabernacle was packed. To the relief and chagrin of his relatives, Amos walked in at that moment, wearing the same clothes he had on the day before, and took his place on the stand with the other dignitaries.

He had awakened early that morning, slipped out quietly and gone to the tabernacle. Finding it unlocked, he went inside, lifted the hanging from his father's picture and let the tears fall. Memories flooded over him as he stood there, and presently, a calm, sweet peace settled over him. Later, he walked eastward and climbed up to old "Flat-Bottom" where he sat for an hour looking over the valley below, lost in thought. Then he was ready. He returned to the tabernacle.

The meeting began. The portraits were unveiled and Amos was introduced. A hush fell over the congregation and a few titters were heard as he walked to the podium. After the first few words, his listeners forgot his appearance as he brought back to life his dear friend Lorenzo Snow, Father Jonathan, and Brother Smith, and it was the audience who shed tears and not Amos. He had a clear, ringing voice much like his father's. It was the day of stentorian voices so everybody could hear, and *that* day was no exception. Hundreds who couldn't get inside, listened through open windows and didn't miss a word. Those who were there never forgot the occasion.

People often said they didn't have to go to meeting to hear the bishop talk. They could sit on their porch at home and hear every word as he shouted and pounded the pulpit. Loella tried sometimes to get him to simmer down. "Mose, you shouldn't get so worked up when you speak. Take it easy and don't shout so loud."

"Well," he replied, "I think of so much to talk about I'm afraid I won't get it all said."

Joseph Rich was another unusual character. He and Amos continued to enjoy being together. They were a perfect foil for each other. Amos never forgot that it was he and his father Charles C. who were responsible for getting him back into the Church. Their positions were strangely reversed a few years later when Joseph was excommunicated under unusual circumstances.

Joseph was an optimist and he claimed things always turned out for the best. He could turn the worst misfortune into a happy ending. Amos said, "Yes, Joe, if a train ran over you and cut both your feet off you'd just laugh and say 'Oh well, my feet were always getting cold anyway.'"

Joseph grinned and said, "Why do you do everything that Brother Budge asks you to do? You take his words like he was the Lord himself. When I die I want people to stick down a shingle and say, 'Here lies one man who never Budged.'"

"Not me," laughed Amos. "When I die I want the shingle stuck down, but I want it to say, 'Here's a man who *always* Budged.'"

And like a storybook ending, it was largely through Amos' influence that Joseph C. Rich repented and asked his old friend Mose to come to Paris and baptize him in the same little dammed-up creek they'd both used years before. Amos R. Wright was also one of the speakers at his friend Joseph's funeral, held in the beautiful tabernacle in Paris.

I have been very closely associated with Joseph for forty-five years, sometimes in times of great danger, and I discovered he never deserted his friends, but stood by them even to death. That was only one of his noble traits that has endeared him to me.

One of the greatest blessings of my life has been the close friendship between us and if I could tell of the things he has done for me, it would fill a volume. We both believed in a Divine Providence. We both knew that God is all-powerful and I prayed that I might be the blessing to one of Charles C. Rich's sons that one of them has been to my father's son, and I am pleased to say that He has heard and answered my prayer.

When I came into this Valley I did not belong to the Church and it was this man who took me down to the creek just south of town here and baptized me, for which I have ever since been thankful, and I have honored him from that day to this as one of my greatest benefactors." (*Joseph C. Rich, Versatile Pioneer on the Mormon Frontier*, Ezra J. Poulsen, p. 274.)

Amos was offered a job with the government as Indian Agent at Ross' Hole in Wyoming. It meant a good salary for those days, but he would have had to move his families. He turned it down because he wanted his children to grow up where they would become virtuous, good citizens, free from the sin and corruption of the world.

Amos was set against novel reading. He said all his grown-up girls did was read novels, write love letters and strum on the organ. He said he only read one novel in his life and when he got to the end it said, *to be continued*. He may have been influenced by what Brigham Young said about novel reading:

> If I had charge of such a society as this, I would not allow novel-reading; yet it is in my house, in the houses of my Counselors, in the houses of these Apostles, these Seventies and High Priests, in the houses of the High Council in this City and in other cities and in the houses of the Bishops, and we permit it; yet it is ten thousand times worse than it is for unprincipled men to come here to teach our children the ABC's, good morals and how to behave themselves. Ten thousand times worse! You let your children read novels until they run away, until they get so that they do not care, they are reckless and their mothers are reckless, and some of their fathers are reckless, and if you do not break their backs and tie them up, they will go to hell. That is rough, is it not? Well it is a comparison. You have got to check them some way or other, or they will go to destruction. They are perfectly crazy. I would not like to get into a society where there were no trials; but I would like to see a society organized to show the Latter-day Saints how to build up the Kingdom of God." (*Journal of Discourses* Vol. XV p. 224.)

Amos urged the family not to read about crime and vice. He said their time and energy should be used for uplifting subjects. He was a steady reader himself. He subscribed to the Literary Digest and read it from cover to cover each issue. The first year Coulsen went to Logan to the A.C. he brought home with him at Christmas time, a text book titled *The History of Greater Britain*. Amos picked it up and read it through in a few days. Then he said, "Coulsie, you sit down now and ask me questions about this book and see if you think I could pass an examination." Coulsen started, but never got more than two or three questions asked because Amos answered them so fully that he took all the available time.

Cate's youngest daughter, Frances, loved music and had a natural talent for it. The Evans brothers lived in Malad and were well-to-do cattlemen. They were Cate's brothers. They invited Fanny to come down and stay one winter, so she could take music lessons. Amos said no. Begging and teasing didn't do any good. Cate said, "Oh, Mose, don't be so ornery. She could learn so much down there."

"Too much!" he replied succinctly.

Fanny didn't dare say anything more, but mumbled to herself, "You don't care anything about me. All you want is to get your own way."

Malad was an anti-Mormon town. A combination of gentiles and the Evans brothers' money would expose his daughter to temptations greater than she could resist. The risk was too great and he stood firm, knowing both Cate and Fanny wouldn't understand and explaining would only make matters worse.

Sometime later he and Cate had visited her brothers in Malad and when he came home he was very melancholy. Soon after, he and Conover were fixing fence together and Amos, who had a habit of talking to himself, repeatedly said all day long, "Money, money, money, nothing but money, talk twenty-four hours a day about money, money, money!"

Cate agreed that her preoccupation with money matters during her pregnancy with Frank made him the same way and contributed to his selfishness.

Frank not only liked to fight but always tried to cook up a fight between others and if he could arrange a gang fight at one of the dances, so much the better. Provincial rivalry between towns was a matter of constant concern to the Church authorities. A Montpelier delegation would attend a Bennington dance with the intent of "cleaning the Bennington boys" and vice versa. On one of these occasions a vicious gang fight resulted in the utter defeat of the Montpelier boys. There was some physical damage because the Montpelier parents brought the Bennington ring leaders to trial before a Church court. Amos was in Burgoyne's store at the time and Burgoyne said, "Why, Brother Wright, why aren't you down there at the court defending your boys?"

"Because they're guilty and deserve to be punished," he replied.

One fall, Ed wanted to go to Canada on a construction job. Amos reluctantly gave his consent and went out and bought Ed a

fine team of roan horses, no doubt with borrowed money. Ed went
to Canada and was gone for several months. When he came back,
his teeth were stained with tobacco and he sat around and
smoked cigarettes in front of his father. Amos said Ed had been in
bad company and it was a wonder he had escaped the law since
he had been gambling and drinking and in all sorts of mischief.
Later, when Ed went to the Brigham Young Academy in Logan
and came under the influence of Karl G. Maeser and other
members of the faculty there, Amos came in one evening very
pleased and said, "Well, my boy Ed has got the right collar now,
thank God. He gave a fine talk in meeting today and Silas wasn't
far behind!"

During a political campaign Amos was offered a tidy sum to
make stump speeches for a man who represented the liquor
interest in Idaho. He said, no! "Liquor isn't good for man and I'll
never talk for it nor vote for it."

But he took a nip occasionally. He had developed a taste for it
in his rebellious days when he was "on the loose." He rationalized
that an occasional drink was "not by commandment nor
restraint."

Coulsen and Conover found a bottle of brandy in the wheat
bin one day when they were playing and sampled it without
telling their father. And once on their way home from 'Pelier
when the weather was extra cold, Amos opened a bottle of
whiskey and took a swig and offered it to Coulsen and Conover
saying, "It's all right to take a little drink with your father when
it's cold. But remember, don't ever get drunk, you haven't got any
too much sense when you're sober."

Bear Lake Valley was settled before the Word of Wisdom was
crystallized as Church law. Older people joined the Church after
habits of drinking and smoking were formed. Liquor was
"medicine" but sometimes an unrepentant Saint was cut off from
the Church for drinking habitually.

Silas had just been made bishop in place of Amos. As they
rode toward Paris in the bobsled, the weather was cold as usual.
Brother Welker pulled out a flask of whiskey saying, "Maybe this
will warm us up a little." He took a snort, passed the bottle to
Amos who did likewise. But as Silas reached for the bottle, Amos
laid a restraining hand on his arm.

"No, Silas, I don't think you'd better take any. You've just
been made a bishop and if somebody heard you had anything to
do with liquor you'd be put in an embarrassing spot."

Amos found an old piece of dried-up chewing tobacco one day and pounded it to powder with a hammer. Then he rolled it in a piece of newspaper and smoked it. He said he wanted to see if it would make him sick and seemed pleased that it didn't.

One man in the ward told him he was having a hard time keeping the Word of Wisdom. "My nerves are something awful and the only thing that helps is a cup of coffee. The doctor in Sody told me a cup wouldn't hurt me. Then I asked Dr. Hoover about it and he said to go ahead. Now what shall I do?"

"Make up your mind! It's two doctors against the Lord," replied his bishop. Amos had implicit faith in the Lord. When things got tough he would say, "Trust in the Lord. He will take care of us." When they were first married Loella believed it too, but in later years she sometimes added, "Well, he'd better, because nobody else ever has."

Amos would cite for example the time he was on his way to the canyon early one morning to get a load of wood. He said he had hitched the team to the wagon, got on, standing on the tongue hounds, and as he started out on a good trot, in some way the front wheels became detached from the hind part. He thought the jolting caused the kingbolt to bounce up far enough to allow the reach to pull out. Of course his weight on the tongue caused it to drop down into the heels of the horses, making it impossible for him to manage them. They started to run and kick and he could see nothing but sure death for him. He cried out "Lord, save me," and to his astonishment and relief the wagon tongue suddenly rose to the level and he was thrown free without being hurt.

One day, Amos and Coulsen were mending the pigpen fence when Cate came down the path wearing her usual starched sunbonnet and a fresh apron and looking very neat and nice. She handed an opened envelope to Amos saying, "See what you think of that." Amos took out a check for $600.

"Well, I guess we won't starve to death, this winter." He folded the check and put it in his wallet.

"Did you think we would?" Amos hitched up the horses as he muttered, "Now I'll be able to hush up some of those dang creditors."

The check from the government paying him for fighting in one of the Indian wars many years before, was considered as significant as manna from heaven.

Amos believed in paying a strictly honest tithing. He sometimes had to borrow money at the end of the year to balance his tithing for the year, but believed if he didn't receive blessings then, he would in the hereafter for doing so.

One time, Coulsen and Conover and their father were hauling hay. One load in ten was the Lord's load and they always took it to the tithing yard and stacked it there. "Conover and I were tromping while Father pitched out of the field," recalled Coulsen. "Father had the lines down on the ground beside old Duke. A swarm of flying ants got after the horse's heads. They jumped and Father grabbed the lines and held on. This turned the wagon toward him and when he couldn't hang on any longer the hind wheel ran over his thighs. I remember two black and blue streaks across the back of his legs just the width of the wagon tire. He didn't suffer any serious effects and he attributed it to the protection of the Lord."

He made his teen-age girls mad at him sometimes, but they later thanked him for being particular who they went out with. The girls of both families were pretty and popular. Amos laughingly said he wished he lived at the mouth of the canyon because he would never have to make a road when he went to town because the young blades kept the road hot coming and going to see the girls. None of the "depot element" ever got to take them out, and Amos had a way of putting a cocky young fellow in his place if he needed it. Amos happened to come in out of the corral one evening when Jonny Barrett came to take Libby to a dance. He had a wing collar and white spats on.

"Hey, Bub, come pull off my boots," said Amos. Then he had the boy straddle his leg facing away from him and as Jonny pulled and tugged, Amos put his other foot on the boy's rear and pushed till the boot came off with a jerk and Bub pitched forward onto the floor. Then he repeated the process with the other boot.

Once, a good-looking young man drove over from Sody to court Addie. He had a pair of black ponies all harnessed in the fanciest snaps, slides, rosettes and tassels, and a shiny one-seated buggy with rubber tires. He was dressed in style, too. But he was a gentile and didn't even get a look at her. She watched through the window as he drove off down the road and thought her father was the meanest man in the world.

A new teacher named Billings came to town who made a big hit with the girls. He, too, drove a fancy rig and when he planned a bobsleigh party for the eighth graders to go to a dance in Montpelier, all the young folks were dying to go. When Nettie asked Amos if she could go, he shook his head no. She begged and pleaded but the answer was still the same.

Billings saw Bishop Wright at church one afternoon and told him how disappointed Nettie was that she couldn't go. All the rest of the young people her age were going. Amos said, "Sorry, but Nettie can't go." The night of the dance, the whole crowd drove past the Wright home and stopped in front of the gate as Billings came to the door for a last try. The answer was the same, despite Nettie's tears and Billings' annoyance.

Next morning the word got out that Billings had been so drunk at the dance that he had to be taken off the dance floor. Amos said, "See Nett, my girl, your old father knows a thing or two about people. And besides, you're a bishop's daughter."

Nettie got a part-time job as a telephone girl in Paris while she was going to the Fielding Academy. She was a pretty girl and a good worker as well. Frank got a job for her that summer, cooking at a big ranch in Wyoming for a dozen haymen. The couple she worked for had money but no children and they fell in love with her.

"We'll send you to any school in the United States," they urged, "pay for voice lessons and dress you like a queen. We haven't got anybody to love and your father won't mind. He has so many children he'd never miss you."

Nettie felt like Cinderella at the ball at the mere thought of such a fantastic offer. She agreed to write to her father for his permission, half-guessing what his reply would be. By return mail, a letter came from Bennington.

> Even though I have twenty-four children, I am a poor man, and age is overtaking me. I would not for one moment consider giving one of my children to someone else, much less my Nettie. But I would offer my right arm for her protection anytime and as long as I have breath in my body it shall be spent to teach her to live right, with the faith and hope that someday we can all sit down in the heavens together. If she would go with you, I could not have that hope and the price is too great to pay.

At the end of the summer she had earned and saved a hundred dollars, and got it all in greenbacks. Before she got on the train for Montpelier, she tucked the money in the bottom of her shoe so she wouldn't get robbed. Proudly, she counted out ten dollars of her hoard and handed it to her father. "Here's my tithing money, Father," she said simply. His hand shook as he reached for the tithing box and tucked it inside. With a tremble in his voice he looked at her lovingly and said, "Thanks, my girl, and God bless you!"

"When I got home and saw how Mother and the family needed so many things," she recalled many years later, "I began to weaken about going to school, and the first thing I knew my money was all spent and I had to go to work again. I still longed to go to college. But I got to go after I was married. My husband was a professor at the college in Logan, so I took classes off and on for a long time."

One afternoon Cate had a quilt on the frames and the girls from both families were helping quilt. Addie began telling about woman sufferage, how interested she was in it and how she would surely favor women's rights. Amos, who was reading the paper in the adjoining room, heard her and came to the door.

"I'm glad you brought that up, Addie. I have intended to talk to you about it. Woman suffrage will not better women's lot. If this proposition becomes a fact and women get their franchise, it will only be a little time until they'll cut their hair and dress like men, actually to wearing pants like men. They will enter fields known as men's employment and compete with them for jobs and salaries. Then home duties and children will suffer and problems will arise that you've never dreamed of. And if our women under such solemn covenants as our marriage relations imply, should ever raise their hands or voice against such things, the day will come when their daughters will run the streets as common prostitutes and they cannot help themselves." (Gwen Andersen, "My Grandfather Said.")

When Nelly married Fred Jacobsen and went to southern Arizona, it broke Mose's heart. She was his and Loella's first child, born when he was in Wyoming on a mission, and she had held a special place in his life ever after. She and Fred were going to Logan to be married in the temple. Young folks in those days didn't have a big send off, but just got on the train together and went and got married.

Amos hitched up the team and wagon and put Nelly's baggage in the back and she and Fred sat in the spring seat with him. He helped her and Fred unload their stuff, but when they were ready to get on the train, Nelly couldn't see her father anywhere.

"Where did Father go?" she asked with tears in her eyes. "I can't believe he'd leave without saying goodbye." But the conductor shouted, all aboard! and Fred helped her up the steps as the train slowly pulled out of the station and over the hill. She carried a little stab of resentment away with her. "Surely he could have cared enough to say goodbye."

It wasn't until a month later when a homesick Nelly in Safford, Arizona, received a letter, postmarked Bennington, that she fully understood what had happened. "I hid behind the depot while the train pulled out, and when the last vestige of smoke curled over the hill bearing my Nelly away from me, this old heart burst and has never commenced to beat normally since."

From then on they wrote to each other quite often.

He continued to use big words and more than he needed to, but that made him feel like an educated man, even though he always insisted that he wasn't. That was the style of the day. He liked to stretch things for effect, but he did it so people knew he was exaggerating and not deceiving. He could write freely to Nelly. She understood, and he needed a sounding board. But he decided it would be wise to include Fred. He was his son, now, so when he wrote to him, he let himself go, exaggerating to the point of absurdity. As usual, the weather was given a lambasting and then he started in about his daughter, Mary. She had always been small and delicate like Loella and still was.

Someone once asked him why he chose to settle in Bear Lake since he disliked the climate so much. "Chose!" he snorted.

When Loella became pregnant again, she couldn't stay in Bennington when the baby was born, May 9, 1908, because the polygamy scare was in the air again. Virginia was born in Brigham City under the care of Aunt Mary Jane, Father Jonathan's wife and Amos' kindly stepmother.

Amos seldom, if ever, went to a picture show. He recognized they were mostly trash. But a Negro minstrel show came to Bennington one time which Amos went to and loved. They danced, cakewalked, clog danced, impersonated various people and he threw his hat in the air and yelled approval. He said black men were intended to be entertainers and were the natural musicians among the human race.

Ed Austin often tried to get Amos to take life easier; have a little fun, instead of being so serious all the time. But habits don't break easily.

Neither did he like to see children idle. Gladys Weaver was Dora's girl. She came to Bennington one summer to visit and she and Norey were both five. They fell in love with each other at once. She loved her Aunt Loella, too, but when they got rowdy, Amos said sternly, "Go pull weeds."

Gladys asked Norey why they had to pull weeds, who explained they were for the pigs. They pulled and pulled and threw weeds over the fence to the pigs till the fence was all covered up, too. Then they climbed up in the hay loft for a change. They heard Amos calling. "I thought I told you kids to pull weeds, you're not supposed to play in the hay." And as they climbed down the ladder, Amos gave both girls a little swat on the bottom.

When Gladys told her mother about that mean old man afterward, Dora started to laugh. "I know what you mean. I felt the same way when I was a little girl. Uncle Amos was my schoolteacher. I was very shy and bashful and got scared at nothing, but I could spell better than the rest of the kids and so I was in lots of spelling matches. One time I got so excited when he asked me to spell 'squash' that I stammered and said, 'S-Q-U-ASH.' That made our side lose the spelling match and Uncle Amos looked like he wanted to shake me. I ran home that day and said I wouldn't go back till there was a new teacher. And I didn't, because there wasn't another one."

One evening Amos had been to the canyon all day getting out stove wood and was very tired, so he went over to Cate's. She and the girls had already had their supper but Cate got something for Mose and sat across from him while he ate. When he got through eating he sighed and said, "I'm awful tired Cate, I believe I'll stay here tonight. The children are so noisy over at Loell's and I need some rest." Cate quickly answered, "Oh, no you won't; you go home! It's no worse for you than it is for Loella. Your place is there, not here." Amos sighed again, pushed his chair away from the table and went out the door.

At a sacrament meeting one cold day in January 1912, Amos went as usual to take charge of the meeting. It was cold and there probably wouldn't be many there or they'd be late, but "I'll start on time if I'm the only one there," he said. He had the habit of talking to himself. "I wonder how long this thing will go on. It's been thirty years now. I don't know how much longer I can stand it."

Just then he saw a horse and buggy coming down the road. It was President Budge and his two counselors. They tied the horse at the hitching post and went inside. Brother Budge informed Amos they had come to have him released as bishop. He was surprised and relieved. He was duly released with a vote of thanks for his services. His grandson, Silas L. Wright, was proposed as bishop in his place. When Brother Budge said, "any opposed" one member held up his hand. He said he didn't think the office of bishop was hereditary, and thought it would be a good idea to have somebody beside the Wright family run the ward for a change. But since he was the only protestor (a number of others got cold feet and kept still) Silas L. Wright became bishop, and Amos' work was done.

A released bishop was usually made a high councilor or a patriarch, but nothing was said about either office to Amos. Why, he wondered, and concluded his years as a bishop were a failure. He brooded over it and became more moody than ever. He determined he wouldn't let on to anybody else, but he couldn't hide it from those who knew him best. He felt strangely lost without the "mantle" he'd worn so long and faithfully. He was "on the shelf" from now on and he had to face it.

One matter of a very personal nature came as a distinct shock to his pride and daily reminded him he was old, in his seventy-second year. Loella's twelfth child was born February 10, 1911. They named her Ruth Esther. A few weeks later Loella informed him with a finality new to her, that twelve children was enough. She was forty-two and from then on she would not risk another pregnancy.

One evening Nettie went out to check the chicken coop door for the night. That was one of her chores. She hated to go out after dark, but that night there was a beautiful full moon so she wasn't so scared. The snow sparkled and squeaked under her feet as she walked. Suddenly she heard a strange moaning sound, and she froze in her tracks. It came again, a pitiful wail, and then she heard her father's voice and realized he was out by the haystack talking to his friend, the Lord, in whom he always trusted. She couldn't make out the words but they sounded pleading and urgent. It was cold. She hurried and checked the chicken coop door and ran back in the house, still hearing her father's voice breaking the night silence.

Chapter Thirty-two
Intimate Glimpses

Getting out wood from the canyon was always part of the fall and winter work. In between blizzards there were usually some clear sparkling days with the sun shining on the snow, so bright it was eye-hurting.

There had been a few wet storms that settled the snow and made it solid enough to form a crust on top. After a cold snap, the crust was so hard a team and bobsleigh could be driven anywhere without bothering to open gates or stopping for fences. The horses and bobsleigh went right over the top.

When Amos woke up he decided it was a good wood-getting day. It was still dark as he rolled out of bed, pulled on his clothes and bundled himself against the ever-present cold. He'd have to get the boys up. They slept in the haymow in the barn up above the stable where Beauty cow and Printz pony were kept.

There was a ladder to climb and some blankets and a buffalo robe for a bed. Many mornings the boys had to brush the snow off the robe before they could crawl out, hustle down the ladder and into the house before it froze whiskers on their arms and legs.

Amos climbed the ladder and crawled over on the hay to where the boys slept. Conover could sleep through an earthquake so Amos rapped him a couple of times on the head, saying "Conover, Conover, *Conover!*" Then quietly, "Coulsen, it's time to get up."

Loella packed a lunch and after bolting a bowl of germade with sugar and cream, the boys donned stocking caps and mittens and Amos bundled into his warmest coat and cap with ear flaps and the three of them headed for the canyon.

Amos had hitched Old Rock and Bird to the bobsleigh, tossed a forkful of hay in the sleigh box for the horses, and a chain to cinch the logs on with, together with ax and saw. Off they went straight east to the mouth of Dry Hollow, a small canyon between

Home Canyon and Red Canyon.

The boys unhooked the horses from the sleigh and tied them to the back so the animals could munch on the hay. Taking the ax and saw, they climbed the south side of Dry Canyon. It was very steep and hard to climb even when the ground was dry, but when covered with ice and snow it took all they had to get to the top. They spotted a clump of dry evergreens near the top of the hill and made for them. Lugging the tools by turn, they finally made it and stopped a few minutes, huffing and puffing in the thin air, their breath making smoke rings.

Amos hadn't forgotten his skill with an axe and the boys watched fascinated as he cut a notch on the upper side of the tree trunk and made the chips fly. Coulsen and Conover got on each end of the crosscut saw and pulled it back and forth till the tree started to topple and came crashing down into the snow. Amos trimmed off the branches and the log was ready to slide down the hill. They repeated this operation three or four times the same way.

"I think we've got enough logs, boys," said Amos. "Let's take time out for something to eat."

The sandwiches Loella had made, disappeared magically.

"Now, boys, we'll all three push as hard as we can and get this log moving. We want to make it slide straight down and not roll, then it will go clear to the bottom of the canyon where we want it. Altogether now, *PUSH!*"

Slowly, it began to slide, picking up speed and making a snow-spray on each side of the log as it went, and stopping with a crash at the bottom. Logs number two and three did the same. The last one was the biggest and Amos dared the boys to ride it down. They hesitated, looking startled. They were really afraid but ashamed to admit it to their father. If *he* thought they could, they could, so they climbed on. It was so big their legs stuck straight out on each side.

"Roll off before you get to the bottom," shouted Amos as he gave the log a push, straining every muscle to do it. It was like riding a roller coaster. Their stomachs turned inside out and they yelled as trees and bushes whizzed past in a blur.

"Jump!" yelled Coulsen, and both boys tumbled into the snow a few seconds before the log crashed to the bottom of the canyon.

"Wow! WE DID IT!" they gloated, brushing snow out of their ears and eyes and mouth. Amos followed, carrying ax and saw.

He knew how to place the bobsled so they could roll the logs onto it, fasten the chain securely and hitch the horses for the homeward ride. That was easy, gliding over the top of the drifts and reaching home just before dark. The boys couldn't wait to brag to their mother about the ride on the log.

Loella had a big pot of soup bubbling on the stove and the aroma made their mouths water. They dipped warm water out of the stove reservoir into the wash basin for getting the top layer of grime off, and wiped the rest off on the roller towel hanging behind the door. The girls had the table set and Amos announced, "Time for prayers" as he knelt down at the head of the table and thanked God for a day's work well done.

There was never a time when the boys didn't have work to do and Amos saw that they did it. The big logs from the canyon were always waiting to be sawed into stove-lengths and then split and piled ready for kindling and fuel. It seemed as if the split wood melted away faster than it could be cut and piled. But they managed to squeeze in a little fun between work. If Amos told them to go to Montpelier in the winter on an errand, they took the bobsleigh with Rock and Bird in the harness. On the way home when they got to Crane's Corner, it was slick as glass and the horses knew it was time for fun.

Coulsen cracked the whip and the horses made the sleigh whirl in a circle so fast, it was all he could do to stay in the wagon box, with Conover hanging onto the back runner. They kept it spinning like a merry-go-round gone crazy, and the horses enjoyed it as much as the boys.

Coulsen had gone as far as the eighth grade, which was the top in Bennington. He loved school, though Amos thought the local school was poor. He visited at least once or twice each winter to check on what was going on. It always embarrassed Coulsen when his father walked in, but he recognized that Amos was respected, because the teacher always asked him to speak. He was the only parent who ever visited school.

He sometimes kept Coulsen out to punish him if he thought he needed it. Amos knew that would hurt him worse than a whipping. And it did. Very few boys from Bear Lake had ever gone to the A.C. in Logan. That stood for Agricultural College. Coulsen ventured to tell his father he wished he could go to Logan someday, though he didn't dare hope his wish would be granted. Where would the money come from, anyway?

Remembering his own yen for learning, Amos was pleased that his son wanted to go. "Well, Coulsen, we'll see what we can do. Maybe you could get a job down there doing something to help out." From that moment, Coulsen's every thought and action was geared toward going to college. He worked early and late so the crops would be good and there might be enough money so he could go. He worked cheerfully and happily, dreaming dreams and hoping hopes.

Amos was father to fifty families in the ward in addition to his own two, and it took all the wisdom and patience he could muster to keep them in the strait and narrow way. This made a total of 344 men, women and children for whom he was responsible.

He had become disgusted with the constant talk about proper dance rules which occupied so much time at priesthood meetings and amounted to nothing but talk. He began calling the Valley dances, "dog heists." The first presidency had first counseled stake presidents and bishops to ban round dancing entirely. They realized the danger of arousing passions when boys and girls were allowed to dance in the intimacy of a waltz or two-step. The bishop's job was to enforce the rules and "the buck stopped with him." He found himself caught between doing his duty and meeting the criticism and pressure from young folks and their parents. "What's wrong with a little waltz?" they asked. "Why be so strait-laced?" Gradually, the general authorities diluted the counsel and allowed one or two waltzes each evening. But much wants more, and eventually all restraints were removed, though warning as to the consequences remained.

Amos decided to try an alternative. At least, young people could be taught the proper way to waltz. He knew a man who fit the need perfectly. John Dunn was a musician, a teacher, a gentleman and a fiddler who could make anybody want to keep time to his tunes. He had taught the older folks to dance every other kind of dance in the dictionary. Young people loved him and he liked them. Amos asked him if he would conduct a weekly dance class and suggested a prize be given at the end of the series for the boy and girl who were the best dancers. The idea took fire at once and at the end of six months Amos was delighted to find out that his own son Coulsen had been chosen along with John Dunn's granddaughter Mabel as winners of the prize. They had their picture taken in Montpelier at the photograph gallery and it was circulated among Bennington families to demonstrate "the real McCoy". At the bottom of the picture was printed: AS ADOPTED BY THE NATIONAL ASSOCIATION OF TEACH-ERS OF ROUND DANCING, J. Dunn & Co's School, Bennington, Idaho, 1907.

With the bishop's responsibilities off his shoulders, Amos was lost. His active mind demanded something to work on, and suddenly a brainstorm was born. Bear River, a mile below Bennington, was a frustrating barrier. There had been a ferry there for years, and he had kept the cable mended and workable part of the time. It was risky to cross in the spring, because of high water, and dangerous to cross in the winter. A man never knew when his team and bobsled or wagon would break through the ice. If a bridge could be built like they just finished west of Montpelier, that would really be something! But where would the money come from? There had to be a way, and Amos' mind began wrestling with the problem. He talked to himself more than ever for six months and by then he had convinced Jared Parker and his grandson Silas L. that the idea would work. They all talked it up around Bennington and Nounan. Some folks thought it was crazy, but by November they took a petition to the county commissioners, signed by farmers on both sides of the river, and their request was granted. By December the contract was let to build a bridge across Bear River at Pescadero. The following summer the approaches to the bridge were completed under the direction of George E. Stephens.

Amos watched the work with interest, constantly encouraging, prodding and urging speed. He ate and slept with the Pescadero bridge. Loella sensed he needed something to take his mind off of it. She proposed he take her to a dance the ward was having to raise money for the bridge.

After all the years as bishop, trying to control ward dances, he never wanted to see another one, and told Loella so. But she had learned not to take his word for law the way she had for so many years, and pointed out that *this* dance was different. It was for the *bridge*. They went.

There was a big crowd. The music was good and everybody was having fun. He and Loella danced and remembered it was at a Mutual dance in this very hall over twenty-five years before when he asked her to marry him. They still liked to dance and felt young at heart.

Loella's sister Kitty was there, and when Amos asked her for a polka, she agreed with gusto. She liked to cut up as much as Amos, and a polka was just the vehicle they needed. Starting out slowly, to get the feel of it, they gradually speeded up. Faster and faster they went, putting in a lot of extra steps. Again and again they clapped for just one more encore, until finally they both collapsed on a bench from sheer exhaustion.

Amos hadn't been so exhilarated for ages. He felt he was eighteen again and could have gone on indefinitely. It took him a long time to unwind that night after he got to bed, but he finally dropped off into a troubled sleep, dreaming he was climbing a mountain whose top constantly receded. He staggered upward, gasping for breath and was awakened by Loella shaking him.

"Mose, Mose, wake up! What's the matter?"

He tried to answer but couldn't make a sound. A stabbing pain raced down his left arm. He couldn't move it or his leg. It was a stroke, later confirmed as such by Dr. Hoover. Loella and the girls nursed him as best they could. For weeks he was unable to get out of bed or speak without mumbling. Propped up in bed he wrote to his brother Brig in Brigham City:

> My mouth seems thick and deprived of proper and natural articulation. However, upon the urgent request of authority and some friends, assisted to the stand and seated in an armchair, I preached the funeral discourse of a Gentile gentleman who died here recently. I presume it was a matter of policy since the deceased was a very wealthy and somewhat influential man.

> With this exception I have not been to meeting or taken part in religious exercises for several months; that is I mean, but very little. I have but little use of my hand and can't raise my arm up even with my body. My poor penmanship is the result of the stroke.

But, at length, his strong physique began to assert itself and he was able to walk with the aid of a cane and his speech returned to normal. On a good day he would venture a little way up the lane, five-year-old Virginia running after him picking night-wood shades, buttercups and sweet williams. When she handed them to Amos he would bow and say, "Thank you, Madame," and pat her on the head. She sometimes asked him for a nickel and he would pull a button or a peppermint out of his pocket and tell her to pretend it was a nickel. He pointed to the sky, the trees, the grass or mountains in answer to her childish questions. Then when they got home he would take her on his knee and sing "My Little Turtle Dove." Someone asked her who she was and she said, "Father thinks I'm a disciple of Jesus."

His friends were very kind during his recovery. People he didn't realize even liked him stopped to chat and brought him little treats. Of course Ed Austin came often. He had been quite successful by that time and loved to put on the dog, so it was no surprise to see him drive up one day in a fancy rubber-tired surrey and a blooded bay mare in the shaves. They had a good time talking as usual but Ed finally said he'd have to go.

Amos followed him out to the road, limping some and using a cane. Ed untied the mare and climbed into the buggy. Amos noticed the mare was check-reined with her head high in the air. Just before Ed picked up the reins to go, Amos said, "Ed, you ought to be ashamed of yourself, reining your mare like that with her head reared back until it almost breaks her neck!"

Ed looked at him sidewise, said nothing, but took the decorated lap-robe off from his knees, climbed down out of the buggy, went and unchecked the mare's head. Her head remained in approximately the same position. He looked squarely at Amos for comment.

"Well," said Amos, "That's all right. If she is naturally high-headed—that's all right." Ed grinned, got back in the buggy and drove off.

Winnie and George Stephens stopped by one afternoon for a chat. Ruth Esther was a toddler and George took her on his lap, charmed by her childish beauty. Turning to his son-in-law, Amos said, "George, you can have her to raise after I die."

Loella laughed and said, "I guess you won't have much to say about it when you are in your grave." But George smiled and said, "She's my little girl. Grandpa gave her to me."

But between such visits, there was lots of time to think, and things were different now. He had always taken his toughness for granted. Other people might get sick, but that would never happen to him. It had been his job to help and pray for them if they needed him. Now the boot was on the Wright foot. He painfully uncrossed his leg.

Sure, the bridge wasn't finished, but it was far enough along so they didn't need him anymore. Seventy-two was *old*. The thought hit him with a shock. Maybe he'd never get over this.

From that low point, he began reviewing his life to see what comfort there was left. He didn't find much. He'd been a failure all along and hadn't had sense enough to see it. No wonder they didn't make him a patriarch. No wonder they released him as bishop. No wonder his wives and children criticized him. No wonder he'd never made a decent living for his families. The no-wonder game got to be as absorbing as the what-if game used to be, only the negative thoughts increased his depression. So many members of his family had not turned out the way he hoped they would. What would happen to them when he was gone, especially the young ones? He spent a good deal of thought on that subject. He advised Loella to stay in Bennington with the little ones when he died. "They will have a better chance of growing up in the Church here than anywhere else."

Sitting in his congress chair in the shade at the east side of the house, one summer day, he thought of Coulsey and his dream of going to college. How could that ever happen now? No wonder he wanted to get away from here. He was young and still had a chance to live somewhere else other than in Bear Lake's isolation and nine months of winter. Just then he saw the boys driving the loaded hayrack down the lane with old Spot barking at the horses' heels. Coulsey and Conover were two of the best boys God ever gave a man.

He took his cane and hobbled out to stand under the tree by the barn so he could watch them unload. They pitched the hay onto the stack in the barnyard and Conover went in the house. Coulsen stayed to rake up the extra hay that had dropped as they unloaded. He stuck the pitchforks in the stack where they belonged, hung up the harness and cleaned out the stable. He didn't notice his father standing there until he was ready to go in the house. Amos was directly in his path. As Coulsen neared him, his father reached in his pocket, drew out a silver dollar and silently handed it to him. It was a poignant moment; a moment too deep for words. A silver dollar was rare and precious and that one symbolized a father's gratitude for and pride in his obedient son in whom he was well pleased. To Coulsen it dramatized his father's appreciation and love as well as the desire to give his all to make his dream come true.

It was late October before Coulsen could leave, but finally the day came. Amos had looked forward to driving him to the train in 'Pelier. He looked for an excuse to get out of the house now he couldn't work, and he wanted a few precious moments with his son before he left. Who knew, it might be the last time he'd see him. He watched Coulsen drive Old Rock, hitched to the single buggy, around to the front of the house and then go inside to change his clothes and pack his bag. Amos put on his hat and hobbled out to the buggy and stood there waiting. Coulsen came out, loaded his suitcase and an extra box into the back of the buggy. Then turning to his father he said, "Well, goodbye Father. I guess Conover will drive me to town."

"Goodbye, my boy," he said as he embraced Coulsen, "and for

God's sake stay out of bad company!" Whereupon he broke down
and cried out loud, loud enough to be heard a block away.

"Now, Father, don't feel that way", said Coulsen.

"Go on, go on, you don't need me!" he cried waving him away.
Slowly, he shuffled back to the house.

What a mass of contradictions he was! It was hard for those
closest to him to know what to expect from such a volatile,
unpredictable nature. And since his stroke, he was more emotional than ever.

There had been jarrings and contentions ever since the two
families began living on the same lot. Poverty, cold, close
quarters, discomfort, jealousy and human weaknesses made
living, well nigh unbearable at times for all concerned. The
wonder is it wasn't worse. There were intervals of relative peace
and good times in between. Sympathizers sometimes said to Cate,
"Why don't you leave him?" To which she replied in her quick
Welsh accent, "You don't know what you're talking about!"

Amos needed to go to 'Pelier one day. He asked Frank to hitch
up for him and drive up to the door. He was slow getting out and
down the two steps and out to the buggy. Impatiently, Frank took
hold of Amos' bad arm to help him in and he screamed with pain.
He almost fainted and Frank dragged him a few steps and laid
him under a tree to recover.

Cate heard his cries. Her little peek-hole between the logs
revealed what had happened and she came running out. Kneeling
down beside him she began wiping his forehead with her apron,
as she moaned, "Mose, Mose, are you all right? It's me, Cate,"
meanwhile kissing him and laying her head on his breast.

Slowly he opened his eyes and mumbled, "Never mind, I'll be
all right now. Just give me a few minutes." Whereat she stood up,
pulled her shawl around her shoulders and walked back into the
house.

A few days later, Cate was sitting at the table, writing. Amos
came up behind her and stooped to kiss her on top of her head,
saying softly, "My poor little mourning dove!" She didn't move or
respond.

For many years Loella accepted his every word without
question. It was a father-daughter relationship in many ways.
When she came to realize that he wasn't infallible and sometimes
questioned his authority, it was almost more than he could bear.
The noise and confusion at Loella's was upsetting as it would
have been to any man of seventy-three. She would say, "Mose,

why don't you go over to Cate's. It is quiet there and you can get some rest." To which he replied, "You try to get rid of me by saying 'go over to Cate's.' When I go to Cate's she says, 'Go back to your darlin'!'"

Fortunately, Amos' good arm was the right one so he could still write letters.

Loella's mother, Sarah, was alone down in Whitney after Gib died. Her health was failing and she couldn't stay alone. Mary stayed with her for awhile but something else had to be done. Loella waited till she and Amos got to bed one night to talk to him about it. Nona and Hattie and Virginia slept in the little bed next to theirs in the only bedroom.

"Can I bring Mother here, Mose? She's so sick and can't take care of herself anymore."

"How can you take care of your mother and me, too? Can't Kit or some of the other girls take her? Besides, where would we put her?" whispered Amos, so he wouldn't wake the little girls.

"She has done so much for us all these years, we'll never be able to pay her back. We could move the girls into the attic with the rest of the children for awhile. Norey is so sweet, she wouldn't mind and she's the oldest."

"That's right," said Amos. "Anybody who can't get along with Norey couldn't get along with anybody." Amos and Loella didn't know it, but Norey was still awake in the other bed and heard what they said. She treasured those words from her Father as long as she lived.

So Grandma Sarah came. "Your Grandma has been very bad the last week," wrote Loella to her daughter Nettie. "She suffers untold agony every day and night unless we give her morphene or rub cloyrforme on her legs. Her feet have begun to turn dark and she has gangrene. I don't see how she lives. Your Pa just administered to her and she went to sleep.

"It does my heart good to know you still love me as you use to do, then when I am old like my dear Mother I will have one to take care of me. They all think they can't take care of Ma, but I feel like I would take care of her if I only had one room and had to go on one leg and had no money. It is hard and a trile but someone has to do it and I am glad I am that one."

Grandma Sarah breathed her last about two weeks later and was buried alongside Gib, her companion for eternity, down in the Whitney graveyard, where their grandchildren kept the two graves covered with wildflowers every Decoration Day.

Then Norey and Hattie and Virginia moved back in the bedroom they'd vacated, and as Loella had predicted, "Norey didn't mind."

"I don't remember that any of us quarreled or that I felt unhappy as I grew up, in fact, I was always happy," Norey recalled many years later. "Father loved to get behind Mother and throw both arms around her and dance her around as he sang a funny Indian song. I grew up seeing Father and Mother love each other. He would kiss her on the neck and I always thought that was the way all married people did. He used to kiss the bottom of her feet to wake her up. She had such little two-and-a-half size feet and he thought they were so beautiful.

"I loved to go over to Sister Wright's. She was always so good to me. She had a sparkle in her eye and she had naturally curly hair, more so than Mother's. She had deep, dark blue eyes that danced. She must have been a lovely looking girl. She did hand work and made quilts. Of course I don't remember anything about the older children, so by the time I was old enough to remember, I loved them all and they loved me.

"I was making a little blouse one time and it had some embroidery on the collar and cuffs. To get away from the noise and little kids, I went over to Sister Wright's and sat on the porch with her and worked on it. She was so proud of me while I worked. She sat there and watched me. "Oh, Noney, you are going to be a good wife and mother. You will always be a good girl." She spoke kind of quick; not a brogue, but with a certain inflection which made her speech distinctive. She could sing too.

"There was always music over there. Father bought an organ for them and they had mandolins and guitars and Fanny and Libby and Caty could play and sing. They said Nelly and Nettie used to sing with them and they sounded beautiful, singing parts. Course that was before my time.

"One time I was helping Father when he was sharpening some mowing-machine blades or points, and I was about ten years old and I was turning the grinding-stone after he poured water on it and I was supposed to turn it slowly and evenly. I guess I got tired and he yelled at me a couple of times to keep turning it evenly. I guess Mrs. Wright heard him, because here she came, shaking her finger and saying, 'Mose Wright, don't you touch that child, and don't you yell at her once more or I'll take her in my house and you won't get your knives sharpened today.' I guess she had heard him doing it to others, her kids, too.

"But Father wasn't above spoiling me. He was strict what the girls wore. I remember my first pair of high heels and Mother said, 'I don't know what your father will say about these.' But I was always very confident about myself and didn't worry about what he would say.

"I was coming over from showing my new shoes to Sister Wright. I could see Father sitting by the stove. I said, 'Father, would you like to see my brand new shoes?' He looked up from his paper and said, 'Come over here, put your foot up here.'

"So I put my foot up on his knee and he took it in both his hands, very kindly and sweetly and turned it around and looked at the shoe and at the high heels. Then he looked at me. I was waiting for his answer, and he said,

'They're pretty shoes.' And then he took both my hands and looked up at me and said, 'But Pa's afraid it will spile you.'

"I kissed him on the forehead and said, 'Oh, I'm glad you like them,' and ran off again. By the time I was growing up a little he had mellowed considerably. He never was cross with the girls and of course never touched them to slap them. I've never heard the other girls say he did either. But he did whip the boys. I wasn't old enough to have boy friends before he died, so I don't remember anything about that.

"I remember one time going to a dance at Bennington. I had a new dress on and it had long sleeves, so I rolled them up above the elbow and before I left, Father said,

'Now, Norey, you put those sleeves down where they belong before you go to that dance.' So I didn't say 'why' or anything, and I just said, 'Oh, okay,' and I rolled them down. And this is a little secret, I hadn't any more than got in the buggy than I rolled them up again. So Father did spoil me I guess.

"He was very particular that we get our drinking water from the lower spring. There was an upper spring, but the lower was the coldest and the purest. It was my turn to get the water, so like the others, I went to the upper spring. I guess he was on to us by then but I thought, 'Well, he's an old man and he won't know the difference.' But just as soon as he tasted it he said, 'Norey! did you go to the lower spring for this water?' I didn't say anything, yes or no, but he dumped the water in the reservoir on the stove, and said, 'Now you go to the lower spring and get a bucket of water.' So I went and all the way there and back I sang him this song:

Speak to me kindly dear Father,
Only speak kindly to me."

The long days for Amos after his stroke, eventually fell into a pattern. After breakfast he read the *Deseret News* clear through. He subscribed to it because it was the Voice of the Church. The *Salt Lake Tribune* was anti-Mormon. He couldn't resist reading it, though, if he happened to see a copy around somewhere. He wrote letters and took them to the post office in time to pick up the mail. It was slow going at first but he got better as time went on. On the way back he'd usually stop in at Winnie's and Addie's to chat a little, often being invited to stay for supper.

Amos went over to see how the bridge was coming along whenever he had a chance. One day when he got there he could see it would soon be finished. He walked out on the planking and some of the men called to him from the bank of the river. He turned around and realized too late they had taken his picture. He had a phobia against photographs. That one was circulated and labeled, "The Father of the Situation."

His brother Brig wrote a letter inviting him to meet him in Logan the following week where they would spend a few days working in the temple together. Then they could go back to Brigham City and visit some of his old friends.

"The change will do you good, Mose," Loella encouraged. "I'll get you ready and Conover can take you to the train and get you settled before the train pulls out. Brig will meet you at the depot in Logan, and you'll get along fine."

Amos didn't say anything but began turning the idea over in his mind. "Maybe that *would* be good for a change," he said softly. "Loell will be glad to get me off her hands. I could do some temple work that needs doing and Brig and I could have a good visit. We could stay at Nett's and I'll get to see Coulsey."

He perked up noticeably after he told Loell he guessed he'd try it. It felt good to have something to look forward to. Things worked out perfectly as planned. Brig met him and after a week in the temple they went together to Brigham City. One of his sister Charlotte's daughters lived in Brigham and she called him on the phone one day.

"Uncle Mose, I've got a brand new Franklin and I'd like to come and pick you up and take you to the Washakie Indian Colony near Malad tomorrow so you can visit some of your old friends."

His heart did a tap dance and he said he'd be ready. He was surprised how excited he felt.

"I'll get to see those dear people of mine again and talk

Shoshone with them. Maybe I've forgotten how. It's been over ten years since I saw any of them. And going in a big fancy auto! I'd better be careful or I'll act like a gentile, but I bet I'll like it."

He was waiting for Venna next morning when the Franklin stopped in front of Brig's house. When they turned onto the main dirt road leading to Malad, Venna pressed down on the gas, and the speedometer climbed to fifty miles an hour. "I'll give you a thrill, Uncle Mose," she laughed, as the scarf tied over her big hat flew in the breeze. She had left the top down purposely, and watched Amos out of the corner of her eye. He was holding onto the car door and kept his eyes glued to the road, but didn't say a word.

The car stopped just before they got to Malad. "Well, here we are, Uncle Amos. That didn't take long, did it?"

Reaching in his hind pocket for his handkerchief, he blew his nose and said, "Is that as fast as that thing will go, Sis?"

The next two or three hours he and Jim Brown and Jim Joshua, his half-breed missionary companions, slipped imperceptibly into Shoshone talk and amazingly Amos didn't have to "brighten up" in the language at all. As word got around the Indian village, old men and women flocked around him.

"Peah-Tibo, Peah-Tibo," they sobbed as they embraced him, weeping unashamedly. It was laughter through tears from then on, till Venna called a halt and said, "Uncle Mose, we'd better be getting back. My lights might not work too good, and I don't want to try driving in pitch dark."

He had lots to think about and talk to himself about after that. He'd have to write to Nelly and tell her all about it. When he got back to Bennington he talked up a storm. He said Coulsey was doing all right at the college waiting tables at the cafeteria for 10 cents an hour, and how proud he was to have him getting an education. Then Loella confessed what her daydream had been that time when they went to Logan to get married and heard there was going to be a college built up on the hill above the temple. "I suddenly thought, 'maybe one of my sons will go there!' And then I was ashamed because we weren't even married yet, but I've always hoped it would come true, and now it has."

The summer before Amos' death, Coulsen and Conover raised the biggest crop of wheat ever, 2,200 bushels. They filled a rented granary and hauled the rest to the flour mill in Montpelier. After they had unloaded the last load, Coulsen went in the office and asked the manager how much his father owed him. The manager looked surprised and said, "About $72. Why?"

"Well, if you will take that out, we would like to settle for the wheat." Miles took out his handkerchief and blew his nose and said, "Well, what do you know! I could settle my little account with you boys right now if it hadn't been for Frank."

"Frank?! What has he got to do with it?" asked Coulsen.

"I don't know," Miles replied, "but he was just here and served a legal order signed by Judge Kuntz to hold that wheat until all of your father's debts are paid."

Conover's nostrils began to quiver like they did when he was mad. The boys walked out and Conover said, "If we meet Frank on the way home we'll stop and give him the beating he has had coming all these years!" They didn't meet him.

Frank said one time, "I never did like school. I could never keep my mind in the schoolroom. I was always thinking about what would take place after school, like a fight or a dogfight."

The stake authorities were going to cut him off from the Church one time and Amos immediately went into action. He asked them why they were taking that action. They said it was "indifference." Amos had his Doctrine & Covenants with him and he turned to the page giving reasons for excommunication. "You can't do this to my son, I won't allow it. Besides, he always donates liberally when there is a call for it."

Frank met Coulsen on the street in Montpelier one day sometime later and was in the mood to talk. "You know, the older I get, the more I believe there must be something to the teachings of the Church and the principles that Father has always stood for so solidly. You may think that sounds funny coming from me when I act the way I do, but I am telling it to you so you won't act like I have. One of the greatest things among men is example. I can look back over my lifetime and see where many young fellows have followed my example and I never knew at the time that I was setting an example at all."

The last three letters Amos wrote were a projection of the real Amos, of his daily thoughts, sometimes whispered or half-audibly spoken. The first is a letter of gratitude to his beloved Nelly. The second is to his brother Brig, a half brother, and a son of dear Mary Jane. The last one is to his own Charles Coulsen Rich Wright. Out of the multitude of letters he wrote during his lifetime, the ones preserved were written by some of those who also loved him.

His letter to Nelly was written at the end of Christmas day,

1914, the year the Great World War began.

Bennington

Nelly Jacobsen, Dr. Daughter:

We received your letter and Christmas presents last night. Ma had just gone to Logan to see Nett and the folks. She will probably remain through the holidays. Your remembrance of us is very highly appreciated.

We had killing frost 20 June last summer so we didn't have half a crop even. Our hay grew no more after that and was only about six inches high where we cut it. We have no meat to eat and don't know how we are going to get through the winter.

Coulsen is trying to work his way through school at the A.C. but is home for the holidays.

"Father had had the hay baled and was selling it in 'Pelier,'" recalled Coulsen. "I remember working hard all during the two weeks I was home, to get this baled hay hauled to Montpelier. We used bobsleds and horse power. Conover was helping me. When it came time to go back to school, Father forbade me to go until I had finished delivering the hay. I tried to explain how serious it was to me because if I came back even half a day late, I would lose my previous semester's credit.

"Uncle Brig was visiting there at the time and he listened very sympathetically to what I had to say, but Father would not listen and insisted that I stay and deliver the hay. I tried to explain to him that I had already made arrangements for the hay to be delivered by somebody else, but he still insisted I stay.

"Finally, I burst out crying and said, 'You simply do not understand the situation, Father!'

"Father said, 'Brig is going down that way and he can stop at Logan and see some of the faculty members and straighten it out all right.' I was still crying and all at once he softened and said, 'You know I wouldn't do anything in this world to harm you.'

"Uncle Brig then interceded and Father relented and I went back to school." (Letter written by Coulsen to David L. Wright, 1956.)

Conover has gone in with a man from Kansas, buying hides and peltry. They seem to be making a living, so far, not much more as yet. Conover is getting to be quite a large man. He weighs 175 pounds and is very powerful. No one in the country here can handle him. So far he has taken good care of himself and will soon weigh 200 pounds.

Amos was proud of Conover's strength. All the boys and men in Bennington said he could lick anybody in the valley and bragged about it to the people in Montpelier and Georgetown.

Many said he would cut a big swath as a professional boxer or wrestler, which of course didn't hurt Con's feelings.

When Loella heard about it, she talked to Conover. "I hope you won't decide to be a fighter, Con. Sure, you're strong and can beat the other fellows, but there are better ways to make a living. You'd be thrown in bad company, and you know your father wouldn't like that."

"But, Mother, I've promised to fight the best man from Star Valley next week. I can't go back on my word. What will the guys say? They'll say I'm a coward."

"But I know you aren't, and you aren't afraid. But they want you to fight so they can bet and win money on you. They don't care what happens to you, even if you got hurt or killed. Going back on your word this time would be better than finding out later that you'd made a bad mistake."

This was a bitter pill to swallow, but Conover's respect and love for his mother made him decide to call off the fight. It happened just as he predicted. All of Star Valley said he was "chicken". A Georgetown big guy said he was a coward and bragged that he could lick the whole Wright tribe and the rest of Bennington thrown in. By that time there was a big crowd gathered on the meetinghouse lawn, and everybody was egging Conover to take him on.

"Go on, Con, you can lick the tar out of him. Don't let Bennington down like that!" It was too much for Conover, so he pulled off his coat and lit in to the big guy. Of course he gave him a bad beating which he had coming, and the crowd went wild and Conover was the hero for a day. That was the last time he fought and he didn't tell his mother about it. Neither did he tell anybody why he stopped fighting. That was between him and Loella. When Amos heard about it, he was proud of his boy for more reasons than just licking the town bully.

I have just got back from Georgetown. I took what children your Ma left at home, up there with me and we took dinner with Mary. Her husband Charl is teaching school there this winter. There is barely snow enough to sleigh ride but it has been awful cold all this month, running down thirty and forty below freezing point nearly all the time.

My own health is about the same as it has been for several years past. I can't work any more, but I can ride to town and do errands for the boys and that is all.

I am very much impresed with your affectionate sentiments, and if I were where you are I suppose you would have to wash and keep me in shape if it was done at all. Some of the children help me to dress and undress every day though I can walk out to the meeting house by taking plenty of time, about an hour.

It is no surprise to hear about the case you allude to. People lose their intelligence as well as anything else if they don't obey the laws upon which the mind rests and is perpetuated. There are two ways open to us, progession and its opposite. Indeed it is possible to resolve ourselves back into the original element of which we were composed, which would partake very largely of the Second Death.

But I must not preach to you or you will think I am too religious. So I must say a little about that not found in the papers.

Christian Wallentine whom I helped return to the Church by baptism, is quite low. He wants me to come over to Paris and give him a send off when he dies. A number of others have made the same request.

This was his way of telling Nellie that he could still preach funeral sermons, even though he had been "laid on the shelf." People loved to hear him speak at funerals. He knew how to make death seem logical and acceptable. Those who heard him, often made a request that when they died they wanted him to speak at their funeral, too.

Sammy Hall got a draw on something the other day and won a big prize. Now your Ma has gone and bought four draws at a big figure. She expects to win the Union Pacific Railroad with all of its rolling stock, and commence running it the next day. She says she learned how in a picture show down at Pocatello the other day while she was chaperoned around the sights of the Gate City of Idaho, the gem state of the West by Frank Hargroves and his class.

Frank Hargroves was a young man whom Loella thought was a good dancer before she married Amos and whom she had never seen since. He still loves hyperbole.

You see I am quite jealous because she says she has no further use for one so near dead as your old Papa is nowdays. She only took three pair of shoes with her to help her dance herself into the ground before she gets back.

Norey is going to school at 'Pelier, reading the classics and studying the dead languages. She has already got so that she nor anyone else can understand her. She thinks that by spring Montpelier can't hold her. The powers that be have moved all the hitching posts off main street so you can't find any place to tie up any more. They were considered to be a nuisance and were removed to please the automobiles.

At seventy-five, he was keenly aware of what was going on in the world as well as locally. Progress, as seen through his eyes, was tongue-in-cheek, depending on how it affected people, for good or ill.

Your Mother's sister, Ida, and her husband Fred, now live in Logan. Fred found it hard work to get over the line from Canada where they lived, on account of conscriptions resulting from the War in Europe. Ten thousand have already been drafted and have already been shipped to fight for the Allies against Germany.

Your Aunt Nett's boys took the first prize at Snake River Falls Fair, riding and lassoing steers. They seem to think that if they can bust a bronco and wear a pair of schapps they are sure of the seventh heaven. This is a consequence of raising them among the mustangs, sandsnakes and sage brush, apart and far away from civilization and proper teaching. What a life! If you are fortunate enough to raise your children I hope you will not fail to keep before them a different ideal.

'Pelier is building up quite rapidly. The lower town has a chapel now nearly completed, costing $13,000. You wouldn't know the country between here and Paris. The railroad runs into Paris. Phone and telegraph lines are everywhere. Bear River has been turned out of its natural channel into the Lake. And from thence, a Bee Line Ditch has been cut as large as the River itself down almost opposite here and will continue straightening the river clear to Soda. The railway is now double-tracked from Wardboro on to nearly our bridge. They are blasting and dredging it through, almost night and day. It is said that they have expended already $3,000,000 on the work and will spend several more. The County expects to supply electric power for hundreds of miles in every direction.

One of our neighbors has a new piano. But it's no evidence that because a person has an ear like a jackass that there is any music in his carcass.

I went down to Logan last summer and was baptized for some friends and relatives in the Temple. I went up to the Malad Colony of Indians to see some of my old Missionary Companions. One I baptized into the Church twenty-five or thirty years ago is now turning white. Much of his back is already as white as mine, proving positively that the promises of the Lord will be fulfilled.

Mrs. Wright (Cate) is in her usual health. Walks out to meeting quite frequently. Bishop Austin has bought a home in Salt Lake City and is going there in the Spring to live and die there, I suppose. Ed, our son, has located in Burley Idaho practicing law there. Seems to be doing pretty well so far. James Dunford has quite a large tract of land close to Maple Field. He comes over in his eleven hundred dollar auto quite often.

I can get a free pass on the Railroad now and am almost a notion

to go out to Nampa and Boise to see some of my grandchildren. If
your Ma would go to take care of me I think I should go. But it seems
that she don't want to go anywhere only with Frank Hargroves.

Well, my dear daughter, I am always sorry you are so far away.
Writing is a slow way of communication and not satisfactory to say
the best of it. I hope you will get through all right (she was expecting
a child) and come to see us again before Death makes another call.
As ever your loving Father,

A.R. Wright.

The letter to Brig is dated just nine days before he died. The
penmanship is strong and definite but the spelling, not as good as
usual. It is a reply to one from Brig, received the same day.

Bennington
Feb. 15, 1915

I just got your letter by this evening's mail. As usual I am very
glad to hear from you. I was sorry to hear by Loell that your general
health is not the best. I am glad to know you think of coming to see us
again. I am surprised to hear of Jim Brown's death though I felt that
he was failing when we saw him last summer.

I see by nearly every paper that many of my old acquaintances
are passing away when I expected to go before any of them. I have
been very poorly for the past two weeks with some kind of a pain in
my stomach and throat. Loell says it's because I'm such a hog.

When I mentioned that you send me some seeds, I thought you
raised some yourself and might have some to throw away, but I
would not have you buy any for me. It sounds strange to hear of
ploughing anywhere when it is so awful cold here, frequently 12 to 40
degrees below what would freeze water, yet there is less snow than
ever before in the Valley for fifty years.

I feel very lonesome most of the time and don't particularly care
when I shall be called, though since I had been obliged to wear one
pair of pants for years past, Sunday and Monday and every day, last
week I got a $2.75 remnant pair so I wanted to live till I could wear
'em to show I had one thing new once more. I have now had them on
once and no doubt they will last me as long as I have any use for
anything of the kind.

Some fellers dug a grave up in the cemetery here the other day
and after getting through the snow they found the ground froze solid
for two or three feet deep. Can't plow much that way.

I suppose Loell told you all the news she knew and more, so I
won't write much. I thank you much that you have done so much for
me in the Temple. On the 23rd of this month railroad rates will
commence and will be good for twenty days to Logan. If I was able to
stand it I'd go and work in the Temple all the time but work is over
for me I suppose.

Cate is getting thin and failing fast. She says she is going to choose a husband from some of her own nationality in the next world. Loell is going to have the President of the Church. So I'll have to find a charity wife somewhere that no one else on God's earth wants, or go without and be a mighty small potato forever. I hope God will bless you and yours forever.

Yours, A.R. Wright

Just three days before his death, he wrote to Coulsen in Logan. Coulsen needed some money to finish school. Amos had borrowed some money on which interest was due. Coulsen was staying with LeGrande and Nettie in Logan.

Bennington,
Feb. 21,1915

Coulsen Wright,
Dr Son:
Your letter to Conover came through all right. We are all sorry you seem to be cramped to get through but we hope you will not get discouraged. We have tride to sell old Dave all winter but buyers seem to require big fat, though he is beginning to look better now. Everybody thinks horses will be high in the spring.

I have bargained some little hay to Larson of Georgetown. When he pays maybe we can help you a little. It would be suicide to sell one of the cows. The heifers now have calves. Your Ma has coaxed us to get a separator. She thinks she can pay $7.00 a month for it and have a little left to keep from going in debt so much during the summer.

We are just as anxious to help you as you can be. We have to pay Grey tomorrow. He threatened to demand the principal if so of course we would have to sell out to meet it. I think LeGrande and Nettie will be lenient with you and if so you may not be alarmed and keep your mind on the business of getting an education and sooner or later all will be well. God bless you.

Your Father, A.R. Wright

Chapter Thirty-three
Death Pays a Call

It was three years since Amos had suffered his stroke. He had largely recovered his health, though Loella noticed he was more emotional and was cross and irritable much of the time. It took patience and all members of both families were more or less affected.

His daughter, Mary, lived in Georgetown. She thought Loella needed a change and invited her to come up for a few days. Sixteen-year-old Norey agreed to stay at home to look after her father and the younger children.

She got supper the evening Loella left and afterward Amos went in the other room to sit by the window. Pretty soon she heard him breathing heavily. She was doing the dishes in the kitchen. She hurried in to him as he groaned, "Pa's sick. Help me get to bed."

"Where do you feel sick ... do you have a pain?" she asked.

"My head aches," he replied. Norey helped him to the bed and took off his shoes and stockings and began rubbing his head.

"Rub my leg, Norey". She could see his face was purple. He turned his head toward her and murmured, "Norey, Norey, Norey." They were the last words he ever said.

She ran to get Cate, who came at once. She brought a little glass of wine, and put it to his lips but he couldn't swallow. Sitting in the little rocking chair by the bed, Cate put her hand on his chest and bent over him saying, "Mose, Mose, this is Cate!" He didn't speak and she said, "He's gone." He had had another cerebral hemorrhage.

There wasn't a phone in the house. Cate said, "Norey, get someone to call Loella in Georgetown and let all the children know. When Virginia saw Norey crying, she did too, and four-year-old Ruth Esther followed suit. When Loella got the word, she and Mary came right away. As they came down the lane, Loella said, "Your father's gone. That window wouldn't be open if he was alive."

Amos had left strict instructions that his funeral was to be as simple as possible. He didn't want a lot of expense. He especially said "no flowers". Rosy Hall, a little German woman, laid a tiny bouquet of red geraniums on the coffin in defiance of his wish.

After a simple service in the meetinghouse where he had served so long as bishop, he was buried in the little Bennington graveyard among the June grass, sage and Indian paintbrush. For Amos Russell Wright, thus ended seventy-five years of alternate turmoil and strife, peace and tranquility, struggle and frustration, achievement and success, poverty and want, relative prosperity, danger and exposure, shelter and quiet, bewilderment and rebellion, understanding and loyalty, melancholy and despair, elation and joy, anger and violence, love and long-suffering, but above all, enduring faith in the Lord Jesus Christ, which in his case amounted to certain knowledge.

A week or so after the funeral, Cate came over to Loella's. She was wearing her usual gray shawl. Little Ruth ran out to meet her and she gathered the little girl into her arms and wrapped the shawl around her. The two women decided to go over to Aunt Kitty's together that afternoon. They left the little ones with Norey. Before they were ready to go home a sudden Bear Lake storm blew up and there was no way to get back.

"Well, you can just stay all night. You'll have to sleep together. I've only got one bed," said Kitty.

But they didn't sleep. They lay in each other's arms and talked out all the pent-up feelings of the past thirty years, as the blizzard raged outside.

"Oh Cate, dear, I should have been more thoughtful of you, like you were of me."

"But you were so young. I should have known. You did the best you could."

"I knew just as soon as Mose was gone, how mean and spiteful I had been. I guess our Mose had to go so we could know we loved each other and him, too. He always said he was the bone of contention. But he was a man of God and I'm thankful you were willing to share him with me."

"Yes," sighed Cate. "Mose was always his own worst enemy. But I was to blame, too. He wasn't the only one who lost his temper. I thought I knew better than he and didn't listen to his counsel and sometimes let my children influence me against him.

I found out afterward I'd been wrong and resolved to do better, but I didn't improve much. I tried to bury my love for him but I couldn't. The hardest thing was to learn to share. I worshipped *things*, but I finally found out they weren't important, after all, and I needed to learn unselfishness. Mose knew that all the time and tried to tell me, but I wouldn't listen."

"And I didn't know how to take care of *things* even when you gave them to me," sobbed Loella. "That must have hurt you terribly." And on and on into the night they retraced the rocky path they'd traveled, washing away the bitterness and sorrow with tears of repentance, and sharing the miracle of forgiveness.

Cate died two years later at her daughter Winnie's house. Loella came over and stood with Winnie, looking at the woman in the casket.

"She was so good to me," said Loella, wiping her eyes, "so sympathetic and understanding—like a sister or a second mother." Then she told Winnie about the time Cate kept her from running away, as she followed her out to Bennington Hill and brought her back. "She might have let me go so she could have had Mose all to herself. But she helped me keep from breaking my covenant and she kept hers at the same time."

Cate was buried beside Amos. Loella was left to walk alone for another twenty-seven years, with a family of children to care for. Those years were harder than all the others put together, becuase she had to go it alone. But that's another long story by itself.

Later, when she lived with her son Coulsen at Ft. Duchesne, she slept downstairs near an extra bathroom. He told her to call him when she wanted to get up in the night, but she seldom did. He was afraid she would fall. One night he heard the sound of her cane tapping across the room. He hurriedly ran downstairs and waited till she came out of the bathroom. She had her head down, watching where she stepped. When she looked up and saw him she said, "Good heavens! You look just like your father. I thought sure he had come to get me."

Later, living at Norey's, she often said, "Well, I can't go to the Spirit World today, I've got too much to do." She spoke as if it were just across the street. Sometimes she would look thoughtful and say, "I can't decide which one I want to see first, Cate or Mose."

She kept her Bible on a little night stand by her bed. Norey found this verse tucked inside:

I LONG FOR REST

Oh Father, take me now I pray thee.
Take my tired soul and lay me
Underneath some cooling shade tree
For I long for rest.
In my tired hours I've sought thee,
And in kindness thou hast soothed me,
Thou wilt not then now forsake me
When I long for rest.
Of this maddening rush I'm dreary,
Perhaps it is I see not clearly
But I only know I'm weary
And I long for rest.
Life and love thou freely gave me,
And from pain Thou oft hast spared me.
In my life I've tried to serve Thee
Now I long for rest.
Soothe my loved ones when I leave them,
Do not let their thoughts deceive them.
For my soul but seeks a haven
And I long for rest.
Take me Father, now, I pray Thee,
Wilt Thou please, no more delay me.
Open Thy bosom to receive me
For I long for rest.
—*Floyd Matson.*

It. was Norey, again, who was with *her* at the last. And
strangely, Loella spoke the same words as Amos: "Norey, Norey,
Norey!"

At her request, she was buried in Logan, Utah, in the cemetery
near the temple where she and Amos were married.

"I couldn't be recognized as Mose's wife most of the time while
I was alive, and there isn't room to be buried by him in
Bennington. That doesn't matter now, but I want it to be plain
that I *am* his wife when I'm gone."

Accordingly, her headstone reads:

MARTHA LOELLA WEAVER, wife of AMOS RUSSELL WRIGHT

Copied into her own little scrapbook is her epitaph:

I have hoped, I have planned, I have striven
To the will I have added the deed.
The best that was in me I've given,
I have prayed but God didn't heed.
I have dared and reached only disaster,
I have battered and broken my lance.

I am bruised by a pitiless master
That the weak and timid call Chance.
I am old, I am bent, I am cheated
Of all youth urged me to win
But number me not with the defeated
For tomorrow again I begin.

Amos, Cate, Loella. They endured to the end. Yet it wasn't the end, it was a new beginning, where as exalted beings with their children in the Celestial Kingdom of God they will inherit thrones, principalities and powers, and as king and queens they will reign forever and forever.

Appendix

"History demonstrates that people, all people, are fallible. There is no one without weakness, no one except the Savior who can claim perfection. In studying our ancestors, therefore, we cannot in honesty ignore the fact that they had weaknesses. This is not a "negative" or discouraging message; quite the contrary. For history always demonstrates that people can change and improve and that even imperfect people can accomplish much good.

"As we are made aware of some of our ancestors' faults, we may acquire more confidence that our own shortcomings will not necessarily be a hindrance to achievement. A knowledge of the struggles of our ancestors to overcome their weaknesses gives us confidence and courage in our own struggles." (Leonard J. Arrington, "Learning About Ourselves Through Church History," *Ensign*, September 1979, p. 8.)

Notes on Chapter Three

Historical background of Doctrine and Covenants 132

1. The Lord commanded Joseph to make a new translation of the Bible in the summer of 1830.

2. Joseph received visions of Moses in the fall or early winter of 1830.

3. After the Prophet arrived in Kirtland in February 1831, he immersed himself in a study of the Old Testament.

4. Sometime in February or March 1831, Joseph studied the life of Abraham.

5. On 7 March 1831 the Lord commanded Joseph to stop translating the Old Testament and to study the New Testament.

6. Joseph translated the Book of Matthew between 8 March and 1 September 1831.

7. Sometime, in 1831 Joseph received the revelation found in Section 132.

8. At the request of the Prophet, William Clayton, who acted as Joseph's scribe, formally wrote the revelation on 12 July, 1843. (Doctrine and Covenants and Church History, Gospel Doctrine Teacher's Supplement p. 65)

Joseph Smith the Prophet had not only commenced the practice of plural marriage, himself, and taught it to others, before President Young and the Twelve had returned from their mission in Europe in 1841, but Joseph actually received revelations upon that principle as early as 1831. (*History of the Church* 5:xxxi, "Introduction," 1878).

President Lorenzo Snow lived to bear his testimony to the world that Joseph Smith taught him the doctrine of Celestial marriage. He lived to declare to the world that he knew, positively, that Joseph Smith did receive it by revelation and that that doctrine was true and of God. And if he had done no more than this, he would have accomplished a great work, because he was a living witness, an eye-witness and an ear-witness and he knew whereof he spoke. You and I will have to meet his testimony and so will the people of the world, and when we go to give an account of that which we have heard and known in the world, we cannot dodge this, but will be held to an account for it, just as sure as the Lord lives, and that Pres. Snow did his duty. (Conference Report, Oct. 1902, p. 87, Joseph F. Smith)

Affidavit of President Lorenzo Snow

In the month of April 1843, I returned from my European mission. A few days after my arrival at Nauvoo, when at President Joseph Smith's home, he said he wished to have some private talk with me, and requested me to walk out with him. It was toward evening. We walked a little distance and sat down on a large log that lay near the bank of the river. He, there and then, explained to me the doctrine of plurality of wives; he said that the Lord had revealed it unto him, and commanded him to have women sealed to him as wives; that he foresaw the trouble that would follow, and sought to turn away from the commandment; that an angel from heaven then appeared before him with a drawn sword, threatening him with destruction unless he went forward and obeyed the commandment.

He further said that my sister, Eliza R. Snow, had been sealed to him as his wife for time and eternity. He told me that the Lord would open the way, and I should have women sealed to me as wives. This conversation was prolonged, I think one hour or more, in which he told me many important things.

I solemnly declare before God and holy angels, and as I hope to come forth in the morning of the resurrection, that the above statement is true.

LORENZO SNOW

Territory of Utah) ss.

Box Elder County)

Personally came before me J.C. Wright, Clerk of the County and Probate Courts in and for the County and Territory aforesaid, Lorenzo Snow, and who being duly sworn deposeth and says that the foregoing statement by him subscribed is true of his own certain knowledge.

Witness my hand and seal of Court, at my office in Brigham City, Box Elder County, Utah Territory, this 28th day of August, A.D. 1869.

(Seal)

J.C. Wright, Clerk.

As Joseph pondered the life of Abraham and the teachings of Jesus, both in the New Testament and Book of Mormon, many questions arose in his mind, not only about the legality of Abraham's having more than one wife, but also about the nature of the marriage relationship. How could Abraham have more than one wife and not commit adultery?" (D & C & Church History Gospel Doctrine Teachers' Supplement, p. 66.)

In addition to this internal evidence pointing to an early date for the revelation, Elder B.H. Roberts, in his analysis of the date of the revelation, declared, "There is indisputable evidence that the revelation ... was given to the Prophet as early as 1831" (History of the Church 5:xxix). op. cit. Ibid.

Include xerox copy of Jonathan Calkins Wright's dream in his own hand-writing and published in the Wright Book.

Still later in our own dispensation, the Lord, through his prophet Joseph Smith, in 1843 reestablished the practice of plurality of wives *by a worthy few who were especially chosen*. This practice was *commanded as a principle of sacrifice which the Lord compared as similar to that he had commanded at the hands of Abraham*, who was told to offer up his own son Isaac. (Harold B. Lee, *Youth and the Church*, 1955, p. 109.) italics added.

"If the strict order of the Priesthood were carried out in the building of Temples, the first stone would be laid at the southeast corner by the First

Presidency of the Church ... the fourth (the northeast corner) expressive of the lesser Priesthood." (*History of the Church* Vol. IV pp. 330-331.)

UNRATIFIED TREATY OF OCTOBER 14, 1863, BETWEEN THE UNITED STATES AND THE MIXED BANDS OF SHOSHONE AND BANNOCK

Treaty of Peace and Friendship, made at Soda Springs in Idaho Territory this fourteenth day of October A.D. one thousand eight hundred and sixty three, by and between the United States of America represented by Brigadier General P. Edward Connor, commanded the Military District of Utah and James Duane Doty, Commissioner, and the undersigned chiefs of the mixed Bands of Bannocks and Shoshones occupying the valley of Shoshone river, as follows—

ARTICLE I. It is mutually agreed that friendly and amicable relations shall be reestablished between the said Bands and The United States; and that a firm and perpetual peace shall be henceforth maintained between the said bands and the United States.

ARTICLE II. The Treaty concluded at Fort Bridger on the 2nd day of July 1863 between the United States and the Shoshones nation, and also the treaty concluded at Box Elder on the 30th day of July 1863 between the United States and the Northwestern Bands of the Shoshone Nation being read and fully interpreted and explained to the said chiefs they do hereby give their full and free assent to all of the provisions of said Treaties and the same are hereby adopted as a part of this Treaty, and the same shall be binding upon the parties hereto, the said Bands sharing in the annuities therein provided for the Shoshone Nation.

ARTICLE III. The said Bands, in addition, agree (sic) that the roads now used by white men between Soda Springs and the Beaver Head Mines and between Salt Lake and the Boise river mines, as also such other roads as it may be necessary or convenient for the white men to make and use between said places, or between other points within their country, shall at all times be free and safe for travel; and no depredation shall be committed upon white men in any part of their country. And the said Bands hereby acknowledge to have received of the United States by its commissioner at the signing of these articles provisions and goods to the amount of three thousand dollars to relieve their immediate wants before their departure to their hunting grounds.

ARTICLE IV. The country claimed by the Said Bands jointly with the Shoshone Nation, extends, as described by them from the lower part of the Humboldt river, and the Salmon Falls on Shoshone River, eastwardly to the Wind River mountains.

Done at Soda Springs this fourteenth day of October A.D. 1863.

In presence of the Undersigned Witnesses—

David BLACK
  Capt. 3rd In'fty C.V.
  Commdg. Camp Connor
HORACE WHEAT
AMOS R. WRIGHT
WILLIS H. BOOTHE
Special interpreters
James Duane DOTY
  Commissioner
P. EDW. CONNOR
Brig, Conl. W.S.V.
  Comdg. Dist. Utah
Shawowuk
  his x mark
Washetiabo
  his x mark

Notes on Chapter Seven

The Salmon River Mission

The period between 1856-58 presents problems. Conflicting records, facts and traditions do not fit a logical pattern. The Salmon River Mission was set up in the spring of 1855. Amos' name is not listed with the original company. Indications are, however, that he went in the spring of 1856, though his name is not listed. Conover Wright says: *"While Father was at Ft. Lemhi he received his first call to be a missionary among the Indians."* This would have to be prior to *May 12, 1857.* (see date below) *Also see date October 27, 1857.* A very fluid state of comings and goings existed among the missionaries during the three-year-period of the organized mission.

Conflicting statements from family members made in 1956, exist regarding Lois Moran and Amos. Did they fall in love before or after her marriage to Jonathan C. Wright, or both? Strongest indication is that it was *after.* We simply do not know.

March 28 1856 A company "of nine left Ogden on their return to Lemhi in charge of Elder Parry and were accompanied by 22 new missionaries." (Amos is not listed)

May 15 1856 Party reached Ft. Lemhi. Silas Wright's journal says Amos (his father) left for Ft. Lemhi (no date) with L.W. Shurtliff.

August 1856 L.W. Shurtliff and Nathaniel Leavitt carried the mail to Utah and this time had a narrow escape from the Indians.

January 14 1857 Jonathan C. Wright married Lois Moran, Brigham City, Utah

March 21 1857 Jonathan C. Wright and Lois Moran endowed, Salt Lake City Amos Wright, endowed; Virginia Ann Charlotte, Endowed (3 months later md Alvin Nichols as his third wife.

April 23 1857 Amos R. Wright mustered into Capt. Jefferson Wright's Co. A. Utah Cavalry, Brigham City, Box Elder Military District. Record in Adj. General's office (Utah— Discharged 1858.

May 8 1857 Brigham Young and Company arrived at Ft. Lemhi (Amos not listed) 142 people in company and a number of boys.

May 12 1857 Amos R. Wright received Apostolic blessing under hands of Orson Hyde, Lorenzo Snow and J.D. Richards (Blessing recorded)

October 27 1857 Company of missionaries arrived at Ft. Lemhi. Left Utah Oct. 3. "The company when organized consisted of 43 brethren, 15 sisters and a number of children. *Of these, 26 had already spent a portion of their time at the mission* and 32 were going there for the first time. *The 26 who were already acquainted with the Salmon River are named as* follows: names listed and *Amos R. Wright listed as interpreter.*

February 15 1858 Amos named twice as one at Ft. Lemhi engaged in battle with Indians.

March 26 1858 Amos listed as one of 11 men sent as an "Express" to take word to Brigham Young of abandonment of Ft. Lemhi and that the remaining missionaries would follow as a body.

April 1 ? 1858 Express arrived in Salt Lake City.

Notes on Chapter Eight

"Pony Express," *Comprehensive History of the Church,* vol. 5, pp. 76-78.

In 1859-60 there was established a method of communication which, though it lasted but a comparatively short period, is worthy of mention in a history of these times. This was the Pony Express. The system was organized by W.H. Russell of St. Louis and others. The plan was to run a light letter mail service across the continent by solitary horsemen, carrying fifteen pounds of letters at $5 per half ounce. The stations were located about 24 miles apart, and each rider was required to span three stations at the rate of eight miles an hour as his day's ride. These riders heroically covered their route, "regardless of snows and storms, or savages and beasts of prey, yet not without the sacrifice of life." The solitary pony express rider, sometimes ambushed, and sometimes chased down by the savages, yielded his life in the cause of advancing civilization in western America.

The time for letters between New York and San Francisco was reduced to 13 days. The actual ride took ten and one-half days. Telegraph stations shortened message time to nine days. "The high charges prevented the line from being profitably patronized," says H.H. Bancroft. "It seldom carried over 200 letters, and at times less than 20; the best pay came from a mail contract. Indian troubles brought interruptions. With the completion of the overland telegraph in 1861, the pony express was practically abandoned."

The Pony Express service was popular in Utah, and a number of young "Mormons" were among the most successful and fearless riders. "The Pony Express proves to be quite an institution," wrote George A. Smith in April 1861. "The news of the surrender of Fort Sumter reached Salt Lake in seven days."

A Pony Express Club was formed in Salt Lake City at the head of which was President Young, who with a few other persons and the Deseret News, paid for a duplicate of the California press service, and the News would get out the extras. The expense was such, however, that it was finally determined that the club must be enlarged to 100 paying members, which would reduce the expense to 20 cents per capita per week for such a club, or 10 cents a pony. The telegraph supplanted the pony system which it did in October 1861.

Sources for Pony Express:

Evans, John Henry, "Pony Express," *Instructor*, vol. 46, p. 363.

Hafen, L.R., M.A., *Improvement Era*, Part 1 vol. 27, p. 57.

Settle, Raymond W., *Saddles and Spurs, The Pony Express Saga*, p. 76.

Wilson-Driggs, "The White Indian Boy," World Book Company.

Deseret News, November 30, 1940, p. 11.

Notes on Chapter Nine

Almost as many versions of the "excommunication" story are available as there are tellers. The actual quarrel did occur, but as Coulsen writes, "We do not know actually what did happen."

Coulsen wrote the following for David Wright's information when David was researching the life of Amos R. Wright in 1956:

"Father himself never talked in my presence, of that period of his life when he was cross-wise with the Church." Another story of why this occurred is as follows:

"Father herded the town cattle out on Promontory one summer. These cattle were mostly milch cows belonging to various families in Brigham City. Each family paid the boy a small sum depending on the number of cattle owned. President Lorenzo Snow's cattle were included in the herd. President Snow failed to pay Father when it was due. So after several requests without results Father met Bro. Snow on the street one day and asked him again for his pay. Brother Snow made some excuse which angered Father, whereupon he took Bro. Snow down and took the money he had coming out of his pocket. The outcome of this was Father's excommunication from the Church. I heard Frank tell this story. It has possibilities but is probably far from being complete or accurate."

Notes on Chapter Fourteen

"I understand that Reverend Roberts, the Episcopalian Minister at Wind River went into Washakie's lodge when he was near death and unconscious and sprinkled water on his head and administered certain Christian burial rites to him." (David L. Wright letters 1958)

Notes on Chapter Twenty

No record is available of the actual speech made by Amos R. Wright, though reference is made to it. Effort was made to follow his general style of speaking, and to include only that which he could well have said.

Notes on Chapter Twenty-Six

There are a number of versions to the story of who paid the fine, as many as there are sources.

"Father told the story that when he was on his way to jail after the trial at Blackfoot, he and his escort were suddenly aware of a horse and rider galloping rapidly down the street. It was a black horse. His neck was covered with lather. The rider pulled up when he came even with Father and said, "Is that you, Wright? I heard you were in trouble. I came to pay your fine." Whereupon he paid it. It was $500. The man turned out to be a man (not a member of the Church) whom Father had befriended when this man had become stranded as an emigrant on the "Old Oregon Trail" going through Bear Lake Valley. Father thought this man was sent by 'Providence.'

Another one: "The fine was paid (at least the larger part) by Amos' son Silas (24 years old), his son-in-law George Stephens (25 years old) and Horace Weaver (under 18 years old). Russell was a young man (16 years old) and no doubt contributed some. Dave may have paid some into the fund (I think he did). I know George, Si and Horace scraped the bottom of the barrel to raise funds. They sold livestock and at least one wagon. I have heard Mother tell what each one sold to pay the fine but it was so long ago I wouldn't try to give the details."

N3: "He, Amos, spent some time in jail and had quite a big fine and they took him to Blackfoot. His children and Cate all went together and raised the money for the fine. I don't remember how much it was, about four or five hundred dollars. Some sold their horses to raise the money."

N4: "All the witnesses the officer could find were called to Blackfoot to testify. They went three times in one year and a half before he was convicted. His sentence was $600, and six months in jail. The witnesses paid his fine and brought him home with them."

N5: "Amos gave himself up to the officers and was arrested. All the family pitched in and raised the $300 fine and were overjoyed at his release."

N6: "His son Silas and the sons-in-law worked hard all summer shearing sheep and they helped pay Amos' fine which was $500. My understanding of it is that when he finally gave himself up he was taken to Boise for trial and found guilty of plural marriage. His fine was $500 and he did not have the money to pay it. "Just as I was about to give up in despair I saw a beautiful black team of horses coming. They were hooked up to a buggy. They were coming very fast. They were reined-up right in front of me. Governor Hawley of Idaho jumped out of the buggy and said, 'Amos I hear you are in trouble. Here is $500. After shaking my hand he drove away. I paid my fine and did not have to go to jail for obeying God's commandments."

N7: "When the fine was levied Dave immediately took up a collection among Amos' family and friends far and near and paid the fine.

N8: "One evening a young couple came to Amos' house to be married since he was a bishop. He married them and when they offered to pay the usual fee, Amos wouldn't take the money. When some of the family asked him why, he said, 'That man's father helped pay my fine.'"

N9: Another possibility is that other bishops sponsored dances to raise the money. There was a Defense Fund for this purpose. The money was donated by the wards and dispensed by the stake.

N10: "Although times were hard and money was very scarce, all the adult members of the Wright family knew they must be ready to help when the time came. The case was tried in the district court at Blackfoot. The date of the trial was set and Silas 26, Addie 20, and John, a boy of 16, were subpoenaed as witnesses. The court was at Blackfoot and all concerned made the trip. They were paid $3.00 per day while they were there. The case was called and again and again it was postponed until it was autumn when it was finally tried. He was fined $500 and although every member of the family helped, it left them destitute. Silas sold a team and harness and Amos sold every critter on his place that would sell. Addie and John turned over all the money paid them for being witnesses at the trial."

The Idaho News, Vol. 2, Blackfoot, Idaho, October 6, 1888. No. 17. District Court Proceedings, Wednesday October 3: United States vs Amos R. Wright, unlawfull cohabitation: given until to-morrow to plead. Pleads not guilty following day.

The Idaho News, Vol. 2, Blackfoot, Idaho, June 29, 1889. District Court Proceedings: Thursday: United States vs Amos R. Wright, continued by consent.

The Idaho News, vol. 2, Blackfoot, Idaho, Saturday Nov. 2, 1889. District Court Proceedings: United States vs Amos R. Wright, plead guilty.

The Idaho News, Vol. 2, Blackfoot, Idaho, Saturday Nov. 9, 1889. U.S. vs Amos R. Wright, defendant fined $200.

No bail mentioned. No jail sentence mentioned.

Notes on Chapter Twenty-Seven

"Polygamous marriages were performed in the Logan Temple from 1884 to 1890. These records were all recorded in one book and hidden away so the law would not have access to them. The former recorders and early presidents of the temple knew the whereabouts of the record but would not reveal its location. During the demolition process in 1978-79 all workmen watched for this record as each wall and floor was removed. The book was never found. *Our polygamous marriage records are still lost.* They were last seen about 1934 and may have been placed in the *South East corner stone* of the building with other momentoes at the Golden Jubilee. *This box is to be opened in 1984 for the 100-year anniversary.*" (Olson, Nolan, Logan Temple Recorder, "Logan Temple," p. 223.

Notes on Chapter Twenty-Nine

In 1956, David L. Wright (R107 p. 140) did intensive research on the life of Amos R. Wright, planning to write his story later. His untimely death prevented it. He carried on extensive correspondence with first-hand sources, including C.C. Wright (R18 p. 112), eldest son of the second family, who wrote his comments on each of the 1901-02 letters at that time.

Notes on Chapter Thirty

Father was a man with a cause, always standing true to this cause, and ready to do whatever was necessary to further it or vindicate it. He was able as many are not, to forget himself. He was only the instrument or vehicle through which certain thoughts and principles came to light. There was some mysterious force within him which still vibrates in some of his descendants.

Father had an unwavering, abiding and driving faith all the time I knew him at least, and this was the central characteristic in his nature I believe. He consistently lived by this faith or this inner driving force that was his constant

companion. He was of course, always devoted to the Church; regardless of
what other men did he did his duty as he saw it.

He seemed to have a natural judgment for justice and fairness in any
controversy. It was often said of him that he should have been a judge instead
of a farmer. He seemed to know instinctively who was right and who was
wrong, in a case of conflict. He was an almost unfailing good judge of a man. It
seemed he only had to have one look at a man and he could just about size him
up completely. We used to marvel at his accuracy in this respect with strangers.

I believe he was considerably above average in honesty and in his sense of
honor. I do not remember his ever doing a dishonorable act or condoning one.

Father was a thinking man. He almost always seemed lost in thought. He
was not mechanically inclined, ingenious or dexterous with his hands, but I
believe he was above average in mental capacity.

He was not what some might call a kind and loving father. Most of the time
he was cross and cranky. But he gave himself entirely to making a living for
his family when he was not taking care of some duty for the Church or
fulfilling some other obligation which he considered to be his duty as a man.

He was not an effective provider, but he was never lazy. Yet he worked
slowly and did not make rapid accomplishments.

His scope and earthly activities and experiences were rather narrowly
delimited. He did not come in contact with anyone very prominent or very
learned outside the Church.

He was never shallow or crude. He was a natural gentleman inside but not
outside. He was never flippant or sarcastic. He had strong abiding convictions
which he squared with his own sense of values and then stuck to them as if
they were moulded in concrete. He practiced what he preached and was
thoroughly disgusted with anyone who did not.

He never acted superior to others. If he had to exercise any public authority
toward anyone, he always explained that it was his duty and not his personal
desire. (Coulsen Wright's letter to David L. Wright, 1956.)

Your observation about the difference between the Weavers and the
Wrights with respect to showing their affections is significant. I remember
Sister Wright saying on one occasion when someone mentioned her love for
Father: "Love? is there such a thing?"

Father I believe was naturally affectionate and it would have been natural
for him to openly demonstrate it. But after long years without it he became
guarded against it. Had things been otherwise he may not have been the stern
cross man he was in his older life. He could be softened in an instant with one
sincere word or gesture that indicated any warmth or personal fondness
toward him. (Letter to David Wright from Coulsen, 1956)

The case Amos was appointed to arbitrate was between .....H... and
E........ H. was a returned missionary who converted E. to Mormonism in
Germany. H. in some way financed E's passage and voyage to America and
Idaho. E. worked for H. five years. H. claimed E. owed him much more still.

Amos called them together with some witnesses. An eye witness says: "I was
present at least one night during these hearings. Feelings ran high. The principals
would have come to blows more than once if Amos had not interceded as he did. H.
was well dressed and groomed. He was crippled in one leg. E. was illiterate and
spoke English poorly. Amos obtained a compromise settlement of the case, which
was mostly in favor of E. I was impressed with Amos' skill and natural judgment
in handling this case."

Notes to Chapter Thirty-One

"Father often said to his children, 'Never never do anything that will make
you lose your membership in the Church. It's the worst feeling you could have, like
being outcast or like losing a great fortune and not being able to put your hands on
it.

"And if any of you raises his voice against polygamy, woe be unto him!'"

"Mother always said, 'I pray that none of my children will be asked to live that principle. I don't think we should be conceited about belonging to a polygamist family but we do know that it will be a great blessing to us and our descendants. How it can be I can't explain but I'm sure it is. It will give us an advantage in being able to repent because of this great sacrifice of our parents. Others might sin the same sins we did but they would not be able to repent of it sufficiently, but because of this great sacrifice, the Lord will accept of our repentance more readily than others who had not been born under that great principle.' I know how hard it was for them to accept it, and I think it wasn't any harder for Joseph Smith to accept it than it was for my parents and Mrs. Wright. But the way they understood it was that they were to be good parents, and have more children who would be righteous and help build the Kingdom. Otherwise if they had only one wife or one child, it wouldn't be built very fast that way. And the Lord chose the best men and women to live that principle." (Personal Interview with Alnora (Nona) Wright Brown, Salt Lake City, Utah 1978)

Of all the sources from which one can truly gather impressions of the personality of a man, the foremost is that of the collection of his letters and papers, the speeches and writings of the man himself. This is the high document, always to be lived with and brooded over, to be scrutinized and forgotten and gone back to and searched again with all the gifts of imagination, intuition, experience, prayer, silence, sacrifice and the laughter next door to tears.

Carl Sandburg

Bennington, Idaho
October 26, 1880.
Dear President Taylor:
I have returned from my late mission among the Indians. I reported to President Rich but he intimated that I ought to report to you. So I thought a line or two would not be improper. I left this place the 6th of Sept. last, to visit the Indians on the Wind River Agency, W.T. I was gone four weeks save two days, baptized, confirmed and recorded the names of 311 Indians including the chief Washakie. Blessed several children, baptized some for their health, administered to many of their sick and under the same peculiar circumstances probably not necessary to mention, I ordained 4 Individuals to the Priesthood. This comprises the substance of my trip—but if the Details of the same or if I am in possession of any Information concerning the Indians that would be of Intrest to you, I am at your service.
Yours in the Gospel,
A.R. Wright

Bennington, Idaho Nov. 18, 1880
Pres. John Taylor
Salt Lake City, Utah.
Dear Brother:
Your kind letter was received. I have appropriated what time I could (seeing it was Conference times here) in copying my baptismal record which I forward herewith to you to make such disposal of as you may deem proper....
My reason for making this last trip among the Indians was because I understood I was legally called so to do. I went alone because there are but few men that would be willing to adopt the plan I thought best and those who would were busy haying and harvesting and I did not wish to call them from their work when I could get along alone.
The former agent, Mr. Patten, upon being introduced to one of my brothers at Evanston one day, told him that if ever he could get hold of me he would put

me in irons. I heard also from other sources that the present agent has made similar threats and considers our missionary work among the Indians as an insurrection against the government, though I am not prepared to vouch for the truth of this last report.

Nevertheless for this and other reasons I thought it best to go out there as quietly as I could. Accordingly I left the road about thirty-five miles above this place and tried to follow an Indian trail but owing to its dimness and the fact that I knew little or nothing of the country I could not follow it, but was obliged to strike across the country and find my way as best I could.

I undertook to cross the Wind River range of mountains about forty or fifty miles north of South Pass City, but I encountered so much fallen timber, rocks and other obstacles of a rugged character I thought best to try some other route, which I did, by heading that range, leaving South Pass Miners Delight and Lander City in the valley, all to my right, keeping close to the foot of the main range of mountains all the time so as not to be discovered by white men.

However I unavoidably came in contact with several during the time I moved up the valley but was not recognized by any of them though I was considerably acquainted with one of them and made some inquiries of him respecting the route etc.

After twelve days travel I arrived at a place called Quakingasp Springs by the Indians. I suppose it is about five miles from Camp Brown, the Government post there though I did not know exactly where I was at the time. I found four lodges of Indians at this place and though strangers to me they received me very kindly.

I inquired of them how far it was to the main village and agency, Camp Brown. I soon found out exactly where I was. I made my business known to the principal man of the camp called Sam by the whites there, but Tor Namppe (Blackfeet) by the Indians, who said he was a Mormon and appeared to be almost beside himself he was so glad I had come among them.

I told him I wished to send a message to Washakie. He replied that he was just getting ready to go to town that day and would take any word I desired to send. I told him that when he got to the village, to take one of the chiefs with him and acquaint Washakie of my arrival and business but be sure he said nothing to anybody else. He was soon ready and off. In the meantime one of the young men of the camp accompanied me upon the side of the mountain where I had as good a view of the village and garrison of the troops as could be had in that valley at that distance, the whole country being a succession or series of gulches, buttes and bluffs so one cannot see but a very short distance from any point, only high up on the mountain except a narrow strip of land on either side of the river which the people call the valley.

The messenger did not return till after dark. I thought that I could see he had been disappointed. He said that he had done as I told him, but Washakie said that Pres. Young had told him of our faith years ago, but he did not believe our doctrine and as for himself he chose to remain as he was.

Furthermore his advice to me would be to keep out of camp for if I were discovered by the whites there, I would be arrested and chained up. The old man and the government interpreter were both very sick, unable to go away from the lodge in which they were respectively confined. The other chiefs who visited me said that these two were the only ones of their people who were indifferent to our preaching. You will perceive that if I obtained an interview with Washakie I must of necessity go where he was, he being entirely unable to come where I was.

The Indian with whom I was staying was quite uneasy for fear I had become alarmed and would return without any further effort toward accomplishing the object for which I was sent. He was untiring in his efforts to please me all the time I was there: sent to or generally went himself to the settlements and bought vegetables and such things as he thought I would most relish. His wives, for he had two, took great pains to cook as much like white women as they could and in fact the victuals was got up in pretty good shape. The man erected a good comfortable tent in the center of the grove for my special benefit, furnished me a horse whenever I wanted to go anywhere, (my own horse having become so lame I had to leave him entirely) and finally loaned me the best horse he had to come home upon. He said his family had never had the privilege of being baptized and he hoped I would not forget him now that I was there. In fact he gave me no peace till I performed that ordinance for them and then he was just as much concerned as before, because one of his sons was or had gone to the railroad after supplies and he was afraid I would go away before the boy came back. But the boy came all right and was baptized, contrary to this Indian's fears.

I was not at all alarmed or discouraged at the reception I had met with from Washakie for I had fasted and prayed and I felt that God was with me, and if so who could be against me. However I concealed my real intentions from this man, but told him to catch a couple of horses early the next morning and with one make haste to the village and I with the other would prospect the country a little. Moreover I directed him to visit the next chief to Washakie himself and tell him I was near camp and wanted to see him immediately. This chief (who by the way belongs to the Church and has the name of being a very good man) soon came to where I was stopping. I told him why I was there and how I had thus far been received. He said if he were in my fix he should go and have a personal interview with Washakie myself. He thought I would look very destitute to come away and not be able to say that I had even seen the chief. He questioned me very closely in order to find out what I would do but as before I said nothing about my contemplated mode of procedure. The next day after baptizing this man's family with whom I was stopping and some others in that same camp I started for the village, which contained about a thousand Indians I suppose more or less. I left about four o'clock in the evening so as to arrive about dark.

I rode up to the Chief's lodge about dusk. He had changed so much since I had seen him sixteen years ago that I did not know him. I asked where Washakie's lodge was. He replied that he was Washakie, pointing to himself. I dismounted, introduced myself and told him my business; asked him if he had any objections to this people joining our church if they wanted to. I thought he answered rather reluctantly but before I left him he appeared to be anxious to give me all the information concerning the people and premises there that he could. I asked him what he thought of our doctrine. He said he thought it was an invented story and not true. Still the Mormon people were and had always been his friends and he wished to be considered their friend. I gave him an account of the visit to Joseph by the Angel Moroni, restoration of the Gospel etc. He said President Young had told him the same years ago.

After saying all to him that I thought I was prompted to say and obtaining his consent to labor among his people, I returned to my stopping place. The next morning I dispatched a messenger telling him to circulate the word in the camp that those who wished to be baptized could find me there at those Springs above mentioned, but come in small squads one after the other so as not to excite suspicion.

That day I performed the ordinance for eighty-seven persons, besides baptizing many for their health as well as administering to many. The Indians said there had been some healed several years ago when they had been baptized for their health.

That evening I received a message from the interpreter who is a half-breed Indian, saying that he was so sick he expected to die, but hoped I would come and see him immediately. Accordingly I took my Indian friend (Tor Namp pe) with me for a guide. We started about sunset. Upon entering the village I procured a wrapper and went on in disguise. When only a few rods from the sick man's lodge, which seemed to be only just across the road from the Fort, I told the guide to go in and prospect the premises and if the Post doctors had retired, come back and let me know. He soon returned saying the coast was clear ... follow him.

The interpreter, I found lying upon his back in a perfectly helpless condition. His right arm was paralyzed so that he was unable to raise his hand to shake hands with me. His left arm also was so to the elbow. However he could raise his left hand but not his arm. His legs too were so completely paralyzed that they appeared to be of no use to him whatever. He said he wanted to hear of our doctrine. Much had been told him but he said he did not think he had got it as it was.

I commenced at the beginning and talked fast until one or two o'clock I suppose, arranging what I had to say so as to accommodate myself to the time as near as possible. He said he believed every word I said, and if he got able before I got through with the people there, he would be glad to be baptized. He wanted to know also where I had stationed myself as he wanted to send his family to me to be baptized, which he did the next day. His brother, John Sinclare, also came and joined us. The lodge was full of Indians and half-breeds.

My guide said on the way home that night that the Indians present could feel that I gained upon that man until he was overcome, though we spoke in English on that occasion. I told him it was not me that gained upon him, but the Spirit of God. He replied that he knew that.

I had asked Washakie if he thought there was any danger of some young reckless Indian informing on me. He said no. He said these half-breeds and white men with Indian women for wives, Mexicans etc. were the ones to watch. But instead of being in the hands and at the mercy of this desperate class of men, they seemed to be in my hands and one of them inquired of me, manifesting great concern, what I was going to do with him.

When we left the lodge that night I found myself completely surrounded by Indians for several hundred yards. It seemed as though I could not get away although it would soon be light. One would take hold of me and another and another, till I could not begin to answer them all.

The next day they commenced coming early. I was in the water almost constantly, except when confirming and recording, until after sundown. I baptized and confirmed about one hundred twenty persons that day. I have no idea how many I administered to and baptized for health. I became so weak towards evening that it seemed to me that I could not say another word. Still I said if they should come all night I would not turn one person away, and they did come till after sundown. Some of them appeared to be perfectly out of breath and their horses all of a foam. Sometimes two or more would come into the water at once and some would try to get under the water themselves.

One morning just before daylight, after I had spent almost the entire night in the village preaching and baptizing, I had only just retired to bed at my own camp when I was aroused again by the Indians who had followed me up in the night, to have me do something for them that they might be healed. Candidates were accompanied by their friends so I was enveloped almost constantly by a perfect swarm. How such crowds could leave the Agency and Post day after day and not excite suspicion I don't know, without God was in it. But they told me that they had sent young men on horses to watch the movements of the troops and settlers up and down the valley and if suspicion should be aroused I should know it first or before anyone could take me. Furthermore if anyone was to be imprisoned they would go in first. How true this would have proved to be I can't say. But they acted like they thought I was the hero of the whole country. They brought me various kinds of food from different parts of the village, and nothing seemed too good for me. I had canned salmon, nuts, fresh beef, good bread, milk, potatoes, onions, turnips, groceries if I wanted them. They paid fifty cents apiece for watermelons and brought them to me, which by the way was quite a treat as I had not seen any for twelve or fifteen years, nor was they unmindful of me when I left, but furnished me with a good supply to come home with. Sent a young Indian to show me the trail across the range of mountains so that what it took me five days to travel going out, I made in two coming back.

After I had been employed for nine or ten days in this manner, or at least the day before I intended getting ready for home, Washakie sent me word by his herder that he had come to the conclusion I had told him the truth. I had declared to him with all my might that I was telling him the right way and there was no other that would do; that it was not merely my word or President Young's word, but the word of God. Hence he wanted to see me again right away.

Myself and guide went down that night. Upon our arrival the old man wanted to know how he could be baptized as he was unable to come up to where the rest came. I told him that he might select his own place and I would attend to it no matter where it might be. Accordingly he sent his young men and boys to prepare a place in a creek close by, which took them about two hours. They built a log heap fire on the bank and after the moon was up so we could see better, I performed the ordinance for himself and all his family: seventeen persons. Before I left I administered to him.

I came back by the interpreter's lodge. He said if he died he wanted someone to be baptized for him. I told him it could be done when our Temple was finished. He said if he got well he would attend to it himself. He asked me to pray for him. I administered to him. I never went to the village any more after that night, having baptized all but two of that camp ... the interpreter and his mother who was waiting on him. But very many Indians were off hunting so I could not see near all of them.

The next day was issue day. My friend Sam went to town that day to receive supplies while I went into the mountains about six miles to see if my horse would be able to come home. When I got back home that night I am told that Washakie was on his horse that day attending to business as normal. I have seen one Indian from that country lately. He says Washakie and the Interpreter were healed and are both well and hearty now. When I left for home I thought proper to ordain my friend Sam. I did so. The kindnesses done me by himself and family brought tears to my eyes many times and what could I do for him. I only had fifty cents. I gave him that but I could exercise the power of the priesthood in his behalf. I did so.

The first night out coming back I camped alone in the tops of the mountains of that range. After I had made preparation for the night I heard the neighing of a horse some distance from me through the timber. I saddled up as soon as I could and made my way for the place from whence the sound proceeded. I soon discovered a light which proved to be the campfire of three Indians. I stopped there that night.

Shortly after retiring I was taken very sick. The Indians were very much alarmed. They said that if I died there the whites would say they killed me. Not only that but they were very sorry for me because they considered that I had been a benefactor to the Indians. My sufferings were so severe that I thought the sickness was a judgment upon me for something I had done sometime in my life, though I did not know what it was. One of the Indians said or suggested that I pray to God to heal me. They had hunted through the brush and timber for something for me but could find nothing and now what else could be done. I did pray that I might be relieved or taken out of the world, for my suffering seemed to be beyond endurance. Finally I asked the Indian who seemed to be so much concerned for me, if he was a Mormon, for they were all strangers to me. He replied that he was. I then asked him if he would pray for me. He said he did not know how but would try. I ordained him and told him to put his hands on my head and pray for me which he did. I felt very much relieved. I then asked him if those other two belonged to the Church. He said they did. I ordained them. They all put their hands on my head and prayed for me.

As the Gentiles would have it, the moment they took their hands from my head I happened to be entirely well, but I would be afraid and ashamed to say that I was healed in any other way only by the power of God. And whether the sick were healed through my ministrations or not I think I was healed through the administrations of those three Indians.

On a stream called the Labarge, about one day's travel this side of Green River, the way I came back, there is quite a large settlement of mountaineers. I stayed there all night. Their women were very anxious to know where I had been. I told them all that heard me talk wanted to be baptized, (I mean Indians and half-breeds) no whites. I sought and obtained permission from the principal man among them, and baptized eighteen persons almost against their doors.

Thus closed my missionary labor of that trip. I left home with only a loaf of bread tied behind my saddle and two dollars the people gave me. Before I was five miles away I had five dollars and a half and before I was two days away I had eleven dollars, but I felt that I could get along without it. I did not ask anybody for a cent either. From the way I had been threatened I supposed it was all my life was worth to go. But President Rich, who by the way has always been a father to me, blessed me and told me that I should have wisdom to know what to do when I got in that country. It was so, and though I knew not the country or how I was going to live or how I should accomplish the mission, I never lacked for three good meals a day without I chose to fast. Strangers treated me like I was an old friend. I was fed and clothed and men gave me money though I never asked for any of these things. Enemies to the south seemed to be afraid of me and perfectly powerless though I was alone. Of course I could write volumes but I am afraid I have already said too much.

Again I don't like to talk so freely about myself but I never was so blessed before and never was so thankful and never enjoyed myself so long at one time. I don't wish to weary you but you understand these things. In fact, I thought of the time you were in France and of Brother Cannon on the Sandwich Islands, and of many of the experiences of the Elders of the Church and how the Lord had proposed to bless me too, though I was only a poor private man.

Of course you are at liberty to make such disposition of the accompanying record and these papers as you may deem proper.

Thanking you for your kind letter, I remain your Brother in the Gospel of Christ, A.R. WRight.

(The original of this letter is the property of L.D.S. Historical Archives, Salt Lake City, Utah, and here reproduced by their kind permission. An article based on this letter titled, "A Voice From the Dust" by Geneva Ensign Wright, has been purchased by *The Ensign*, official L.D.S. Church organ. Letter signed by Stephen H. Fletcher, Director Copyrights and Permissions Office, Aug. 22, 1980)

Pine Ridge,
Dec. 20th, 1885
Dear Loella:

I have postponed writing to anyone except one letter to Pres. Taylor, because I have not as yet been able to tell how I might be situated for the winter. And indeed I can't tell even now how I shall move only one day beforehand, so I thought I would just say a word or two now, and more after I see more how things are going to be with me here. I felt as though the train was hauling me off to the grave as I waved my last farewell to Jonny with my handkerchief. I wished then more than ever for your cheerful disposition to console me among enemies and strangers. However I had a safe and speedy conveyance to my present place of abode, except some inconvenience from cold and fatigue on the stage. Since my arrival we have held meetings regularly with the Indians. They do the singing ... it is quite grand. But you would be astonished at their ignorance, superstition and degradation. I have lived with them all the time though it takes a cast iron stomach to eat after their cooking. Last night I dreamed of home but awoke to find myself laying in an Indian lodge in the mountains among savages who sing and whoop all night long sometimes in their games and cutups. Of course it seems very strange to be without one single acquaintance with whom one can converse and trust. If I could see you now I expect I should talk you to death and make you wish that you had run away with the fellow you seen in the dance more than ever. However I hope that you are well and comfortable ... you have my confidence and prayers. "Can I depend on yours." The weather here at present is pleasant not much snow to speak of but it has been very cold. I have generally had a horse to ride from one place to another and have generally been very busy. If you can write to me tell me all the news. Address your letter to George Terry, Shoshone Agency, Box 8, Wyoming. May the God of Heaven bless and preserve you is the sincere hope of your loving etc. T. Benton. Kind regards to all the folks and be sure and remember all I told you. Your own, T.B.

Willow Creek, Jan. 14th, 1886
My Dear Sweet Girl:

I expected to have heard from you ere this time. Perhaps you did not get my letter. You may be surprised when I tell you I had only had one letter from home since I left and have seen no papers from our country or people. Perhaps you are not well if not maybe some of the family would write a line for you, though I should be delighted to see a line from your own hand. I hope the winter is passing away pleasantly for you. I have not heard how much snow you have. The weather here is quite cold and has been for some time. I have suffered some considerable from exposure but not as much as I expected. I have no chance to converse with any white person and therefore it is quite lonesome. Can you blame me for being anxious to hear from those I love and who are dearer to me than life itself. I suppose you can comprehend the fact that I am alone in the midst of strangers savages and enemies. You perhaps don't realize that to be deprived of the privilege of speaking your own language is calculated to make one think of those who do. And no doubt you will laugh at me a little if I say that a letter from you would be read over and over until every word and every letter in it were counted and the paper on which it is written worn out. I am not situated so I can write much but though I can't write I never leave off my prayers or concern for you. What more I could do or pass through than I am at present to convince those who are so dear to me as you are, I am unable to say. If I should tell you the plain simple truth and no more, I fear you would think I am grumbling. But I don't wish to complain. Indeed I feel tolerably well and have the most excellent uninterrupted good health. Moreover I think my labors here have not been in vain. And I fully believe that the Lord has heard and answered my prayers many times and if this should find you well and enjoying yourself my faith in His kind Providence would be still more increased. Now my Dear Girl you must hasten to send me a few lines dictated by your ever cheerful disposition, and may the God of Heaven bless and preserve you and yours to enjoy many happy hours together again is the sincere and most earnest hope and prayer of Your Affectionate, T. Benton. Shoshone Agency. Direct to George Terry, Box 8. (be sure to put Box 8 on the address) Give my love to yours.

UNITED STATES INDIAN SERVICE

Shoshone Agency,
Jan. 17, 1886
Lorenzo Snow Dear Brother:
Owing to many circumstances unnecessary to explain I have never yet thanked you for the last and very encouraging letter I received from you. I now thank you very much for the sentiments therein expressed. I have heard that The "Philistines" (Anti-Mormons) have caused you some trouble. I am really sorry and assure you that if I were the judge you would be entitled to, and receive the rest and peace your past labors and present advanced age demand. I confess that I hardly understand why good Brethren and aged gentlemen must be persecuted forever. I feel as Washakie said to me the other day, I think the Lord ought to care before long and lift us out of our troubles. Nevertheless the Lord's will be done. I am taking the share of bondage the Lord has allotted me I suppose. And I don't feel to complain. I have been very anxious to hear from the President. I have written several letters but get no answer, perhaps he does not approve of our policy. Of course I am ready to change it any time he sees fit. I have endeavored to operate according to the suggestions you made in case I should be sent to this mission, except that I went onto the Reservation and have remained on it ever since. Have held meetings regularly, sometimes two or three per week. You saw something of the ignorance of the Indians when you were here, but you would be still more astonished if I should go into details. They are certainly in a sorrowful condition. I don't know how far the Lord's mercy may extend, but if anyone else would say without His authority that they can be civilized and redeemed I should disbelieve it. Brother Brown is with me; tolerably well but his wife is a great nuisance though I am satisfied he would fail without her, so of course we must keep her. I have not had the privilege of conversing with any White man and live entirely with Indians. This with the filth and exposure to which I am now exposed of course makes it quite lonesome sometimes. I wrote to the President for enough to get us a little camp outfit so we could live by ourselves, but he assisted my family when I

came away and I presume he thinks I am extravagant, so all right, but the circumstances make me crave warm weather more than ever before. I hope you will not say anything to anyone about it. I don't wish to complain. I hope your present situation is not so bad as reports led me to believe. If you write, direct to George Terry, Shoshone Agency Box 8. Your Brother in the Gospel *T. Benton.*

Sage Creek, Feb. 1st, 1886
My Darling Girl:
Your kind interesting and affectionate letter was received late last night. I started yesterday morning to come to this camp. I was so sick all day that I thought I should have to lay on the trail all night, but your loving and cheering letter has made me well again. It seems as though you are almost a prophetess. You cautioned me to be careful and not get sick but I was too careless. The day before I wrote to you before, I started to go to a neighboring village. I rode very steadily till the after part of the day and then called in at a lodge to get something to eat. The meat had been killed so long that it was almost rotten. I believe this hurt me, but I still continued on for I was in a great hurry. I got into camp sometime in the night and went on. It was so cold I had to walk to keep from freezing. I did not get to the next campsite until late and then I had been without eating since the morning before except this tainted bite I told you of. I hastened to write home and there was taken very sick. The Indian where I staid had lost four of his children lately that I blessed five years ago. He told me where he had laid them in a cave on the mountain. I thought sure I would have to tell him to lay me there with them. Then I thought I would have to send for my Indian Friend who is with me here and who was about thirty or forty miles away, to come and take the last word I could ever say to you, to deliver it to you himself. Then again I thought I would take my letters and try and get them to an office about fifteen miles away if I died in the attempt. The Indian saddled my horse for me and I started, and that I believe is the first time in my life that I ever failed to go through when I undertook to do anything. I did not get one mile away. The ground in camp was so wet that you could squeeze water out of it with your hands almost. The Indians were very kind to me and done everything they could for me and prayed very earnestly for me. I got well in eight days and I am all right now again. Many things of interest take place here. I was directed to write to Pres. Taylor and keep him posted from time to time. I wrote three letters to him but could get no answer. He had told me to locate four miles from the line, but I could not reach the Indians from that point, so I came onto the reservation. The first meeting we held with the Chief was quite a strange one. He is seventy or eighty years of age but straight as an arrow and active as a boy. It is said he has killed six men in personal engagements say nothing of those killed in battle. He had lost one of his wives lately. Her small children were around him. A White man had killed his son this season. Delegations from several of the surrounding tribes have been urging him to lead them to war. The troops here were putting on their wagon covers and buying stores to put in them and getting ready to march onto Salt Lake. A Mountaineer had come to him with a report that we had already commenced to fight, upon which he jumped on his horse and rode forty or fifty miles as hard as he could go to see if it was so. An Indian had brought me word from the Agent that if I did not leave in ten days I should never be permitted to get off this Agency again. I destroyed Bro. Taylor's letter of instructions, intending to take all the consequences of arrest myself. Strange to say the Chief demanded my authority from Pres. Taylor which I could not produce because I had destroyed it as I say. In alluding to the resurrection it led him to thinking of his dead friends and some unwise remarks were made by one of his Counsel, whereupon the old Chief flew into a rage and drew his knife, and the whole meeting went into confusion so I thought I would not be able to control them and for two meetings after, it seemed as though I could do nothing with them. But the fourth meeting we seemed to get power over them. I assured him that the reports were all a lie, though it did look strange to see how things were going here.

I could get no word from Bro. Taylor and no papers and only one letter from Home since I had left. These circumstances taken together, made me feel very sorrowful for I thought I had done wrong in destroying Bro. Taylor's letter containing my appointment to this Mission. Also in coming across the line where he said or suggested that I stay four miles the other side. And now as I thought I had went against Counsel and was about to be made responsible for bringing on a conflict between our people and the Government, and that God and all my Brethren, family and friends had forsaken me. We could hardly tell who the old man was going to kill at the time but we think it was one of his counselors. Again Bro. Brown's wife was sick nearly all the time and we could not leave her nor carry her with us. We had to live with the Indians, their filth is awful. One place they passed the antelope hair around in the lid of an old chamber pot that looked like it had been used all night for its natural purpose. There were six or eight dogs in the lodge to commence on when we went to bed, but before morning the pups that had come into the world in the night on the beds increased the number so materially that the proprietor of the wickiup thought it necessary to have his wife help him remove some of the filth while I was supposed to take the lead in offering up the morning prayer in behalf of the noble Red Man of the Forest.

These my loving Girl are some few of the reasons why I thought you had forsaken me. But when I got into camp last night I found a kind and encouraging letter from Pres. Taylor, blessing me and encouraging me in all I had done. And also a letter from Cate and several other friends at home. As well as such a sweet one from you and when I read that you would pray for me I thought I could face death itself if necessary. I have thanked God over and over for giving me such a faithful companion. Dream about you? ... I should think so ... a thousand times only to wake and find myself lying in an old smoky wickiup without a soul to speak to only Indians. Take care of you? ... why don't you ask me if I would cut off and throw away my right arm, or purposely gouge out my right eye. Like to see you? ... I'll bet if I ever get hold of you again you will think I am never going to let go of you any more. Company for me? ... If I could sit down by you now, all the circuses, theatres, dances and public amusements on the globe with free tickets could not get me away from you for a month. Pray for you? ... when you become a mother do you think you will forget your own child? Possibly such a thing might happen but I don't think that it is more likely than for me to forget you my darling and part of my very life itself. It seems to me that if I were turned loose and honorably released I would never get off my horse till I had you in my arms. I am sorry to hear that your Father is not very well. I hope he will be nearly well when this reaches you. Be sure to tell him I shall not or cannot forget him, neither any of the family.... You wrote that the snow was eighteen feet deep. I hope it is not quite so bad. I expect you meant eighteen inches. This seems very strange of course, how there can be so much difference in countries. The ground here is dry, the air at present is warm enough to be comfortable in without a coat. The range is fine and stock running on it is fat. I am sorry to hear the Brethren still continue to be persecuted. The Indians say to tell Pres. Taylor to hurry up the Lord to come to their relief. Indeed it seems strange that good men must be persecuted forever. Now my sweet Lel, you must not think I am grumbling or discouraged, for as long as I know I can have your support, I feel that I can go through anything necessary. I hope I shall be true to my people and the Kingdom of God and never do anything to cause you to be ashamed of me or give you one painful thought. I better die a dozen times than to dishonor my calling. We have promised to baptize several converts now soon. There is some really good kind people among them. And some very wicked ones. Two murders were committed here last week and the third person wounded. They gamble awful. One fellow gambled off all his horses and all his property and then one of his wives and one of his children, and finally the only remaining wife he had. The winner took her home and slept with her all night and then went into another game and she ran away. The other fellow is wandering around among the camp begging his way. Another fellow shot his wife dead as she came into the lodge door the other day. Now you see I am about to the end of this sheet and must close. Maybe I have tired you out. So hoping that the God of Heaven will bless and preserve you by the power of his Holy Spirit to help you to go safely through what is before you, and that you are caused no unnecessary pain but speedily restored to your normal health and strength, with the life of that which will be so dear to you secured, is the prayer and blessing for and upon you and by the best friend and loving companion you have this side of the world to come. A.R.W.

Lost Creek, Feb. 27, 1886
My Dear Lel,
Your kind and encouraging letter of the 17th inst. was duly received. I don't think you ought to make any excuses about not being an able letter writer. Why you could bet the hind sights off the Democrat Editor writing up the News, or expatiating on sentiment, or any subject you start in to handle. I can hardly do or think of anything else for several days after getting one of those good ones from you. I am delighted to hear you were still well and thankful to say that I am about as healthy now as I have ever been before in my life. And not only that, but we are much more comfortably situated than we have been at any time before during the winter. We have a lodge to live in by ourselves and some cooking utensils. And of course I am able under these favorable conditions to control things so as to dodge a little of the filth to which we were subjected to before, when the places where we had to stop belonged to others. You say I ought to kill a dog. Well I had none to kill. Dogs are quite valuable here and are eaten by the Arrapahoes, by whom they are esteemed a delicious dish.
I thought I would not tell you my dream that I had about you the other day for fear you would laugh at me but I'll tell you and then if you want a little fun over me I'll try and stand it. I dreamed that I left here and went to heaven and you were laying on my right arm and I drew you still closer to my side and smoothed your hair back from your brow and kissed you on your forehead. Then told you all my troubles and you talked to me so good and kind that I said, why this is not dream but surely I am at home. My troubles are over and this is my Lel. I awoke and found myself lying on my back. I turned quickly to my side to find you but you was not there. I was alone as usual. And lo and behold it was all a deceitful dream. But I don't care. It was awful glorious while it lasted anyhow. Now don't you think that this was almost as much of a joke on me as your dream was on you? I am going to try and get five dollars if I can before this goes out and send in Cate's letter. She will give you two of it. Get something you want with it and remember your best Friend has not forgot you yet. I shall be very busy now for a few days so, so long my Dear for this time. I'll remember you again as soon as I can get around to it. You will of course understand that it will not be wisdom to say much about what I write to you outside of the house. Bless your good heart. *T.B.*
You say I did not say anything about coming home. Well my Dear I don't know myself when that happy time shall be. Of course you would be ashamed to see me without I was honorably released. As soon as I find out I will not fail to tell you the first thing. You ask if the Indians gamble off their wives ... of course they do. Well it is the excitement of the game and the rule with all gamblers not to quit when they are losing.... Bro. Brown says I am no companion to him for four or five days after hearing from you. I am sorry that your Father has had an attack of rheumatism. I pity anyone from the bottom of my heart that has to endure such indescribable pain. I think I should have been dead wtih it long ago, considering the amount of exposure I have passed through, had it not been for refraining from all kinds of stimulants as much as possible. I hope and pray that your Father will recover and be able to resume his usual labors. I have just received word that Pres. G.Q. Cannon has been arrested. My God when will this ungodly crusade cease? How long O Lord shall the best men and women of the age and earth with their families be separated, broken up, imprisoned, plundered and robbed? I have been in daily expectation of arrest ever since I have been here. Why must this be? Is it wrong to love those so dear to me? Must I be asked to sever the ties made sacred and eternal over the altar of the great Jehovah. As well ask me it seems to sever the limbs from my body. And again what can be wrong in trying to get people to do right, repent of sin and prepare for eternity, if I can't have you for my companion. As I feel now, and I hope I shall always feel so, then give me death and annihilation. If you must be torn from me to be branded as a prostitute and

called the mother of a bastard, turned out upon this cold savage ruined world without husband or Father to love, protect and care for you and yours, then life is not worth having, and we are not creatures capable of exaltation. I am weighed down now with anxiety for you in your critical crisis. It seems to me that I could do so much more for you than anyone else. But be of good cheer my Dear, God can and will more than make up to you what you seem to lack through my absence. I have never neglected or forgotten you in any way, and my prayers for you have been constantly offered up in your behalf. I feel assured they will be answered. I am thankful you feel so generally cheerful but when I hear you have gone through safe and you and yours are all right, I shall feel like a thousand pounds were lifted from my shoulders. For goodness sake don't keep me in suspense a single minute after you are prepared to tell me this joyful and so much longed for news. Till then I shall not cease to pray and fast as much as possible for the preservation of your lives and speedy restoration to health and usual buoyancy of spirits. Now my Darling Girl Farewell. To the care of the God of Heaven I commend you, whose blessing and protection will bé upon and around about you for good. Your affectionate and anxious Companion, *T. BENTON.*

UNITED STATES INDIAN SERVICE (*Stationery*)

Owl Creek Agency, March 20th, 1886

My Dear Sweet Loella:

I came up here about twenty miles from our own camp to Terry's, on purpose to see if I could find another word from those so dear to me. I found upon my arrival your ever-welcome and encouraging letter. But as you say I have to still remain in great anxiety and suspense for another month I suppose. I have fasted and prayed and prayed that I might yet hear that you had gone through all right and this anxiety lifted from my mind, though my constant concern for you generally can never leave me till I can get to see you again. But never mind my Dear don't feel discouraged. God will take care of you. Though I can't understand for the life of me what you mean by saying nobody cares for you even if you would die, can anyone be so inhumanly cruel as to mistreat you? If so, tell me all about it, my loving Girl. You have never said a cross or unkind word to me or gave me an unkind look in your life, and the thoughts of the comfort and pleasure I had with you uninterrupted by even one unpleasant act during the time I was permitted to be in your company, help me materially now I am so far from you to go through all that I may be called to endure to prove myself worthy of such an amiable and loving companion. How can you say I make fun of your kind letters which seem to be a perfect Godsend to me? Dear Lel, I meant just what I said. I don't see how you could make them more precious to me than they are. I wish they were twenty pages each and I could get one every day. But then I would be so homesick that I would be no account for this labor. I am glad to hear your Father is better and that my prayers for him were answered. I am thankful to be able to say I am well and apparently as tough and stout as a mule. I have only been sick once and only been lost twice ... once in the night and once in a fog. But found myself all right again in both cases. The country here is very rugged and rough which has been an advantage to me thus far. The Indians continue to treat me kindly and I must not complain when I know that hundreds of my Brethren are traveling and begging their way from door to door in the midst of enemies and more adverse circumstances than in which I am placed. We have now got four horses to use and can all ride and move camp at the same time. Bro. Brown's wife will soon be the mother of a little brown papoose. I suppose I shall have to take what cold comfort I can by looking at him pass away the dreary hours with his baby boy while mine is hundreds of miles away in his Mother's lap. But I believe God will spare me to see you both, sometime sooner or later. And then oh won't I be gloriously paid for all my pains. You said you could not feel like enjoying life deprived of a loving husband. My Dear sweet one, you shall never be deprived of a kind and loving one throughout all the ages to come, while I exist without I shall be so unfortunate as to fall into wickedness and thus render myself unworthy of one so good, so kind, so confiding, so pure and virtuous. But I suppose it is foolish to give way to my feelings. I expect you will laugh at me. But I pity the one or two or even three horses that ever start from

here towards where I know you are with me as their passenger. I'll bet they will
never want to carry another man toward his Love. You saucy little witch what
made you say, "If you don't want my card send it back." Don't you think or
know you come pretty near cutting me assunder. I'll bet if I ever get hold of you
again I'll give you a good spanking and kiss you all over for that. You won't let
me Eh. I'll show you who will carry you off and put you in a good humor when I
get back. I scarcely ever close my eyes but what I am looking in those two black
ones of yours till I awake again and am forced to think, Oh it is so lonesome to
be separated from their sight so long, when I had enjoyed myself so many
times before in watching every step you took and listening to every word you
spoke. And now I can't hear that voice, here in these old mountains. But as
high as they are if I was loose I would not be without hearing it again, many
days. Now my lovely little Partner, you must write and tell me everything don't
be afraid to talk to me, and tell me all you have passed through. I can feel for
you as no other living soul on this earth can and I think you can trust me and
though I may pass away God will be with you, to comfort and bless you for
Ever and Ever. Your anxious etc. etc. *T. BENTON.*

Owl Creek, March 28, 1886
My Dear Loella:
I have just received a line from Adda informing me of the birth of our little
Girl. I feel very thankful and much relieved to know that my blessing upon you
and my prayers for you have been thus far answered, though Addie says you
were yet, quite weak. But time and care will restore you now that the worst is
over, to your normal health and buoyancy of spirit. Now you assume the duties
of Mother and will begin to experience the comforts such as nothing in this
world can bring you save your Darling child. I am inexpressibly proud to know
that it is a girl. Who don't know that girls are always better than boys. If it
were not for girls there would never be any boys anyhow. Boys swear and get
drunk, run away from home and are always getting into all sorts of mischief,
making trouble for themselves and everybody else. And every Father knows it
costs almost twice as much to raise one boy as two girls. I should like to know
what would become of Society if it was not for girls and women to temper it.
Why without girls, men and boys would soon be worse than a set of barbarians.
Go into a country where there are nothing but men and refinement and the
greater virtues are at an end. And nothing but roughness and coarseness and
wickedness prevail. When I get to Heaven if there are no girls there I am going
to leave. Again we all know that nothing is so lovely and precious to a man as
his wife who could not be a wife if she had not first been a girl. And who can
describe the care and anxiety that pervades a man's bosom when he is absent
from his lovely wife, knowing that she must be alone almost half of the time,
because all her oldest children unfortunately are boys, and can't be kept
anywhere only somewhere they ought not to be. How many times I have met
anxious parents strolling and wandering about town half crazy for fear they
could not find their naughty boys. Not so with girls they are always to be found
at home to honor and keep Ma company. They would never have any trouble
nor do any wrong if it were not for the cussed uncontrollable boys, who never
know anything good till some kindhearted confiding forgiving girl learns it to
them. And it is not till they have been under the care and instruction of some
nice girl for a few years that they know that the world itself would cease to be
fit to live in if it were not for our Angels who are all girls. Now My Darling Lell
you must kiss her a thousand times for me. And as soon as you can write and
tell me all about her then I'll tell you just what to do. God bless your sweet heart
and take care of you both till I can take care of you myself. Your loving, *T.
BENTON.*

Bull Lake, April 13, 1886
Dear Loella:
We are camped alone at the present time on, or on the bank of a lake which
is seven or eight miles long. It is raining as hard as it can pour, so we cannot
get out to do anything to pass away the time. I moved up in this quiet little

place because the grass starts sooner here than other places, and I wished to recruit our horses for we have rode them all down till they are quite poor and weak. It is almost a month and a half since I heard from you, except a word or two from Adda. Of course I am very thankful for that letter, but I am anxious to see a line once more from your own hand. When shall I ever hear from you again? I have just been reading one of your letters over again that I have read and read till the paper is completely wore out. I wrote to you immediately upon the receipt of Adda's letter and now I write again though I am sorry and feel very lonely that I can have nothing to reply to. I hope you have got your usual health again. And if all is well with you and yours. I expect you have such a happy time that your attention is entirely absorbed in that direction. I know you will have lots of comfort, but you must not forget me in this lonely place. You must remember that I have not a child or friend in the world to speak to me here and that one sweet word from you is more to me than all the world besides. You will surely not forget that it is hard on me, when I love you so well that I must be separated from you so far, and cannot see or speak to you, and have only been allowed the privilege of living with you my Dear Girl a few short months. Of course you will bear in mind that it was like tearing my limbs from my body when I had to leave you, and that no one can fill your place in my heart. Your friends and people, home and home scenes, are all near you. All these things I am bereft of. If I see a White man at all I know that if he knew me he is an enemy. And therefore I must shun him and keep him from seeing me if possible. Last night it seemed that I dreamed all night long about my little girl. I asked you to let me hold her and I thought she was so plump and heavy, and her eyes was so bright and black. And she was oh so lively and pretty that I could not give her back or let go of her, but when I awoke she was gone and my arms were empty. You will surely tell me her Father something about her wont you? You will certainly not forget that I cant see her only in dreams. And that if I had her so far from you I would tell you everything. But perhaps I better say a word or two about matters here. We are getting along as well as can be expected. I have baptized and rebaptized forty five or fifty persons. Have just received a kind letter from Pres. Taylor ... it appears that he expects a great deal of me. I don't know how I shall be able to fill his anticipations. I can only hope to do right, and trust to God to order all things well. I cannot say anything yet about coming home. It appears from Bro. Taylor's letter that our enemies are getting worse and worse and so bad that he said he could not say anything definite just now about anyone coming out here this spring. I shall forward him a letter same time this goes out. Maybe the next time he writes I shall know something more about it. The Indians say they will all go off on a hunt as soon as their little crops are in. If they go over on to Green River maybe I shall go with them. Harl Weaver drove from there home in three days last fall and I rode it in 2 and 1/2. If the Authorities of the Church would not allow me to go home, I should be almost tempted to send an Indian in after you to come and spend the 4th of July there with me.

And while you were seeing me, I would see you a little too! But maybe you would not come! Now my ever sweet One you must try and answer this and tell me how you are fixed. And believe me to be the best Friend you have in this cold wide world. And maybe I can help you a little if you need it! Try me and see. For without I am just as busy as I can be I can't keep you out of my mind till sometimes it seems as though I can't stand it any longer. And when I dream your love comes here to me
And fills my soul with joy divine
Then again I have felt my sweet Loell
Your heart beat close to mine.
Yours Faithful and true, *T. BENTON.*

P.S. Give my kind regards to your Mother and all your folks and kiss my Darling ten thousand times for me.

UNITED STATES INDIAN SERVICE

Shoshone Agency, May 1st, 1886
My Dear Loella:
It will be two months next Friday since I had a line from you. I have written

three letters to you, and shall keep writing till I hear what has become of you.
Of course I can't tell whether you are sick or well, dead or alive. I am very
anxious to know how you are. I hope you have not forgotten and given me up
entirely. I am still carrying with me and reading almost every day the last
letter you wrote me on the 7th of March. It is so worn now where it was folded
that it won't hold together much longer. I believe if you knew what a lonely
time I have and how I dream and think of you all the time, and how gladly I
would send you the last dollar I could get in the world if I knew I would starve
the next day, if you needed anything I think you would surely let me know how
you and that which is so precious with you to me, are getting along. Of course I
am not finding any fault with you because I don't know what is the matter. I
hope and never forget to pray that you and yours are well. Oh how quickly I
would give the world and all there is in it if it was mine to give, to see you once
again. Yet notwithstanding my great anxiety about you night and day I can't
even hear from you anymore. Something must be the matter for I know you are
too good to forsake me without ever telling me what for. If there was any
chance in the world to see you without deserting my post assigned me by the
Priesthood of God, how willingly would I go through anything that mortal
man has ever endured to hold you in my arms once again. And if the people of
God were free and I were honorably released we could soon be comfortable and
happy. But never mind my Dear, God will bless us yet if we do what is right.
Many of our Brethren and sisters are tried now severely. Let us be brave and
trust in God and we will come out all right yet. Maybe I can get to see you
someway or another this summer. If you and Cate would put your heads
together maybe you could get to Green River without exciting suspicion ... it is
only two and a half days drive. I would meet you there if possible. I could ride it
in three days and nights if I knew I could see you for my pains when I got there,
but maybe you would not come but would be afraid to travel over the road
without someone to take care of you. What shall I do, I can't see you nor speak
to you nor hear you or hear from you. Have I got to lose you. Surely you will yet
tell me what you would do. May Heaven hasten the word, is the anxious and
fervent prayer of your loving Companion *T. BENTON.*

North Fork, May 5, 1886
My Dear Loella:
Twenty times or more today I have thought of what happened about a year
ago about this time. And though I have written four letters since I have seen a
line from you I thought I would send another in a manner that I know will
reach you if possible to find you. I shall be very sorry to hear that I have ever
said or done anything to lead you to forget me. If I have not thought to mention
it in every letter I have written I intended at least to always have you tell me
how you get along so that if you lack anything to eat or wear I could show you
that I would not be deaf to your appeal. Of course I can tell nothing from here
when I hear nothing. I don't know what in the world to say to you, because I
don't know where in the world you are, or whether you are in the world at all or
not. If anybody has tried to influence you to discard your best Friend on the
earth, and you thereby feel any indifference towards him now in his lonely
situation, surely you will say or write a line to let him know. I can't believe you
have throwed me away on account of some ones talk or persuasion without
giving me a hearing or a chance to defend myself or even say goodbye to me.
Oh no, you are too good and kind and honest to slaughter a friend in that
manner. Many people are being severely tried now among us, both men and
women, and I am taking a severe part of the test, and have risked my life
already to prove myself true to God, my friends, family and His Kingdom. If it
were not for the relation existing between us, cemented by ties of love and
affection that I have always prayed might continue for the ages of eternity, I
would shrink from the responsibility and take the world easy like many others
do. I am trying to live as pure and faithful a life as I know how to and hope and
pray I have not or will never do anything to make you justly ashamed of me.
Well Lel you was good to me and I pray God with the fervency of my soul to
bless and prosper you anyhow, even if you don't think of me now anymore. If
you will accept it from me I will send you some money, if you will write and tell

me where you have gone to. Your Undeviating Loving, *T. BENTON*.

Cottonwood, May 6th, 1886
Mrs. Sarah Weaver, Dear Sister:
I am very uneasy all the time about Loella. It is two months since I had a line from her. I have written five letters to her but have had no answer. I am afraid my poor Girl is laying in her grave. If this is so, for goodness sake why won't no one tell me about it. I know her good heart too well to think she would forget me or neglect me without giving a reason why or bidding me goodbye. I have been anxious to know how she is situated. Addie wrote that she was not doing very well shortly after her confinement. I am afraid that I have felt her kind and noble heart beat for the last time in this world of trouble and sorrow, I pray you have mercy enough on me to let me know the worst and if as I fear it is, let me mourn for her in death as I loved her in life. Yours very anxiously awaiting a reply, *T. BENTON*. Direct to George Terry, Shoshone Agency, Wyoming (*Box 8*) I have trusted you with this letter you will not betray me or say anything about my fears to anyone. A.R.W. Kind regards to yourself, Bro. Weaver and all the children. Word was sent me that two of my brothers were killed this winter. This is why I suppose my friends think they won't tell me about this, thinking it will break me almost entirely.

(At the bottom of the page, this):

May 8th,
This is the letter I sent to the Office yesterday. You mustn't tell anybody about it only your Ma. I wonder if you think I am such a fool as to trust you to the care of an Indian even for ten seconds. I thought you knew my style of joking and would understand me. *Injin Hell* I'd like to see one touch you while I am alive.

Re the above paragraph: (Amos evidently received the long-looked-for letter from Loella just before he posted the letter to her mother. It appears Loella had remonstrated about going that far in the care of an Indian, and this is his reply.)

Shoshone Agency, May 7th, 1886.
My Darling Sweet Loella:
Oh My God Loella I never was so thankful since I breathed the breath of life as I am tonight to hear thank Heaven that you are alive. Yesterday I rode all day as hard as I could go without eating a bite till after sundown, then I wrote to your mother to tell me for the Lord sake if you was dead. I thought my friends was keeping it from me because they thought I could not stand the shock. I started again this morning and sent Jim to the Agency with your Mother's letter, but the Office was so full he couldn't get to mail it without being seen, so he brought it back. I will send it in this, then you never will stop laughing at me I guess. But I was pretty near crazy. I thought I would go wild I was so sure you was dead. I know you feel bad and I would give my life to help you if that would help you. I am glad your baby is all right and well. It don't make any difference what color her eyes is, she will be pretty and good when she grows to be a little bigger. I am very sorry your Father has concluded to go away. If he had been going to stay I thought the cows and what I could make arrangements to get you besides from times to time would make you comfortable till I could come and take care of you myself. Again Bro. Snow intended to come out here this Spring and purchase a farm and buildings and put me on it to manage the Mission here, but he is in prison. I have written to Pres. Taylor. He may send some of the Twelve out and if they come something will be done no doubt. Again I thought Cate would have her house done by spring then you could stay with her once in a while when you wanted to. She would be good to you when you get acquainted with her. Cate got six of the cows and there is two more to come. I will write to Bro. Budge. If you want to live with your folks you could leave the cows with Cate if you did not want them. But would not they be good in Oxford the same as Bennington, why not. You could come and stay with Cate once in awhile and thus pass away the time till I can get loose then I would soon take care of you. Tell your Father that

anything he owes for you to keep an account and when I get free I know of a way to get him every cent of his pay.... It is almost impossible for me to tell you just what to do because of our enemies. If all was peace I would know what to say. You see I can't tell from here how all the circumstances are there, but if you could see Bro. Budge he will tell you just what is for the best. Don't be afraid to talk to him he is my friend. Or Bro. Winters if you can't see Pres. Budge. What does your Father say? When you write tell every little thing you can think of. Again if this Bill now before Congress passes then if you were found living with Cate it would be very dangerous. And Oxford is a Hell of a place too, so you see there is many things to think of. And again I know I have got friends in Bear Lake that would not see you suffer while I am not much acquainted in Oxford. Of course we with all the Saints are going to be severely tried, but for God sake Lell don't never let go of me. I will bring you out all right if I ever get free.

I can't live without you. You will know that I am tied now and make allowance for me and if I was at home maybe I would be thrown into prison and then I could not even write to you without letting the Boss of the prison read it. I am not in such a bad fix as that, though I have not had a chance to sit down to a table but once for six months or more, or nearly six I mean. I can't talk with a soul only Injins except Terry once in a while and he is Half Blood and is gone off to be away a month or more. And now I have got a Half Breed that I baptized this winter to get the letters out for me. I will send you Twenty Dollars in this letter if I starve. It is marvellous how I happened to get it, but you shall have it. I shall have to leave the Reservation to get it registered and have got to be back here tomorrow to hold meeting. Another hard day and part of the night before me. But a man that would not starve or go to prison for such a noble girl as mine is not worthy of her. I am trying to live as pure and good a life as I can. Dont drink nothing but water and I'd rather lose my right arm than to even look at a woman while I am away from you. I have already risked my life here and if it was not for my love for you I could not stand it. If you go to Oxford be very careful. Don't never close your eyes till you ask God to take care of you. If you go to the dances don't associate with the Gentiles—don't let them waltz with you, don't take any presents from them. You will soon get stout again now I promise you your health. And then you will feel different than what you do now. Remember your covenants. We have been in holy places and God will hold us very close. Don't fall. Pray for me. I have all Hell to fight alone here. I need your prayers every day. Be brave my own sweet one. I know you will. Pres. Young had to go on missions for years leaving his wife sick in bed right when the Saints were killed and butchered like beasts of prey. God will remember us when we have been proven. I could write a week to you but I must hurry now to start. Do right my Darling and the angels of Heaven will be around you to take care of you and help you to stand. I have prayed for you every day. I shall never forget you. We shall yet have a home and be happy together so God bless you and take care of you. To this end is my prayer and blessing for you. *T. BENTON.*

Bennington, Sept. 29, 1901.
President Snow, Dear Brother:
I had learned some months since by letter from a half-blood on the Washakie Reservation, that the Indians there wanted me to come out and see them. And now since the receipt of your letter, I have no doubt of their sincerity.

Carefully considering the contents of your communication I infer that you are not averse to knowing something of my circumstances. Owing to frost and drouth I have lost my crop which added to a similar loss only two years since, has reduced me to a condition that I have never before had any occasion to contend with, which caused me to wonder how I shall be able to get through the coming winter since my only occupation is farming and of course my all was invested.

Should you decide that I had better go irrespective of circumstances, what method of procedure may I ask, would you advise upon my arrival in that country. No doubt you are aware that owing to the extreme bitterness that existed there among the Government officials, Pres. Taylor thought it best that I should operate by stealth when I went before. Starting too late in the season to go any other way I took the cars to Rawlins and then the stage. Upon my arrival I commenced to live with the Indians, wore a blanket and being properly disguised, I soon found myself covered from head to foot with vermin and prostrated for days in trying to swallow the filth I was subjected to. Whereupon as you doubtless remember I wrote to you explaining the situation, when you very kindly called the attention of the President to the matter.

He provided then that I should buy a lodge and some ponies to pack a camp outfit upon for myself and missionary companion, an Indian, and live together, which I did. Thus we obtained access to the people, had good congregations, performed quite a number of baptisms, so that ever since I have almost ventured to hope that the Lord and my Brethren presiding, have approved of my labors.

By the way, I find that words are inadequate to express my appreciation of your kindness and the interest you took in me as well as for the confidence you seem to repose in me in that you think I am still fit to assist in some way the great work of God. I sincerely hope that you will not think that I desire to excuse or screen myself from performing any duty required of me in the Church. But since I am not supposed to know whether you would consider the project as justifying any pecuniary support or not, and according to the wording of your letter, I have written as I have.

Hoping that you will find me perfectly reconciled to any counsel you may have for me in the premises, whether it is to stay or go in any way or for any length of time, I conclude by saying that I am in your hands, having the utmost confidence that your decision will be for the good of all concerned. With distinguished consideration for you and Bro. Joseph F. I am as ever your Brother in the Gospel,
A.R. Wright.

October 17, 1901: In regular meeting of the Apostles in the Temple, Pres. Joseph F. Smith presiding, it was decided that Bishop A.R. Wright become a regular missionary to the Shoshone Indians.

October 31, 1901: At a meeting of the Apostles in the Temple, it was decided to allow the sum of $585.00 to meet the expenses of Bishop A.R. Wright on his intended visit to the Shoshone Indians. (Journal History, L.D.S. Archives)

Shoshone Agency, Dec. 16th, 1901.
My Dear Loell:
I have now been gone from home nearly a month but have not heard from you yet. I wrote you shortly after my arrival here, but feel somewhat disappointed, since I got no reply. I am so situated that I don't think it prudent to mail two letters home at one and the same time. If you knew how anxious I am to hear how you and the children are, I believe you would write at once.

I have just come in from a little trip out among the Indians. The snow is quite deep and the weather has been cold and severe. The country here looks just as much like winter as it does anywhere.

The folks where I am staying are sick much of the time. They are off to the doctors today. I am, as a consequence, quite lonesome. It is a difficult matter I find to keep from thinking of those I love so well. I am very busy so far as I have opportunity, trying to brighten up in the language. I see that I had forgotten a great deal of it, but am getting back to it now about as fast as could be expected.

I am beginning to accommodate myself to the surroundings as well as circumstances require. But you would be very much astonished at many things to be seen here. The white women of the country, where there are any, all ride astride same as the Indian women. The wickedness to be seen here and there in the country is a fright. It seems to me that if our young people could behold it, if only for a few moments, they would thank God from the bottom of their hearts that they have the privilege of living among the Saints, where there are so many influences for good thrown around them for their protection.

I don't think of anything to say just now any more than I hope you will write and tell me everything of which you can think. It will all be of interest to me. I hope Coulsie is attending school regular so that he will be able to write me a few words before winter is over. I hope I shall have the prayers of yourself and all the children every day, morning and night.

May the Lord bless and take care of you all is the constant desire of Your Affectionate, etc. etc.

A.R. Wright.

Shoshone Agency, Dec. 24, 1901
My Dear Loell:

I am exceedingly thankful in the receipt of your letter. I couldn't think why you did not write. I am sorry to hear about Nettie but believe with proper care she will get well.

It was hard work to keep back my tears when I read Coulsie's little sensible letter. He has always been with me you know, until now. In my hurry sometimes I look around for him only to find that he is not with me. I could read every word he wrote without any trouble whatever. I am equally thankful for Nellie's letter also. It was interesting to me to see how she brands every word with her disposition.

I was glad to hear you say 'write often'. It evidences a feeling and an affection that I can feel better than I can describe, but I am sorry to say that I can see that in all probability, circumstances will be such with me here that I can't write near as often as I would like to. I shall have to keep up quite a correspondence with some others and with them all taken together I could not do much else but write.

Things here are so curious that I don't know what I can say about them that would interest you, unless you had had some experience of a similar sort. Therefore I can only fill up a letter with sentiments that you know already I have always entertained.

I would not be surprised to know that you are right in the idea that since I have got permission to stay here, I shall be away a long time. There is certainly a big work here to do and someone must do it. And since I am called I should be as willing as other members of the Church to do my duty. If I back out then all is lost.

You speaking of getting rid of anxiety and responsibility: I have learned long since that if we do right we must progress and progression implies the assuming of very grave responsibilities. I have never occupied a position before where I felt its weight more than at the present time, nor where I have felt more obliged to live more carefully and any nearer to the Lord than at the present time.

I am glad you went to see Bishop Austin. I could with the most perfect safety commend you to his care. His counsel will never fail you. You can depend upon him to always speak from an unselfish standpoint. I should regard myself as the most ungrateful retch if I ever forget him or his noble wife and family. Bro. Jensen will hear you too.

...I had so much pain occasioned by lying around without scarcely anything under me that I finally got a mattress, so I have been able to sleep a little better. I have had two drinks of milk since I have been here but no butter. Still I guess I would weigh as much now as when I left home.

It seems curious to see a nicely dressed lady ... white woman ... so far as you can see, riding astride on horseback with a Mexican or Indian for a husband.

They have what they call chinook winds here. One has been blowing now for some time. It has taken the snow pretty much all off. The country, the climate, the people and everything is all different here to anything you see where we live. I am stopping now just a mile from the Government Post. I can hear the bugle call and the cannon fire night and morning but not the toot of the locomotive. Of course I shall soon get used to everything.

I am working hard to get better command of the language. There is quite a difference to what those Indians there have. You would think it strange to see small boys here speaking three different languages. Or a father talking one language, his wife another, the children speaking both in the house and still another outside.

Well my Dear I have finished two letters this evening and must yet take them to mail so they will go out in the morning. Teach the children good principles, and don't forget to pray. Pay your tithing if you have anything to pay on. Earn anything no matter how little, and when you see me again you will be better off than ever. God bless you all,

A.R. Wright

The following letter from Amos is a sample of what Amos and Ed Austin talked about. It is good man-to-man talk between two friends who fully trusted each other.

Shoshone Agency,
Dec. 28, 1901
My Dear Friend and Brother Ed:

The Indian and his wife sent to assist me in my missionary labors here have just arrived bearing a letter to me from you, every word of which is more precious to me than as if it was a five dollar gold piece. I was feeling quite lonesome in the midst of some peculiar circumstances that exist here, being alone ever since I have been on the reservation except the first few days after my arrival, with no one to counsel with but myself; obliged to act upon my own judgment and responsibility and take the consequences. I am overjoyed to see you were thinking of me.

My companion reports having a hard trip of it. He had to leave one horse and the others are pretty well used up. The snow was deep in many places and hard crusted. I wonder that he ever got through at all. Even here, all say there has been nothing like it for years. However the weather is moderating now and the chinook winds are taking the snow all off again.

I came from Lander by stage in the night. The driver told me of a friend of mine who lived hereabouts, but he misrepresented the distance. I decided to look him up as I wanted to keep a little quiet till I could take in the situation. I had my grip, overcoat and bedding to carry, which soon got heavy. I found the place but it was desolate yet I could go no farther, so I rolled up in my blankets and tried to sleep. That however was out of the question though I had had none to speak of since I left home. I warmed up before morning and I got a short nap.

I rose early, hid my things and started North afoot to see if I could find anyone. I soon came to some lodges. The Indians were very kind and directed me to another place where I found a half blood who proved to be a brother-in-law to the friend I was looking for. He invited me to ride with him and he would take me to the place where I wanted to go.

After resting up a little I commenced by fasting and prayer to get myself in proper shape to visit the U.S. Indian Agent of this reservation, a man that was said by everybody here to be a perfect terror, a man that had given our people no end of trouble in their attempts to go by this way to the Big Horn country; a man profane, prejudiced and full of bitterness towards us all.

Notwithstanding all this, sink or swim, the time had come when I had to approach him and find out my fate. Accordingly I was ushered into his presence, being introduced by the aforesaid friend of mine. To my great surprise he received me in the most courteous manner possible, and after entertaining me in an interesting way for an hour or more, I thought I discovered a favorable opportunity for stating my business which I did. Then still more to my surprise he gave me permission to remain here and invited me to visit him frequently.

I deal in good faith with him and told him that I expected to explain to the Indians the existence of the Supreme Being, His character and attributes, the Creation, the Fall, the Atonement etc. etc. Well, said he, I believe that I am about half Mormon myself. When finally he wished me perfect success, he bid me good night.

You can be assured Ed that I retired one of the most thankful poor fellows you have seen for some time, because of what had been told me I expected to be arrested and escorted off the reservation at once.

I find, however, that my task had only just begun because of the great difficulty in keeping down excitement. Some Indians from over on Big Wind

River came to see me one day and they almost obliged me to preach to them and promise to come over there the first thing. I was as careful as could be, knowing their excitable disposition. But no matter, they went back and commenced to gather together for a grand Ghost Dance, with the expectation that I would lead the procession!

Of course you know Ed that this would raise Hell, and just as I expected, here come the Agent, and since it is against the law of the Reservation and with the view the Great Father at Washington takes of it, and believing no doubt that it is all chargeable to me, it puts me in a terrible tight place and has kept me jumping sideways ever since, to stop it. Of course my friend just arrived will help me, but being an Indian he can't see why they can't enjoy themselves as well as other people. I write plain to you Ed because I know that you know something about Indians.

[There was not any law on the statute books, but an order by the Secretary of the Interior or the Bureau of Indian Affairs had the force of law. A violation of this order could bring on arrest and penalties. For many years in early days the government tried to stop the Indian dances. The Ghost Dance, the Sun Dance, the War Dance, the Bear Dance, were all under a ban. If Amos was suspected of encouraging one of these and especially taking part in them he could be prosecuted or run off the reservation. In more recent years these dances have been regarded as recreational and have not been interfered with.] The letter continues....

My friends at home all congratulated me when I was called, upon the ground that I would be relieved of all responsibility and have such a fine pleasant rest. Poor things, they did not know what they were talking about.

When I had only been here a few days, the Government commenced to pay out about eleven thousand dollars to the Shoshones here all in cash. Of course I knew what that meant and was exceedingly careful to mind my own business. Nevertheless they had a fight and beat one another over the head with guns and pistols, and if they had had my ammunition they would have killed each other. The troops were called out, sentinels were stationed from the Agent's office to the Post, and after a grand council they were pacified and dispersed.

I have not written this way to anyone, but I like to talk to you because I know that you know where to draw the line between the "noble Red Man" and the "Ignoble Savage." I know that they are of the House of Israel all right and my heart yearns for their redemption, but I am not here to make any false motions and if I would manage as some think they ought to be handled, I would get the top of my head blowed off in less than an hour.

I would give a fortune if I had it, if you were here so I could counsel with you. And were it not for your poor health Ed, I'd sure call for you. Lander has not improved much. I heard there was a man murdered there last week. Another fellow got mad at his horses, chopped the head off one of them and hewed the ribs out of the other with an ax. I might tell you of worse things but "never mind." I thank you Ed again and again for your kind remembrance of me. Gold would never buy the impression and effect your deportment made upon me the first time I ever saw you. It was my salvation. Thank God for you, my dear Brother.

Confidential. I don't want to make a noise. May the God of Heaven bless you my friend.

A.R. Wright.

Shoshone Agency
January 2nd 1902.
My Dear Dear Loell:

Yours of the 28th ult. was received. I hasten to answer. I realize your loneliness but it seems that is the price we have to pay for the blessings of the Lord, and more if He requires it.

I feel so thankful when I think that one year ago today about this hour in the Temple of the most High God we received the blessing that millions and millions of God's creatures will never, world's without end realize, and which will never be taken from us by any power on earth or Hell save it be through transgression. I feel that I am willing to die for the fulfilment of those sacred promises if necessary and I know you are ever with me in everything that is right.

The English language fails to enable me to put on paper my feelings toward you and my dear children, but it won't do to allow my feelings to weaken me against the performance of my duty. Others must be made acquainted with these glorious truths that have done so much for us; else we become selfish and disobedient and then we would lose all we have suffered so much to gain....

The Government employees about the Agency invited me to go to the Post with them last night to see a little sort of a show given by the soldiers. They done very well but I did not stay long though they had a fine supper and ball after the show and all of it free.

I am kept exceedingly busy every day with the language. I find that in order to preach intelligently that I must brighten up considerable. A fellow came in the other day while I was talking and inquired if I was really a white man. This shows how difficult it is for a white man to speak in their dialect.

I am grieved to hear about Nettie. "Pray for her" why of course I pray for her. What do you take me for? May the God of Heaven be with you and every one of my dear ones at home is my constant prayer. Tell the Brethren that I shall be sure to remember them all at the right time.

Your affectionate Companion
A.R. Wright.

He received a letter from Box B, The First Presidency of the Church in Salt Lake dated January 14th.

Brother:-
The First Presidency send you herewith enclosed cashier's check for $200. to enable you to labor and live among the Indians, as contemplated by you in yours of the 31st ult.

Yours,
Geo. F. Gibbs, Secretary.

The following letter and others, show that Amos is developing an obsession concerning the behavior of the younger people, especially his own children. Instead of his later life turning out to be full of peace, love, serenity, prosperity and comfort, in many respects it was turning out just the opposite.

He seemed to feel that misfortunes like Nettie's eye accident and others, would not occur if the people of the community, especially the young people would live the teachings of the gospel more nearly and strictly.

Coulsen thought the doctrine he expounded, as illustrated in the following letters concerning what young people, should be taught, was sound. He thought his father relied too much upon the spoken and written word to accomplish this teaching. "But if," wrote Coulsen, "his children acquired and held any high ideals I believe they came in part at least from these preachings."

Loella's next letter said Nettie was completely blind in one eye because of the accident.

Shoshone Agency, Jan. 17th 1902.
My Dear Loell:
Your welcome letter is before me. I am exceedingly thankful to hear from you but am almost overcome with grief to hear of the loss that Nettie has sustained. If you go to Hoover and tell him how that I am gone and not knowing when I will be back I think he will do the best he can for you and with but little charge if any.... You don't want to be afraid to explain to him how you are situated.

I am more than sorry that you lost your dog. Not that I worship a dog, neither do I compare anything of that kind to losses of much more serious character, but I know and you know how we have always been imposed upon with stock when we have been without one, and you know too that those who ought to be the most ashamed of the way they have treated me ever since you have been in the family, are the very ones who always wanted to kill him. Though it would not be prudent for you now that I am gone to complain, you can think all you want, but it's no use to talk. For if you do you will be charged with ingratitude at once. Bear what you can as well as you can. You ought to get another dog somewhere if you possibly can though I suppose they would kill him as soon as you get one. But if you try to get along through the winter it will be still worse in the Spring so that you would not have hay enough next fall to feed even a cow through the winter. For people that would treat you as we were treated last summer would rob the dead if they only got the chance. But say nothing, do right and the day will come as sure as God lives when such persons will be glad to get down on their hands and knees and beg your forgiveness and would give two or three such worlds as this to get you to even speak to them. Of all the sins there is in the catalogue I had rather be guilty of any of them than to mistreat in any way one who had done me no harm and one who is unable to defend or help themselves.

The Lord was certainly right when he said better that a millstone be tied to your neck and you thrown in to the depths of the sea than to offend one of these little ones. And the Savior said also that a man's enemies should be of his own house and household. But because I wanted to do right and felt sorry for them they took advantage of me and left me flat and then laughed at me and damned and God-damned their benefactor.

Warn the little boys against making the common mistake of misplaced confidence. Don't lead them to believe that they are under the same obligations to their enemies that they are to their friends, and love their neighbors as themselves. And that is all right and sound doctrine too, but it should be understood. "Who is your neighbor" the Savior asked. Not him that will treat you with the hatred and ingratitude we received from time to time. In order to protect themselves from these things I write about, learn them to be very careful about making promises and exceedingly careful about making bargains. Always have every little thing understood. I have paid debts that I never owed and lost hundreds of dollars simply because people will lie you out of your eyes on some little omission on a bargain. This world is full of sin and wickedness, and religion in many cases is only a cloak. Thousands in the Church put on the finery of Heaven to serve the Devil in.

I want you to tell the boys and teach them these things now while they are small for they will remember them. It will come to them with great force as soon as they begin to come in contact with the world, and the right kind of teaching now will protect them when they get older without sustaining the loss and sorrow that I have many times.

On the other hand tell them not to quarrel, it don't do any good, but watch their own interests beforehand. It's too late to lock the door after the horse is stolen or to help yourself after you are quarrantined, but be sure to serve God in the meantime. He will never forsake them. Teach them to obey the Gospel, that will never forsake them. Teach all the children to be virtuous and clean, honor the Priesthood and don't talk against it. Show them how so many have went to Hell because they never learned this lesson. Show them the end of those that do wickedly.

Now I leave the rest to your own judgment. I am pained too to hear about Nettie. I feel that I have been born only to have sorrow, instead of happiness. Our children will be ours forever and forever except it be through transgression. Therefore let us do our best by them. Don't think that they are too small. Tell them now they will remember it.

My body is becoming hardened to roughness, of course some parts harder than others. But the Goddess of Dreams told me of a heart in the West, warm and affectionate towards me, and yet with other attributes of a still higher temperature that would equalize all and every irregularity if she were here with me. Tell me in your next letter if you expect to employ Sister Ipsen or not.

May the God of Heaven bless you,
A.R. Wright

Sister Ipsen was a midwife. Loella's baby was almost a year old. Amos didn't want her to go to Dr. Hoover for whatever was wrong with her. His statement that he would probably have to stay on his mission longer than Loella thought, is typically pessimistic. He was often called a pessimist. His response was that the truth was not always pleasant.

Shoshone Agency, January 31, 1902
My Dear Loell:

I received yours and Nettie's letter tonight and hasten to answer you as I have usually done. I am exceedingly glad to hear from you as often as possible, but sorry to hear that Hoover don't think he can venture an operation for Nettie. I still believe that she will be all right sometime when an experienced Oculist can take it in hand. I want to write to her and will and send it as soon as I can maybe in this letter. I am glad the Brethren think of you and have cut your wood.

I am more and more anxious about the little boys. All the time I think of them. The sin and sorrow to be seen here every day among this people is simply heart rending, yet it is nothing more nor less than the consequences of disobedience and resistance and opposition to lawful authority. Any Father, Mother or other constituted authority who will take under their arm the principle of rebellion is not only an enemy to the person himself, but he becomes a traitor to both God and the truth, and there is no sin except murder that equals it.... I thank our Heavenly Father more and more every day that I live that I had no one to defend me in disobedience. I have to preach more than I would like to but if that is a duty why I will have to perform it.

I ate one meal cooked by a white person since I have been here. I am not complaining. I don't want you to complain to anyone for me. I have got along tolerably well.

I am very sorry that you have declined to employ Sister Ipsen. I had rather her than that a man doctor should be monkeying with you when I am away, and until I am there with you and on the spot to prevent other intruders who might have masculine inclinations, when my own solidity would be amply sufficient to keep you from being imposed upon.

Now my Beloved and Good Girl I would kiss you all over if I could reach you. May the God of Heaven to whose care I commend you, bless and take care of you forever, is the constant prayer of your affectionate,
A.R.W.

Shoshone, Wyoming
Feb. 1st, 1902
My Dear Daughter Nettie:

I have been almost overwhelmed with sorrow ever since I heard of the sad misfortune that has overtaken you, and have prayed and prayed that it might be alleviated and made light upon you through the Providence and mercy of our Heavenly Father. Let us be thankful that it is no worse and that there is still hope that through the employment of proper skill your sight may be restored.

Be assured my darling daughter that as soon as I am at liberty there shall be left no stone unturned to find relief and comfort for you, and I firmly believe the restoration of your sight is not impossible.

Think how much worse it might have been had the accident been more unlucky something that would have unbalanced your mind and left you in a condition to be endured throughout your life that would be worse than death. I would have you remember that God has not forgotten or overlooked you, but has blessed you with faculties and endowments that will never fail you in this life or the life to come."

His letters dwell on the fact that he had been betrayed and persecuted because he was too trusting and unsuspecting. He wanted his little boys to be spared such treatment. He writes:

You know or ought to know that certain ones that I tried to bless all the day long would have destroyed me if they had had the power. Not because they were exactly wicked but because they didn't know the difference between a man that would lay down his life for them and a three-legged stool that could be bought for a postage stamp.

If presiding or good men come to visit the Ward, go to hear them. And then take the boys and go and shake hands with them and thus familiarize them with goodness and good men they will remember it and learn to draw the line correctly between righteousness and wickedness, happiness and sorrow. Walk right up on the stand if you can't reach them any other way. Let fools stand down in the body of the hall and laugh if they want to.

It won't be long till Coulsie will be eight years old. I want you to have him baptized and make a record of it, but I don't think you had better have it done in bad or too cold weather.

Loella wrote to Amos telling him about the frozen foot.

Shoshone Agency,
March 6, 1902
My Dear Girl:

I was pained upon the receipt of your sorrowful letter. I understood that Coulsie broke his toe and if that was all I did not feel so much alarmed, but now at this late date I learn that he froze it. You should have been very careful to make it plain, for a freeze is very dangerous and hard to get over. You should have told me. You had better show it to Hoover and have him tell you what to do with it, or it may have to come off, and I am afraid you have waited too long.

It seems as though the more I think of anyone or anything, the more sure something will happen to give me pain concerning it. I am pained too to hear about Nettie. Oh how hard, how very hard I have tried to control the accursed dancing and especially the round dancing and the extremes and exposures that accompany it, on account of the damnable condition of modern society and ignorance, and this is what I get for my pains. When I think of poor Caty whose health is gone for life, and many other things still worse, all on account of the opposition that met me whenever I tried to save and bless them, Oh how I wish you could live so that God would bless and take care of you all. I thought that after I was gone, the bone of contention would be no more and you would all get along better than when I was at home. I want you to write at once and tell me what Hoover says about Coulsie.

As to the hay, I told Cate to sell enough hay as soon as possible to pay for the remainder due on the harness. Maybe that is what she is trying to do. After that you ought to share everything according to your families needs and necessities.

May the God of Heaven have mercy on me to take care of and heal my boy.
Yours affectionately,
A.R. Wright.

A week later another letter came from Loella which Amos answered.

I am very thankful to hear that you are as well as your letter indicates. When you are all well I think that I can get along but when I hear you are sick it pretty near runs me crazy. I was afraid the bone of Coulsie's toe was frozen and if so it would have to come off and make him a cripple for life. If it was only flesh affected and you had known, a little Frazer's axle grease would have healed it in a few days.

I don't know anything about what the authorities will say about this mission. It is my opinion however, that I shall have to stay here a long time, because no one knows the language and no white man can learn it except he learns it when a small boy as I did. Not only that but the Indians act like they want me to stay and if any considerable number of them feels that way I will probably have to stay.

I thank Coulsie for his sensible and affectionate letter. I hope the weather will soon be warm enough so that he can be baptized. I hope that he will be careful not to get hurt so much. Tell him not to use any tobacco, tea nor coffee nor whiskey, but keep the Word of Wisdom and I believe he will grow to be a good and useful man yet.

God bless you my Dear forever and ever and every one of my sweet little children, boys and girls. Yours affectionately,
A.R. Wright

Shoshone Agency,
March 23, 1902.
My Darling Girl:

Your ever-welcome letter has just reached me. I can't see why you say all the time that you don't amount to anything. If you knew how glad I am to hear from you, I don't think you would say that any more. I suppose you will laugh at me when I say your letters always make me feel like a new man. I don't know what I would do if it was not for the support I have from that source.

The circumstances here would make a man thank God to see even a horse or animal from home. I have tried not to give way to my feelings.

As to the hay, I don't see how there could be anything out of the way in telling Cate how bad you need it. I hope you can get along together. All I can say is that what there is there, belongs to all of you alike. I hope you will divide justly and remember one another. If I could divide it for you I would be glad to do so, but that is out of my power now.

I have heard nothing from Cate for a long time. I don't know why she fails to write. She only says a very few words when she does write. I asked a long list of questions but she don't answer them.

President Budge wrote me the kindest and best letter you ever read. I thank God for him and always have.

I had a little half-blood boy about the size of Conover sleeping with me for the past ten days. He lays and tells me how hard his father whips. He says he likes me and I know that he would go home with me if I was going and he had the chance....

I must bid you good night. Peaceful rest and happy dreams for you my good Girl. Yours affectionately forever and forever,

A.R. Wright

When Amos heard about the Wards raising money to help Nettie, he wrote a letter of thanks to Sister Pugmire.

Shoshone Agency
May 3, 1902.
Dear Sister:

I have just heard of the kindness received from you by members of my family, for which I am unable to express my gratitude as fully as the circumstances demand. However I am not as much surprised as might be supposed, because I have had favorable opportunities for knowing the stock that you are of, and realize the truth of the old saying, "blood is always sure to tell."

I have known for years that you were your noble and illustrious Father over again, from whom I received so many blessings that it would make this letter too lengthy altogether if I were to ennumerate only a small part of them. I regret sincerely that I have never been able to make returns in a practical manner financially, but have had to content myself as best I could, by asking God to bless his family and his sons as he ever blessed my Father's son.

I had the pleasure of being acquainted with your kind indulgent and faithful husband. It seemed that I had always known him, and from him too I received favors that have not been published in the newspapers, but they are indelibly impressed upon my memory, and as I firmly believe, recorded in the archives of Heaven not to be blotted out.

I congratulate you upon the promptness and support that you received from members of the department over which you so ably preside. No doubt you are aware that I have had some little experience in trying to accomplish objects of a similar character, and therefore know that your own example constitutes the motive power by which you have ever attained almost unprecedented success.

In conclusion dear Sister, let me repeat it, that I thank you cordially from the bottom of my heart again and again for the interest that you have taken for my afflicted family in my absence.

May the God of Heaven bless you and yours forever, Your Brother in the Gospel.

A.R. Wright

Bennington
January 14, 1906
Dear Fred:
Your letter came to hand some days since.... We are in the midst of the
most blinding and raging snowstorm that has visited these parts for many
years. The snow is now over two feet deep and still no indication of any
intermission whatever. I am very poorly prepared for it, especially if it shuts us
out of the Canyon which it will certainly do unless it clears up within a few
hours more. It seems almost impossible to keep up with the climate here. The
season is so short in the summer and therefore so long and savage in the winter
that it is almost enough to scare one out of heart to try to raise a large family
under such adverse conditions. We have already had about eight weeks or two
months pretty stiff winter and can't possibly hope to be let out for four long
months yet, it is almost enough to discourage anyone, except a county officer in
trying to reach what might be called a Bear Lake Resurrection. Indeed I am
inclined to believe that when the actual resurrection takes place, Bear Lakers
will be found to be the first people on the ground since they have already been
experiencing a much more lengthy burial sleeping period than any other class
of criminals known. Therefore for once their turn must certainly come first.
I am so wet that I shall have to stop and dry my clothes before I finish this
sheet. By the way, Loell has a nice range now, just arrived from Montgomery
Ward and Co. We celebrated my birthday unloading it and setting it up. It's a
dandy.
Our Mary has commenced to go to the dances. She is hardly old enough,
according to rule, but she says that she weighs a ton and goes in on her weight
instead of her age. She is running with Tom Quayle and says she will have him
in spite of Fate. I have threatened to tie her up and have given her to
understand that even an elephant can be staked out. This advice is in the
interest of both parties for if in her blind pursuit of him she should happen to
stumble onto the fellow, she would crush him to stone and Quayle would be no
more. My father weighed 315 pounds before he died, but if Mary keeps on, 315
will not be impossible for her to surpass. She is no longer able to go into the
Shanty through the back door, but must go out at the front one and clear
around the house to make the trip. She says the Smoot Committee is right, for
one man is enough and that she is amply able to take care of any man all alone
and without the assistance of a third party.
Bishop C. and other Saints of Montpelier are going to consolidate with the
depot element and build a large dance hall which will cost six or eight
thousand dollars and is to be completed by June, and is supposedly for the
purpose of elevating and purging our youth. The youth say, however, that of
course the almighty dollar is a subordinate consideration. "Evil communication corrupt good manners" in this age as in all previous ones. Whenever
we step over onto the Devil's ground there is no limit to our foolishness, so if
you ever commence to go downhill, everything is greased for the occasion.
I should be glad to know that we can see you ere long. It is hardly enough to
know that you are well and prosperous when you are so far from me. Loell
dreams of you all the time and my hair is already white instead of grey because
of you!... But this does not bring you to us, so what can't be cured must be
endured I suppose.
Yours affectionately,
A.R. Wright

The following paragraph to Nelly would take prize for exaggeration. Amos
laid it on with grim humor.

...The weather as usual has been excessively cold, from twenty to thirty
degrees below, much of the time. Of course this becomes harder and harder on
me as I get older. But in the face of these circumstances, the pride of your Ma
and the girls has increased so rapidly that when the weather would freeze a
polar bear to death or the horns off from a goat, the Female contingent of the
family are running around like a set of maniacs, tearing down the windows
and throwing open all the doors, hollering and screaming at the tops of their
voices, *FRESH AIR FRESH AIR WHY CAN'T WE HAVE FRESH AIR!?"*

Woman's jealousy knows no limit. But the principle of ignorant pride and fashion is still worse, so since your Aunt Ida has been here telling your Ma what a nice cool country Canada is, she thinks doors and windows are an abominable superfluity especially in the blizzards of a Bear Lake winter.

I am in the Canyon, most of the time wet up to my crotch, or crossing those endless inimitable Paris bottoms chilled to the core, with the never-failing little Zephyr commonly called the Bear Lake Blizzard, to keep my company.

Is it not some consolation to you to know that some of your trials are inherited from your father? I will try and get a dollar or two and send you before long.

Take all the physical exercise you can reasonably, but don't worry or study too hard. Keep the Word of Wisdom, and seek change frequently. Don't marry Shakespeare. I would rather see you marry a "hoe it" than a poet.

The children will all be glad to see you when the time comes. Remember you are not forgotten in any of our prayers. Therefore God will take care of you. Coulsie and Conover are standing on either side of me to hear this letter read that I have written to you. Coulsie says he would write but he has to hurry to school. Maybe he can write next time. Conover says if he could see you he would say, "Helloo, did you have a good time?"

Your affectionate Father,
A.R. Wright

Bennington, Feb. 1, 1906
Loella Jacobsen, Dear Daughter:
We are in receipt of your postal card announcing the birth of your first son. Pleased to hear that both Mother and babe are doing well. Congratulate you upon the rapidity and dispatch with which you have commenced to people Graham County Arizona. Among your numerous descendants, prospective, we hope that you will have many and worthy representatives.

"Children are an heritage from the Lord. Blessed are those who have their quiver full of them" especially when they are good children. I would have you remember however that *kind* and *character* is a paramount consideration. Better have one Jacob than twenty Esaus. One of the first commandments ever given was to multiply and replenish the earth, showing quite conclusively the object of the marriage institution, and how directly it points to life and its fountain, so much so that the first marriage ever performed on this planet was solemnized by God himself, thus indicating the sacredness and eternity of such a covenant. The foundation laid in the relation is understood but by very few people in the world.

A man without a wife is mighty small potatoes and a woman without a husband is just as small. I came to this world to get, among other things, a wife. And though naked we all come into the world it does not follow we must go out of it the same way. Therefore if I can take no more with me when I leave this sphere of action than I brought here, nonentity would be preferable.

When I am laid away I care not whether there is a flower within a thousand miles of my body. But if my claim to the holy and eternal Priesthood, wives and children with blessings and powers of government and creation to continue throughout the ages shall not be forfeited then I shall be more than paid and satisfied that I had not lost sight of the permanency of these kinds of covenants not made *with* or not *of* man alone, but with God.

Amos indicated that he believed in prenatal influence in his letters to Loella. Now he talks about it again to Nelly.

And now since you are a Mother I would like to talk a little philosophically to you if I had time, but writing is such a slow way of communication that we can't say much. Suffice it to say, however, that a mother can have just about the kind of children she may choose to have. My Father's ancestry away back always kept sheep but it appears that they were particularly prejudiced in favor of White Sheep. But when my Father was born and grew older, he concluded to introduce another color into the flock. The method employed for the purpose was successful, which was to hide in a ditch as the herd was coming down the lane, until just opposite him he threw a black hat among them. The next increase in the bunch was a jet black, the first one for a generation. "SEE MY GIRL!" Now don't laugh at this idea, because it is not confined to physical freaks of nature but it relates to that which is intellectual, moral, spiritual, and social, scientific, religious and everything praiseworthy in life or otherwise, just as you choose. Therefore, how important it is that mothers should be well-informed as to every truth necessary to be understood by anybody. Governor McConnell told us when he was down here on the campaign, that the best friend a child ever had was its mother. This is not true though unless the mother is a wise and good mother.

You ought to learn now that there is much in the saying that "the hand that rocks the cradle rules the world." Therefore be always sure that you rock it right, or your descendants will rule it wrong instead of right.

See don't you! The great Napoleon, Washington, and almost all men who have been truly great, attribute their greatness and success to the fact that they had good and wise mothers. But what is wise in a mother? that's the grand question. Well allow me to say, don't never lie to your child and tell him that he is innocent when he's guilty—and then call it affection. For if you do you become an enemy instead of a friend, tare down instead of build up, separate and destroy instead of unite and make powerful and permanent.

Nearly fifty years ago I was in a certain town when a murderer was executed for his crimes. In the remarks that he was permitted to make ere he was launched from the gallows into eternity, he pointed his finger at his mother who was standing in the crowd to witness his execution, and said he,

"It is you my Mother that brought me to this sad and sorrowful fate for you told me that I was innocent when I was guilty. And this untimely death of your son is the result of your false sympathy instead of your genuine motherly affection."

Do you wish to live long enough to see the day in this world or any other, that you must take that from your own flesh and blood?

Moreover I would have you remember that Nature's laws are God's laws, and if you cultivate and acquire a correct understanding of them, you can well afford to repeat yourself "ad infinitum". Because there is an independent power for good, possessed by a mother that is almost incalculable.

I would direct your attention to the mother who in cleansing and coloring a large quantity of yarn, undertook to compute the amount it would all be, at a certain price per skein, involving a delicate fraction in the computation as it did. She racked her brain from center to circumference for twenty-four hours continuously until she arrived at a correct solution of the problem. When as a natural consequence and in perfect harmony with the laws of Nature, her own son yet to be, became one of the most wonderful men of the time on these lines, able to give you the correct answer to the sum of any array of figures almost, and with any slate or pencil or scarcely any meditation or hesitation!

Can you tell me why Mosey is the only child your mother had that will never fall into a washtub? Or why that Ed now occupies the honorable position of Principal in an Academy of learning, assisting to mould public opinion for good, being a power for good among men instead of evil. Or why Frank's knowledge will be principally confined and not get very far outside of the weight of a beef steer?

Can you now begin to realize the significance of the great and important truth that one of the greatest singers of any time or people, Mrs. Adeline Patti was born upon the stage in the midst of song and melody?

Therefore, if you wish to have the honor of being mother to a large family of statesmen, philosophers, scientists, lawyers, doctors, orators, professors—great and good men that will make the world better for their having lived in it, then direct your thought and action to the business of a proper application of the laws of Nature, and Nature's God as they really are, and not as they are not.

I should like to talk to you all day but your Mother will finish this letter. I leave you to take the key from what little I have so hastily said on this subject. Think of great things that involve nobility—or character and great depth of thought and in course of time you will realize the truth and importance of this subject.

Kind and affectionate regards for you all, your Papa
A.R. Wright
Loell added a note at the bottom of Amos' letter.

My Dear daughter and son
We was more than glad to here from you and to here you had got through
with your trubel as well as you have. hope and pray you will continue to
improve. and soon regain your health again. When I told Unkel Morris he said
he just give you nine months and ten min. Of course Fred being a soldier he
had to be on time it could not be other wise. We hope you can come and see us
this summer. All of the children calls me grandma, said papa would have to
buy me a rocking chair. We are looking for Nettie home now ever day will be
glad when she comes. I expect when she comes she will wish she never had, for
it seems so crowded this winter, in our little log cabin. But we have all been quit
well, so we ought to be thankful for that. Your pa has written a good long letter
to you so I will not write any more. Kiss the baby for me and write soon.
Mother.

Did Nelly know how lucky she was? She must have known because she saved
his letters. They may have become scripture to her. Surely her father loved her
with a very special brand of love. Imagine what it would mean to get such a letter
or two or three when far away from home and confronted with situations which
could affect all the rest of life and beyond for good or ill a straight arrow pointing
the way. What a treasure!

Bennington
April 17th, 1907
My Dear Daughter Nelly:-
Your long hoped for letter to me has at last arrived. Its content does not
surprise me any. I am glad to know that the long period of time elapsed since
our separation does not seem to destroy your confidence in him who is now and
has ever been your best friend. Not naturally so altogether, but because of
certain existing truths that all must receive if they expect to make any progress
in, or according to the Plan of Eternal Progression that God has provided.
The relationship between father and daughter is not at all easily broken or
disposed of, especially when the child has been born under the Covenant. No
other obligation can ever be successful in the absence of proper recognition of
this established and ever-enduring principle. Therefore all contracts, stipu-
lations and agreements of whatever name or character must necessarily be of
short duration unless this underlying principle of fatherhood is properly
understood and maintained.
Can you understand the philosophy of the circumstance that occurred
immediately after the resurrection of the great Redeemer of the world when he
said, "Touch me not Mary for I have not yet ascended to 'My Father'?"
Who was Mary? Who ever tried to do more for a man than she did? Have
you considered how much the Master loved her? So much indeed that she
became the first messenger to the people of the great and glorious resurrection
of the Lord Jesus Christ himself. But notwithstanding all this, Father was to
be first recognized and all others afterwards. This then is the foundation stone
and the fundamental principle of all our worship, as evinced by the continued
declaration of the Savior of mankind from the beginning of His mission to the
crucifixion on Calvary.
Can you begin to see now why it was that your Father was so intensely
interested and deeply concerned when you left the old homestead, never to hear
his voice or counsel again, unto your protection from a fate that peradventure
might produce for you unfavorable, interminable and, when fully consumated,
almost indescribable and unbearable sorrow.
On Sunday the 11th of February I was in Boise City. No services according
to the Gospel were held throughout the day, but the skating rink, natatorium
and other pleasure resorts were crowded to overflowing. Among the unbelievers this is so everywhere until the Sabbath of the Lord is no longer a day of
rest and worship, but a day of frivolity and debauchery, misnamed happiness
and pleasure though the Lord has ever said from the beginning that those who

take pleasure in unrighteousness should be damned.

But as I gazed upon the revelry of the wicked, there in that wicked city, little did I think that any influence in the whole world could induce my oldest and beloved daughter of her most adorable Mother to be a Gentile or risk the dangers of following foolish associates in breaking the Sabbath.

Don't you know, my dear, that the sacrament of the Lord's Supper is not going to follow you to your picnics and amusements? And don't you understand that Eternal Life cannot abide in you in neglecting the Sacrament? One day in seven is none too often for you to renew your Covenant with that God on whom you are dependent for every breath you draw. Do you not know that the Lord condemned and punished a whole nation, not because they had forsaken Him altogether, but because they had not observed the "regularity" of His worship and service?

Don't ever get a mistaken idea into your head that your acquaintances will think more of you when you follow a multitude to do evil. If I could reach you now I would at once proceed to subject you to a series of privations, that you might, by better experiences be put in the way to acquire knowledge. It takes knowledge to bring on to anything like a high standard of perfection. The Lord has no use for fools or their folly because it is the very opposite of His intelligence, which constitutes his Power and Glory.

I want you to know that your father, up to date, has not forfeited any of the rights belonging to the name of father. And if the conditions upon which I gave you away are not complied with, the day will come as God lives, when I shall call for you with power, to exercise a father's rights and privileges, and bring you back to that bosom from which you were taken away, on the strength of promises that according to your letter, are not being fulfilled.

Now my darling daughter, distance cuts no figure. I have only given you a few hints to show you that I never leave off my concern for you, for you are my girl yet and will ever be. Don't therefore dishonor me by daring to forsake or depart from the devotion taught you by that father who offered to lay down his life to maintain the relation under which you, my darling daughter, was born.

I implore you to keep the commandments of the Lord. Give the Kingdom of God and His righteousness the preference always. Money is good in its place but don't worship it. Remember that when the Devil wants to destroy a person he first throws a bag of gold at them and then stands and laughs at their downfall and destruction.

Remember that great men and women are generally the product of adversity, not prosperity. When the Lord cursed the earth to bring forth thorns and thistles, and decreed that Adam should eat his bread by the sweat of his brow, it was for the good and development of Adam, not his injury or punishment.

And thus I might enumerate thousands of prophets and the truly great and wise of the earth and show you that they were made subjects of many bitter experiences in order that they might gain knowledge, which is power in all worlds as well as this one. So when the Savior of the world was to be placed in personal contact with the Arch-enemy of all mankind, he first fasted and starved Himself nearly to death in order to prepare Himself for the memorable encounter, wherein He, through adversity, came off victorious.

When your estimable and admirable Mother entered a relation despised and opposed by the great majority of the masses everywhere, hunted and hounded like a wild beast of prey, she could and did give birth to daughters who could work their way into the highest institutions of learning in the land and, without much sympathy or assistance except from the God of Heaven, they became able to receive from 85 to 100% in all of their studies, easily outdistancing all prosperity-competitors, even those who have been raised only to know how to read novels, write lovers letters, or drum on an organ, luxuriating in comparative ease and idleness and consigned because of it to a most humiliating and disgraceful failure.

SEE EH, NELLY ... is it Greek to you now?

Moreover when your poor old father, falsely accused, abused, betrayed, shot at, sentenced to pains and penalties, reduced to indigence and almost bankruptcy and dependence, shamed and ridiculed for the lack of money-sense as the world says, he could be chosen out of all the men in a large Stake of Zion to go and settle matters of many years standing, wherein three bishops, twelve High-councilmen, and Presidency of a large and populous Stake of Zion, all most miserably failed and retired discouraged and defeated. Yet your Father, the product of persecution and adversity, could and did go, and in five short evenings properly weigh and ferret out all the complications and effect a complete and perfect statement of all the trouble from which he has received congratulations ever since. So thank God for adversity! See Eh, Nelly ... can't you understand the Greek? (See Notes at end of Chapter)

As ever your loving father,

Amos R. Wright

Amos tried to get Fred and Nelly to leave Arizona and come back to Utah or Idaho, without success. He cited in a letter to her, a number of instances where his counsel and advice had been disregarded but later had been proved correct.

Cate heard by telegraph that her brother at Rexburg was dead. It would have taken two men to hold her until I took her to the train at 'Pelier. When she got up to her brother's home he met her at the door, alive and well and had not even been sick. So she was obliged to say, after ten or twelve dollars for her haste and excitement, "Well, that's just what Mose thought."

I have left no stone unturned to prevent the trustees from employing Gentiles in our school. But as in some other things, they thought they knew best, bid defiance, and set at naught my counsel. Whereupon I went off by myself and prayed to God that there might be a vindication of the truth of my position and counsel in His own time and way. Only a very short time after that, our Gentile laid down and died. I say, "laid down and died" because she told me that she had no pain whatever but she soon breathed her last and now her remains lay resting in a quiet little cemetery in Michigan. Possibly the trustees have awakened to what I have always told them for they now have a male Latter-day Saint for Principal of our school as I counseled them in the beginning.

Nett has been here during the holidays. She pretends to go to school at the Academy in Paris. Has not learned anything so far, nor will she for the present. She is very much enamored of Bishop Humphrey's son who appears to be one of the Principals in the school. He has been quite attentive and she has danced herself clear into the ground and her health pretty near all away. They say they are going to marry, but if they don't marry soon there will be nothing of Nett left to marry. However, Pa don't know anything in such cases.

Mary has gone to conjoint with Lester Munk. He has been trying to get her in the notion to have him, but she thinks long courtships is the only stuff these days. "BAH."

Bishop Austin started from the Tithing Office for home the other day. He had $600.00 in his pocket. When he attempted to put his hand in his pocket to reach for his handkerchief, a blizzard blew the money all away. I have not heard that he has yet found it.

In great haste and loneliness, A.R. Wright

(Loella was pregnant with Virginia and couldn't stay in Bennington when the baby was born. In a letter to Nelly dated April 17, 1907, Amos explained the situation.)

If you lived somewhere near in Utah you could now be a great blessing for your Mother. Dubois is moving heaven and earth almost to procure our disfranchisement. New laws continue to be enacted inimical to our interest so that we have to report births, deaths and much information that places us at a disadvantage and exposes us to punishment unmerited, because of wickedness in the world.

(For this reason Loella went to Brigham City and stayed with Aunt Mary Jane, Father Jonathan's wife who was such a kind stepmother to Amos. Virginia was born May 9, 1908.)

Bennington, May 15, 1908.

My Dear Nelly:

I have just returned from a trip to the Lower valley where I have been to attend the funeral of my daughter Caty who died at six o'clock last Monday morning after a short illness of only a week, perhaps of Erysipelas and blood poisoning combined. She was a great sufferer.

I have been in the midst of an accumulation of circumstances that are certainly of a very trying character to me, which makes it doubly hard to bear this, my latest bereavement. I sped over in great haste to Brigham City to see your Mother and the three children I have there, the last of which had been born just a day or two before Caty died....

Mrs. Wright (Cate) is all broke down over the death of Caty—all the more so because Caty never recognized her after she got there and naturally enough Cate thinks that if we had been near her she might have been saved.

Your new little sister is a beautiful child—black hair and lots of it.

I shall never get used to having you down there.

As ever, Father A.R. Wright

Bennington,
October 21, 1913.
My Daughter Nett:

Your letter received and just read. You say you could think of nothing logical or philosophical to write. But the fact as elucidated in your note though short, that you think favorably of your father, is a great consolation. I can scarcely think of anything more severe on a Father than to be met with ingratitude from his own flesh and blood.... Of course it is hardly to be expected that with your limited experience you can as fully realize as you will in time to come, the great and inestimable value of loyalty to truth and correct principles but I am rejoiced beyond my powers of expression to see you begin to see the light and realize to some extent its force and value.

I thank you again and again for your kind offer to come and see you with the probability of doing some work in the Temple. I spoke to Pres. Budge of some old-time mountaineers, friends I used to have in early days, some of whom were very brave and true. He said I might represent them, which I would like to do if I could be permitted to do so, as well as some work I should like to do for some of my kindred.

I was very urgently requested to attend the late Jubilee held in Paris and take a part in the program by reciting some of my experiences among the Indians, but I have long since learned that you can't expect people to believe anything when they themselves have never been there.

The trustees of the Montpelier Schools are now trying to get me to visit all of the schools of the upper and lower districts of that section. But how do you think I'd appear in the presence of teachers, educators, and professors with little or no education and no knowledge whatever of the art of Oratory, and with such a limited vocabulary. Why, you will very readily perceive my dear daughter, that I would be placed under the humiliating necessity of coming home with a very much damaged reputation.

Your Grandma is very poorly. Mary has gone to Pocatello to the institute. Coulsen expects to come about the 1st. Conover is night-watcher at the hotel. Frank was elected Sheriff a few months ago and is as proud as a blooded horse on fair day.

I am as ever your loving father
A.R. Wright.

(He was quite a hand to fish for compliments as he grew older. He could give Noah Webster a run for his money and he knew it.)

Bennington
October 21, 1913
Dear Sweet Daughter:

I will try and write a few words to you while your Grandma sleeps. She has been very bad the last week. She suffers untold agoney every day and night unless we give her morpheme or rub cloyrforme on her legs. Her feet have begun to turn dark and she has gangreen. I don't see how she lives. Your Pa just administered to her and she went to sleep.

It is now eleven o'clock and I must go to bed if I can and get a little sleep. I keep quite well. If grandma dies here we will take her to Whitney to bearey her. Of course I will see you then. I don't think it will be long.

I am so glad Coulsen is going to try and go to school. . . . We are all well but Grandma. Amos is working for Mortisens this week while there is not any school. He is a dear boy.

It does my heart good to know you still love me as you use to do, then when I am old like my dear Mother I will have one to take care of me. They all think they can't take care of Ma, but I feel like I would take care of her if I only had one room and had to go on one leg and had no money. It is hard and a trile but someone has to do it and I am glad I am that one.

I have to go now and fill the hot water bag to try and get her feet warm. She is cold all the time so goodnight Nettie. Kiss the children for me and give my love to L.R. You have a good man Nettie.

From Mother.

Bennington, Nov. 26, 1914
My Dr Son Coulsen:
Yours of the 25th is before me. You ask will I answer it. Of course I'll answer even if it would cost me my life and save yours.

I am pleased to hear from you and overjoyed to know of the sentiments your note contains and expresses. I am highly pleased to see you decide wisely as to the football business. The game is a relic of danger and barbarism. One of the sons of one of the best friends I ever had was recently killed in a baseball game which is not nearly so bad as the foot game.

Speaking of amusements, I would not have you think that I wish you to forego a reasonable amt of harmless and legitimate amusements. They are perfectly right and proper in which you will always have my support and blessing. But excesses comprehend the great danger, they should ever be regarded as incidental but not the sole object of life. Moreover the pleasure-seeking spirit of this generation involves a strong invitation and an almost irresistable temptation to sexual sin, which if committed there is not more than one man in ten ever gets over it, after which he can never look his fellow-creatures squarely in the face. It will rob you of the support which is indispensable and nothing but a pure and clear conscience can give you. It is a species of dissipation that antagonizes one against his best friends and wise counsel, producing a spirit of rebellion and opposition against truth and safety as well as a waste of time and means, morals and character. It is the very absence of economy since it always invites extravagance, wreckless expenditure of money you can't afford to spare.

Believe me my son when I tell you that no more persistent and dangerous enemy ever approached the well-being, success and prosperity of men or nations than the habit of extravagance and excesses. Considering the opposite sex the only safe rule is "touch not, taste not, handle not until the girl or woman is your own." You will be wise never to be seen in the presence of a woman unless a third party is present. You have absolutely no right to take in your arms a woman unless she is a relative, until after the consumation of marriage.

I am rejoiced to know that you have resolved to have an education at all legitimate cost or hazard. Indeed it is an irrevocable law of Heaven that no one can be saved in ignorance. Knowledge is power in this world or any other, and will give you access to a voice in the affairs of life and government here and hereafter, and if properly applied spells success and happiness all the time and forever.

Mary and Charl came for Thanksgiving yesterday. Brought a turkey and Ma killed a rooster, cooked some cranberries, baked some sweet potatoes and a squash pie so we are still feasting on the remnant of the repast.

It looks like a storm though we have had an ideal fall. Sixty acres of wheat in and all our ground plowed for spring. I have lots to tell you which would not be prudent to write. . . . Get the Spirit of God and keep it. God bless you.

Your Father, A.R. Wright

One of his sons in later life wrote: "I do not harbor any ill-will towards Father for the floggings he gave me. I think it was a very mistaken type of administering punishment. But I think he was under a great emotional strain much of his later life, if not all of it. He should, of course, have been master of his temper and should have exercised the proper restraint, but he was apparently unable to do so. He was tried in his family relations much more than the ordinary man. He was so rigidly determined and so thoroughly convinced that he was right concerning Church doctrine that he could hardly stand it when one of his own children refused to accept the same views whole-heartedly.

"Mother always respected Sister Wright but never liked her. It is only simple truth to say that there was always jealousy between them. As I grew older, however, I respected and admired Sister Wright more and more for treating Mother as civilly as she did. For a person of her nature and proud disposition she exercised unusual restraint and forebearance." (Coulsen Wright writing to David Wright in 1956.)

Bibliography

Pushman, Richard L., *Ensign* (Sept. 1978) p. 9.
Carter, Kate B., *Heart Throbs of the West*, vol. 10, pp. 280-81.
Nibley, *Faith Promoting Stories*, p. 143.
History of the Church, vol. III, p. 305.
Journal History, L.D.S. Church Historical Archives.
Wright, Conover, "History of Amos R. Wright," ms.
Andersen, Gwen, *My Grandfather Said.*
Wright, Jonathan Calkins, *Ancestors and Descendants.*
Bancroft, *History of Utah*, p. 324 and p. 397.
Woodruff's Journal, May 29, 1847.
Comprehensive History of the Church, vol. III, p. 449 and 302.
Carter, Kate, *The Salmon River Mission*, p. 47.
L.D.S. Church Archives (Apostolic Blessing May 12, 1857 to Amos R. Wright).
Bybee, Robert L., *Salmon River Mission*, dictation.
Arizona Highways, (October 1978) "Men in Death Valley."
Wilson-Driggs, *The White Indian Boy*, p. 141, pp. 147-48.
Brodie, Faun M., ed., *City of the Saints*, pp. 257-59.
Hafen, L.R., M.A., *Improvement Era*, pt. 1 vol. 27, p. 57.
Evans, John Henry, *Instructor,* "Pony Express" vol. 46, p. 363.
Settle, Raymond W., *Saddles and Spurs, The Pony Express Saga*, p. 76.
Comprehensive History of the Church, vol. 5, pp. 76-78.
Comprehensive History of the Church, vol. 4, p. 375.
Day, Robert B., *They Made Mormon History*, p. 220.
Box Elder Lore of the 19th Century, pub. Box Elder Sons of Utah Pioneers.
Comprehensive History of the Church, vol. IV, pp. 57-58.

Madsen, Brigham D., *The Bannock of Idaho*, p. 141.

Waldo, Anna Lee, *Sacajawea*.

Evans, John Henry, *Charles Coulson Rich, Pioneer Builder of the West*, pp. 365-69.

Arrington, Leonard, *Charles Coulson Rich*.

Historical Sketches of F. Ross Peterson, Pullman, Washington.

Rich, Russell, "Settlement of Bear Lake Valley," *Church History*, U.S. Film 962.234, Item 2, ms. thesis.

Irvine, Arnold, "Church News," *Deseret News*, February 20, 1965.

Olson, Nolon P., *Logan Temple, The First Hundred Years*.

Talmage, *The House of the Lord*, pp. 217-19.

Paris, Idaho, Stake Minutes, Melchizedek Priesthood, LDS Archives, Salt Lake City.

Letter from Moses Thatcher to President John Taylor, November 17, 1884, LDS Archives.

Gibbs, Grenville H., "Mormonism in Idaho Politics," *Utah Historical Quarterly*, vol. XXI no. 4, October 1953, pp. 294-95.

Rich, Russell R., "Ensign to the Nations," *History of the LDS Church*, pp. 379-80.

Rich, Russell R., *Land of the Sky Blue Water*.

Norton, Thomas J., *The Constitution of the United States*, p. viii preface.

Ridpath, *Popular History of the United States*, p. 128.

Whitney, Orson F., *Life of Heber C. Kimball*, pp. 221-23.

Christensen, Larry, "The Mormon Battalion," *The Ensign*, July 1979, p. 55.

Comprehensive History of the Church, vol. VI, p. 115.

Journal History, LDS Historical Archives, LDS Church Office Building, Salt Lake City.

Letter from W. N. B. Shepherd to Conover Wright, March 16, 1937.

Nibley, Preston, *The Presidents of the Church*, pp. 116-17.

"Manuscript Histories," LDS Church Archives no. 759-871.

Letter from Amos R. Wright to President John Taylor, 1880, LDS Church Historical Archives.

Wells, Merle W., "Anti-Mormonism in Idaho," *Studies in Mormon History*, 1872-92.

Allen, James B., and Glen H. Leonard, *The Story of the Latter-day Saints*, p. 406.

Whitney, Orson F., *Life of Heber C. Kimball*, p. 397.

Sjodahl and Smith, *Doctrine and Covenants Commentary*, pp. 336-37.

Comprehensive History of the Church, vol. VI, p. 227.

Deseret Weekly, November 14, 1891, vol. 43, no. 21, pp. 59-60, LDS Archives.

Reemain, Paul E., *Plural Marriage Limited*.

Vital Records, Bennington, U.S. file 982.442, item 3.

"History of Bear Lake Pioneers," *Daughters of the Pioneers*, p. 259.

"Learning About Ourselves Through Church History," *Ensign*, September 1979, p. 8.

Simms, Loella Jacobsen, ms. letters.

Wright, David L., letters, 1956.

Snow, Lorenzo, Report of his mission to the Wind River Reservation, October 27, 1885. LDS Historical Archives.

Thatcher, Moses, Report of his mission to the Wind River Reservation, (October 1884), LDS Historical Archives.

A Dream of Jonathan C. Wright

A dream by J.C. Wright
March 23. 1831
One of the Elders in authority said to Each one of the Brethren present, go. Make haste get your wives. Each one started & appeared to take with him a new basket & started off immediately in different directions. I went to a Large splendid building. & went to a door in the S.E. corner of the building & apparently the key was Lost yet I had no difficulty in opening it, in fact it flew open at my command after passing in this closed again. & I stepped forward, a few steps; to another room, wich was hid from, or rather separate from the first, by a veil, which I came to & after a moments pause I raised it up, & passed on into the other room & in the N.E. corner of the room I found my wife Rebecca laying in a bed I came up to her. & spoke to her,—she immediately rose up dressed in white. & looked as lovely as an angel *Even* nearly or altogether transparent,- she asked me what time a day it was I told her it was nearly noon. She said she might as well got up in the morning, but she never waked till Just this minute. I thought the department in which she lay was splendid beyond description. & all the apparel belonging to it was white as snow. I turned a little around being filled with inexpressible joy. ---- my joining 1st child which has just arrived my wife had no tears but was filled with noble dignified Joy. & rose from her bed conscious of having to lay down no more. & soon would have all her children with her again to be parted no more forever. Our Joy was full & we Knew all was well.
Jon. C Wright
JONATHAN CALKINS WRIGHT
Rebecca Wheeler
Sarah   Boyce
Cynthia Nichols
Mary Jane Neeley
Lois Moran
Caroline Olsen
Prudence North
Amos   Russell Wright
Virginia Ann Charlotte
David Darwin
Jonathan

Martha Wright
Catherine Roberts
Martha Loella Weaver
Silas
Jonathan Daniel
Winifred Rebecca
Adelaide
Amos Russell
John Wheeler
Frank Marion
Edgar Monroe
Catherine Jane (Caty)
Charles Elmer
Elizabeth (Libby)
Frances
Sarah Loella
Jeanette Tippets
Mary Ellen
William
Charles Coulsen Rich---Geneva Ensign Wright
Conover
Alnora Lane (Nona or Norey)
Amos Weaver
Harriet
Arunah Caesar
Virginia
Ruth Esther